American Cultural Pluralism and Law

Third Edition

JILL NORGREN AND SERENA NANDA

Westport, Connecticut
London

Library of Congress Cataloging-in-Publication Data

Norgren, Jill.
   American cultural pluralism and law / Jill Norgren and Serena Nanda.—3rd ed.
      p.cm.
   Includes bibliographical references and index.
   ISBN 0–275–98692–6 ((cloth) : alk. paper)— ISBN: 0–275–98699–3 (pbk.)
   1. Minorities—Legal status, laws, etc.—United States. 2. Multiculturalism—
Law and legislation—United States. I. Nanda, Serena. II. Title.
KF4755.N67   2006
342.7308′7—dc22   2006007760

British Library Cataloguing in Publication Data is available.

Library of Congress Catalog Card Number: 2006007760
ISBN: 0–275–98692–6 (cloth)
      0–275–98699–3 (pbk.)

First published in 2006

Praeger Publishers, 88 Post Road West, Westport, CT 06881
An imprint of Greenwood Publishing Group, Inc.
www.praeger.com

Printed in the United States of America

The paper used in this book complies with the Permanent Paper Standard issued by the National Information Standards Organization (Z39.48–1984).

10 9 8 7 6 5 4 3 2 1

To our families

Contents

IV. Community and Citizenship

Preface

During the 1987 Iran/Contra hearings, Senator George J. Mitchell of Maine spoke eloquently about the importance of the rule of law in a multicultural nation like the United States:

Most nations derive from a single tribe or a single race. They practice a single religion. Common racial, ethnic, and religious heritages are the glue of nationhood for many.

The United States is different. We have all races, all religions, a limited common heritage. The glue of nationhood for us is the American ideal of individual liberty and equal justice.

The rule of law is critical in our society. The law is the great equalizer, because everybody in America is equal before the law.

Senator Mitchell's words express a fundamental ideal in American society. How closely these words match the reality experienced by many Americans is a question that interested us as a political scientist and a cultural anthropologist. This book draws upon our separate disciplines and our common interests in multiculturalism and law as it operates in the United States.

Debates over American cultural diversity and the role of law in American society have greatly intensified since the publication of the second edition of this book in 1995. Important new court decisions and some significant new trends in the issues we discussed led us to write the third edition of *American Cultural Pluralism and Law*.

The central theme of the book, that is, the negotiation between law and the many subcultures that make up this diverse American society, remains the same. The basic organization of the book and much of the material from the second edition, in full or in part, is retained. We have judiciously edited some material, and regrettably deleted the chapter on Courts and Culture, in order to make room for updating the sections on Native American land rights; African American issues, particularly affirmative action; Latino immigration; the impact of religious ideology on the public schools; and women's rights. An entirely new section on gay marriage has replaced our earlier analysis of gays in the military, and we have added a discussion of Puerto Rican sovereignty to the chapter on Native Hawaiians, as both groups have shared a history of U.S. colonialism. We have also added a new section on disability rights to the chapter on homelessness, as both homeless people and disabled persons have actively fought the discrimination against them in courts. We have retained the chapter on Japanese American internment in full, and indeed this history takes on new meaning in the context of the 9/11 terrorist attack on the United States. We have added an entirely new chapter on the relationship between cultural pluralism and law as it has affected Muslim/Arab communities in the United States, U.S. actions abroad, and the reexamination of the balance between national security and civil liberties after 9/11.

We happily acknowledge the many people who have been so helpful to us in our work. We thank our students for their insights, interest, and willingness to share with us their own, culturally diverse, perspectives on the law. Numerous individuals, inside and outside academe, encouraged us in this project, reviewed parts of the manuscript, made useful suggestions, and provided us with needed resources. Our thanks to them all:

James Bowen, Dorothy Bracey, Milton Ferrell, Joan Gregg, Carol Groneman, Joel Grossman, Tom Litwack, Frank Lono, Gerald Markowitz, Philip Tajitsu Nash, Ruth O'Brien, Darby Penney, Daniel Pinello, John Paul Ryan, Philippa Strum, Haunai-Kay Trask, Jon van Dyke, Geoffrey White, and Jean Zorn. We also offer our deepest thanks to the late William Lewis, Billie Kotlowitz, Richard Turer, and especially Petra Shattuck.

We are very grateful to the institutions and grants that supported our work. Many of our ideas were developed in the National Endowment for the Humanities Summer Seminars, "Courts in American Society," and "Cultural and Political Identity: Perspectives from the Pacific," and the American Bar Association Committee for Undergraduate Nonprofessional Legal Studies conferences that we were invited to attend. We also thank this group for awarding us a mini-grant to develop problem-solving exercises to accompany this book.

We would also like to thank the many groups and individuals who sent us materials essential to our research: the American Jewish Congress; the Lambda Legal Defense and Education Fund; the Legal Action Center for the Homeless; the New York Coalition for the Homeless; the New York

State Attorney General's Office; Gerald Sata and Richard Halberstein, attorneys for Japanese American redress plaintiffs; the Utah Civil Liberties Union; the U.S. Office of Redress Administration; the Civil Division of the U.S. Department of Justice; and Mr. Juan Cartagena of the Community Service Society of New York.

Our thanks also go to the anthropology department—particularly to Linda John—and the government department, and to the outstanding library staff, of John Jay College, who helped in so many ways. We are grateful also for the award of a PSC/CUNY Research Foundation grant, which was essential to the completion of this work.

Introduction: *E Pluribus Unum?*

Since its colonial beginnings, the United States has been an increasingly culturally diverse nation. Like other liberal-democratic nations, it faces a fundamental tension: On the one hand there is the need to create national institutions, including law, that unify culturally different groups and conflicting group interests, and on the other the need to protect human rights by allowing some degree of religious, personal, cultural, and local political autonomy. Law (federal and state constitutions, statutes, administrative rules, and judicial opinions) is one of the most important mechanisms for addressing this tension.

The theme of this book is the interaction of law with cultural pluralism in the United States, specifically, the continual negotiation that occurs between culturally different groups and the larger society. We pursue this theme by asking some key questions: In a democratic nation-state, what is the extent of cultural difference that can be tolerated, consistent with the integrity of the larger body politic? How, in the face of technological, economic, social, political, and cultural change, does a nation-state, operating under the rule of law, and specifically in the United States under a written constitution, cope with cultural diversity?

From its earliest history, the first settlers and subsequent founders of the United States decided not to regard Native Americans or African Americans as serious partners in its nation-building enterprise, despite their essential contributions to the economy. The reality of class, religious, and ethnic differences and conflicts was submerged by the construction of the myth of a nation created *de novo*.

When conflict arose, the apparent availability of land, only sparsely settled by Native Americans, permitted the early settlers and, later, migrants
from the East Coast, to protect their differences by moving, permitting
the development of local cultures. Simultaneous with this development of
local cultures, for example, the religious dissenters of New England or later
the Mormon theocracy in Utah, was the development of an "American"
culture. The first settlers were Anglo-Saxon, Christian, imbued with the
idea of political liberty, and, with the exception of a few communal groups,
adherents of economic individualism. These values formed the basis of
the national culture they sought in the "new Eden" of colonial America
and, later, the United States.

The clarion call of freedom encouraged the belief that the new nation
would be tolerant, even respectful of cultural diversity, political dissent, and religious differences. This is most eloquently expressed in the
American Constitution, specifically in the Bill of Rights, whose function
is to limit the ability of governments—the instrument of the dominant
culture—to tread upon, or annihilate, the cultural, political, and religious
differences of weaker groups and individuals. But those who wrote the
Constitution had the power to define the limits of tolerance, which they
did, most egregiously, by putting off the legal question of slavery.

The greatest source of America's diversity, central to its national myth,
is immigration. Immigration was—and still is—viewed as a testimony to
the positive belief in the possibilities of American pluralism linked to the
idea of economic advancement regardless of one's birth. But then, as now,
immigrants were regarded ambivalently. Between 1820 and 1850, most
immigrants were from nations of northwestern Europe and were therefore generally similar, culturally and physically, to the earlier immigrants.
Many, like those from England, Scotland, and Ireland, also spoke English,
by this time firmly but unofficially established as the national language.
But even some of these immigrants were viewed with hostility: American
Protestants feared that the Roman Catholic affiliation of many Germans
and the Irish would bring interference in American affairs by the Catholic
Church in Rome. In addition, many of these immigrants were paupers
or political dissidents and it was feared that their radical political and
economic philosophies would cause upheaval in the newly established
nation.

Despite this hostility, later immigrants from Asia and southern and
eastern Europe faced much greater prejudice and harassment. Freely
available land had decreased; many of these new immigrants were physically, culturally, and linguistically different from the earlier northwestern
European immigrants; and filling the need for unskilled industrial workers, the new immigrants tended to concentrate in ethnic urban ghettos.
By the late nineteenth century, immigration was perceived as a threat to
the emerging American culture, now definitively perceived as based on
Protestantism, liberal democracy, and free-enterprise capitalism.

As a result pressure built for a national policy of immigration restrictions. These were first directed against the Chinese, and later, with the 1924 National Origins Act, against southern and eastern Europeans, all of whom were perceived to be "racially unassimilable." But because the nation needed workers, white immigrants were grudgingly accepted, and the national myth of America as the great "melting pot" continued to emphasize the nation as a beacon of freedom and opportunity for culturally different groups.

But while immigrant literature frequently testifies to exclusion and rejection, the most unequivocal, persistent, and pernicious rejection—including rejection by violence—was being experienced by racial minorities and indigenous peoples.

Although national origin, religious commitment, "race," and indigenous status form the most obvious subjects for an examination of American cultural pluralism and law, with the broadening of the civil rights movement in the 1960s, we have also included in our discussion other groups, based on gender, sexual orientation, social class, or personal status. They too are perceived as outsiders whose values or cultures confront some aspect of the dominant culture, and they too, have actively sought their rights in court.

The claims of culturally different groups in our society have involved, ironically, both getting in and staying out: The Amish, for example, are outsiders whom the law has permitted to protect their cultural autonomy, while other groups, like the Mormons, Native Americans, Rastafarians, and homeless were only partially permitted to do so. Still other groups, including African Americans, Japanese Americans, women, homosexuals, and disabled persons, who have been considered outsiders by virtue of society's discrimination, have used courts to "get in."

In the negotiations between law and culturally diverse groups, it needs to be noted that American courts are dependent on a body of law that emphasizes *individual* rights and does not historically address *group* cultural interests. Unlike other societies, whose constitutions give legal status, and even certain privileges as well as rights, to cultural groups, the U.S. Constitution does not mention culture and does not accord explicit rights to groups, cultural or otherwise.

While law, and courts in particular, are the institutions most specifically charged with the protection of cultural pluralism and the rights of individuals belonging to culturally different groups, we may ask what are—or what might be—the constitutional or other legal bases to which subcultures in the United States can look for protection?

For indigenous groups, such as Native Americans, Native Hawaiians, or Mexican Americans, some protection has been found in the law of treaties, federal legislation, and state constitutions. Even these, however, do not affirm group rights to the extent of international law. Historically, the United States has been reluctant to become a signatory to many U.N.

resolutions on self-determination for cultural minorities or to participate in international forums on rights for indigenous peoples. While it may be argued that the protections of the First Amendment free exercise of religion clause, and legal strategies like the class action suit, do speak to group rights, it is also clear that U.S. law, in being predicated on the protection of *individual* rights, mainly promotes assimilation rather than cultural pluralism.

Unsurprisingly, then, a close reading of the operation of law in the United States demonstrates that in practice, courts have steered a middle and sometimes inconsistent course between two sides: on the one hand, the American ideal of tolerance, embedded particularly in the Bill of Rights and other later constitutional protections such as the Fourteenth Amendment; and on the other hand, the obligation of law to protect the integrity, and indeed the very life, of the nation-state.

The interaction of several factors may help explain the different results for these different groups in their use of the law. One important factor is the distance of the cultural activity the group seeks to protect from the Judeo-Christian tradition, individualism, republicanism, and capitalism, all of which form the core values of the dominant culture. The litigation involving the Mormons, or the Rastafarians, for example, shows the firm limits of diversity that the law is willing to allow. And even when courts have accommodated diverse cultural practices that challenge American values, they have most often done so, as in the Native American peyote and the Amish school cases, only in the most narrow terms.

But clearly the values of the dominant culture, as expressed in judicial interpretations, are not static. Evolving standards are clear in the case of women, African Americans, homosexuals, and undocumented immigrants, particularly Latinos, and the historical stereotypes of these groups, which were part of the dominant culture, are no longer expressed in judicial opinions.

The particular historical period also helps explain the legal treatment of culturally different groups. In periods of national insecurity, culturally or racially different groups, such as the Jehovah's Witnesses during WWI, Japanese Americans during WWII, or Muslim/Arab Americans post 9/11, are more likely to find their rights trampled on.[1]

The "slippery slope" principle may also affect legal outcomes for minorities. This concern over the force of precedent and the possibility of a domino-like effect, for example, has inhibited American courts from deciding in favor of the return of land to Native Americans and the awarding of sovereignty to Native Hawaiians, which also brings with it demands for return of land. In this regard public protests, as in the case of the Puerto Rican island of Vieques, may be more effective than courts.

The initiation and judicial reception of litigation also partly depends on the interest of third parties, whose participation takes many forms. Non-Amish lawyers, for example, were essential in bringing Amish claims to court, as was also true for Native Americans, among whom there were virtually no lawyers until the late 1960s. Homeless persons also have largely depended on third parties in their litigation. In many of the religious establishment cases, like the current attempts to impose religion into the public schools, public interest and civil rights organizations have been increasingly important, as religious fundamentalism has increased its political clout over the past two decades.

Our cases thus suggest that courts are not autonomous, isolated bodies composed of justices neutral toward dominant cultural norms and immune to contemporary politics. This was clearly demonstrated by the growing conservative influence of the Rehnquist Court, which began when he became chief justice in 1986, furthered by Justices Scalia, Thomas, Rehnquist, and Kennedy through the application of the jurisprudence of "new federalism." This new direction, in which the Court has sought to elevate state authority, often at the expense of congressional powers, has resulted in the narrowing of a number of effective remedies for acts of discrimination, involving, for example, the rights of disabled persons, the regulation of hate crimes, the diminishment of civil liberties, and the undermining of the boundaries between church and state. This politicization of the courts is also seen in the enormously contentious and partisan debates over President George W. Bush's Supreme Court nominees.

Indeed, the increasingly acerbic politicization of courts during the Bush administration raises an old question with new urgency: that is, how to explain why the nation-state, through its courts, entertains challenges to dominant culture values by culturally diverse and autonomous groups. One important explanation, of course, lies in our being a government under the rule of law especially committed to civil liberties and civil rights as expressed in the Bill of Rights. More pragmatically, our liberal-democratic state undoubtedly gains legitimacy to the extent that it adheres to its own rules, both domestically and with regard to its role abroad, as in the allegations of torture, secret prisons, and indefinite detentions resulting from the invasion of Afghanistan and Iraq. As representatives of the nation-state, American courts must steer a middle course as they constantly calibrate the interests of culturally diverse groups within a social contract that permits and even encourages diversity but also demands national unity and national security.

NOTE

1. For a full discussion of the Jehovah's Witnesses in this context, see Norgren and Nanda, *American Cultural Pluralism and Law* (Westport, CT: Praeger, 1988), chapter 5.

PART I

Race and Ethnicity

CHAPTER 1

Native Americans, Land, and Law

The difficulty in writing about Native Americans begins with terminology. Today Native Americans constitute more than 560 federally recognized tribes, so that even to label them collectively is to distort their cultural and geographical diversity. The commonly used phrase "American Indian" does not reflect their term for themselves. Rather, European explorers who misunderstood where they were and whom they met imposed it on them. The terms "Indian" and "Native American" are, then, expedients used to refer to the indigenous peoples of the North American continent.

Historically, these people were, and are today, characterized by a wide range of economic and cultural systems.[1] In spite of real and important differences, however, the many diverse Native American societies shared similar attitudes toward land and nature, which they viewed as having "sacred primacy." For Native Americans the land was Mother Earth: They believed that humans had a spiritual relation to the land, and that the land was there to be used, with respect, in perpetuity, and was owned by no one. In the words of Chief Frank Fools Crow, a Lakota medicine man: "We have one law ... to live on this earth with respect for all living things. That means we cannot harm the earth because we have respect for the place of those things in the world.... Heart, body, mind and soul all together with the world: that is the Indian way to live. You see, these hills are our church; the rivers and the wind, and the blossoms and the living things—that is our Bible. Nature is God, God is nature."[2]

In this relationship to land lies the most important cultural difference between Native Americans and the Europeans (later the people of the

United States). In contrast to Native American beliefs, in the culture of the United States, land is real estate and has no sacred qualities. Land is a tradable commodity and a proper source of individual wealth and profit. Drawing upon Western religious ideas, Americans believe nature to be God's gift to man, subject to man's dominion.

These different views on the meaning and use of land created a fundamental conflict as American political institutions resisted acknowledging the right of Native American governments to control their own land and to use it in the traditions of their cultures. The roots of this conflict were exposed in the first encounter between Native Americans and Europeans.

Columbus, and the men who followed him, came with a strongly developed sense of the supremacy of European values, religion, culture, and law. They assumed that they would dominate the land and peoples they encountered in what they called the New World and were prepared to deal with indigenous peoples only on terms dictated by Europe. The Europeans sought riches, opportunities for trade, land for the expansion of empire, and the chance to bring salvation, through conversion, to Native Americans, uniting them in a universal Christian community, driving out "the demons of difference," that is, those who were not Christians.[3]

For the Europeans, Native American land, which was held in common, not used for individual profit, and sometimes not used for agriculture, was land used inefficiently in violation of the European law of nature. Nothing more fundamentally reflected the cultural differences between Europeans and Native Americans than this European view that human beings could only be motivated to work by the promise of individual reward. This view of human nature, written into the earliest law, provided a rationale for the Europeans and, later, the Americans of the United States to dispossess Native Americans of their lands.

With the arrival of the British and the French in North America (joining the Spanish) by the early seventeenth century, a competition began among the several European sovereigns and trading companies for access to Native American land and goods, such as animal skins. To secure their investments in land and commerce, the Europeans imported the legal mechanisms that were part of their own cultures: formal deeds and contracts between individuals as well as government-to-government treaties.

When the British colonists organized an independent government, first, in 1781, under the Articles of Confederation and then, in 1789, under the U.S. Constitution, they continued the colonial tradition of dealing with Native Americans through Anglo-American law. Physically exhausted by the revolutionary war against England, concerned about the continuing presence of other European powers in North America, and with its treasury depleted, the leadership of the new Republic of the United States appreciated the value of lawful and diplomatic relations with Native American governments compared with the costs of the warfare and social disorder that would result from continuing conflicts with them. The U.S. decision, then, was to deal with Native American tribes peacefully, as sovereign nations, through internationally binding legal treaties. The degree to which Native Americans understood the nature of these agreements is disputed by scholars; Native American legal concepts differed from those of the Europeans, and translation of the proceedings was universally inadequate.

In these first years of diplomatic relations, Native American governments demonstrated considerable good will toward the United States. But it did not take long for Native Americans to realize the implications of white land hunger. By the 1790s, the Seneca leader Red Jacket, addressing the U.S. Senate, spoke sadly of how the Native Americans' faith in white law had been betrayed:

Brother! Listen to what we say. The Great Spirit ... made ... [this land] for the use of Indians .... But an evil day came upon us. Your forefathers crossed the great waters and landed on this island. Their numbers were small. They found friends and not enemies .... They asked for a small seat. We took pity on them, granted their request and they sat down amongst us. We gave them corn and meat ... They called us brothers. We believed them and gave them a large seat. At length their numbers had greatly increased. They wanted more land. They wanted our country. Our eyes were opened, and our minds became uneasy.[4]

By the first years of the nineteenth century, with the increasing population of the United States and subsequent scarcity of Native American land on the East Coast, Red Jacket's description became pertinent for more and more Native American nations, though to a different extent depending on the region. The United States was like a patchwork quilt: In the Northeast, much Native American land had been lost by the eighteenth century, while in the southeastern part of the continent, Native American nations resisted the pressure from state and federal governments to take over their land.

In the 1820s through the mid-1830s, a series of events took place that highlighted the collision course involving land rights and cultural differences between Native American nations and the United States. The allure of fertile farmland and the discovery of gold in the Cherokee Nation (in what is now Georgia) proved a strong magnet attracting both settlers and speculators to Cherokee land. The Cherokee Nation, in the face of the persistent pressure from state and federal governments of the United States to cede its land, realized that no degree of compromise would ever satisfy their American neighbors' hunger for land. As a result, in 1823, in a letter to U.S. treaty commissioners, the Cherokee National Council expressed "an unalterable determination ... never again to cede one foot more of land" and refused to sign treaties containing such language.[5]

At the same time, early in the nineteenth century, the Cherokee formed themselves into a republic with a constitution based upon that of neighboring governments and the United States. They established public schools and developed a syllabary that made possible the publication of a bilingual newspaper, the *Cherokee Phoenix*. They had become, for the most part, a settled agricultural and commercial people who welcomed Christian missionaries into their community. However, despite Cherokee attempts to accommodate whites by accepting certain aspects of Western culture, their earlier decision "not to cede another foot of land" led to pressure on members of the U.S. Congress to create legislation by which the United States could gain title to the lands of the Cherokee and other southeastern tribes under cover of law.

This legislation, the Indian Removal Act (4 Stat. 411), was passed by Congress in 1830, with the strong support of President Andrew Jackson. The act provided for the *voluntary* removal of Native Americans from their land east of the Mississippi River to lands west of the river. The Louisiana Purchase, in 1803, had encouraged a myth among Americans that there was a vast tract of western land, now under the jurisdiction of the United States, to which the Native Americans could be removed. Ignoring facts, President Jackson argued that since people like the Cherokee did not put their land to productive use, they were not entitled to hold it. "What good man," he asked, "would prefer a country covered with forests, and ranged by a few thousand savages to our extensive republic, studded with cities, towns, and prosperous farms ...."[6] Opponents of the bill included those who did not believe removal would protect the Cherokee from the encroachment of whites, or be voluntary, those who believed that the act violated prior binding treaties and U.S. recognition of Native American sovereignty and property rights, and those who were political opponents of Jackson and wished to embarrass him. After a close vote, however, the removal policy became law and a new era of U.S.-Native American relations began.

THE PROMISE OF LAW: THE CHEROKEE CASES

Even prior to Cherokee removal west in 1838, the increasing tensions between the United States and Native Americans presented an early opportunity for leaders of the Cherokee Republic to test the ideals of the United States, which emphasized a commitment to law as a way of resolving conflicts. Before the Removal Act had been passed, the state of Georgia had passed legislation intended to assert state jurisdiction over Native American societies adjacent to the state, with the intention of eventually incorporating that land. In the face of this hostile state and federal legislation, the Cherokee Nation, unwilling to resort to force and determined to take the whites' expressed reverence for law at face value, decided to test Native American national sovereignty and land rights in court. The Cherokee government hired two of the foremost lawyers in the United States, William Wirt and John Sergeant, to help them bring suit as a foreign nation against the state of Georgia in the Supreme Court of the United States. Through their lawyers, the Cherokee argued to restrain Georgia from executing and enforcing that state's new jurisdiction laws, contending that these laws violated international treaties between the Cherokee Republic and the United States as well as the Article VI Supremacy Clause of the U.S. Constitution.

In two cases, *Cherokee Nation v. Georgia* [30 U.S. 1 (1831)] and *Worcester v. Georgia* [31 U.S. 515 (1832)], Chief Justice John Marshall established the legal framework that, to this day, theoretically governs Native American property and political rights in the eyes of the United States. Marshall wrote that the Cherokee nation was "capable of managing its own affairs and governing itself." But, in order to protect the interests of the United States, he also defined Indian nations as "domestic dependent nations," whose relationship to the United States "resemble[d] that of a ward to his guardian."[7] Regarding land rights, in *Cherokee Nation* Marshall also attempted to lessen Native Americans' claims to their lands when he wrote that they "occupy a territory to which we assert a title independent of their will."[8] A year later in *Worcester,* Marshall provided a doctrine more sympathetic to Native American sovereignty and land rights. He described Native American nations as "independent political communities retaining their original natural rights as the undisputed possessors of the soil."[9] Even here, however, Marshall did not concede an absolute tribal title to Native American land, arguing instead that such nations held *occupancy,* not fee simple (absolute) title to their land. This meant, in Marshall's legal confection, that Native American societies had the right to use the land and live on it as long as they wished, if and until they willingly consented to extinguish occupancy title, in which case the United States, as heir to discovery title, would gain full legal possession.

The 1830 Indian Removal Act and the Supreme Court decisions in the Cherokee cases are significant because they set a pattern in which legal language appeared to offer protection for Native American rights, yet at the same time permitted the abrogation of those rights. Both the legislation and the court decisions established that Native American governments had a land title to be recognized by the United States that could only be yielded by tribal consent. In fact, however, Native American land was eagerly sought by whites, and both the legislative and executive branches were willing to respond to political pressure to pursue Indian land through fraudulent and coerced treaties as well as successful appeals to minority faction leaders within the tribes. Such manipulations permitted the Cherokee to be removed from their land in 1838 following the endorsement of a removal treaty by only 75 men in a nation of 15,000 people. The Cherokee name for the journey out of their homeland, the Trail of Tears, indicates

Stereotypes of Native Americans are often exploited for commercial purposes. Not only is the term "redskin" offensive, but the advertising misrepresents Cherokee culture. It was the Plains Indians, not the Cherokee, who wore feathered headdresses. Photo courtesy of Joan Gregg.

this move was a forced march rather than a voluntary exodus. With Cherokee removal, the imprimatur of law was placed, not for the last time, on the expropriation of Native American land.

THE WHITE PROBLEM DOESN'T GO AWAY

The supporters of the Removal Act hoped—in vain—that it would be a pragmatic solution to "the Indian Problem." Certainly, for Native Americans it was not a solution to the "white problem" because the two groups continued to confront one another as white settlers pushed westward. Many of the problems that had plagued Native Americans in the East, such as the damaging impact of unscrupulous traders and the sale of liquor as well as the effects of contagious diseases, followed them, in the 1840s and 1850s, to the West. In an attempt to address these problems and to honor binding treaty commitments concerning Native American land title, the U.S. government embarked upon a wholesale policy of settling Native Americans, using coercion and force, in precisely defined geographical areas, called reservations. Here, ideally, the Native American would be free from what the government considered the damaging effects of some aspects of white culture.

Reservations were not an entirely new idea. Even prior to the creation of the United States, the colonists had attempted to deal with the clash of cultures by creating small reserves of land for Native Americans. While some of the supporters of the reservation policy were well-meaning, it is clear that they were also ethnocentric: They wished to save Native Americans physically in order to transform them into Christians, capitalists, and democrats. The reservations provided a way of disarming and controlling Native Americans and making them a captive audience to be taught Western values. Representatives from the U.S. government called Indian agents, traders, and missionaries, who were permitted within the boundaries of the reservations, would be the agents of change. This transition was, for the U.S. government, the linchpin of its Indian policy. While some supporters of the reservation policy hoped to help Native Americans, for other supporters the policy was one more skirmish in a cultural war ultimately designed to save the Indian by eradicating Native American languages, religion, and economic systems.

Within a relatively short time, however, it became clear that the reservation policy did not work. Unwilling subjects of assimilation, most Native Americans resisted acculturation. Furthermore, the centralization of Indian populations on reservations made them even more vulnerable to the purveyors of alcohol. In addition, the reservation system could not and did not protect Native Americans against loss of land. Having lost aboriginal (original) title to Eastern lands, Native Americans found treaty-title reservation land just as eagerly sought after. Pressure to yield this treaty-title reservation land was intense and in various ways including, again, new fraudulent treaties, vast parcels of reservation land came into white ownership. Native Americans continued to be too much in the way of the "march of progress."

By the early 1870s, the inadequacies of the reservation system became apparent. The slow pace of acculturation on reservations combined with continuing assaults by settlers on Native Americans on the frontier, and the negative impact of the transcontinental railroad on the ecology, economy, and social well-being of Native Americans convinced American social reformers and government officials to consider a policy that would result in more rapid Native American assimilation. Reviving an early-nineteenth-century policy, a consensus emerged that the quickest way to turn Native Americans into "good Christians, capitalists and democrats" would be to allot them individually owned sections of land from what had been communally held tribal land. U.S. Senator Henry Dawes expressed a widespread feeling among Americans when he said, in a speech supporting this policy of allotment: "They [the Indians] have got as far as they can go, because they own their land in common.... There is no selfishness, which is at the bottom of civilization. Till this people will consent to give up their lands, and divide them among their citizens so that each can own land he cultivates, they will not make much more progress."[10]

In the words of Native American scholars Kirke Kickingbird and Karen Ducheneaux, men like Dawes insisted that, "the magical qualities of individual property would transform the stolid warriors into happy church-going farmers."[11] Kickingbird and Ducheneaux aptly capture the spirit of American unwillingness to accept the cultural difference of Native Americans. This unwillingness became law with the passage of the General Allotment (Dawes) Act (24 Stat. 388) in 1887.

As with the earlier Indian Removal Act, the Dawes Act only won congressional support after long and heated debate. A key issue centered upon the degree to which Anglo-American law should be applied to Native Americans as they agreed to abandon tribal community and to live like white men and women. The assimilationists considered themselves reformers. They believed that without the protection of American law Native Americans would continue to be both physically and culturally exploited and deprived of "the benefits of civilization." Others argued that "the Indian must live among us" but was not "yet competent to vote intelligently," and supported a more gradual extension of citizenship rights to Indians. Dr. Thomas A. Bland, organizer of the National Indian Defense Association, defended the unpopular view of an "Indian's right to be an Indian." He argued that earlier assimilation policies had not worked and that any new assimilation policy should move slowly and take into account generational differences within Native American communities as well as the differences between Native American tribes' interest in acculturation. Unlike other lobbyists, Bland argued for more rather than less Native American control of their own affairs and less U.S. interference in the absence of a specific request by a tribe. Bland's arguments were the closest that Native Americans came to having a voice in the debate over their future.

Supporters of immediate Native American assimilation won the day with the passage of Dawes General Allotment Act, which provided, for the tribes specified in the law, that each Native American head of household, (and other eligible persons) would be allotted 160 acres of land with individual, not communal-tribal, title. Unlike whites, however, the government forbid Native American allottees to sell their land for a period of 25 years, a policy that again emphasized the government's position that

Native Americans were wards in need of paternalistic protection. The act also provided that all Native Americans who participated in the allotment, as well as those who left the land and adopted "civilized life," were eligible to become American citizens. Another provision of the act was that "surplus" land—reservation land left over after each eligible Indian had received an allotment—could be sold immediately by the U.S. government to non-Indians.

Despite its stated goal of helping the Indians, the Dawes Act was aimed at destroying tribal societies. By offering individual Native Americans citizenship and individual landholding, the act made it more difficult for tribal governing bodies to function and, thus, quite intentionally undercut tribal sovereignty and unity.

As a result of the Dawes Act millions of acres of what was previously tribal land passed into the hands of whites, some of it by swindle, some by individual sale, and some to the U.S. government, which sold it as "surplus" land. It was ironic, that at a time when white farmers and ranchers were attempting to consolidate landholding in order to make them more efficient and productive, the Dawes Act required relatively small allocations to Native Americans. Cherokee DeWitt Clinton Duncan spoke about this problem in 1906 before a Senate committee:

I spent the early days of my life on the farm up here of 300 acres, and arranged to be comfortable in my old age; but the allotment scheme came along ... I had to relinquish every inch of my premises outside of that little [allotment] ... I have exerted all my ability, all industry, all my intelligence ... to make my living out of that [allotment] ... and, God be my judge, I have not been able to do it. I am not able to do it ... What am I to do? I have a piece of property that doesn't support me and is not worth a cent to me under the cruel provisions of the ... law that swept away our treaties, our system of nationality, our very existence, and wrested out of our possession our vast territory.[12]

By the 1920s it was apparent that the Dawes Act was a failure. It neither transformed a majority of Native Americans into "happy churchgoing farmers" nor did it fulfill its supporters' expectations that allotment would be "the mighty pulverizing engine for breaking up the tribal mass." Most Native Americans, without a right to be different in the eyes of the United States, nevertheless made it clear that they did not want to be Americanized. For Native Americans the white problem had still not gone away.

THE TWENTIETH CENTURY

Even as the failures of the Dawes Act were acknowledged, the goal of assimilation was not abandoned. In 1924 Congress passed an act extending citizenship to all Native Americans who were not yet citizens. But with the election of President Franklin D. Roosevelt in 1932, the U.S. government began a reappraisal of its assimilation policy. Led by social worker John Collier, appointed by Roosevelt to head the U.S. Bureau of Indian Affairs, legislation was prepared to address the myriad problems and inequities that the Dawes Act had not in any way resolved and, indeed, had exacerbated. In 1934 the controversial Indian Reorganization Act (the Wheeler-Howard Act) (48 Stat. 984) was passed, which had the intent of strengthening tribal government, promoting the revival of Native American culture and asserting Indian religious rights, restoring Native American lands to communal holding, and aiding economic development within tribal communities. Again, in spite of good intentions, albeit informed by a governmental perspective, the end results, from the Native American point of view, were mixed. To begin with, the legislation was written without consultation with Native Americans, and the tribal governments provided for in the act were based on Western values reflecting individualism and majoritarianism as opposed to consensual decision making. And although tribal landholding increased slightly as a result of the termination of allotment, Native American lives did not, in fact, improve appreciably.

Shortly after World War II when Dillon Myer, former director of the War Relocation Authority—which had responsibility for the removal of Japanese Americans from the West Coast during the war—became commissioner of Indian affairs, U.S. government policy again shifted back to assimilationism. With the election of Dwight Eisenhower as president this point of view culminated in congressional action aimed at getting the federal government "out of the Indian business." The new policy was colloquially called "termination."

Despite clear evidence that Native Americans had maintained their distinctly different culture—even as many moved to urban areas—in adhering to religious practices, tribal languages, traditional values of community, reciprocity, and kinship, and were resistant to assimilation, a basic assertion of termination policy was that no important cultural differences existed between Native Americans and other Americans. The supporters of this policy were political conservatives whose central value was individualism and the priority of private property over group interests, and they refused to acknowledge—or validate—other world views.

The intention of the policy was to end both legal and moral obligations by the federal government to Native Americans, an obligation that the government incurred as the legacy of *Cherokee Nation* and America's march west. Although rarely expressed in explicit terms, many of the services—health, education, law enforcement—that the government had offered Native Americans were in fact necessary to ameliorate the disruptions caused to Native American culture and economy by the incursions of Western culture and the subsequent loss of land. The major thrust of termination policy was the withdrawal of the federal government's trust responsibility to Native American people and their tribes and any special help given to Native Americans as a result of this relationship. In five states, federal and tribal civil and criminal jurisdiction over the tribes within their borders was replaced by state law and policymaking.

In addition to its individualistic ideology, termination appealed to American policymakers and the public because a century of federal involvement caused federal politicians to be increasingly impatient and skeptical about the efficacy of the federal trust relationship with tribes, and because termination offered the possibility of decreasing federal spending on Native American communities. Moreover, the rejection by the U.S. Supreme Court, at that time, of the separate but equal doctrine in connection with school segregation (see *Brown v. Board of Education*), offered the supporters of termination a convenient rationale for the extension of the idea of equality under law to Native American peoples and communities, despite the completely different history and relationship of the federal government to Native Americans and African Americans. Thus, in spite of the high tone of the rhetoric of termination, it was in fact, yet another government assault on Native American land, sovereignty, culture, and identity.

With the explosion of the African American civil rights movement in the late 1950s, America embarked on a road of increased self-awareness. Issues of equality and social justice came to dominate the political and social agenda of the nation. Encouraged by the legislative and legal success of the African American rights movement, in the 1960s Native Americans became more vocal and formed new organizations, such as the American Indian Movement (AIM), which protested against the historical injustices to which they had been subject. From the mid-sixties to the mid-seventies, this Native American protest increased. During this time Native American activists occupied Alcatraz and Wounded Knee and organized the 1972 march to Washington on the Trail of Broken Treaties, which culminated in the occupation for five days of the Bureau of Indian Affairs. In this political climate, President Richard Nixon signaled the end of the termination era in a 1970 speech requesting that Congress commit resources to strengthen Native American autonomy.

In the 1970s, the apparent openness of the federal government to Native American claims for cultural and religious freedom and economic redress resulted in a major congressional study of the status of the American Indian in the United States and the establishment of more Native American political and legal organizations. Important among these were two major public interest law firms headed by Native Americans and concerned with Native American legal issues: the Native American Rights Fund and the Indian Law Resource Center. As a result, there was a significant increase in both political lobbying and litigation on issues ranging from religious freedom to hunting, fishing, and water rights. Of all these issues, land claims occupied a central place.

Among land-claims litigation, perhaps none achieved the national prominence of *United States v. Sioux* [448 U.S. 371 (1980)]. Familiar to Americans through school books and films, the Sioux had become emblematic of *the* American Indian. The images portrayed a people—proud, capable, and formidable—that, tragically, bore little relation to the contemporary Sioux. Stripped of their land in the last quarter of the nineteenth century, the economy and social and cultural fabric of Sioux society had deteriorated greatly under the conditions of restricted reservation life.

It was General George Armstrong Custer who, in 1874, announced to the world that there was gold in the Black Hills, land that belonged to the Sioux Nation. Just six years earlier, the U.S. government had signed, by solemn treaty, the right of the Sioux to "the absolute and undisturbed use" of this land. Custer's announcement set off a clamor among white prospectors to take the Hills away from their Sioux owners. The government responded by first attempting to pressure the Sioux to cede the Black Hills. When that failed, the government forced the Sioux out. Federal agents disarmed the Sioux, took away the ponies without which they were unable to hunt buffalo, and finally, threatened to cut off the government rations on which the Sioux were largely dependent. In 1876 the United States made one last effort to obtain a legal title to the Black Hills by attempting to obtain the required signatures of 75 percent of the adult men of the tribe. When only 10 percent gave their consent to the transfer of their land to the United States, Congress passed the Act of 1877, which accomplished the land-grab by fiat.

At this time, the U.S. government justified its extraordinary action in taking the land by claiming that the Sioux were not self-sufficient. This contention was rich in irony since the 1868 treaty had already seized 48 million acres from the Sioux Nation, virtually eliminating its hunting ground after the buffalo had been decimated by whites. When the Army dismounted and disarmed the Sioux, they became totally dependent on the United States for food. In short, the U.S. government took away the ability of the Sioux to be self-sufficient, then pointed to their dependent state as proof of their inability to manage their own affairs and in particular, to control their land.

"THE BLACK HILLS ARE NOT FOR SALE"

Since the late 1880s, Sioux councils had met continuously to discuss their grievances over this taking of the Black Hills.[13] But it was not until the early 1920s that litigation began with a young, non-Indian attorney, Ralph Case, representing the Sioux. Case, sometimes working with other attorneys, framed and filed a legal claim that would give the Sioux money compensation for what the Sioux argued was an illegal taking by the United States of more than seven million acres of land. According to his reading of the law—in particular, the Fifth Amendment's "taking" clause and legislation controlling the U.S. Court of Claims (the federal court with jurisdiction for money claims against the U.S. government)—Case persuaded his Sioux clients that they could not demand that the U.S. government return the land, but could only hope to get just compensation—market value of the land at the time it was taken, plus interest.

For the next 30 years, Case pursued Sioux claims through a tangle of political and legal pathways in which he tried to establish a clear history of the government's "double dealing" and coercion in relation to the taking of the Black Hills. But the U.S. Indian Claims Commission, established in 1946, and the several federal courts before which Case argued on behalf of the Sioux rejected the legal theories upon which he based the Sioux land claims; additionally, they apprised the Sioux that, in their view, the Sioux had no claim because the United States had acted toward them in a "fair and honorable fashion."

By the mid-1950s, little progress appeared to have been made and some Sioux began to explore the possibility of bringing in new attorneys to work on the case. With Case's death in June 1957, a new team of lawyers from a Washington law firm that had experience in tribal legal issues assumed responsibility for the Sioux claims. For the next two decades these lawyers, led by Arthur Lazarus Jr. and Marvin Sonosky, used a variety of legal and political stratagems to further a money compensation award to their clients. In 1979, the Court of Claims awarded the Sioux the long-sought judgment of $17.5 million plus interest for the taking of the Black Hills.

The U.S. government, however, rejected the court's decision. The position of the U.S. Justice Department was that the taking of Sioux land in 1877 was compensated for by food and clothing rations that had been sent to the Sioux for many years afterwards. In the government's view, the Sioux would have lost the land anyway to the predations of white gold miners and farmers, and thus the United States had not only acted in "perfect good faith," but had actually saved the Sioux from starvation and the loss of their land without *any* compensation. The government argued that there had been no violation of treaties or the Fifth Amendment. It appealed the Court of Claims decision to the U.S. Supreme Court, which agreed to hear the case.

At midmorning on Monday, March 24, 1980, lawyers for the Sioux Nation and the U.S. government stood before the justices of the U.S. Supreme Court prepared to argue *United States v. Sioux*, a case that by that morning had been in litigation for nearly 60 years. Many thought, and some hoped, that the high court's decision would be the final chapter in the ongoing struggle of the Sioux Nation to win redress for the taking of 7.5 million acres of Black Hills land.

That morning Deputy Solicitor General Louis Claiborne presented the government's argument that the United States had, in its continual dealings with the Sioux, been motivated solely by a concern for the best interests of the Sioux, claiming that "the Indian tribes have been incapable of prudent management of their communal property" and that the United States had, by necessity, to do it for them.[14]

The attorneys for the Sioux, however, dismissed with contempt the government's argument that it was motivated by concern for Sioux interests and that the rations proffered over the decades were a fair equivalent of the value of the land. Instead, they argued that the taking of the land in the 1870s violated the Fifth Amendment, which says that just compensation must be paid when government takes property for public use.

In an opinion written by Justice Harry Blackmun, with only Justice William Rehnquist dissenting in full, the Supreme Court strongly rejected the government's claim of "fair and honorable dealings" and accepted the Sioux's contention that the rations were in no way fair compensation for the taking of the Black Hills. Indeed, the court stated, the rations were never intended to be compensation at all. Rather, Justice Blackmun acknowledged that an underlying but critical issue in this land claims case was the U.S. policy of assimilating the Sioux. Blackmun wrote:

It seems readily apparent to us that the obligation to provide rations to the Sioux was undertaken in order to ensure them a means of surviving their transition from the nomadic life of the hunt to the agrarian life style Congress had chosen for them ... It is reasonable to conclude that Congress' undertaking of an obligation to provide rations for the Sioux was a *quid pro quo* for depriving them of their chosen way of life, and was not intended to compensate them for the taking of the Black Hills.

The majority of the court concluded, then, that the government's 1877 act was a taking (confiscation) of tribal property guaranteed to the Sioux under the 1868 Fort Laramie Treaty and that the government of the United States had an obligation to make just compensation at long last to the Sioux Nation. It affirmed the judgment of the Court of Claims, awarding $17.5 million, the value of the land at the time of the taking, plus somewhat less than $100 million in accrued interest.

While Lazarus and Sonosky and some of their Sioux clients were extremely pleased with the Supreme Court decision in their favor, most among the Sioux were not. For many years, while this litigation had been going on, there were Sioux who were determined that the illegal taking of their land by the United States could only be redressed by return of the land itself, and not by money compensation.

While an orally based culture does not, in its nature, tend to create a written archive, from the moment of the taking of *Paha Sapa*, their sacred Black Hills, the Sioux made it clear that they had not parted with their land willingly, that the land was the basis of their spiritual and communal life, and that only fear and the total desperation of their position accounted for their parting with their land. That they devoutly hoped for the return of their land was expressed in many ways, not least in the rapid spread of the Ghost Dance in the 1880s to the Sioux reservations. The Ghost Dance was a messianic, revitalist movement that, in the words of the Sioux Kicking Bear, expressed the vision of " ... the promise of a day in which there will be no white man to lay his hand on the bridle of the Indian's horse; when the red man of the prairie will rule the world and not be turned from the hunting grounds by any man."[15] White fear that the Ghost Dance would precipitate Sioux rebellion had led to the tragic massacre of the Sioux at Wounded Knee by the U.S. Army on December 29, 1890. For the next several decades, Sioux elders voiced their deeply felt grievances against the illegal taking of the Black Hills in their tribal councils.

But with the increasing control of Sioux reservations by U.S. government agents, and the imposition of assimilationist policy through, for example, the Dawes Act, factionalism developed among the Sioux in which a new generation of younger, more assimilated Sioux contested the power of the elders and their vision of the future of the Sioux Nation. It was this younger group of Sioux, along with lawyers working on a contingency fee basis, that led to a case framed in terms of money compensation, rather than return of land.

With the shaping of the Sioux claims by attorneys Case, Lazarus, and Sonosky according to a strategy of money compensation, rather than return of land, the question arises why a formal statement of claims for *return* of the Black Hills did not emerge until the 1970s. Given the absence of a continuous written record of Sioux debate on the issue, this question cannot be definitely answered. However, a review of Sioux history suggests several factors that would support the view that hopes for eventual land return had never ended.

The public silence of the Sioux in the early twentieth century, immediately after Wounded Knee, was not only a response to the trauma of the massacre but also the result of the intensification of the government's Dawes Act assimilation program that put U.S. government agents firmly in control on the Sioux reservations.

It is also clear that the Sioux, like the Cherokee in the 1830s, were affected by the lack of Native American lawyers trained in the law of the United States. It is logical, then, that the articulation of an alternative legal theory that presented a Sioux case for *return of the land* only occurred in the mid-1970s after the first Sioux graduated from an American law school and began to practice law. It was this attorney, Mario Gonzalez, who went before a Sioux tribal council and argued that the Fifth Amendment only permitted the taking of land for *public* use; the Black Hills, he contended, were seized for the private use and benefit of American miners, farmers, and ranchers. Gonzalez maintained that the Sioux should terminate all litigation that did not demand return of the Black Hills. While Gonzalez's position won support among the Sioux, Sonosky and Lazarus continued arguing the case for money compensation in the Court of Claims and, when the United States appealed, at the Supreme Court. Thus, ironically, at the same time that Gonzalez and his followers were insisting on return of land, U.S. courts were awarding more than $100 million, hoping to quiet Sioux legal title to the Black Hills forever.

The government hope of closing the Sioux land claims case has not been met; the legal struggle over the Black Hills is not over. Virtually all of the members of the Sioux Nation have rejected the "just compensation" awarded by the courts of the United States. The award, now vastly increased in size because of accrued interest, remains untouched at the U.S. Treasury. Holding to their cultural value of the "sacred primacy" of the land, the Sioux continue to argue, "the Black Hills are not for sale," and as recently as 2005, Gonzalez was acting for the Oglala Sioux in their efforts to block the transfer of recreation lands claimed by the tribe to the State of South Dakota.[16] The struggles of the Sioux to protect and regain land mirror similar judicial and legislative contests waged by other tribes as well as the Native people of Alaska who, in 1971, agreed to the extinguishment of all of their land claims in exchange for 44 million acres of Alaskan public lands and $962 million in compensation.[17]

In the twenty-first century the meaning and value of tribal land remains a matter of spirit, community, and economics. A number of tribes have sought to clarify the status of their land rights in order to establish casino-gambling businesses. More than 200 tribes currently operate over 400 casinos with revenues of $19 billion in 2004.[18] Not everyone is happy about the increasing dependence of Indian communities on gambling revenue, and some observers believe that the casino business and its publicity greatly distort understanding of Indian affairs, including the poverty and poor health that continue to plague many Native Americans.

The value of that land and its resources also remains an area of highly contested law and negotiation. In what may become the landmark case of this era, Elouise Cobell, a member of the Blackfoot tribe, filed a class-action lawsuit (in 1996) asking that the U.S. government fulfill its obligations as trustee to Indian people. She argued, and lower federal courts have agreed, that the government has failed, since the 1887 Dawes Act established specific trust responsibilities, to pay Indians more than a staggering $100 billion of royalties from oil, timber, grazing, and other leases on land allotments. In July 2005, frustrated by the government's "default" and unwillingness to negotiate in good faith, Royce C. Lamberth, the federal district court judge hearing the case, wrote with barely disguised despair of the legacy of the trust relationship imposed in the nineteenth century:

The government as a whole may be inherently incapable of serving as an adequate fiduciary because of some structural flaw. Perhaps the Indians were doomed the moment the first European set foot on American soil. Who can say? It may be that the opacity of the cause renders the Indian trust problem insoluble.

On numerous occasions over the last nine years, the Court has wanted to simply wash its hands of [the department of] Interior and its iniquities once and for all. The plaintiffs have invited the Court to declare that Interior has repudiated the Indian trust, appoint a receiver to liquidate the trust assets, and finally relieve the Indians of the heavy yoke of government stewardship. The Court may eventually do all these things—but not yet. Giving up on rehabilitating Interior would signal more than the downfall of a single administrative agency. It would constitute an announcement that negligence and incompetence in government are beyond judicial remedy, that bureaucratic recalcitrance has outpaced and rendered obsolete our vaunted system of checks and balances, and that people are simply at the mercy of governmental whim with no chance for salvation. The Court clings to a slim and quickly receding hope that future progress may vitiate the need for such a grim declaration.

This hope is sustained in part by the fact that the Indians who brought this case found it in themselves to stand up, draw a line in the sand, and tell the government: Enough is enough—this far and no further. Perhaps they regret having done so now, nine years later, beset on all sides by the costs of protracted litigation and the possibility that their efforts may ultimately prove futile; but still they continue ...

Real justice for these Indians may still lie in the distant future; it may never come at all. This reality makes a statement about our society and our form of government that we should be unwilling to let stand. But perhaps the best that can be hoped for is that people never forget what the plaintiffs have done here, and that other marginalized people will learn about this case and follow the Indians' example.[19]

Cobell is only one in a long line of cases in which Native American plaintiffs have attempted to hold the U.S. government to laws of its own making. Judge Lamberth is not willing to predict the outcome of this struggle, but he has gone out of his way to honor the Indian plaintiffs for their faith in the law and the possibility that their effort will serve as a role model for other marginalized groups.

NOTES

1. Clark Wissler, *Indians of the United States* (New York: Doubleday, 1966).

2. Peter Matthiessen, *In the Spirit of Crazy Horse* (New York: Viking, 1983), 519.

3. Robert A. Williams Jr., *The American Indian in Western Legal Thought* (New York: Oxford University Press, 1990).

4. W. C. Vanderwerth, ed., *Indian Oratory* (New York: Ballantine Books, 1972), 39.

5. Petra T. Shattuck and Jill Norgren, *Partial Justice* (Oxford: Berg, 1991), 39.

6. *7 Cong. Deb.* App. X (Washington, D.C.: 1830).

7. *Cherokee Nation v. Georgia*, 30 U.S. 1, 17–18 (1831).

8. *Cherokee Nation v. Georgia*, 44.

9. *Worcester v. Georgia*, 31 U.S. 515, 561 (1832).

10. A. Debo, *And Still the Waters Run* (Norman: University of Oklahoma Press, 1984), 22.

11. Kirke Kickingbird and Karen Ducheneaux, *One Hundred Million Acres* (New York: Macmillan, 1973), 19.

12. Peter Nabokov, ed., *Native American Testimony* (New York: Viking, 1991), 266–67.

13. Edward Lazarus, *Black Hills/White Justice* (New York: HarperCollins, 1991), 119.

14. For a summary of oral argument in the case see Lazarus, *Black Hills/White Justice*, 387–92.

15. Vanderwerth, *Indian Oratory*, 197–98.

16. *The Oglala Sioux Tribe v. U.S. Army Corps of Engineers*, Case No. 1: 01CV02679.

17. Alaska Native Claims Settlement Act of 1971 (85 Stat. 688).

18. Fox Butterfield, "Indian Casino Revenues Grow To Sizeable Segment of Industry," *New York Times* (June 16, 2005), A20.

19. *Cobell v. Norton*, Civil Action No. 96–1285 (RCL), Memorandum Opinion (July 12, 2005), 32–34.

CHAPTER 2

Trouble in Paradise: Native Hawaiian and Puerto Rican Sovereignty

The issues of sovereignty, cultural identity, and law that intersected in the colonial experiences of Hawaii and Puerto Rico have reverberations in the contemporary conflicts between these island paradises and the U.S. government.[1] Although these experiences are different in important ways, there are also some important similarities. In both societies, the imposition of Western law resulted in the loss of sovereignty and culture and the transfer of important economic assets from control of local populations to American capitalist enterprises and American cultural hegemony. Law in these colonial possessions became an important instrument of social control, as it is in all colonial societies, as it was used to define acceptable behavior and to enforce that behavior.[2]

Among both Native Hawaiians and Puerto Ricans today, there is no complete consensus about the best way to resolve the still highly contested issues of sovereignty and cultural identity. Different groups have different goals and different means for achieving those goals. In general, Native Hawaiians have used courts more than have Puerto Ricans, but both in Puerto Rico and among Native Hawaiians, political protests and legislative action have been important in moving their political agendas forward.

LAW AND LOSS IN HAWAIIAN HISTORY

The history of cultural clashes, broken promises, violation of legal trust relationships, and loss of land that is so central in relations between Native Americans and the U.S. government is also the source of conflict between the United States and the indigenous people of Hawaii. The struggle for cultural integrity and return of land is at the center of the contemporary efforts of Native Hawaiians to assert their sovereignty and claim their rights. This struggle has involved state legislatures and Congress, as well as local, state, and federal courts. Native Hawaiians can claim few important legal victories, however, and recently they experienced an important setback in a Supreme Court decision that may undercut the small gains they were able to achieve in the past 50 years. But that is getting a little ahead of the story. In order to look beneath and beyond the contemporary tourist sell of Hawaii as a harmonious paradise untroubled by conflicts over power, land, and economic "development," we have to begin with the "rediscovery" of the Hawaiian islands by Western powers.

THE HAWAIIAN ISLANDS

The Hawaiian Islands were settled around 300 A.D. by seafaring Polynesians from the Marquesan Islands looking for a new home. In these islands they developed a distinctive culture, consisting of the Hawaiian language; a rural subsistence economy based on taro, a tropical plant with a starchy, edible root, and fishing; the sharing of material goods and cooperative labor; feasting as an expression of community; child adoption as an important means of forging kinship relations; a spiritual as well as economic relationship to land and natural resources; and a tradition of government through chiefs and, later, monarchs that rested on a philosophy of mutual benefit through stewardship and productive labor.[3]

The indigenous Hawaiian political structure consisted of independent, and frequently warring, chiefdoms. The *ali'i*, or high chiefs, and priests, occupied the highest rung of society. *Ali'i* did not "own" the land, but controlled its distribution, parceling it out to *ahupua'a* or district chiefs who were their relatives or allies. Below the district chiefs were the *konohiki*, or land agents, who were chiefs of independent political units of the *ahupua'a*. At the bottom of the social ladder were the *maka'ainana*, the common people. Each level of society had its obligations, rights, and responsibilities.

The *maka'ainana* worked collectively under the direction of chiefs and priests to clear the land, construct irrigation systems, cultivate taro, and build fish-breeding ponds. In return they were granted rights to land with sufficient water for taro cultivation; hunting and gathering; offshore fishing rights; and the use of *ahupua'a* resources for their own subsistence. Commoners who felt they were unfairly treated could (and would) move from one district to another, giving them some leverage in dealing with those above them in the social system.

Chiefs typically reserved some land for their personal use and distributed the remaining land to loyal district chiefs, relatives, or allies, but no one "owned" the land in the Western sense of total and exclusive dominion. When a high chief died or was conquered, his land did not go to his heirs, but to the conquering chief and his allies. This lack of security in land through inheritance was the most important source of early conflicts between Native Hawaiians and Europeans and, later, Americans.[4]

LAW AND THE LOSS OF LAND AND CULTURE

The first sustained Western contact with Hawaii began with the landing of the English explorer Captain James Cook in 1778. European contact and the imposition of Western law laid the foundation for the subsequent American domination of the islands. As a result of European contact the Native Hawaiian population was devastated both through a declining birth rate and increased mortality due to venereal disease, tuberculosis, and other bacterial and viral infections brought by the Europeans; there were also substantial fatalities from the introduction of guns and alcohol. From a precontact population conservatively estimated at 400,000, the 1990 census counted only 8,000 pure-blood Hawaiians and 200,000 part-Hawaiians.

Shortly after Captain Cook's landing, traders, missionaries, whaling ships, and investors from many countries came to Hawaii, and Western contact began in earnest. By 1795, with Western support and substantial weaponry, the Hawaiian Islands were united under Kamehameha, the high chief of Oahu, who became King Kamehameha I, founder of the Hawaiian monarchy.[5] This unified leadership benefited Europeans, first because it increased stability in the islands by ending warfare, and second because it was more convenient for Europeans to deal with the Hawaiian people through a single ruler than to negotiate with several independent chiefs.

During the reign of Kamehameha I, European economic and political influence in Hawaii expanded considerably. Kamehameha I did not alter Hawaiian land tenure, but his economic dependence on Europeans and the growing involvement of Hawaiian chiefs in European trade was the opening wedge for later legal changes introducing a Western system of private land ownership.

When Kamehameha I died in 1819, his son, Liholiho, became King Kamehameha II, ruling with his mother, Queen Ka'ahumanu, until 1824, when he died of measles contracted on a state visit to London. Liholiho's reign saw important changes in Hawaiian culture and traditional land tenure. In Liholiho's first year on the throne, the Hawaiian religion was traumatically destroyed. This religion was based on *kapu*, or taboos, which regulated all aspects of personal interaction and all relationships between the people and the natural environment. The *kapu* system began to erode when it was observed that foreigners, who persistently violated taboos, escaped unharmed. Much influenced by Western culture, in 1819 Queen Ka'ahumanu and Liholiho abolished the *kapu* system altogether by publicly violating the taboo against women and men eating together. Liholiho then ordered the destruction of temples and images of the gods and the killing of priests.[6]

In a miracle of perfect timing, one year later the first organized group of Christian missionaries arrived from the United States, opening the door to large-scale conversion of Hawaiians to Christianity. American missionaries soon became key influential advisors to the Hawaiian government. Their descendants, who moved from missionary work to business enterprise, subsequently became the major foreign landholders and economic oligarchs in Hawaii.

During Liholiho's reign, European landholdings increased as both the king and many chiefs exchanged land for European goods—clothing, rum, weapons, and hardware—and services. But the Europeans and Hawaiian chiefs continued to press Liholiho to make their land rights more permanent by instituting a Western system of inheritance. Liholiho responded by allowing his father's chiefs to keep their land, but the Europeans continued to press for explicit inheritance rights to land.

When Liholiho died in 1824, his 12-year-old son, Kamehameha III, ascended the throne. He soon succumbed to continued European pressure for more permanent protection of individual land rights and in 1825 signed a new law formally allowing chiefs to retain their lands upon the death of the king and giving them hereditary rights in their land.

During King Kamehameha III's reign, the emerging Hawaiian political structure and land tenure system drew increasingly upon Western liberal ideas about protecting individual property rights, which benefited both foreigners and the chiefs, who could now "give" their land to Europeans in order to pay their mounting debts. As the Europeans and, increasingly, Americans acquired more land, they increased their investments in large-scale agriculture, which, with the opening of a growing market in California, now became a profitable business.

THE TRANSFORMATION OF HAWAIIAN SOCIETY
AND THE INROADS OF THE LAW

Between 1820 and 1850, the Kingdom of Hawaii was transformed from a traditional governing system based on sacred laws, hereditary rank, and religious authority to one based on Anglo-American common law, a written constitution, and an elected legislature modeled on the American and British systems. Western law made important inroads among both the Hawaiian elites and the common people and ultimately reshaped the whole of Hawaiian society and culture.[7] Hawaiian elites used Western law to protect their property rights, while the common people began to use the local, Western-oriented courts to resolve property disputes. As more Hawaiians learned to covet Western goods, they left their rural communities to participate in the cash economy of the port cities. Here traditional social controls held little sway and led to the introduction of a missionary-influenced criminal code, which punished such behaviors as theft, gambling, illicit intercourse, murder, the selling of rum, and prostitution, bringing more Native Hawaiians before the courts. As disputants accepted court judgments reflecting Western individualism, a Western legal ideology began to replace the Hawaiian system of folk law and culture.

By mid-century, Western land-tenure law also became more deeply entrenched in Hawaiian society. As a result of continual foreign pressure, in 1848 the Hawaiian government instituted the Great Mahele, a division of land that provided for absolute private ownership and individual inheritance. Under the Mahele, the King held 60 percent of the total land, or 2.5 million acres, while the chiefs received an additional 1.5 million acres. As protection against some future foreign conquest of Hawaii, the King divided his land into two parts: He retained about one million acres, called the Crown Lands, for himself, his heirs, and successors, and "set apart forever to the chiefs and the people" another one million acres of land, called the Government Lands.

In 1850, the Hawaiian legislature passed the Kuleana Act, which formalized individual land ownership for common people who could prove that they were living on and cultivating a piece of land. The stated aim of the Kuleana Act, similar to the Dawes Act for Native Americans, was the survival of the Hawaiian people through their transformation into independent farmers, living in nuclear families, cultivating their privately owned lands.[8] Like the Dawes Act, the Kuleana Act was a spectacular failure. Although 30,000 Native Hawaiian males were eligible to claim a homestead, only 8,200 awards were ultimately made. Many Hawaiians were not sufficiently familiar with written law or land claims to understand what they needed to do; others could not afford the survey fees to make their claims; still others were afraid of reprisals from their *konohiki* if they filed. Thus, like the Dawes Act, the Great Mahele and the Kuleana Act resulted in the transfer of millions of acres of land from Native Hawaiians to Westerners.

The Great Mahele confirmed the legal titles of Europeans to the enormous acreage they already owned; Hawaiian kings and chiefs continued to transfer land to Europeans to pay their debts for foreign goods; and commoners often lost their small homesteads to foreigners through debt, coercion, legal technicalities, and the inability of their small and often marginal acreage to support a family. By 1890, fewer than 5,000 of the nearly 90,000 Native Hawaiians owned any land at all, and what they owned amounted to very little acreage. In contrast, a very small number of Americans and Europeans owned three quarters of the privately held land in Hawaii.[9]

Still, the Americans, who had now largely replaced European and British investors and advisors in Hawaii, were not satisfied. With the opening up of the American West and the passage of legislation to permit the free export of sugar from Hawaii, by 1875 sugar plantations expanded exponentially. The increased demand for labor led to enormously increased immigration, primarily from Japan, China, and the Philippines. Between 1877 and 1890, as 55,000 new immigrants entered Hawaii, Native Hawaiians became strangers in their own land.

As the condition of Native Hawaiians worsened, the Hawaiian monarchs became increasingly resistant to expanding American influence. As a result, the Americans sought to restrict the monarchy's power. In 1887, under threat of military force, the American oligarchy forced King David Kalakaua to sign the "Bayonet Constitution," which imposed property and income qualifications as criteria for voting, disqualifying most ordinary Native Hawaiians; permitted Caucasian (but not other) aliens the right to vote; and expanded the role of American advisors in the Hawaiian government.

Over the next 25 years, Hawaii was transformed from a sovereign nation into an American colony in everything but name. In 1891, the American government passed a subsidy for American sugar growers that disadvantaged the sugar industry in Hawaii, leading American sugar interests there to seek Hawaii's annexation to the United States. Many in Washington also favored annexation of Hawaii as a necessary counterthrust to the growing European claims in the Pacific.

In 1892 Queen Lili'uokulani ascended the throne and in January 1893 tried to replace the Bayonet Constitution with one less favorable to American sugar interests. In response, John Stevens, the U.S. minister to Hawaii and a supporter of annexation, advised President Benjamin Harrison to approve the landing of American Marines in Honolulu, claiming that American lives and property needed protection from the chaos attending the queen's activities. Harrison approved, and under the threat of military force, Queen Lili'uokalani reluctantly abdicated the throne. The annexationists declared a provisional government, which they called the Republic of Hawaii.

Full annexation might well have occurred at this time, but in 1885 proannexation President Harrison was replaced by Grover Cleveland, who questioned the legitimacy of the U.S. role in the overthrow of the Hawaiian monarchy. President Cleveland ordered an investigation and was persuaded by its findings that "the landing of the United States forces occurred upon false pretexts respecting the danger to life and property" and that the occupation of Honolulu was "lawless."[10] This report confirms the contemporary Native Hawaiian view that the overthrow of their monarchy and the subsequent annexation of Hawaii by the United States was both illegal and immoral, buttressing their claims for redress against the American government and their demands for sovereignty.

For almost a decade the "Hawaii question" languished in Congress, but it was given new life with the election of William McKinley in 1896. President McKinley's views about expanding U.S. dominance in the Pacific, including control over Hawaii, had strong popular support. By 1898, as a result of the treaty settling the Spanish-American war, the U.S. government, already using Pearl Harbor as a port, also acquired the Philippines, and the strategic importance of Hawaii as a Pacific military base increased. On July 7, 1898, after heated debate in Congress, Hawaii was annexed to the United States and in 1900 officially became a territory of the United States.

The United States took title to the Crown Lands, set aside for the monarchy, and the Government Lands, set aside for the chiefs and the people in the Great Mahele. Congress established that these "ceded" public lands, exclusive of the portion that the United States could withdraw from public use for military purposes, would be held in trust by the U.S. government for the benefit of the "inhabitants" of Hawaii.

Twenty years after this trust was established, it was clear that Native Hawaiians received few benefits from annexation. Their population continued to decline, and their social, economic, health, and educational status grew worse every year. Hawaiian culture loss also proceeded apace, as traditional cultural forms like the hula and the Hawaiian language were suppressed.[11]

In 1921, some territorial and other representatives in Congress, dismayed at the condition of Native Hawaiians and fearing for their extinction as a people, achieved passage of the Hawaiian Homes Commission Act (HHCA), intended, like the Kuleana Act, to "save" the Hawaiian people by transforming them into independent farmers. The Act provided for 200,000 acres of scattered tracts of trust lands throughout the islands to be carved up into homesteading agricultural or ranching plots and given to Native Hawaiians with 99-year leases at $1 a year. The act also committed the federal government to provide the infrastructure to make these homesteads economically viable.

In order to limit the land available for homestead distribution, the landed American interests immediately thwarted the stated intention of the HHCA by legislatively defining a Native Hawaiian as any person with 50 percent or more of Hawaiian blood, excluding thousands of Native Hawaiians with more mixed ancestry from the program. Congress also capitulated to the sugar growers' demands to exclude all sugar-producing lands from the acreage set aside for the program. As a result, much of the homestead acreage was virtually useless for agriculture. Furthermore, the act's application process was so bureaucratically cumbersome that few allotments were actually made, and the erosion of Hawaiian land ownership and Hawaiian culture continued.

HAWAIIAN STATEHOOD

After WWII, the military importance of Hawaii was clearly demonstrated and a movement for Hawaiian statehood gained momentum

among non-Native Hawaiian political and economic interests. Even some
Native Hawaiians, who saw statehood as a way to increase their own
political power, concurred. In 1959, after a statehood plebiscite in which
Hawaiians could only vote "yes" or "no," Hawaii became Hawaii, the 49th
state of the United States. The federal government transferred the "ceded"
lands to the new state, retaining title to about 400,000 acres, most of which
was used for military activities and the remainder for national parks.
The state became custodian, with federal oversight, for over two million
acres of trust land and was awarded responsibility for implementing the
Hawaiian Homes Commission Act. The federal government now considered itself relieved of its trust responsibilities to the Native Hawaiians and
removed Hawaii from the U.N. list of "non-self-governing" territories.[12]

With statehood and with improvements in air travel came increased
tourism, real estate development, and multinational corporate investment, although none of these developments did much to improve the
lives of Native Hawaiians. By 1989, fewer than 6,000 Native Hawaiians
had received homestead land under the Hawaiian Homes Commission
Act and 19,000 were on the waiting list. Sixty percent of the land allotted
under the HHCA is leased at very low rents to non-Native Hawaiians,
including some of the richest and most powerful families in the state,
for use as shopping malls or other lucrative private economic development, or was given to government agencies. Only 17 percent of the land
is held by Native Hawaiians and only 3,700 of the tens of thousands
of eligible families (about 50,000 Native Hawaiians altogether) actually live on this land, as the basic infrastructure included in the federal
commitment when the act was signed into law was never built by the
state.[13]

THE NATIVE HAWAIIAN SOVEREIGNTY MOVEMENT

Under American law, Native Hawaiians are even more disadvantaged
than Native Americans in their relationship with the U.S. government.
Although recognized for some purposes as an indigenous people entitled
to certain benefits by the state and federal governments (a status endan-
gered by the recent Supreme Court decision, *Rice v .Cayetano*; see below)
Native Hawaiians do not have the "tribal status" of Native Americans,
which means that they cannot sue the federal government or the state for
return of land, reparations, or violations of trust relationships.[14] The many
groups that make up the Native Hawaiian sovereignty movement are
intent on changing this disadvantageous situation, though there is serious
disagreement on how this should be done.

Native Hawaiians are bitter toward the state government about the
lack of homestead distribution, but because they are not a "tribe," they
cannot sue the state for its failure to implement the HHCA. Native
Hawaiian requests for the federal government to sue the state for its

trust violations have also continually been resisted. By the 1960s, with the increased momentum of human rights activism, long-standing Native Hawaiian resentment over their marginalized position in their own society became organized resistance, particularly in conflicts over land.

Throughout the twentieth century, pockets of Native Hawaiian culture based on subsistence agriculture and fishing had persisted in rural areas and small communities surrounding urban areas. Because these communities often sat on land of potentially great commercial or recreational value, their residents were often threatened by eviction by the state and private owners. In the 1970s, Native Hawaiians living on prime oceanfront land were "forcibly removed" to make way for state parks. They resisted and many were arrested. Joined by some university activists, this resistance became the opening wedge in the contemporary Native Hawaiian sovereignty movement.

Newly formed Native Hawaiian organizations demanded implementation of the Hawaiian Homes Commission Act, monetary reparations for loss of land, greater political self-determination or "nation-within-a nation" status, and rights to the "ceded" land held by the state. Protests against the state included public confrontations, mainstream political participation, and court challenges. For Native Hawaiian activists, statehood had not ameliorated what they considered the illegal usurpation of the Hawaiian monarchy, nor had it resulted in substantial improvements in their living conditions.[15]

In 1978, partly as a response to Native Hawaiian claims, the state enacted a new constitution, which included the creation of the Office of Hawaiian Affairs (OHA). OHA membership was limited to Native Hawaiians, and only Native Hawaiians were eligible to vote for OHA trustees. The OHA was given authority to receive 20 percent of the income from the ceded lands; to disburse this income for the benefit of Native Hawaiians; to act as the trustee for Native Hawaiian property and income from the trust lands; and to become the vehicle for disbursing whatever reparations might be awarded by the federal government in the future. Many Native Hawaiians rejected the OHA as a state agency having this control over their future and speaking for their community.[16]

Political rather than legal action has been the major source of whatever success Native Hawaiians have achieved. The Hawaii Supreme Court and the U.S. Supreme Court accepted very few cases regarding Native Hawaiian rights, and hardly any of these decisions expands or advances those rights.[17] Without standing to sue the state and federal governments for trust violations or return of land, Native Hawaiian rights litigation has mainly turned on challenging denial of access to water and land for subsistence purposes and claiming religious rights involving access to sacred land.

NATIVE HAWAIIANS GO TO COURT

In 1976, a group called Protect Kaho'olawe 'Ohana started a movement to end the U.S. military's use of the small island of Kaho'olawe for bombing target practice. The 'Ohana hoped to use Kaho'olawe for traditional subsistence and religious practices and as a sovereign land base in an eventually established Hawaiian nation. Six 'Ohana members occupied Kaho'olawe and were arrested and convicted for "unauthorized entry onto a military reservation." They were fined, given short prison sentences, and banned from returning to the island without the court's permission.

The 'Ohana appealed, claiming violation of their religious rights, but the Hawaii Supreme Court concluded that the compelling government interest in keeping outsiders off dangerous land outweighed any burden on the defendants' free exercise of religion. Further, the court dismissed as "frivolous" the O'hana's claim that the government's possession of Kaho'olawe was illegal because it had been acquired by the illegal overthrow of the Hawaiian monarchy and the subsequently illegal annexation of Hawaii.[18] But while the 'Ohana's attempt to demilitarize Kaho'olawe failed in the courts, through the media attention it eventually succeeded in the court of public opinion. On October 22, 1990, President George H. W. Bush directed the U.S. Navy to halt all bombing practice on Kaho'olawe, and in May 1994, the U.S. Navy returned the island to the state of Hawaii.[19]

In 1982, another case involving Native Hawaiian religious rights also attracted wide media attention. Sam Lono, a Hawaiian religious leader, and his followers were forcibly evicted from a several-months-long religious retreat in Kualoa Park, an area in Oahu sacred to Native Hawaiians, because summer camping is prohibited by state law. Most of the citations were dismissed and only small fines were imposed, but Lono challenged the eviction and fines in court as a violation of his religious freedom, citing state and federal constitutions and also the 1978 federal American Indian Religious Freedom Act. This Act commits the federal government to protect and preserve the traditional religions of Native Americans and Native Hawaiians, "including but not limited to access to sites, and the freedom to worship through ceremonials and traditional rites."

The District Court rejected Lono's claim, holding that "Defendants' religious interest in participating in dreams at Kualoa Regional Park are not indispensable to the Hawaiian religious practice ... [and] ... [D]efendants' practices in exercising their religious beliefs ... are philosophical and personal and therefore are not entitled to First Amendment protection."[20]The Hawaii Supreme Court, in its affirmation of the District Court's decision, further asserted that the state had a "compelling interest" in enforcing its camping regulations.[21] These opinions highlight the difficulty indigenous peoples, whose spiritual systems of belief and practice differ from

Native Hawaiians practice their ancient traditions at Halema'uma'u Crater.

Please respect this sacred Hawaiian site. Do not build rock piles or leave any items that may desecrate this area or diminish the values it holds for native Hawaiians.

One of the most important issues that Native Hawaiians have challenged in court is the use of their sacred land by non-Native Hawaiians, often in ways that they consider sacrilege. Photo courtesy of Serena Nanda.

America's dominant Judeo-Christian tradition, face in gaining legal protection of their religious rights.

In 1987, a group called the "Pele Practitioners" mounted a legal challenge to the state's proposed development of geothermal power plants near the volcano Mauna Loa, claiming that such development desecrated an area sacred to the Goddess Pele, who lived in the volcano, and therefore violated the religious rights of those who worshipped her. The Hawaii Supreme Court acknowledged the legitimacy and sincerity of the Pele Practitioners' religion, but rejected their claim. The court concluded geothermal development would not pose a "significant harm" to Hawaiian religious practices and that denying that development because of one religious group's objections would place government in the unconstitutional position of "fostering support of one religion over another."[22]

In spite of these legal decisions and the court's dismissal of the 'Ohana's "sovereignty defense" in the Kaho'olawe case as "frivolous," the Hawaiian sovereignty movement gained momentum. In 1987, a group called Ka Lahui Hawaii, consisting of several hundred Native Hawaiians representing many Native Hawaiian organizations, drafted a constitution for a separate Hawaiian nation within the United States with a status similar to that of federally recognized Native American tribes. Their proposal called for all of the Hawaiian Home Lands and half the ceded lands to be given to their new nation. Ka Lahui Hawaii asserted their rights to self-determination as indigenous people before the United Nations and other international tribunals, charging the United States with crimes of genocide, ethnocide, impermissible intervention in a sovereign nation, illegal appropriations of land and natural resources, and violations of trust responsibilities established by international law.[23]

Supporters of Hawaiian sovereignty also pursued their rights in Congress, though without much success. A Hawaiian reparations bill had died in the 1974 Congress and a 1980 Congressional commission report on the concerns of Native Hawaiians found, with the three Native Hawaiian members dissenting, that since the U.S. government did not authorize the 1893 overthrow of the Hawaiian monarchy, Native Hawaiians have no legal or moral basis to reparations or return of the ceded (or in their view, stolen) lands.[24]

In November 1993, however, Congress passed a resolution, signed by President Bill Clinton, stating that the 1893 overthrow of the Hawaiian monarchy *was* illegal and apologized to the Hawaiian people for the loss of their land and culture.[25] Many Native Hawaiian activists rejected the resolution and the apology as containing "serious historical errors," "damaging misinterpretations," and the "grave deficiency" of making no reference to the return of land.

At the state level, the pressure for sovereignty continued in various ways. In 1996 the state sponsored a plebiscite, called the Native Hawaiian Vote, in which ballots were sent to 85,000 descendants of the original Native Hawaiian population asking: "Shall the Hawaiian People elect delegates to propose a Native Hawaiian government?" with the definition of that government to be debated through a delegate's conference. Some activists called for a boycott of the plebiscite, claiming that the vote was an attempt by the state to co-opt the sovereignty movement and that many people were confused as to the function of the vote. In any case, only 40 percent of the eligible Native Hawaiians voted, with 73 percent (22,294) voting yes and 26 percent (8,129) voting no. Based on the majority approval of those voting, an "independent, not for profit, non-governmental entity" known as Ha Hawaii was formed to give direction to and raise resources for, the eventual election of delegates to such a convention.[26]

In March 2000, over protests of some Native Hawaiian activists who reject Native Hawaiian "tribal" status as lacking the full sovereignty and land return they are demanding, Hawaii's Senators Daniel Inouye and Daniel Akaka introduced a bill to Congress calling for federal recognition of a Native Hawaiian government with an indigenous status similar to those of Native Americans. This "nation within a nation" model holds that Native Hawaiians possess all of the legal criteria of a "tribe": they were a previously sovereign people; they have suffered as a result of European encroachment and from U.S. seizure and exploitation of their lands; they are an aboriginal group whose ancestors, before the arrival of Europeans, inhabited territory that became part of the United States; and they have had their traditional collective land rights recognized in law. Hawaiians are already included in the 1978 Native American Religious Freedom Act and many other acts that benefit Native Americans as a class.[27] In addition to establishing Native Hawaiian "tribal" status, the Akaka Bill would establish an office in the Department of the Interior to address Native Hawaiian issues and create an interagency group composed of representatives of federal agencies that currently administer programs and policies affecting Hawaiians.

Groups of Native Hawaiian activists have protested the bill on the grounds that they are not an indigenous people of the United States, nor are they Native Americans or Americans. They reject the term "Native Hawaiians" as a colonial reference that defines them in "racist and subordinating" language. For these Kanaka Maoli, the 1993 apology by the U.S. government with its promises of reconciliation is undermined by any attempt, including the Akaka bill, to define Hawaiian sovereignty only within the framework of U.S. law.[28]

ARE THE NATIVE HAWAIIANS AN INDIGENOUS PEOPLE OR A RACE?

Even as the Akaka bill works its way through the Senate, however, Native Hawaiians experienced a significant setback through the courts to a wide range of benefits they receive as Native Hawaiians. In 1999, Harold F. Rice, a Caucasian whose ancestors had come to Hawaii in 1831, challenged the rules under the state's Constitution by which only Native Hawaiians can vote for the trustees for the Office of Hawaiian Affairs. Mr. Rice claimed that under this rule, he and the 80 percent of the non-Hawaiian population of Hawaii were victims of racial discrimination, in violation of the 14th Amendment's guarantee of equal protection and the 15th Amendment's guarantee that the right to vote shall not be denied "on account of race, color, or previous condition of servitude." When the lower courts rejected Rice's claim, he appealed the case to the U.S. Supreme Court.

In finding for Mr. Rice in *Rice v. Cayetano* [528 U.S. 495 (2000)] the Court rejected the state's contention that because Native Hawaiians are not a "race," but rather a "distinct and unique indigenous group" for which Congress and the Hawaii state government have assumed a special obligation, the OHA did not involve racial discrimination. With the support of the U.S. Justice Department under President Clinton, the state emphasized that excluding non-Hawaiians from OHA voting was not based on a racial classification, but on the special trust relationship Congress has with Native Hawaiians, a legal position with substantial precedent in court decisions.

Justice Anthony Kennedy, who wrote the opinion for the majority, joined by Justices Rehnquist, O'Connor, Scalia, Thomas, Breyer, and Souter, persisted in characterizing Native Hawaiians as a "race," referring to the state's definition of "Hawaiian" as based on ancestry. "Ancestry," Justice Kennedy said, "can be a proxy for race. It is that proxy here...." Turning the creation and official purpose of the OHA as an agency for the benefit of Native Hawaiians on its head, Justice Kennedy continued,

The ancestral inquiry in this case ... demeans a person's dignity and worth to be judged by ancestry instead of by his or her own merit and essential qualities. The state's ancestral inquiry [for voting eligibility for OHA trustees] is forbidden by the Fifteenth Amendment for the further reason that using racial classifications is corruptive of the whole legal order democratic elections seek to preserve. The law itself may not become the instrument for generating the prejudice and hostility all too often directed against persons whose particular ancestry is disclosed by their ethnic characteristics and cultural traditions.

Justice Kennedy then went on to say that even if Hawaiians were classified as an American Indian tribe, which they presently were not, the OHA voting restrictions would still be unconstitutional "because such a voting scheme, in which the State limited the electorate for its public officials to a class of tribal Indians to the exclusion of all non-Indian citizens, would still be unconstitutional." Finally, Justice Kennedy dismissed the state's argument that the voting restriction "does no more than ensure an alignment of interests between the fiduciaries and the beneficiaries of a trust." Rather, he said, the restriction "rests on the demeaning premise that citizens of a particular race are somehow more qualified than others to vote on certain matters... There is no room under the [15th] Amendment for the concept that the right to vote in a particular election can be allocated based on race."

Justices John Paul Stevens and Ruth Bader Ginsburg dissented, supporting the state's position that special trust relationships were not confined to Native American "tribes" and had, in the past, been legally extended to Native Hawaiians. Their dissent also emphasized that both the creation of the OHA and the voting restrictions for its trustees were "tied rationally to the fulfillment" of that trust.

The Court's decision, though focused on the narrow issue of voter eligibility for OHA trustees, has much wider implications. It throws into question the constitutionality of all Hawaiians-only benefits—through which tens of millions of federal dollars have gone to Hawaiian health, education, housing, economic development, and cultural programs. The Bush administration, as well as individual Republicans in Congress, repeatedly refer to Hawaiians as a "race" and have acted accordingly. Subsequent to the *Rice* decision, the Justice Department asked that Native Hawaiians be removed from a bill benefiting Native American small businesses because it "could be viewed as authorizing the award of government benefits on the basis of racial or ethnic criteria"; a White House policy statement questioned an energy bill that provides "racial preferences" in its inclusion of Native Hawaiian organizations; and the Justice Department sent a letter to Hawaii Senator Inouye raising concerns over a bill to provide affordable housing grants to low-income Native Hawaiians. Encouraged by the *Rice* decision and the hostility of the Bush administration to all gender- and race-based preferences, several lawsuits have already been initiated against preferential benefits for Native Hawaiians, such as the Hawaiian Homelands Program, and the very existence of the OHA itself. In August 2005, a federal court struck down the Hawaiians-only admissions policy of the Kamehameha School, founded by a member of the Hawaiian royalty to revitalize the Hawaiian people and culture. However, after protest marches at the decision in Honolulu, San Francisco, and Los Angeles, the court agreed to rehear the case with a panel of 15 judges.[29]

For tourists and many state residents, Hawaii is a paradise. But for many Hawaiians, it is a troubled paradise, burdened by a continuing U.S. colonial domination that exploits their culture, alienates them from their land, and denies them the self-determination they deserve as a once-sovereign nation.

PUERTO RICO: ANOTHER TROUBLED PARADISE

If Hawaii is America's paradise in the Pacific, Puerto Rico is its paradise in the Caribbean. Hawaii and Puerto Rico have much in common, including conflicts over political status and national identity, and nationalists in both societies identity with each other as examples of American colonialism.[30]

Early contact with Spain soon resulted in the near extinction of the Taino, Puerto Rico's indigenous people, much as European contact with Hawaii decimated the Hawaiian population through the effects of war and disease. The Spanish maintained Puerto Rico as a colony for over 400 years, using it mainly as a fortified garrison guarding access to Mexico and Spanish America. Ironically, in 1897 Spain granted a large measure of self-rule to Puerto Rico, but potential independence was stymied when the Spanish ceded Puerto Rico to the United States in 1898 after their defeat in the Spanish-American war. The United States viewed this new territory, along with Hawaii, as an essential outpost for protecting its sea routes and for projecting a global American power.

For the next 50 years, the United States ruled Puerto Rico through a succession of largely inept and corrupt military and colonial governors. Nevertheless, U.S. rule brought modest economic development and limited political reform. In 1900 Congress passed the Foraker Act, which gave Puerto Ricans the right to elect members of the lower house of the bicameral legislature, although the U.S. president had the right to appoint

This mural in San Juan, Puerto Rico, emphasizes Puerto Rico's indigenous, pre-Hispanic culture as part of a contemporary Puerto Rican identity. Photo courtesy of Joan Gregg.

the governor, the six cabinet members who would form a majority of the upper legislative chamber, and Supreme Court Justices. In 1917, hoping that further political reform would undercut any movement toward independence, Congress passed the Jones Act, which gave U.S. citizenship to Puerto Ricans, provided for an elective Senate, and enabled the governor to appoint most cabinet members, subject to confirmation by the new upper chamber. In 1947, Congress approved the Elective Governor Act, which gave Puerto Ricans the right to elect their own governor. Puerto Ricans serve in the U.S. armed forces and are subject to the draft, though they continue to be denied a voting representative in Congress and are not permitted to vote for the president of the United States.[31]

Through political reforms, the extension of New Deal programs to Puerto Rico during the Roosevelt era, and various economic incentives and benefits (Puerto Ricans do not pay U.S. taxes), political support for independence in Puerto Rico has been weak. In 1948 however, the Nationalist Party of Puerto Rico pressed its claims for independence in the United States, and also before the United Nations, which placed Puerto Rico on the list of non-self-governing territories eligible for decolonization. In 1952, after congressional approval of a Puerto Rican constitution voted on by Puerto Ricans, Congress officially created the Commonwealth of Puerto Rico. A year later, as a result of U.S. lobbying, the United Nations removed Puerto Rico from the list of non-self-governing territories, though it reaffirmed "the inalienable right of the people of Puerto Rico to self-determination and independence." Since 1972, however, Puerto Rican nationalists, who consider Puerto Rico a U.S. colony, have annually petitioned the U.N. Special Committee on Decolonization to reconsider its status. In 1989, a Permanent Peoples' Tribunal Session on Puerto Rico was held in Barcelona (similar to that held by Native Hawaiians in 1993), aimed at exposing and documenting the "long-suppressed truth of [the] U.S. assaults on our people and nation in the context of international law."[32]

As a commonwealth, Puerto Rico is an "unincorporated territory" that belongs to, but is not part of, the United States.[33] Economic development accelerated during the 1960s under Operation Bootstrap, under which tax incentives were awarded to American-based multinational corporations to invest in Puerto Rico. Both American investment and American cultural influence increased as Puerto Rico was transformed from a largely monocultural economy of sugar plantations owned by absentee corporations to an industrialized society supported by private investment. Operation Bootstrap resulted in a higher standard of living for many Puerto Rican workers, though to critics of the dominant role of American capital it merely transformed Puerto Rico from a political colony of the United States to an industrial colony.[34]

Similar to Hawaii, increasingly efficient plane travel brought more American cultural influence to Puerto Rico, as Puerto Ricans increasingly traveled between the island and the mainland. As agriculture declined in Puerto Rico, many Puerto Ricans migrated to cities; when they could not find jobs there, they moved to the mainland, where two-fifths of the Puerto Rican population now lives.[35]

POLITICAL STATUS: THE DEFINING ISSUE IN PUERTO RICAN POLITICS

Unlike Hawaii, where sovereignty issues involve only a minority of the state's population, the political status of Puerto Rico is the dominant issue in political life. With the economic development of the 1960s, Puerto Ricans largely supported maintaining their commonwealth status, but this eroded as the economy declined in the 1970s, when a strong statehood movement emerged.[36] The issue has languished in Congress since the 1990s, but the island's political status has been at the core of every Puerto Rican election.

Retaining some form of commonwealth status (perhaps with expanded Puerto Rican control of their international trade as in a compact of free association similar to U.S. relations with Guam and Micronesia) and statehood are by far the two most strongly supported options, although there is a small but vociferous movement for total independence. Drawing authority from the U.S. Constitution's so-called Territorial Clause (Article IV),

Congress retains the power to limit political rights for Puerto Rico. And though commonwealth status has brought large federal transfer payments and economic subsidies to Puerto Rico, the perceived colonialism associated with this status makes it a source of tension.

STATEHOOD AND CULTURAL IDENTITY

The momentum for statehood, which initially had appeal in low-income communities and is viewed by its supporters as the only practical route to political equality and economic development, seems to have waned for the present both in Puerto Rico and in Congress. Major obstacles to statehood involve issues of language, culture, and national identity. The U.S. strategy of assimilating Puerto Ricans to Anglo-American culture and language has been a sensitive issue since the beginning of colonial rule.[37] In 1902, the United States made English an official language along with Spanish and mandated English as the language of instruction in public schools, even though few students understood it. Only in 1949 did Puerto Rico's first elected Governor, Luis Munoz Marin, establish Spanish as the language of instruction.

Language was the pivotal issue in the 1998 House bill in the Congress approving a Puerto Rican referendum on statehood. Although an amendment to make English the official language of a Puerto Rican state failed, congressional supporters of statehood had to agree to a compromise that required Puerto Rico to increase English proficiency if it became a state. As a move in this direction, the pro-statehood governor of Puerto Rico proposed the Project for Developing a Bilingual Citizen.[38] The language issue has become even more contentious in the current climate in the United States, where anti-Latino immigrant movements and state English-only initiatives have growing support (see Chapter 4).[39]

Statehood supporters claim that statehood need not mean assimilation. They insist that as a state, with representatives in Congress, Puerto Rico could resist legislation to impose English as the island's only official language. Currently, Spanish and English are both used in Puerto Rico in different contexts and institutions: Local courts for example, operate in Spanish, while federal courts operate in English.[40] Fundamentally, however, Puerto Rico is a Spanish-speaking society with English as a secondary language spoken easily by only 25 percent of the population, spoken with difficulty by another 25 percent and not spoken at all by 50 percent.

For critics of U.S. cultural colonialism in Puerto Rico, the language issue is only the tip of the national identity iceberg, and they cite other more insidious pressures toward the Americanization of Puerto Rico such as the cultural practices of consumerism, suburban housing development, the proliferation of cars, fast food restaurants and shopping malls, and "going on vacation to Disneyland." Because much commercial advertising takes place in Spanish accompanied by salsa music and images of the Puerto Rican flag, Puerto Rican identity, falsely, appears to be affirmed.

This commodification of national culture undercuts the subversive potential of nationalism, a process that proceeded apace in Hawaii and is now a marketing characteristic of transnational corporations operating in a global economy.[41]

Most supporters of statehood and commonwealth status focus on economic benefits rather than on issues of cultural identity. Some statehood supporters point to Hawaii as an example of the multicultural harmony that the United States is able to achieve, but as we have seen above, this view is dismissed as a myth by many Native Hawaiians, who see their own state not as a model but as a warning to Puerto Rico. The point is not lost on Puerto Rican nationalists: One responded to the statehood question, "[I am] 100% for independence; [w]e don't want to disappear like the Hawaiians did." Nationalists claim that once Puerto Ricans recognize that statehood is not a real option, independence is the only solution to decolonization. Like many Hawaiian sovereignty activists, *independistas* vow that they will never give up: "We've been fighting for this for 100 years ... and there is a nationality here that refuses to throw in the towel."[42]

THE MILITARIZATION OF PUERTO RICO: VIEQUES

Since acquiring Puerto Rico, the United States has been determined to "hold on to" the island mainly for strategic, geopolitical reasons. This policy recently erupted in conflict over the use of the Puerto Rican island of Vieques as a site of naval operations reminiscent of Native Hawaiian protests over the military use of Kaho'olawe.

In the 1940s the U.S. Navy acquired two-thirds of Vieques, an island 20 by 4 miles, for use in rehearsing amphibious landing exercises, parachute drops, and submarine maneuvers. It conducted artillery and small-arms firing, naval gunfire support, and missile shoots, and bombed the island in target practice from the air, land, and sea. The military practiced large-scale maneuvers or "war games," in Vieques, rehearsing interventions in the Balkans, Haiti, Iraq, Somalia, and Grenada.[43] The Navy regarded the socioeconomic development of Vieques, which has 10,000 residents, as a threat to naval operations and actively thwarted development plans in the civilian sector. In the 1960s, only a presidential order prevented the navy from a secret plan to remove civilians from Vieques and relocate them elsewhere.[44] The claims of Vieques residents that Navy operations have contaminated the environment seem confirmed by an abnormally higher incidence of cancer on the island, and only recently did the Pentagon admit to having tested chemical weapons there in the 1960s.

The long-simmering tensions between the Navy and Vieques residents reached a climax in April 1999 when a navy jet on a training mission mistakenly dropped its load of five-hundred-pound bombs on a military observation post one mile from its target site. The explosions injured one guard and killed a civilian employee of the base, David Sanes Rodriquez. Outraged over Sanes's death, protesters initially occupied a military target range. Subsequently the protest spread, and tens of thousands of Puerto Ricans marched in San Juan, Puerto Rico's capital city, demanding an end to military training exercises in Vieques.[45] Puerto Ricans mobilized across the United States and were joined by political figures and celebrities from the United States and abroad. The protests temporarily halted all military activity for over a year.

By 2001, national and international media attention to Vieques led President George W. Bush to declare a halt to all Navy operations by 2003. A month after the President's announcement, 68 percent of Vieques's residents voted in a nonbinding referendum to immediately end the Navy bombing. Their continued protests were met by military police using tear gas, but on May 1, 2003, the Navy formally withdrew from Vieques, announcing plans to move its operations to Florida and other parts of the U.S. mainland. The former navy area of operations will be turned over to the U.S. Department of the Interior, which promised to clean up the contamination and turn the area into a wilderness refuge.

Unlike Hawaii, the protests against Navy operations in Vieques muted the underlying nationalism issues and instead focused on the material harm done to the island and its residents by Navy operations. But the Vieques conflict could not help but highlight the colonial relationship between the United States and Puerto Rico. Now that the Navy has left, it is likely that Vieques will expand its economy through resort development. This possibility compels reflection on the similarities between Hawaii and Puerto Rico, two island paradises in which Americanization through consumer culture and tourism may be as significant as political relationships in transforming cultural diversity into cultural homogenization.

NOTES

1. We use the Native Hawaiian form of spelling of Hawaii, except when we specifically refer to the state of Hawaii or are quoting.

2. Sally Merry, *Colonizing Hawaii: the Cultural Power of Law* (Princeton, NJ: Princeton University Press, 2000), 250.

3. H. Trask, "Lovely Hula Hands: Corporate Tourism and the Prostitution of Hawaiian Culture," in *From a Native Daughter: Colonialism and Sovereignty in Hawaii* (Monroe, MA: Common Courage Press, 1993), 179–200.

4. Melody Kapilialoha MacKenzie, *Native Hawaiian Rights Handbook* (Honolulu, HI: Native Hawaiian Legal Corporation, 1991), 4.

5. Eric Wolf, *Europe and the People Without History* (Berkeley: University of California Press, 1982), 58–59.

6. See Stephenie Seto Levin, "The Overthrow of the *Kapu* System in Hawaii," *Journal of the Polynesian Society* 74 (1968), 402–30; and William Davenport, "The 'Hawaiian Cultural Revolution,'" *American Anthropologist* 71 (1969), 1–19.

7. Mari J. Masuda, "Law and Culture in the District Court of Honolulu, 1844–45: A Case Study of the Rise of Legal Consciousness," *The American Journal of Legal History* 32 (1988), 17–41.

8. Maivan Clech Lam, "The Kuleana Act Revisited: The Survival of Traditional Hawaiian Commoner Rights in Land," *Washington Law Review* 64 (1989), 233–287.

9. Mackenzie, *Native Hawaiian Rights Handbook*, 10.

10. Native Hawaiians Study Commission, *Claims of Conscience: A Dissenting Study of the Culture, Needs and Concerns of Native Hawaiians*, Vol. II (Washington DC: Department of the Interior, 1983).

11. Raymon Lopez-Reyes, "The Demise of the Hawaiian Kingdom: A Psycho-cultural Analysis and Moral Legacy—Something Lost, Something Owed," *Hawaii Bar Journal* 18 (1983), 3–23.

12. S. James Anaya, "The Native Hawaiian People and International Human Rights Law: Toward a Remedy for Past and Continuing Wrongs," *Georgia Law Review* 28 (1994), 309–64.

13. Susan Faludi, "Broken Promise: How Everyone Got Hawaiians' Homelands Except the Hawaiians," *Wall Street Journal*, September 9, 1991, 1.

14. Mililani B. Trask, "Historical and Contemporary Hawaiian Self-Determination: A Native Hawaiian Perspective," *Arizona Journal of International and Comparative Law* 8 (2) (1991), 77–95. In 1988, the passage of the Native Hawaiian Judicial Relief Act permitted Native Hawaiians to sue in state courts for trust violations, but only based on claims arising after 1989. Also, under the act, courts are not permitted to award successful native plaintiffs either land or money, but must surrender the plaintiffs' award to the state agencies who are responsible for implementing the trust. The irony of this vicious cycle, which makes the very bureaucracies who have been responsible for the problem the solution to the problem, has not been lost on Native Hawaiians.

15. H. Trask, *From a Native Daughter*, 89.

16. M. Trask, "Historical and Contemporary Hawaiian Self-Determination."

17. Melody Kapilialoha MacKenzie, "The Lum Court and Native Hawaiian Rights," *University of Hawaii Law Review* 14 (1992), 337–94.

18. *United States v. Mowatt*, 582 F.2d 1194 (1978), 1196.

19. "Navy Test Ground Returns to Hawaii," *New York Times*, May 9, 1994, A12.

20. *State of Hawaii v. Lono*, Appendix A, 4.

21. *State of Hawaii v. Lono*, Memorandum Opinion, 2.

22. *Dedman v. Board of Land and Natural Resources et al.*, 69 Haw. 255 (1987), 261.

23. See the film, *The Tribunal: Peoples' International Tribunal Hawaii* (1993) for a Native Hawaiian perspective (available from Na Maka o ka' Aina, 3020 Kahaloa Drive, Honolulu, Hawaii, 96822); for an anthropological interpretation, see Sally Engle Merry, "Legal Vernacularization and Ka Ho'okolokolonui Kanaka Maoli, the People's International Tribunal, Hawaii 1993," *PoLAR: The Political and Legal Anthropology Review*, 1995; see also Serena Nanda, "Trouble in Paradise: Native Hawaiians v. the United States of America." *Journal of Criminal Justice Education, Educational Media Review* 7, no. 1 (Spring 1996), 155–160; and Ward Churchill and Sharon H. Venne, eds., *Islands in Captivity: The International Tribunal on the Rights of Indigenous Hawaiians* (Cambridge, MA: South End Press, 2004).

24. Native Hawaiians Study Commission, *Report on the Culture, Needs, and Concerns of Native Hawaiians (Majority)*, Vol. I (Washington, DC: U.S. Department of the Interior, 1983).

25. S.J. Res. 19, 103rd Cong., 1st Sess., 107 Stat. 1510 (1993).

26. Scott Crawford, "The Native Hawaiian Vote—The Result Announcement," September 12, l996, http://nativenet.uthscsa.edu/archive/nl/9609/0046.html; for a rejection of the referendum, see Jose Luis Morin, "The 'Native Hawaiian Vote': The Deception Continues," November 14, 1996, http://www.inmotionmagazine. com/hivote.html.

27. Richard H. Houghton III, "An Argument for Indian Status for Native Hawaiians: The Discovery of a Lost Tribe," *American Indian Law Review* 14 (1990), 1–55.

28. Dean E. Murphy, "Bill Giving Native Hawaiians Sovereignty Is Too Much for Some, Too Little for Others," *New York Times,* July 17, 2005, A12.

29. Alexandre Da Silva, "Appeals court rules against Hawaiians-only admissions policy," *Associated Press Wire,* Aug. 3, 2005 (from the Internet). For a Native Hawaiian view, see Georgia Ka'a puni McMillen, "A School of One's Own." *New York Times,* August 29, 2005, A15. See also Janis L. Magin, "Court to Reconsider Hawaii Schools Case," *New York Times,* February 26, 2006, A17.

30. Kekuni Blaisdell, "The Kanaka Maoli Struggle Against the United States: Some Similarities and Differences with the Puerto Rican Independence Movement," *La Patria Radical,* (Monthly newspaper of Movimiento de Liberacion Nacional Puertorriqueno), July 25, 1993.

31. Kenneth Jost, "Puerto Rico's Status: Statehood, Commonwealth or Independence," *Congressional Quarterly Researcher,* 8, no. 40 (October 3, 1998). Online at http://library.cqresearcher/cqresrre1998102300. Accessed March 24, 2006.

32. Blaisdell, "The Kanaka Maoli Struggle."

33. Edwin Melendez, *Colonial Dilemma: Critical Perspectives on Contemporary Puerto Rico* (Boston, MA: South End Press, 1993), 1.

34. Ramon Grosfoguel, *Colonial Subjects: Puerto Ricans in a Global Perspective.* 2003 Electronic Resource, 61.

35. "Puerto Rico's Status."

36. Melendez, *Colonial dilemma,* 1.

37. Grosfoguel, *Colonial Subjects.*

38. "Puerto Rico's Status," 1936.

39. Grosfoguel, *Colonial Subjects,* 61.

40. "Puerto Rico's Status," 935.

41. Grosfoguel, *Colonial Subjects,* 63.

42. "Puerto Rico's Status," 942.

43. "Chronology of events of U.S. Navy's use of Vieques," Associated Press Worldstream, April 30, 2003.

44. Katherine T. McCaffrey, *Military Power and Popular Protest: The U.S. Navy in Vieques, Puerto Rico* (New Brunswick, NJ: Rutgers University Press, 2002), 5.

45. Ian James, " Amid tear gas and booming artillery guns, entrenched Vieques protest movement shifts focus to future," AP Worldstream, January 14, 2003; Martin Delfin, "Hundreds storm bombing range in Vieques after US Navy withdraws," Agence France Presse, May 1, 2003; Dana Canedy, "Navy Leaves a Battered Island, and Puerto Ricans Cheer," *New York Times,* May 2, 2003, A22.

CHAPTER 3

African Americans: The Fight for Justice and Equality

I been 'buked and I been scorned. I'm gonna tell my Lord when I get home just how long you've been treating me wrong.[1]

When Mahalia Jackson sang the words of this traditional spiritual at the 1963 March on Washington she was expressing African Americans' understanding of their position as the most systematically excluded group in U.S. history. The story of African Americans in America begins with a forced migration, as slaves, to this country. Both the numbers of African Americans brought here as slaves and the prejudice and discrimination they faced is unmatched by any other immigrant group.

The telling of American history has long emphasized slavery as a Southern institution, underplaying its importance in building the economy of the North. Early in the eighteenth century, for example, more than 40 percent of New York City households had slaves.[2] And while Vermont and Massachusetts outlawed slavery late in the eighteenth century, New York State did not forbid the practice until 1827. In these years African Americans living in the North slowly gained citizenship and suffrage. In the South, too, in the early nineteenth century amidst the pervasiveness of slavery, a small class of "free people of color" emerged. These individuals, while denied the privileges of citizenship, nevertheless developed cultures based on literacy and wealth in many urban areas.[3] Thus, the specific history of African Americans varied by time and region. Yet despite these differences, the weight of this group's experience has been one of exclusion matched, since the middle of the nineteenth century, by persistent effort of members to break the legal and extralegal barriers that have kept them out of the social, political, economic, religious, and cultural life of the nation.

THE DRED SCOTT CASE [*DRED SCOTT V. SANDFORD* 60 U.S. 393 (1857)]

The most explicit and infamous legal statement of African American exclusion, and the attempt to overcome it, is the case of the slave Dred Scott, which was decided by the Supreme Court in 1857. Dred Scott had been taken by his owner to live in Illinois and the Wisconsin Territory where, by an act of Congress—the 1820 Missouri Compromise—slavery was prohibited. Scott lived with his owner for five years on free soil and then returned to Missouri, which was a slave state. On the basis of his having lived on free soil, in 1846 Scott and his supporters began a suit for his freedom in state court. Subsequently, during the 11 years of state and federal litigation, proponents of slavery raised the constitutionality of the Missouri Compromise as an issue. These people also challenged Dred Scott's ability to sue in federal court, raising the issue of all African Americans' right to be citizens of the United States.

The controversial case was argued twice in 1856 before the U.S. Supreme Court. Some evidence suggests that the justices were prepared to exercise judicial restraint and merely affirm the prior Missouri Supreme Court decision declaring Scott a slave. Justices from the slave states, however, led by Justice James Wayne of Georgia, decided to confront the slavery question squarely and supported a full opinion on the merits in which, by a 7–2 vote, the high court struck down the Missouri Compromise as unconstitutional and declared that Dred Scott had not won his freedom by residing in a free territory.[4] Even more critically, the justices stated that *any* person—free or slave—whose ancestors were born in Africa and sold into slavery was not meant to be, and could never become, a citizen of the United States. The Court emphasized that a slave, such as Dred Scott, was "strictly property, to be used in subserviency to the interests, the convenience, or the will, of his owner" and "that a slave, the … property of a master, and possessing within himself no civil or political rights or capacities, cannot be a CITIZEN." The justices concluded that since slaves were property, and the Constitution "was pledged" to protect property rights, setting a slave free would be a violation of the rights of his master and, thus, unconstitutional.

Chief Justice Taney began his majority opinion with a comparison of "the Indian races" and "negros (sic) of the African race," pointing up the differences. Indians, "although they were uncivilized, they were yet a free and independent people," and, as members of sovereign states, could become citizens, "negros," never. Claiming that "it is not the province of the court to decide upon the justice or injustice … of these laws," the Court held that even though free African Americans were citizens and could vote, where qualified, in several states—New Hampshire, New York, New Jersey, North Carolina, and Massachusetts—this did not entitle them to the rights and privileges of national citizenship. Next, Taney argued directly on behalf of the rights of slaveholders as property owners and against the actions of Congress:

The Government of the United States had no right to interfere for any other purpose but that of protecting the rights of the owner, leaving it altogether with the several States to deal with this race, whether emancipated or not.

[T]he right of property in a slave is distinctly and expressly affirmed in the Constitution. The right to traffic in it, like an ordinary article of merchandise and property, was guarantied to the citizens of the United States.

... the Government in express terms is pledged to protect it in all future time, if the slave escapes from his owner. This is done in plain words—too plain to be misunderstood. And no word can be found in the Constitution which gives Congress a greater power over slave property, or which entitles property of that kind to less protection than property of any other description ... it is the opinion of the court that the act of Congress which prohibited a citizen from holding and owning property of this kind in the territory of the United States north of the line therein mentioned, is not warranted by the Constitution, and is therefore void; and that neither Dred Scott himself, nor any of his family, were made free by being carried into this territory; even if they had been carried there by the owner, with the intention of becoming a permanent resident.

The *Dred Scott* case demonstrates the sharply drawn legal and moral perspectives that divided not only the nation, but also the Court. Justices Curtis of Massachusetts and McLean of Ohio systematically rebutted the major points upon which the Court's opinion was based. They not only contended that persons of African descent could be citizens of the United States, but also stated that the Missouri Compromise was constitutional. Referring to earlier federal and state court opinions and the existence of free African American citizens in many northern states, and using moral arguments against slavery, Curtis and McLean rejected the conclusions of the majority. While admitting the "infamous traffic in slaves" inherited from Great Britain, Justice McLean was more optimistic than the majority about man's ability to throw off "domestic relations [having their source] in so dark a ground." He pointed out that leading men in both the South and the North had hoped that slavery would gradually decline, a hope that was blocked by the increased value of slave labor in the cotton and sugar culture. McLean rejected the majority view that "a slave ... [is the] same as a horse, or any other kind of property," arguing that, "A slave is not a mere chattel. He bears the impress of his Maker, and is amenable to the laws of God and man; and he is destined to an endless existence." Complementing McLean's moral argument that men of all races share a common humanity, Justice Curtis noted that the Constitution, in its opening declaration, refers not to the Caucasian race, but to "the people" of the

United States. He, too, reminded the Court that free persons of African ancestry were citizens in many states, and that therefore slaves of African ancestry such as Dred Scott could indeed become citizens of the United States.

The *Dred Scott* decision is today often dismissed as no longer important, having been technically reversed by the Thirteenth, Fourteenth, and Fifteenth amendments to the Constitution following the Civil War. This dismissal, however, underestimates the historical significance of an opinion that established Supreme Court approval for the idea of African American inferiority and exclusion from all civic rights.

HOPES DASHED: THE RISE OF JIM CROW

Despite the depth and persistence of racist attitudes in American culture, the period after the Civil War, known as Reconstruction, witnessed some small possibilities for change.[5] The passage of the Thirteenth, Fourteenth, and Fifteenth amendments did provide African Americans with a legal base from which to challenge their continued exclusion from American society. With the formal structure of laws maintaining slavery now banished, new terms of social relations between the races could perhaps develop. In this period much of the racial separatism was informal, with a "strong reliance on custom." States avoided passing overtly discriminatory racial laws that would contravene the principle of legal equality established by emancipation. During Reconstruction there were even laws passed in some states that provided African Americans equal access to public facilities, although little, it is true, was done to enforce them. Where discrimination occurred it was often extralegal or even illegal and was not yet accompanied by the legal provision (de jure) of separate facilities for African Americans. Thus, the discrimination against African Americans had not yet hardened into the rigid, systematic, and comprehensive system of enforced separation of African Americans and whites known as Jim Crow. While African American exclusion, widely practiced in the North, was never as rigidly codified in law as in the South, it nevertheless proved intractable to significant change and, some have argued, was even more powerful in excluding African Americans from mainstream American society.

With the waning of this short period of Reconstruction, after the presidential election of 1876 African Americans became subject to a new, highly structured code of laws that both segregated them and discriminated against them in every area of political, economic, and social life. These "Jim Crow" laws affected African Americans (and, subsequently, in some communities, Asian Americans) from cradle to grave. These laws included the use of literacy and "character" tests as well as poll taxes and irregular hours for voter registration to keep African Americans from voting; exclusion of African American children from the schools attended by white children; and segregation of park facilities, health services, and mass transportation. Courts were racially segregated and pains were even taken to prohibit African Americans from swearing on Bibles used by whites.[6]

Several of these nineteenth-century state segregation laws, as well as nongovernmental (private) action discriminating against African Americans in quasi-public facilities, such as theaters, were tested before the U.S. Supreme Court, which, in an effort to mollify sentiments supporting African American exclusion, found them constitutional. When, in July 1890, the Louisiana legislature passed "An act to promote the comfort of passengers," requiring racial segregation in railway cars, a group of middle class African Americans from New Orleans, alarmed at the growing number of segregation laws, formed the Citizens Committee to Test the Constitutionality of the Separate Car Law. This Committee was part of an active African American civil rights movement that, in 1890 alone, had held five national conventions. The New Orleans Committee, after an unsuccessful attempt to prevent the passage of the law by the Louisiana General Assembly, decided to test its constitutionality before the federal courts. The Committee, with funds raised in the African American community, hired Albion Tourgee, a white northern lawyer who had been active on behalf of former slaves during Reconstruction, to make a test case of Jim Crow.

It was arranged for Homer A. Plessy, a very light-skinned Louisiana African American, to purchase a train ticket and then to take a seat in the coach reserved for whites (with the knowledge of the railway company, which, concerned that the law would prove expensive, was anxious for a test case). When Plessy refused to comply with the conductor's request that he move to the car reserved for people of his race, he was arrested and charged with violation of the Louisiana railway car segregation statute. When Judge Ferguson of New Orleans ruled against Plessy, an appeal was made to the Supreme Court of the United States. By a 7–1 vote the high court turned back the claim made by Plessy that Jim Crow laws were unconstitutional. Rather, the justices established the now famous doctrine of "separate but equal," laying the foundation for a half century more of de jure segregation by race. Ironically, the Court's majority opinion upholding Jim Crow was authored by Justice Henry Brown from Michigan, while the sole dissent came from Justice John Harlan, a Southerner, a former slaveholder, "and at heart a conservative."[7] The majority opinion came first.

PLESSY V. FERGUSON 163 U.S. 537 (1896)

The constitutionality of this act is attacked upon the ground that it conflicts both with the 13th Amendment of the Constitution, abolishing slavery, and the 14th Amendment, which prohibits certain restrictive legislation on the part of the states.

That it does not conflict with the 13th Amendment, which abolished slavery and involuntary servitude, except as a punishment for crime, is too clear for argument.

A statute which implies merely a legal distinction between the white and colored races—a distinction which is founded in the color of the two races, and which must always exist so long as white men are distinguished from the other race by color—has no tendency to destroy the legal equality of the two races, or re-establish a state of involuntary servitude.

By the 14th Amendment, all persons born or naturalized in the United States, and subject to the jurisdiction thereof, are made citizens of the United States and of the state wherein they reside; and the states are forbidden from making or enforcing any law which shall abridge the privileges or immunities of citizens of the United States, or shall deprive any person of life, liberty, or property without due process of law, or deny to any person within their jurisdiction the equal protection of the laws.

The object of the amendment was undoubtedly to enforce the absolute equality of the two races before the law, but in the nature of things it could not have been intended to abolish distinctions based upon color, or to enforce social, as distinguished from political, equality, or a commingling of the two races upon terms unsatisfactory to either. Laws permitting, and even requiring their separation in places where they are liable to be brought into contact do not necessarily imply the inferiority of either race to the other, and have been generally, if not universally, recognized as within the competency of the state legislatures in the exercise of their police power.

So far, then, as a conflict with the 14th Amendment is concerned, the case reduces itself to the question whether the statute of Louisiana is a reasonable regulation, and with respect to this there must necessarily be a large discretion on the part of the legislature. In determining the question of reasonableness it is at liberty to act with reference to the established usages, customs, and traditions of the people, and with a view to the promotion of their comfort, and the preservation of the public peace and good order. Gauged by this standard, we cannot say that a law which authorizes or even requires the separation of the two races in public conveyances is unreasonable.

We consider the underlying fallacy of the plaintiff's argument to consist in the assumption that the enforced separation of the two races stamps the colored race with a badge of inferiority. If this be so, it is not by reason of anything found in the act, but solely because the colored race chooses to put that construction upon it … The argument also assumes that social prejudices may be overcome by legislation, and that equal rights cannot be secured to the negro except by an enforced commingling of the two races. We cannot accept this proposition. If the two races are to meet on terms of social equality, it must be the result of natural affinities, a mutual appreciation of each other's merits and a voluntary consent of individuals … Legislation is powerless to eradicate racial instincts or to abolish distinctions based upon physical differences, and the attempt to do so can only result in accentuating the difficulties of the present situation. If the civil and political rights of both races be equal, one cannot be inferior to the other civilly or politically. If one race be inferior to the other socially, the Constitution of the United States cannot put them upon the same plane.

Justice Harlan, in vigorous dissent, accepted Plessy's Thirteenth Amendment argument as well as that based upon the Fourteenth Amendment's demand of equal protection. Unlike Justice Brown, who refused to acknowledge that government-mandated forced separation of the races stamped "the colored race with a badge of inferiority," Harlan asserted that the U.S. Constitution tolerated no racial classifications, as it was "colorblind," and that segregated facilities did impose "a badge of ... servitude," and thereby violated the constitution:

In respect of civil rights, common to all citizens, the Constitution of the United States does not, I think, permit any public authority to know the race of those entitled to be protected in the enjoyment of such rights.... such legislation as that here in question is inconsistent, not only with that equality of rights which pertains to citizenship, national and state, but with the personal liberty enjoyed by every one within the United States.

The 13th Amendment does not permit the withholding or the deprivation of any right necessarily inhering in freedom. It not only struck down the institution of slavery as previously existing in the United States, but it prevents the imposition of any burdens or disabilities that constitute badges of slavery or servitude ... the 14th Amendment ... added greatly to the dignity and glory of American citizenship, and to the security of personal liberty.... These two amendments, if enforced according to their true intent and meaning, will protect all the civil rights that pertain to freedom and citizenship.

... It was said in argument that the statute of Louisiana does not discriminate against either race, but prescribes a rule applicable alike to white and colored citizens ... Everyone knows that the statute in question had its origin in the purpose, not so much to exclude white persons from railroad cars occupied by blacks, as to exclude colored people from coaches occupied by or assigned to white persons ... No one would be so wanting in candor as to assert the contrary. The fundamental objection, therefore, to the statute, is that it interferes with the personal freedom of citizens ...

The white race deems itself to be the dominant race in this country. And so it is, in prestige, in achievements, in education, in wealth, and in power. So, I doubt not that it will continue to be for all time, if it remains true to its great heritage and holds fast to the principles of constitutional liberty. But in view of the Constitution, in the eye of the law, there is in this country no superior, dominant, ruling class of citizens. There is no caste here. Our Constitution is color-blind, and neither knows nor tolerates classes among citizens. In respect of civil rights, all citizens are equal before the law ...

In my opinion, the judgment this day rendered will, in time, prove to be quite as pernicious as the decision made by this tribunal in the *Dred Scott Case* ... Sixty millions of whites are in no danger from the presence here of eight millions of blacks. The destinies of the two races in this country are indissolubly linked together, and the interests of both require that the common government of all shall not permit the seeds of race hate to be planted under the sanction of law. What can more certainly arouse race hate, what more certainly create and perpetuate a feeling of distrust between these races, than state enactments which in fact proceed on the ground that colored citizens are so inferior and degraded that they cannot be allowed to sit in public coaches occupied by white citizens?

I am of opinion that the statute of Louisiana is inconsistent with the personal liberty of citizens, white and black, in that state, and hostile to both the spirit and letter of the Constitution of the United States.

THE MODERN ERA: SCHOOL DESEGREGATION

In the nineteenth century, African Americans used litigation to press for their rights, often, as demonstrated *by Dred Scott, Plessy,* and other cases, with harsh results. But for civil rights activists in the early twentieth century, imbued with democratic ideals, and with few alternatives, litigation still offered one hope, however dim, of holding Americans to the spirit of the Constitution. Courts were a limited weapon in the battle against African American exclusion. However, given the disenfranchisement of African Americans from the political process, African American and white civil rights activists, some of whom by 1909 had incorporated into the National Association for the Advancement of Colored People (NAACP), made the decision to litigate while also lobbying elected leaders.

For the first half of the twentieth century a continuous battering at the barriers of segregation, led increasingly by African American lawyers trained at Howard University Law School, was set in motion. Their court-room challenges were directed at discriminatory laws restricting access to voting, to housing, to transportation, to education, and against lynching. In the area of education, the initial strategy focused on equalizing school facilities for African American and white children. However, by mid-century, when it became apparent that public education was a major route to success in American society, that the resources the states would use for African American schools would never permit them to become equal, and finally, that segregated schools, in and of themselves, placed an unfair burden of inferiority on African American children, the strategy changed to that of a wholesale attack on the "separate but equal doctrine" established in *Plessy.*

The confidence to pursue this more far-reaching, though risky, strategy grew out of factors that suggested that there was a changing climate regarding African American exclusion in America. Above the Mason-Dixon Line the Democratic Party increasingly saw political opportunity in attending to rights violations directed toward the growing numbers of urban-dwelling African Americans.[8] Some public officials pointed out that widespread, government-supported racism in the United States undermined our political credibility with newly independent nations in Africa and Asia. The government's desire to expand markets and curb the influence of the Soviet Union among these nations also made officials more amenable to the lowering of publicly supported barriers used to exclude African Americans. Thus, at the conclusion of World War II, under President Harry Truman's leadership, desegregation of the Armed Forces began, discrimination in federal hiring practices was reduced, and the Federal Housing Authority (FHA) ended its ban on insuring racially mixed housing.[9] Truman called upon Congress to make lynching a federal offense, to end segregation on all interstate transportation, and to outlaw the poll tax.

During these years, the NAACP and other civil rights groups had been laying the foundation in a series of cases, largely involving graduate and professional education, from which to strike down the separate but equal doctrine that had been used as the legal basis for segregated schooling. In 1950, in *Sweatt v. Painter* (339 U.S. 629), the Supreme Court signaled a possible change in equal protection law, finding that a segregated school for African Americans could not provide them equal educational opportunities because it would be "missing those qualities which are incapable of objective measurement but make for greatness in a law school." Also giving hope that constitutional barriers to desegregation would not be long in coming down was the 1950 decision in *McLaurin v. Oklahoma* (339 U.S. 637). Like *Sweatt*, the case involved the right to education at a desegregated professional school; while not overturning *Plessy*, the Court held that the explicit segregation of African American students in the classrooms, library, and dining facilities of a white public educational institution violated equal-protection guarantees.

At about the same time as the *Sweatt* and *McLaurin* litigation, challenges were brought in several states, including Kansas, Delaware, Virginia, and South Carolina, by African American plaintiffs who argued that segregation was in and of itself discriminatory. All of these claims had been rejected by lower courts. Unlike *Sweatt* and *McLaurin* these cases struck at segregated schooling at the elementary and high school levels. This went more to the heart of American prejudice for two reasons: Clearly an order to desegregate American elementary and secondary schools would involve far greater numbers of students than the desegregation of professional or graduate schools; more pointedly, the creation of racially mixed elementary and high school environments implied a potential for social and sexual interaction that many whites found absolutely unacceptable. These combined school cases reached the Supreme Court on behalf of several plaintiffs, the first of whom was Linda Brown, an African American student in Topeka, Kansas, who, because of a state law mandating segregated schools, had to walk over a mile to the African American school, bypassing a whites-only school much nearer to her home.

The Supreme Court that first heard argument on these cases, in the 1952–1953 term, was a court divided by personality and judicial philosophy. Fifteen years after President Franklin Roosevelt's attempted court-packing plan, in which Roosevelt challenged the judicial interference of the Court in the economic recovery legislation of the Depression Era, the justices still had not resolved the role the Court should play in societal change. Liberals, who in the 1930s had been anxious to further their economic and social agenda through legislative action and who, then, rejected what was termed the antidemocratic, nonmajoritarian interference of federal courts, now saw the Court as an essential weapon against legislatures representing popular sentiment that favored the continuing, and, to them, unconstitutional injustice of school segregation.

In addition to the philosophical differences among members of the Court, the ineffectual leadership of Chief Justice Fred Vinson further undermined the Court's ability to act conclusively on the school cases. The Court ended its first year of deliberation on *Brown* determined that the issue should be reargued in the new term. Here fate stepped in! A year of turmoil quickly dissipated when, after the death of Chief Justice Vinson, Earl Warren became the new head of the Court. He brought the Court to consensus, insisting that the justices confront the basic issue: "that the doctrine of separate-but-equal rested upon the concept of the inferiority of the colored race." Thus, Warren led the Court to its historical and unanimous decision that *Plessy* had been wrongly decided and that "separate but equal has no place in the field of public education." The Chief Justice authored the opinion, indicating the importance of the case:

BROWN V. BOARD OF EDUCATION 347 U.S. 483 (1954)

In each of the cases, minors of the Negro race, seek the aid of the courts in obtaining admission to the public schools of their community on a nonsegregated basis. In each instance, they had been denied admission to schools attended by white children under laws requiring or permitting segregation according to race. This segregation was alleged to deprive the plaintiffs of the equal protection of the laws under the Fourteenth Amendment.... The plaintiffs contend that segregated public schools are not "equal" and cannot be made equal ...

In approaching this problem, we cannot turn the clock back to 1868 when the Amendment was adopted, or even to 1896 when *Plessy v. Ferguson* was written. We must consider public education in the light of its full development and its present place in American life throughout the Nation. Only in this way can it be determined if segregation in public schools deprives these plaintiffs of the equal protection of the laws.

Today, education is perhaps the most important function of states and local governments. Compulsory school attendance laws and the great expenditures for education both demonstrate our recognition of the importance of education to our democratic society. It is required in the performance of our most basic public responsibilities, even service in the armed forces. It is the very foundation of good citizenship. Today it is a principal instrument in awakening the child to cultural values, in preparing him for later professional training, and in helping him to adjust normally to his environment. In these days, it is doubtful that any child may reasonably be expected to succeed in life if he is denied the opportunity of an education. Such an opportunity, where the state has undertaken to provide it, is a right which must be made available to all on equal terms.

We come then to the question presented: Does segregation of children in public schools solely on the basis of race, even though the physical facilities and other "tangible" factors may be equal, deprive the children of the minority group of equal educational opportunities? We believe that it does.

To separate [children in grade and high schools] from others of similar age and qualifications solely because of their race generates a feeling of inferiority as to their status in the community that may affect their hearts and minds in a way unlikely ever to be undone. The effect of this separation on their educational opportunities was well stated by a finding in the Kansas case by a court which nevertheless felt compelled to rule against the Negro plaintiffs:

> Segregation of white and colored children in public schools has a detrimental effect upon the colored children. The impact is greater when it has the sanction of the law; for the policy of separating the races is usually interpreted as denoting the inferiority of the negro group. A sense of inferiority affects the motivation of a child to learn. Segregation with the sanction of law, therefore, has a tendency to [retard] the educational and mental development of negro children and to deprive them of some of the benefits they would receive in a racial[ly] integrated school system.

Whatever may have been the extent of psychological knowledge at the time of *Plessy v. Ferguson*, this finding is amply supported by modern authority. Any language in *Plessy v. Ferguson* contrary to this finding is rejected.

We conclude that in the field of public education the doctrine of "separate but equal" has no place. Separate educational facilities are inherently unequal ...

In the initial *Brown* decision the Court did not address the question of remedies, instead inviting all the parties to the case to submit new memoranda on the question of how to implement desegregation of American schools. It was not until the following year, 1955, in *Brown II* (349 U.S. 294), that the court dealt with this problem. In this opinion, the Court was sensitive to "different local conditions"—the regional culture of the South—as well as the issue of class. It attempted to accommodate the potentially explosive repercussions of its decision by ordering desegregation (not integration) "with all deliberate speed," a decree that appears, from 40 years hindsight, to have been a strategy of vague generalization. Today, legal historians and civil rights advocates debate the impact of the *Brown* decision on racial justice. Professor Gerald Rosenberg argues that, "there is little evidence that *Brown* helped produce positive change, [and] there is some evidence that it hardened resistance to civil rights among both elites and the white public."[10]

Civil rights lawyer Walter Dellinger refutes these conclusions, writing: "disparagement of *Brown's* impact is seriously mistaken ... The clarion call of the Court's unanimous condemnation of racial segregation as incompatible with our deepest Constitutional principles was to play an indispensable role in the life of the South and the nation."[11] Yet other scholars, Derrick Bell and Harold Cruse among them, insist that the NAACP's strategy in shaping *Brown* reflected the ideals of a "black bourgeoisie" that overemphasized the symbolism of integration and failed to establish greater African American administrative and intellectual control of integrated schools.[12]

The immediate political response to *Brown* varied greatly. In the six border states and the District of Columbia, *Brown* appears to have promoted

Hopes raised, hopes dashed? After the passage of *Brown v. Board*, civil rights activists, both black and white, hoped that school integration would lead to equality for African Americans. Now, 50 years after *Brown*, many express disappointment that not only school integration, but full African American equality has not been achieved. Photo courtesy of Serena Nanda.

desegregation, with the number of African American children attending school with Caucasian children increasing after 1956. In the South, however, stalling and evasion of the desegregation order gave way to massive resistance. The Louisiana legislature, for example, in 1960–1961 alone enacted 92 laws and resolutions to maintain segregated public schools.[13]

By the 1960s it was clear that Southern school districts were not going to follow through on the spirit of *Brown* without more specific enforcement on the part of the elected branches of the federal government and more specific guidelines from the Supreme Court. Congress, strong-armed by President Lyndon B. Johnson, responded by enacting the 1964 Civil Rights Act, which, in part, barred racial discrimination in schools. The U.S. attorney general was given authority under this landmark legislation to bring desegregation suits on behalf of students in segregated schools. The act also permitted the federal government to withhold federal education aid from school districts that discriminated by race. A year later Congress passed into law the Elementary and Secondary Education Act (ESEA). This legislation provided financial incentives for school districts in which there was desegregation.

The U.S. Supreme Court also expanded upon its earlier desegregation rulings and, in the 1971 case of *Swann v. Charlotte-Mecklenburg* (402 U.S. 1), made clear the obligation of local school districts to end state-sanctioned school segregation, if necessary by implementing plans that would result in substantially increasing the numbers of African American students attending schools with whites. Toward this end, the Court specifically approved controversial methods such as busing, gerrymandered school districts, and racial quotas to achieve school integration. Chief Justice Warren Burger conceded the necessity of such affirmative methods in a system that previously had been "deliberately constructed and maintained to enforce racial segregation."

While the Court's decisions put an end to legally sanctioned, de jure, segregation in Southern schools, they left de facto segregation in both the North and the South largely untouched. In both places, but particularly in the North, the exclusion of African Americans had often relied upon subtler forms of discrimination rather than on legal statute. In the 1960s and 1970s, having defeated de jure segregation, civil rights groups moved on to attack this next barrier—the de facto segregation of schools, housing, and the workplace, testing the limits of courts' willingness to deal with this equally pernicious exclusion of African Americans from the opportunities afforded other Americans. While the Supreme Court has acknowledged the prevalence of de facto exclusion of African Americans, through the development of the "intent doctrine" it has resisted meeting, in full, demands for equal participation of African Americans in American society.

Thus, in *Keyes v. School District* [413 U.S. 189 (1973)], where there was a clear showing of intent on the part of the Denver School Board deliberately to segregate the schools by school construction, gerrymandered attendance zones, and excessive use of mobile classrooms, the Supreme Court placed the burden on the local school boards to implement plans resulting in integration. However, the Court has resisted ordering the amelioration of disparate impact such as de facto school segregation where clear evidence of intentional discrimination cannot be demonstrated.

AFRICAN AMERICANS AND SCHOOL CULTURES

Schools are the site of struggles over rights because of their powerful role in American society. Study after study demonstrates that success in adult life correlates with level of education. In different ways, how children learn in school and what they learn affects life chances. Thus, members of the African American community have argued that racial justice extends beyond general issues of school desegregation and integration to specific questions of curriculum. In early curriculum litigation, in a complicated 1970s educational-language case brought against the school district of Ann Arbor, Michigan, African American parents argued that educational agencies must take appropriate action to overcome language barriers that impede equal participation by its students in its instructional programs.[14] In *Martin Luther King Junior Elementary School Children et al. v. Ann Arbor School District Board* [473 F. Supp. 1371 (1979)], African American plaintiffs drew upon a provision of a 1972 federal school bus-ing act to support their belief that school curricula must be adapted in ways that would acknowledge Black English, the language of home and community of many African American children, a language whose syntax is distinct from that of standard English, and to take Black English into account when helping children read in standard English.

Judge Charles W. Joiner, of the U.S. District Court, was persuaded by the expert testimony of sociolinguists that the children spoke a language known as Black English that was different from standard English and did constitute a language barrier that impeded equal participation in instructional programs. Although media distortion and political backlash presented Joiner's decision as a mandate for the schools to teach Black English, nothing could be further from the truth. In fact, *King* is a continu-ation of the legal doctrine established in the 1974 *Lau v. Nichols* case bought by non-English-speaking students of Chinese ancestry, and reaffirms the school's responsibility to "open[ing] the doors to the establishment by teaching the children to read in the standard English of the school, the commercial world, the arts, science and the professions" (see chapter 4). In *King,* Judge Joiner wrote:

This case is not an effort on the part of the plaintiffs to require that they be taught "black English" or that their instruction throughout their schooling be in "black English," or that a dual language program be provided … It is a straightforward effort to require the court to intervene on the children's behalf to require the defen-dant School District Board to take appropriate action to teach them to read in the standard English.

[E]xperts … testified … that efforts to instruct the children in standard English by teachers who failed to appreciate that the children speak a dialect which is acceptable in the home and peer community can result in the children becoming ashamed of their language, and thus impede the learning process. In this respect, the black dialect appears to be different than the usual foreign language because a foreign language is not looked down on by the teachers.

[B]lack children learn to be bilingual. They retain fluency in "black English" to maintain status in the community and they become fluent in standard English to succeed in the general society. They achieve in this way by learning to "code switch" from one to the other depending on the circumstances.

In a far more radical action, one seeking changes in curriculum and school population, beginning in the late 1980s educators and African American parents in several American cities proposed "Black Only"—in some instances "Black Male Only"—schools, or schools within schools. Stating that, "Most of black America's seven million school age youth are in trouble, particularly those in this nation's central cities," advocates argued the need for special programs with African American teachers as mentors, an African-centered curriculum, extended hours, school uniforms, and

Saturday classes.[15] Using such innovations, proponents hoped to improve the rate of academic success of African Americans in school.

Plans for African American male-only schools went forward in several American cities in the early 1990s. Ultimately, however, most school boards backed away from the idea in the face of significant criticism or the possibility of lawsuits. Not surprisingly, for example, African American Dr. Kenneth Clark, whose social science research was cited in *Brown v. Board of Education,* spoke against "Black Only" schools, saying that they negated everything that he and other civil rights activists fought for in the struggle to end de jure school segregation. Other scholars and citizens opposed this new form of segregated schools on the grounds that categorizing children according to race is destructive to the children and to society. These individuals proposed that schools continue to create truly multicultural curricula that can be taught to all students. (Heeding this suggestion, in 2005 school administrators in Philadelphia instituted a mandatory course in African American history to be required of all ninth graders.)[16]

Detroit, Michigan, however, "desperate over the wasted lives of its young black men," decided to go ahead with its plan for male academies.[17] After pressure from the Latino community, among others, the school board said that the schools would be open to boys of all races although they would focus on African Americans. Continuing their justification for sex-segregated schools, officials cited the long history of other all male educational institutions in the United States, including military academies and parochial schools.

As soon as Detroit began admitting students for the new male-only academies, a lawsuit was brought by two African American mothers on behalf of their daughters who, they alleged, were not eligible for the admissions lottery. The mothers contended that the academies' goals of "mastering emotions, maintaining relationships with family and community, accepting responsibility, developing self-esteem—are equally valuable and vital to all children" and that the Detroit school board had acknowledged an "equally urgent and unique crisis facing ... female students."[18] Lawyers from the American Civil Liberties Union and the National Organization for Women Legal Defense and Education Fund arguing the case, *Garrett v. Board of Education of Detroit* [775 F.Supp. 1004 (1991)], challenged the legality of the schools, citing violations of the equal protection clause of the Fourteenth Amendment, Title IX of the Education Amendments of 1972 (requiring equal opportunity in public schools regardless of sex), the Michigan Constitution, and state statutes. They asked for an injunction. Lawyers for Detroit's school board maintained that the schools could be permitted under the law and referred to Detroit's soaring high school dropout rate among young men.

U.S. District Court Judge George Woods heard the case and ruled that excluding girls from the new schools did violate the law. Woods acknowledged that while the school system may be failing African American male students, and while there was "compelling need" to address the "crisis facing African American males," these facts "fall short of demonstrating that excluding girls is substantially related to the achievement of the Board's objectives. The Board has proffered no evidence that the presence of girls in the classroom bears a substantial relationship to the difficulties facing urban males."[19] Judge Woods also concluded that, "male academies improperly use gender as a 'proxy for other, more germane bases of classification,' in this instance, for 'at risk' students. Specifically, the gender-specific data presented in defense of the Academies ignores the fact that all children in the Detroit public schools face significant obstacles to success ... the Board acknowledged a ... crisis facing ... female students ... Ignoring the plight of urban females institutionalizes inequality and perpetuates the myth that females are doing well in the current system."[20] He ordered all sides to meet and to work out a schedule under which girls would be admitted. This was done, and by 1995, the three schools at issue in the litigation—Marcus Garvey Academy, Paul Robeson Academy, and Malcolm X Academy—had enrolled approximately 20 to 25 percent females.[21] Ten years later the number of girls nearly equaled that of boys at Malcolm X Academy.[22]

AFFIRMATIVE ACTION

The plan to establish all-male, African-centered academies was, of course, an affirmative action program. Affirmative action has been generally defined as "government policies that directly or indirectly award jobs, admissions to [schools], and other social goods and resources to individuals on the basis of membership in designated protected groups, in order to compensate those groups for past discrimination caused by society as a whole."[23] Such programs can also be promoted by the private sector. Affirmative action plans to remedy the exclusion of African Americans from the major economic and educational institutions of the dominant culture raise difficult issues for courts, posing as they do the question of the constitutional permissibility of programs that may involve the exclusion of Caucasians as a means of making way for African American participation. The legitimacy of African American demands for equal opportunity is borne out by the extensive data indicating persistent and significant gaps between African Americans and Caucasians in income, wealth, employment, education, housing, health, and other measures of well-being. Supporters of affirmative action argue that these differences are a function of past and contemporary racial discrimination.[24]

American courts have tried to find their way through the thicket of competing interests by accepting those affirmative-action plans initiated in response to an actual finding of discrimination, which do not negatively affect whites already in jobs, or which do not impose inflexible racial quotas. Typical of the latter approach was the U.S. Supreme Court's complicated response in the 1978 case, *Regents of the University of California v. Bakke* (438 U.S. 265).

Alan Bakke, a white male, was denied admission to the medical school at the University of California at Davis in a year when 16 out of 100 places had been set aside for "disadvantaged" minority students. His grade point average and MCAT scores were higher than several of those students accepted under the medical school's affirmative action plan. Bakke challenged the school's program, arguing that it discriminated against him on account of his race. He argued that the quota provision violated the California constitution, Title VI of the 1964 U.S. Civil Rights Act (barring racial discrimination in the federal funding of public and private institutions), and the equal protection clause of the U.S. Constitution's Fourteenth Amendment. The university appealed to the U.S. Supreme Court after a California superior court, and the state's Supreme Court, ruled against the use of such quotas. *Bakke* generated unprecedented interest nationwide and dozens of organizations filed amicus briefs stating their views in opposition to, and in support of, affirmative action.

Justice Lewis F. Powell announced the court's ruling in an opinion that was not signed by the other justices who, deeply divided over statutory and constitutional issues, in five additional opinions offered their own concurring and dissenting interpretations of the legality of affirmative-action plans. The Court's ruling upheld the possibility that affirmative-action programs could be legal, but it struck down the one used by the Davis campus because it involved a fixed quota. Powell rejected most of the university's arguments on behalf of affirmative action. He did agree, however, that an affirmative-action plan that does not employ fixed quotas is permissible at a university because of the need to encourage academic freedom and a diverse student body, actions protected by the First Amendment. His support of diversity as a compelling educational interest provided an important new rationale for affirmative-action programs:

The ... goal asserted by petitioner is the attainment of a diverse student body. This clearly is a constitutionally permissible goal for an institution of higher education. Academic freedom, though not a specifically enumerated constitutional right, long has been viewed as a special concern of the First Amendment. The freedom of a university to make its own judgments as to education includes the selection of its student body ... Physicians serve a heterogeneous population. An otherwise qualified medical student with a particular background—whether it be ethnic, geographic, culturally advantaged or disadvantaged—may bring to a professional school of medicine experiences, outlooks, and ideas that enrich the training of its student body and better equip its graduates to render with understanding their vital service to humanity.

In contrast, Justice William Brennan, joined by Justices Harry Blackmun, Thurgood Marshall, and Byron White, contended that racial quotas are constitutionally permissible remedies for past discrimination. Justice Brennan argued that neither the constitution nor Title VI prohibited government from taking race into account "when it acts not to demean or insult any racial group, but to remedy disadvantages cast on minorities by past racial prejudice." Referring directly to the fact that Justice Harlan's opinion in *Plessy* was a dissent, he wrote, "no decision of this Court has ever adopted the proposition that the Constitution must be colorblind."

The *Bakke* case was much watched and discussed. Because the decision only involved racial quotas in admissions to state-supported universities, and because the Supreme Court was so divided in its views, *Bakke* did not provide a definitive judicial statement on the legality of other affirmative-action programs. Since 1978 the U.S. Supreme Court and the lower federal courts, have issued a considerable number of additional opinions on affirmative action and so-called reverse discrimination, many of them having to do with employment and the workplace, rather than education. Among these decisions are *United Steelworkers v. Weber* [443 U.S. 193 (1979)]; *Fullilove v. Klutznick* [448 U.S. 448 (1980)]; *Firefighters v. Stotts* [467 U.S. 561 (1984)]; *Richmond v. Croson* [488 U.S. 469 (1989)]; and *Metro Broadcasting v. FCC* [497 U.S. 547 (1990)]. In these decisions, in addition to approving affirmative-action targets and plans that do not negatively affect whites already in jobs or that impose completely fixed quotas, the Supreme Court has shown particular deference to affirmative-action plans crafted by Congress as compared with racially conscious programs established by state and local governments (unless the latter are designed to redress proven discrimination). But the Court's deference to federally mandated programs was considerably narrowed in 1995 when, in *Adarand v. Pena* (515 U.S. 200), the justices stated that affirmative-action programs, even when established by Congress, must be subject to strict judicial scrutiny to determine whether they violate equal protection standards, and that such plans must be narrowly tailored to accomplish a compelling government interest.

Affirmative-action programs came under additional attack in 1996 when the 5th federal circuit, in the much-discussed *Hopwood v. Texas* case (78 F. 3d 932) said that race may not be used as a factor in university admissions within its jurisdiction (Texas, Mississippi, and Louisiana). In the same year California voters approved Proposition 209 barring affirmative-action programs in that state.

Clearly then, at the beginning of the twenty-first century, the future of affirmative action programs was uncertain. Opponents continued to question the legitimacy and efficacy of such programs, arguing that they were unfair and that they benefited people on the basis of membership in a group rather than according to individual achievement. Supporters of affirmative action programs, however, maintained that they remained necessary both to remedy past and contemporary injustices and, drawing upon Justice Powell's argument in *Bakke,* to provide the diversity necessary for a successful, democratic society.

With opinion sharply divided considerable attention was focused on the U.S. Supreme Court in 2003 in anticipation of the outcome of two new affirmative action cases. In *Grutter v. Bollinger* (539 U.S. 244) Barbara Grutter, a white Michigan resident, challenged the use of race as a factor in admissions by the University of Michigan Law School, arguing that it violated the Equal Protection Clause of the Fourteenth Amendment and Title VI of the 1964 Civil Rights Act. A companion case, *Gratz v. Bollinger* (539 U.S. 244), raised the same legal questions about the university's use of an affirmative-action plan in determining the composition of its undergraduate classes, in this instance, by awarding 20 points of the 100 needed for admission to all minority candidates (African American, Hispanic, and Native American). Illustrating the importance of these two cases, dozens of the largest American corporations along with a group of retired military and civilian leaders filed amicus briefs urging that the justices uphold both Michigan programs. They argued that the need for diversity in all aspects of education was compelling given the global reach of U.S. businesses. The military leaders also stated the ongoing need for race-conscious recruiting and admissions policies in the nation's service academies, programs that had been successful in creating better racial and ethnic balance in the military's officer corps.[25]

The decisions in *Grutter* and *Gratz*, announced on the same day, presented much the same outcome as in *Bakke*. In a 6–3 vote the Court ruled in *Gratz* that Michigan's use of the fixed 20-point award system violated both the Equal Protection Clause and Title VI, reasoning that it was not "narrowly tailored" and did not provide the individualized consideration Justice Powell had outlined in *Bakke*. The plan used by Michigan's law school, however, which employed neither a quota nor fixed points, was found to be constitutionally permissible. Writing for the Court in *Grutter*, Justice Sandra Day O'Connor said that Justice Powell's opinion in *Bakke* "has served as the touchstone for constitutional analysis of race-conscious admissions policies" and cited it in concluding that the use of race as a factor in student admissions was lawful because "student body diversity is a compelling state interest" justifying narrowly tailored affirmative-action programs. In accepting diversity as a lawful goal, she also asserted that the Court had "never held that the only governmental use of race that can survive strict scrutiny is remedying past discrimination."

Justice O'Connor made a particular point of demonstrating the importance of education in the creation of a corps of elected officials. She wrote that universities, "and in particular, law schools, represent the training ground for a large number of our Nation's leaders … Individuals with law degrees occupy roughly half the state governorships, more than half the seats in the United States Senate, and more than a third of the seats in the United States House of Representatives." She then asserted, "In order to cultivate a set of leaders with legitimacy in the eyes of the citizenry, it is necessary that the path to leadership be visibly open to talented and

qualified individuals of every race and ethnicity. All members of our heterogeneous society must have confidence in the openness and integrity
of the educational institutions that provide this training. [L]aw schools
cannot be effective in isolation from the individuals and institutions with
which the law interacts."

While accepting the law school's affirmative action plan, Justice
O'Connor made it clear that time was on the side of those people who
wished to see the end of its use: "We expect that ... 25 years from now, the
use of racial preferences will no longer be necessary to further the interest
approved today." This did not mollify the dissenters who, in four separate opinions, faulted O'Connor for not applying strict judicial scrutiny in
considering whether Michigan's use of race in admissions decisions was
lawful. Justice Antonin Scalia wrote that "today's *Grutter-Gratz* split double header seems perversely designed to prolong the controversy and the
litigation." Justice Clarence Thomas, the only African American member
of the Court, declared his belief that "blacks can achieve in every avenue
of American life without the meddling of university administrators."

Perhaps more than for any other group, the law has been instrumen-
tal in defining the place of African Americans in American society. The
Constitution of the United States was once the legal source of the enslave-
ment and subsequent exclusion of African Americans from the mainstream of American society and culture. But that same document, with
its post-Civil War Amendments, has also provided the foundation of a
civil rights litigation strategy aimed at breaking the barriers of African
American exclusion. In spite of this foundation, however, America has not
fully come to terms with the legacy of slavery and racism. This is an argument made by supporters of reparations who maintain that Reconstruction, affirmative action, and antipoverty programs have not compensated
for institutionalized discrimination. They make the case that reparations have been paid to Holocaust survivors and to Japanese Americans
interned in camps in the United States during WWII (see chapter 12), and
that African Americans "suffer[ing] the aftereffects of slavery should also
be compensated."[26]

In addition to reparations, affirmative action policies, and the persistence of race segregated schools, issues of political representation and
electoral districts will be debated by lawmakers and ruled upon by judges
(the renewal of key provisions of the 1965 Voting Rights Act comes up in
2007). Moreover, important questions remain about the very role of law
and courts. It is not yet clear to what extent law can modify dominant
culture behavior and attitudes so that the extralegal forces that promote
African American exclusion can be overcome. As the debate over affirmative action so pointedly demonstrates, the willingness to use law not
merely to end segregation, but to promote a truly equal status of African
Americans within the larger society remains an open question. This raises
the possibility, articulated by African American law professor Derrick

Bell—among others—that the African American civil rights movement has relied too much on "the leaky boat of litigation."[27] In contrast, not ready to abandon his faith in the law as a weapon in the fight for racial and economic justice, political scientist H. N. Hirsch suggests that we not jettison the law, but rather seek new ways to use it.[28] Still others contend that the United States has a new future as "transracial America," that in the twenty-first century race will no longer be measured "in black or white, but in living color," a fact that raises profound questions for legislators and judges as they make and interpret the law.[29]

NOTES

1. Mahalia Jackson, *Movin' on Up* (New York: Avon, 1966), 198.

2. Ira Berlin and Leslie M. Harris, eds., *Slavery in New York* (New York: New Press, 2005), 63.

3. Arnold Taylor, *Travail and Triumph* (Westport, CT: Greenwood Press, 1976), 186; Judith K. Schafer, *Becoming Free, Remaining Free* (Baton Rouge: Louisiana University Press, 2003); and the work of Ira Berlin.

4. "Scott v. Sanford" in Kermit Hall, ed., *The Oxford Companion to the Supreme Court of the United States* (New York: Oxford University Press, 1992).

5. Eric Foner, *Reconstruction: America's Unfinished Revolution, 1863–1877* (New York: Harper & Row, 1988).

6. Taylor, *Travail and Triumph*, 40–41.

7. John A. Garraty, *Quarrels That Have Shaped the Constitution* (New York: Harper & Row, 1962), 156.

8. Edward G. Carmines and James A. Stimson, *Issue Evolution: Race and the Transformation of American Politics* (Princeton, NJ: Princeton University Press, 1989), chapter 2.

9. Richard Kluger, *Simple Justice: The History of Brown v. Board Education and Black America's Struggle for Equality* (New York: Random House, 1975), 255.

10. Gerald N. Rosenberg, *The Hollow Hope: Can Courts Bring About Social Change?* (Chicago: University of Chicago Press, 1991), 155.

11. Walter Dellinger, "A White Southerner Remembers *Brown*," *Extensions* (Fall 1994), 5.

12. H. N. Hirsch, "Race and Class, Law and Politics," *Boston University Law Review* 69 (March 1989), 457–59.

13. Data on the response of border and southern states may be found in Rosenberg, *The Hollow Hope*, 50–54, 79.

14. For an excellent general reference to various aspects of the case, see John Chambers Jr., ed., *Black English: Educational Equity and the Law* (Ann Arbor, MI: Karoma, 1983).

15. C. R. Gibbs, "Project 2000: Why Black Men Should Teach Black Boys," *Dollars & Sense* (February/March 1991), 1 and 19.

16. Michael Janofsky, "Philadelphia Mandates Black History for Graduation," *New York Times,* June 25, 2005, A7.

17. Isabel Wilkerson, "To Save Its Men, Detroit Plans Boys-Only Schools," *New York Times,* August 14, 1991, 1.

18. ACLU, Letter to Members (September 27, 1991), 1–2.

19. *Garrett v. Board of Education of Detroit,* 775 F. Supp. 1004 (E.D. Mich. 1991), 1007.

20. Ibid., 1007.

21. Telephone interview, March 30, 1995, with Mr. Harold Ellis, Executive Assistant to the Detroit superintendent of schools.

22. Telephone interview with school staff, December 20, 2005.

23. Hall, *The Oxford Companion to the Supreme Court,* 18.

24. See, e.g., Andrew Hacker, *Two Nations* (New York: Charles Scribner's, 1992); U.S. Congress, *Report of the Federal Glass Ceiling Commission* (March 1995). Also, George M. Fredrickson, "Still Separate and Unequal," *New York Review of Books* (November 17, 2005), reviewing Ira Katznelson, *When Affirmative Action Was White* (New York: Norton, 2005).

25. Ronald Dworkin, "The Court and the University," *New York Review of Books* (May 15, 2003), 8–9.

26. Frances Fitzgerald, "Peculiar Institutions," *New Yorker* (September 12, 2005), 72.

27. Derrick Bell, *And We Are Not Saved: The Elusive Question for Racial Justice* (New York: Basic Books, 1987), 71.

28. Hirsch, "Race and Class, Law and Politics," 464–66.

29. Terry H. Anderson, *The Pursuit of Fairness: A History of Affirmative Action* (New York: Oxford University Press, 2005), 264–65.

CHAPTER 4

Immigration: Latinos and Law

The United States represents itself as a nation of immigrants, but immigration has always been hotly debated and surrounded by much ambivalence: On the one hand was the need for immigrant labor, while on the other were strong feelings about the kinds of immigrants who would or would not fit—racially and culturally—into the American nation.[1] Early idealistic visions of America as a land of economic opportunity and political and religious freedom were narrowly defined. By 1790, the federal Naturalization Act restricted American citizenship to "a free white person"; the 1808 Compromise prohibited the importation of slaves, and by the 1830s increasing animosity was expressed against the immigration of Irish Catholics and Germans to the United States, who some believed would undermine American republicanism—either because their previous poverty in Europe had denied them the experience of political freedom or because their Catholicism would make them hostile to it and draw their loyalties elsewhere.

With the extension of the Naturalization Act of 1870, the policy of immigration restrictions, favoring immigrants only from northern and western Europe, became an integral part of the restrictions on naturalization of Asian immigrants (see chapter 12). American fears that an influx of immigrants would result in lower urban wages or that immigrants would flood and then dominate the Western frontiers, were not, however, limited to Asians.[2] Immigration in fact continued to increase; between 1880 and 1910 America experienced the largest influx of immigrants in its history, and, until recent changes in immigration law in 1965, the most diverse. Many of these immigrants gravitated to cities, where they lived in ethnic enclaves in multiethnic neighborhoods and fed America's growing industries. During this time racial ideology began to dominate immigration policy. While African Americans had always been viewed as a racial group, by 1880 the then-fashionable "racial" typologies began to be applied to Europeans as well. Southern and eastern Europeans were "racially" distinguished from the Nordic "races" from northern and western Europe, and by the 1920s restrictive immigration laws effectively limited immigration to these groups. Throughout this period the Supreme Court grappled with the definition of "whiteness" in a series of cases involving persons from countries like India and Lebanon, who appealed the denial of their immigration status based on their "nonwhite" racial designation.[3]

Working within a model that emphasized total assimilation of immigrants, proponents of restrictive immigration claimed that people from non-Nordic "races" could never become good American citizens and that the United States would "degenerate" if it incorporated them. By the 1970s, however, a "mosaic" or multicultural model emerged, holding that ethnic groups do not and should not assimilate completely, and that diverse cultural elements were central in immigrant group identity and also contributed to the larger American society. The multicultural movement partly reflected the demographics of immigration in the last 25 years as well as the "politics of identity" movements that began in the 1960s and continues today.

In 1965, Congress passed a new Immigration and Nationality Act explicitly aimed at reversing the discriminatory, racist immigration laws of the 1920s. The act expanded the numbers of immigrants from previously restricted nations; gave high priority to the social goal of family unification; and put refugee immigration on a less ad hoc basis.[4] While the act resulted in historic increases in immigrants, the major change resulting from the act has been in the composition of the immigrant population, with far greater numbers arriving from the Middle East, the Indian subcontinent, China, Korea, the Caribbean, and parts of Central and South America.[5]

The "new" legal immigrants significantly differ from those of the early 1900s. Many entered the United States at a time of economic contraction, when corporate downsizing was curtailing the number of jobs for legal immigrants while providing jobs at the lowest wages and under the most difficult conditions for illegal immigrants.[6] In addition, since the 1970s the pursuit of group interests (ethnic, gender, indigenous status), backed by policies such as affirmative action, had greater legitimacy in the United States than it had a century ago. Furthermore, immigrants now live in a world in which communication—by telephone, e-mail, and the Internet—is abundant, relatively simple, and inexpensive, and air travel is within reach of the middle and working classes. This makes it possible for immigrants to retain much closer social and economic ties with their families and cultures of origin, and accounts for some retention of cultural differences.[7] It is by no means clear, however, that the cultural distinctions among immigrant groups will persist over generations. For at the same time that there is a popular—though not uncontested—rhetoric approving of cultural diversity, today's immigrants and their children face enormous pressures from the marketplace, the media, and the schools to conform to a mainstream version of American culture, including, perhaps most importantly, speaking English. Efforts to restrict both legal and undocumented immigration and to curtail the rights of undocumented immigrants have particularly gained ground in California and the southwest, and have mainly targeted Latinos, though they also have been directed to the large Asian population on the West Coast. Undoubtedly, one of the strongest pressures for immigrant assimilation involves language use.

IMMIGRANTS AND LANGUAGE

There is no official national language policy in the United States. At the state level, the languages of European immigrants were sometimes permitted or even encouraged within an implied or explicit context of English as the official language; and sometimes they were outlawed. Expansion westward, annexation of Mexican territory, and later Hawaii, and the acquisition of Puerto Rico added other elements to U.S. language policy. English was not a condition of citizenship in either the Mexican territories or Puerto Rico, but in both places, as well as in Hawaii and among Native Americans, indigenous languages were viewed as significant barriers to assimilation, and attempts were made to suppress them, although these efforts were frequently resisted.[8]

Controversies over acceptance and public recognition of second languages were generally heavily weighted toward an assimilationist model of immigration. English was established as the lingua franca in the colonial period and viewed as essential to binding the nation's peoples together soon after independence. This view is still widely shared today: Only three states, Hawaii, New Mexico, and Louisiana, are officially bilingual.[9] Support for English as the official language of the United States waxed and waned depending on political and economic circumstances. This debate was—and is—primarily fought in public schools, but also in courts, business, signage in public space, and regarding official documents, such as voting registration and ballots. In the United States (unlike in most other nations), speaking a foreign language, even as a second language, gives rise to suspicions of inadequate assimilation or even national disloyalty. The many state laws prohibiting the teaching in languages other than English in the public schools aimed at separating young children from cultures considered both inferior and inimical to American ideals, and to prepare large numbers of people for participation in the American economy and civic culture through the use of English-language instruction.

In the past these laws fell particularly heavily on German immigrants, who had made strong efforts to preserve their own language through a system of private schools. In 1923, in the U.S. Supreme Court decision *Meyer v. Nebraska* (262 U.S. 390), a German-speaking community won the right to use German to teach the Bible in an elementary school. This decision is hailed as an important victory for cultural pluralism, not only because there are so few Supreme Court decisions affirming non-English-language rights, but also because the opinion established the idea that the Constitution's due process clause affirmed not just procedural rights, but also substantive rights, values, and traditions. On the other hand, the Court's opinion is not an enthusiastic celebration of cultural pluralism. Rather, the Court expressed considerable empathy and approval of the intent of the Nebraska legislature to "prevent the baneful effects of permitting foreigners to rear and educate their children in the language of their native land and to foster a homogeneous people with American ideals."

The importance of language rights again became a contentious issue in the mid-1960s. As part of the momentum of the civil rights movement, Congress did away with literacy in English as a required criterion for voting. In conjunction with the "war on poverty," Congress also passed several acts designed to help educationally disadvantaged children. Because many of these children did not speak English as a first language, in 1965 Congress expanded the education legislation to include a provision for bilingual education. This legislation was designed less to celebrate and preserve multiculturalism than to be transitional and compensatory, aimed at children with identifiable limitations with respect to school achievement. Although bilingual education is most identified in popular stereotypes with Latinos, in fact, the initial litigation was brought by Chinese in San Francisco, in *Lau v. Nichols* (414 U.S. 563), which reached the U.S. Supreme Court in 1974.

Unlike the controversy in *Meyer,* which centered upon the right to give general instruction in a foreign language, the question in *Lau* was whether or not the government was *required* to provide general instruction in a foreign language for non-English-speaking students in public schools. The plaintiffs, non-English-speaking students of Chinese ancestry, charged the San Francisco school system with violating their civil rights by failing to provide them with adequate instruction in their native language and thus denying them a meaningful opportunity to participate in the public educational program. At that time, the California education code's mandate to local schools required proficiency in English as well as other prescribed subjects.

In its opinion, the Court agreed with the plaintiffs, stating that, "Basic English skills are at the very core of what these public schools teach. Imposition of a requirement that, before a child can effectively participate in the educational program, he must have already acquired those basic skills is to make a mockery of public education. We know that those who do not understand English are certain to find their classroom experiences wholly incomprehensible and in no way meaningful."

The Justices recognized that the provision of equal facilities where children do not speak English could hardly be considered equal treatment under the law and ordered school districts to take "affirmative steps to rectify the language deficiency in order to open its instructional program to these students." This demand of the Court constituted an important "access right" for linguistic minorities, but did not, as is often believed, create a constitutionally based federal entitlement to bilingual education. Indeed, such claims under the equal protection clause were specifically rejected in *Keyes v. Denver,* although courts have mandated implementation of bilingual and other remedial programs on the basis of violation of Title VI of the Civil Rights Act of 1964 and the Equal Educational Opportunities Act of 1974.[10]

The legal ambiguity regarding language rights in education is paralleled by the lack of a clear judicial pattern on language rights in general, which have been manufactured piecemeal by judges and are inconsistent and even contradictory. The major effect of the courts has been to affirm constitutional rights otherwise guaranteed to non-English speakers, and to prohibit discrimination on the basis of national origin, and by extension, language.

In the 1980s and 1990s, perhaps as a result of the perceived legislative and judicial support for minority language rights, and combined with the increases in immigration from Asia, Mexico, and Central America, pressures to make English the official language in the United States became more vocal and more organized. An English-Only movement emerged based on the view that government support of other languages divides the nation, and that in the face of American cultural and racial diversity, English is the one thing holds us together as a people.

One long-term aim of the English-Only and Official English movements is ratification of a constitutional amendment making English the official language of the United States. This would outlaw mandated government bilingual services, effect congressional repeal of bilingual ballot requirements under the 1965 Voting Rights Act, and sharply reduce federal programs for bilingual education. The movement has had some success at state and local levels. In California, in 1986, a popular referendum passed that required legislators and other state officials to "...insure that the role of English as the common language of the State of California is preserved and enhanced," and to make no law "which diminishes or ignores the role of English as the common language" of California. Similar laws, targeting primarily Asian and Latino immigrants, have been enacted in 27 states and numerous local communities.[11]

Opponents of English-Only laws claim that these laws violate many state and federal constitutionally based freedoms, such as free speech (see below); that they are based on inaccurate group stereotypes; and that they are misdirected, in missing the very rapid language assimilation that is a fact of immigrant life in America. According to the 2000 Census, less than 10 percent of the Hispanic population lived in households where no English was spoken; among children, just 2 percent, and within one generation the passage from Spanish to English is virtually complete.[12] The false stereotypes of immigrants as both unable and unwilling to assimilate into American society fuel broader anti-immigrant measures and rhetoric, particularly directed against Latinos and especially Mexicans.[13]

LATINOS, LANGUAGE AND LAW

Latinos in the United States are a large and diverse ethnic group. The approximately 21 million Latino immigrants and their descendants include approximately 13 million Mexican Americans; three million Puerto Ricans; one million Cuban Americans; and four million other Latin Americans, many from Central America. Latino legal immigration sharply increased subsequent to the changes in American immigration law in 1965, so a larger proportion of Latinos, particularly Mexican Americans, are first-generation immigrants. As of 2002, Mexicans accounted for about 20 percent of *total* legal immigration to the United States, and they are also thought to compose about three-fifths of the undocumented population, which now numbers about 10 million.[14]

The immigration and settlement experiences of Latinos have varied over time, coinciding with particular historical events and economic trends. Mexican-Americans originate in the populations of the southwest and California, whose settlement predated the 1846–1848 Mexican-American war. Originally a settled rural population, their numbers were augmented by migrant workers, but since the 1950s, Mexican Americans have become about 90 percent urban, concentrated in California, Texas, New Mexico, and Arizona. Puerto Ricans and Cubans, in contrast, initially migrated to urban areas; the major Puerto Rican immigration, which began between the two World Wars, centers on East Coast cities, while Cubans, whose immigration swelled after the 1959 Cuban revolution, are mainly concentrated in South Florida. Political upheavals in Central America led to increasing numbers of both documented and undocumented immigrants from Guatemala, Nicaragua, and El Salvador, and since the 1960s there has been large-scale immigration from the Dominican Republic.

Anglos have largely viewed the persistence of Spanish language in the territory acquired through conquest of Mexico and in Puerto Rico as an insuperable barrier to Latino patriotism and to the incorporation of Latinos into mainstream legal, economic, social, and educational institutions in the United States. Although in the early years after the treaty of Guadalupe Hidalgo, Spanish was officially used in the governments of New Mexico and California, as the Anglo population increased in these areas pressure for Anglicization was unrelenting, although not altogether

For those opposing Latino immigration to the United
States, language is a key issue. Although for first-generation Latino immigrants, Spanish is an important
vehicle for their participation in American society,
almost all second-generation Latino immigrants speak
English along with Spanish, and by the third generation, most Latinos are fluent in English and no longer
speak Spanish. Photo courtesy of Joan Gregg.

unopposed. In Puerto Rico, acquired by the United States from Spain in
the Spanish-American War of 1898, English was (also) viewed as the major
vehicle of assimilation of the island's population to American culture.
In fact, Latino language assimilation has occurred rapidly in the United
States, and there is a high degree of fluent bilingualism.[15]

Nevertheless, language is the dominant Latino source of ethnic identity,
and the most significant bureaucratic criterion for access to government
resources, such as bilingual education or legal redress for discrimination based on national origin. In courts of law, this close identification of

Spanish with Latino identity has worked both for and against Latinos. In 1978, in *Guadalupe v. Tempe Elementary School District* (587 F.2d 1022), the Ninth Circuit of the Federal Court denied the request of Spanish-speaking students in Arizona for bilingual and bicultural education, stating emphatically, "Linguistic and cultural diversity within the nation-state, whatever may be its advantages from time to time, can restrict the scope of the fundamental compact. Diversity limits unity. Effective action by the nation-state to its peak of strength only rises when it is in response to aspirations unreservedly shared by each constituent culture and language group … as the scope of sharing diminishes, the strength of the nation-state's government wanes." Other courts have been more willing to defend Latino language rights, especially where these involve voting or fair treatment in the criminal justice system.

THE CRIMINAL JUSTICE SYSTEM

Within the criminal justice system linguistically based misunderstandings have a critical impact that courts have now ruled the government must take into account in all aspects of criminal prosecutions, such as the right of non-English-speaking defendants to understand the charges against them as guaranteed by the Sixth Amendment. In a 1970 court case, a Puerto Rican farm laborer, Rogelio Negron, was on trial for having killed a fellow worker during a drunken brawl.[16] Negron did not speak English, so the prosecutor hired a translator to translate his Spanish testimony into English. No interpreter was available, however, to translate the English part of the proceedings into Spanish for the defendant. Negron was informally apprised of what was going on during breaks. He was convicted of second-degree murder and sentenced to 20 years in prison. Claiming that the unavailability of an official English to Spanish translator prevented him from adequately conferring with his lawyer, Negron succeeded in winning a new trial. A federal appeals court ruled that Negron had been denied his Sixth Amendment right to confront his accusers. In his opinion, Judge Irving Kaufman stated, "The least we can require is that a court, put on notice of a defendant's severe language difficulty, make unmistakably clear to him that he has a right to a competent translator to assist him, at state expense, if need be, throughout his trial." This principle has now been adopted for federal criminal and immigration proceedings, and generally in state courts.

Ensuring that Sixth Amendment rights—to understand the accusations, to meaningfully participate in one's trial with the effective assistance of counsel, and to confront the government's witnesses on cross-examination—are not violated for non-English speakers is severely hindered by the shortage of competent court interpreters and the financial burden on courts to provide translation services. Nevertheless, as ordered by a New York District court in a criminal trial involving 18 Spanish-speaking defendants, Judge Jack Weinstein stated that "costs ... do not override constitutional rights.... If the government cannot afford to provide due process to those it prosecutes, it must forego prosecution." He added that whatever problems the government has in providing qualified interpreters must not be permitted to "defeat a criminal defendant's Sixth Amendment interests" lest a criminal trial become "the Kafkaesque specter of an incomprehensible ritual which may terminate in punishment."[17]

VOTING RIGHTS

Voting is clearly a fundamental right in a democratic society and many of the barriers that hampered or prohibited Latinos, particularly Mexican Americans, as well as other minorities from voting have ultimately been struck down by litigation: These include the poll tax, the all-white primary (in the south), excessive restrictions on voter registration, systems that required annual registration, prohibitions on the use of interpreters by non-English-speaking persons, high candidate filing fees, and racial gerrymandering.[18] The majority of cases involving language restrictions on voting that have reached the courts have turned on the narrow interpretation of the unique relationship between the United States and the non-English-speaking Commonwealth of Puerto Rico. The current U.S. policy of encouraging Puerto Rican schoolchildren to be taught in Spanish (see chapter 2) has resulted in an increasing number of Puerto Rican migrants arriving on the mainland without the language skills necessary to participate in the civic culture. After the passage of the Voting Rights Act of 1965 and subsequent amendments in 1972, which required that bilingual ballots and voting information be provided whenever 5 percent of the relevant population belonged to a language minority, courts have held that English-only elections violate the rights of non-English speakers.

In *Arroyo v. Tucker* [372 F. Supp 764 (1974)], for example, the court decided that the right to vote included the "right to be informed," and that officials of the city of Philadelphia, defendants in this case, in order to provide its Puerto Rican-born citizens with access to an "effective vote," were prohibited from "conducting elections and registration in English only." To implement their ruling the court required Philadelphia to provide all written materials in both Spanish and English, including, but not limited to, sample ballots, voter's certificates, registration certificates, and all instructions to voters; to provide an unofficial Spanish translation of all propositions, questions, and amendments; to provide a sufficient number of individuals who speak, read, write, and understand both Spanish and English at all polling places and places of registration in the City of Philadelphia falling in whole or in part in a census tract containing 5 percent or more persons of Puerto Rican birth; to provide appropriate and conspicuous signs at all polling places and places of registration in

these polling places indicating, in Spanish, that individuals are available
to assist Spanish-speaking voters or registrants, and that bilingual written
materials are available; to publicize elections in all media proportionately
in a way that reflects the language characteristics of plaintiffs, and to communicate the contents of the Court's order to all agents, employees, and
representatives of the defendants involved in the registration and voting
process.

EMPLOYMENT

In 1995, Maria-Kelly F. Yniguez, a bilingual Latina Arizona state
employee, filed suit in federal district court challenging the constitutionality of a recently passed amendment to the Arizona constitution that
all government business would be conducted in English and "no other
language." The Court struck down the amendment as violating the freedom of speech clause of the First Amendment of the U.S. Constitution.
Yniguez did not address, however, whether private, nongovernmental
actors may prohibit the use of languages other than English. Title VII of
the Civil Rights Act of 1964 makes it unlawful for any employer, public
or private, to discriminate in employment on the basis of an individual's
"race, color, religion, sex, or national origin" but is silent with respect
to language discrimination. Given the connection between language and
national origin, courts have struggled with whether Title VII's prohibition of discrimination on the basis of national origin forbids language
discrimination.[19]

In 1980, litigants in Texas petitioned a Federal court regarding whether
and to what extent private-sector employers may control language use
by their bilingual employees in the workplace. The plaintiff, Hector
Garcia, was a bilingual American-born Mexican-American, who was a
salesman for Gloor Lumber and Supply, Inc., in Brownsville, Texas. Mr.
Garcia's duties included stocking his department and keeping it in order,
assisting other department salespersons and selling lumber, hardware,
and supplies. Gloor's rules prohibited employees from speaking Spanish on the job unless they were communicating with Spanish-speaking
customers. The rule did not apply to conversation during work breaks.
Mr. Garcia testified that, because Spanish was his primary language,
he found the English-only rule difficult to follow. On June 10, 1975, in
response to a question from another Mexican American employee about
an item requested by a customer, he responded in Spanish that the article
was not available. Alton Gloor, his employer, overheard the conversation and fired Mr. Garcia. In *Hector Garcia v. Alton V.W. Gloor* [18 F.2d 264
(1980)] the court ruled against Mr. Garcia. In his opinion, Federal Circuit
Judge Alvin Rubin dismissed the importance of language as a vehicle of
personal and ethnic identity compared to the importance of the freedom
of contract for employers:

... the English-only policy was not strictly enforced but ... Mr. Garcia had violated it at every opportunity ... Mr. Gloor testified that there were business reasons for the language policy: English-speaking customers objected to communications between employees that they could not understand; pamphlets and trade literature were in English and were not available in Spanish, so it was important for employees to be fluent in English apart from conversations with English-speaking customers; if employees who normally spoke Spanish off the job were required to speak English on the job at all times and not only when waiting on English-speaking customers, they would improve their English; and the rule would permit supervisors, who did not speak Spanish, better to oversee the work of subordinates. The district court found that these were valid business reasons and that they, rather than discrimination, were the motive for the rule.

An expert witness called by the plaintiff testified that the Spanish language is the most important aspect of ethnic identification for Mexican-Americans, and it is to them what skin color is to others. Consequently, Mr. Garcia contends, with support from the Equal Employment Opportunity Commission EEOC, that the rule violates the EEO Act and the Civil Rights Acts....

Of the eight salesman employed by Gloor in 1975, seven were Hispanic, a matter perhaps of business necessity, because 75 of the population in its business area is of Hispanic background and many of Gloor's customers wish to be waited on by a salesman who speaks Spanish. Of its 39 employees, 31 were Hispanic, and a Hispanic sat on the Board of Directors. There is no contention that Gloor discriminated against Hispanic-Americans in any other way.

The [district] court held that the narrow issue was whether the English-only rule as applied to Mr. Garcia imposed a discriminatory condition of employment [contrary to the EEO Act forbidding discrimination because of such individual's ... national origin; and to limit, segregate, or classify his employees or applicants for employment in any way which would deprive or tend to deprive any individual of employment opportunities or otherwise adversely affect his status as an employee, because of such individual's ... national origin."]

.... Neither the statute nor common understanding equates national origin with the language that one chooses to speak. Language may be used as a covert basis for national origin discrimination, but the English-only rule was not applied to Garcia by Gloor either to this end or with this result. Mr. Garcia argues that it is discriminatory to prohibit employees from speaking a foreign language on the basis of a thesis that, if an employee whose most familiar language is not English is denied the right to converse in that language, he is denied a privilege of employment enjoyed by employees most comfortable in English; this, necessarily, discriminates against him on the basis of national origin because national origin influences or determines his language preference.... Mr. Garcia was fully bilingual. He chose deliberately to speak Spanish instead of English while actually at work. He was permitted to speak the language he preferred during work breaks.

No authority cited to us gives a person a right to speak any particular language while at work; unless imposed by statute, the rules of the workplace are made by collective bargaining or, in its absence, by the employer .... if the employer engages a bilingual person, that person is granted neither right nor privilege by the statute to use the language of his personal preference. Mr. Garcia was bilingual. Off the job, when he spoke one language or another, he exercised a preference. He was hired by Gloor precisely because he was bilingual, and, apart from the contested rule, his preference in language was restricted to some extent by the nature of his employment. On the job, in addressing English-speaking customers, he was obliged to use English; in serving Spanish-speaking patrons, he was required to speak Spanish. The English-only rule went a step further and restricted his preference while he was on the job and not serving a customer.

We do not denigrate the importance of a person's language of preference or other aspects of his national, ethnic or racial self-identification. Differences in language and other cultural attributes may not be used as a fulcrum for discrimination. However, the English-only rule, as applied by Gloor to Mr. Garcia, did not forbid cultural expression to persons for whom compliance with it might impose hardship. While Title VII forbids the imposition of burdensome terms and conditions of employment as well as those that produce an atmosphere of racial and ethnic oppression, the evidence does not support a finding that the English-only rule had this effect on Mr. Garcia.

The EEO Act does not support an interpretation that equates the language an employee prefers to use with his national origin. To a person who speaks only one tongue or to a person who has difficulty using another language than the one spoken in his home, language might well be an immutable characteristic like skin color, sex or place of birth. However, the language a person who is multi-lingual elects to speak at a particular time is by definition a matter of choice used that language by choice ....

The [English-only] rule was confined to the work place and work hours. It did not apply to conversations during breaks or other employee free-time. There is no evidence that Gloor forbade speaking Spanish to discriminate in employment or that the effect of doing so was invidious to Hispanic Americans. We do not consider rules that turn on the language used in an employee's home, the one he chooses to speak when not at work or the tongue spoken by his parents or grandparents. In some circumstances, the ability to speak or the speaking of a language other than English might be equated with national origin, but this case concerns only a requirement that persons capable of speaking English do so while on duty.

That this rule prevents some employees, like Mr. Garcia, from exercising a preference to converse in Spanish does not convert it into discrimination based on national origin .... [Garcia's] argument thus reduces itself to a contention that the statute commands employers to permit employees to speak the tongue they prefer. We do not think the statute permits that interpretation, whether the preference be slight or strong or even one closely related to self-identity.

Mr. Garcia and the EEOC would have us adopt a standard that the employer's business needs must be accomplished in the manner that appears to us to be the least restrictive [to the employee]. The statute does not give the judiciary such latitude in the absence of discrimination. Judges, who have neither business experience nor the problem of meeting the employee's payroll, do not have the power to preempt an employer's business judgment by imposing a solution that appears less restrictive ....

We hold only that an employer's rule forbidding a bilingual employee to speak anything but English in public areas while on the job is not discrimination based on national origin as applied to a person who is fully capable of speaking English and chooses not to do so in deliberate disregard of his employer's rule. Even if we assume that the violation of the rule was a substantial factor leading to Mr. Garcia's discharge, we, therefore, affirm the district court's judgment that Mr. Garcia was neither discharged because of his national origin nor denied equal conditions of employment based on that factor; instead, he was discharged because, having the ability to comply with his employer's rule, he did not do so.

When *Garcia v. Gloor* was decided there were few guidelines and a general dearth of judicial authority concerning English-only rules. In fact, *Garcia v. Gloor* was the only outstanding federal appellate court decision at that time. Subsequent to that decision, however, in December 1980, the U.S. Equal Employment Opportunity Commission (EEOC), the federal agency charged with administering employment discrimination law, established guidelines that were contrary to the position of the court in *Garcia*. The new EEOC guidelines held that a total prohibition on speaking languages other than English would be presumed invalid, and that a limited prohibition on speaking languages other than English would be permitted only when justified by a clear "business necessity" subsequently defined to include communications during emergencies and while conducting inherently dangerous work, but did not include customer preferences. Nevertheless, some courts have refused to hold private employers to this standard, and use *Garcia* as precedent, while other federal district courts reject the decision in *Garcia v. Gloor.*

Another English-only workplace case was brought before the Ninth Circuit Court of Appeals in California.[20] Alva Gutierrez, a bilingual deputy court clerk in the Clerk's Office of the Southeast Judicial District of the Los Angeles Municipal Court, had been fired for speaking Spanish at work outside her official capacity as a translator during work hours. Ms. Gutierrez charged her employers with violating her equal protection rights and rights of free speech by imposing an English-only rule in the clerk's office, claiming that such a rule was both intentionally discriminatory against Hispanics and also had a disparate impact on them. The District Court found in her favor, granting an injunction against the rule. The Municipal Court appealed.

Ninth Circuit Court Judge Stephen Reinhardt's opinion contrasted with that of *Garcia* in every way. Judge Reinhardt emphasized the stringent standards of the 1980 EEOC guidelines that forbid not only intentional discrimination, but also facially neutral rules, such as English-only personnel rules, which have a disparate impact on protected groups of workers. Sympathetic to the importance of language in ethnic identity, and also to the important contributions of multiculturalism to American society Judge Reinhardt stated that:

In the United States, persons of Asian and Hispanic origin constitute large minorities. Numerous members of these groups regularly communicate in a language other than English. For many of these individuals Spanish or some other language is their primary tongue. Members of these minority groups have made great contributions to the development of our diverse multicultural society and its tradition of encouraging the free exchange of ideas. The multicultural character of American society has a long and venerable history and is widely recognized as one of the United States' greatest strengths.

Judge Reinhardt further noted that workplace rules that have a nega-tive effect on individuals with accents, or those who speak different languages, can "create an atmosphere of inferiority, isolation and intim-idation," and "can readily mask an intent to discriminate on the basis of national origin." He dismissed the Municipal Court's claim that its English-only rule was a business necessity, aimed at reducing the fears of non-Hispanic workers. Further, Judge Reinhardt pointed out that not only had the Municipal Court failed to demonstrate that the use of Spanish was creating ethnic conflict among its employees, but held rather that the evidence indicated "…. [that] the English-only rule had increased racial hostility between Hispanics and non-Spanish-speaking employees because Hispanics felt belittled by it." He also stated that Section 6 of the California Constitution, which declares that "English is the official language of the State of California," was "primarily symbolic," and that it applied not to private conversations but to official communications. Judge Reinhardt called attention to the irony that while the Municipal Court's English-only rule totally bars private speech in Spanish during on-duty periods, it not only permits but mandates the use of Spanish for much official communication.

The Municipal Court appealed, but *Gutierrez* was vacated as moot by the U.S. Supreme Court because Ms. Gutierrez had left the municipal court's employ. Although the *Gutierrez* opinion provides a thoughtful, alternative reasoning to *Garcia* on language law, subsequently a later case from the same judicial district ignored this opinion. In *Garcia v. Spun Steak Company* [998 F.2d 1480 (1993)], Judge Diarmuid O'Scannlain, writing for the court, returned to the concepts articulated in *Garcia v. Gloor.* He acknowledged that an individual's primary language can be an important link to ethnic culture and identity, but held that Title VII does not protect the ability of workers to express their cultural heritage at the workplace; it is concerned only with disparities in treatment of workers and does not protect against rules that "merely inconvenience some employees, even if the inconvenience falls regularly on a protected class." Judge O'Scannlain defended the right of the employer to decide to what extent employees may make "small talk" on the job and what language they may talk in. He accepted Spun Steak's English-only rule as a legitimate solution aimed at preventing "employees from intention-ally using their fluency in Spanish to isolate and to intimidate members of other ethnic groups," and he found no evidence that Hispanics were being treated in a way that isolated or intimidated them. He acknowl-edged that his conclusion opposed EEOC's long-standing position and stated that although he did not take the agency's position lightly, he did not feel bound by it either.

Judge O'Scannlain did not, however, have the last word. In a subse-quent Spun Steak case, Judge Stephen Rheinhardt reaffirmed his decision in *Gutierrez,* writing,

Language is intimately tied to national origin and cultural identity. Even when an individual learns English and becomes assimilated into American society, his native language remains an important means of affirming links to his original culture. English-only rules not only symbolize a rejection of the excluded language and the culture it embodies, but also a denial of that side of an individual's personality. Language is the lifeblood of every ethnic group. To economically and psychologically penalize a person for practicing his native tongue is to strike at the core of ethnicity.[21]

The bilingual cases discussed above, some of which support language rights in the relatively restricted context of the school, the voting booth, the courtroom, and the workplace, address the more fundamental and broader issue of the willingness of American institutions to accept or encourage linguistic and cultural diversity. This acceptance or encouragement is opposed not only by efforts to make English the official language of the United States, but also by the current movement to restrict Latino (and other) immigration and also in state initiatives to deprive undocumented immigrants from access to public services and from obtaining a driver's license.[22]

UNDOCUMENTED IMMIGRANTS

In the late 1970s and again in the late 1980s through the early 1990s, anti-immigrant sentiment swept the country, motivated at least partly by the social and economic ills that faced American society and particularly by concerns over unemployment.[23] This sentiment was especially pronounced in Texas, Arizona, and California, and particularly targeted undocumented immigrants from Mexico. One result was the passage of laws in several states denying public benefits—education, health care, and public assistance—to undocumented immigrants.

In 1982, a challenge to a state law in Texas denying the children of undocumented immigrants the benefits of public education unless they paid tuition reached the U.S. Supreme Court. In *Plyler v. Roe* [457 U.S. 202 (1982)] the Court held that the Texas law violated the Equal Protection Clause of the U.S. Constitution. In his opinion for the 5–4 majority, Justice William Brennan began by reaffirming earlier court decisions holding that "illegal aliens" were covered by the Equal Protection Clause, as they were clearly "persons" as referred to in the Fourteenth Amendment, regardless of their immigration status. He then went on to specifically discuss the impact of the law on the children excluded from public education, putting that exclusion into the context of the broader issue of illegal immigration:

.... Sheer incapability or lax enforcement of the laws barring entry into this country, coupled with the failure to establish an effective bar to the employment of undocumented aliens, has resulted in the creation of a substantial "shadow population" of illegal migrants.... This situation raises the specter of a permanent caste of undocumented resident aliens, encouraged by some to remain here as a source of cheap labor, but nevertheless denied the benefits that our society makes available to citizens and lawful residents. The existence of such an underclass presents most difficult problems for a Nation that prides itself on adherence to principles of equality under law.

The children ... in these cases are special members of this underclass. Persuasive argument ... that a State may withhold its beneficence from those whose very presence within the United States is the product of their own unlawful conduct ... do not apply with the same force to ... the minor children of such illegal entrants ... legislation directing the onus of a parent's misconduct against his children does not comport with fundamental conceptions of justice.

It is thus difficult to conceive of a rational justification for penalizing these children [under the Texas law]. Public education is not a "right" granted to individuals by the Constitution. But neither is it merely some governmental "benefit" indistinguishable from other forms of social welfare legislation. Both the importance of education in maintaining our basic institutions, and the lasting impact of its deprivation on the life of the child, mark the distinction. [The Texas law] imposes a lifetime of hardship on [these] children. The stigma of illiteracy will mark them for the rest of their lives. By denying these children a basic education, we deny them the ability to live within the structure of our civic institutions, and foreclose any realistic possibility that they will contribute in even the smallest way to the progress of our Nation. In light of these ... costs the discrimination [in the State law] can hardly be considered rational unless it furthers some substantial goal of the State.

The Court then considered and rejected the three rationales Texas gave for the law:

.... appellants ... suggest that the State may seek to protect itself from an influx of illegal immigrants ... [as a way of] mitigating potentially harsh economic effects of sudden shifts in population. [But this state law] hardly offers an effective method of dealing with an urgent demographic or economic problem. There is no evidence in the record suggesting that illegal entrants impose any significant burden on the State's economy. To the contrary, the available evidence suggests that illegal aliens underutilize public services, while contributing their labor to the local economy and tax money to the state. The dominant incentive for illegal entry into ... Texas is the availability of employment; [not] to [obtain] a free education ... [c]harging tuition to [these] children constitutes a ludicrously ineffectual attempt to stem the tide of illegal immigration, at least when compared with the alternative of prohibiting the employment of illegal aliens.

The Court also rejected as without evidence Texas's claim that the undocumented children place a special financial burden on the state's ability to provide high-quality public education. And finally, in response to Texas's claim that "because children of undocumented aliens were less likely to remain within the State, they were also less likely to put their education to productive social or political use within the State," Justice

Brennan noted that this interest was very difficult to quantify. Further, he said, that it was in fact likely that "many of these children would remain within the country indefinitely and perhaps some may even become U.S. citizens." He then went on to say:

... It is difficult to understand ... what the State hopes to achieve by promoting the creation and perpetuation of a subclass of illiterates within our boundaries, surely adding to the problems and costs of unemployment, welfare, and crime .... whatever savings might be achieved by denying these children an education, they are wholly insubstantial in light of the costs involved to these children, the State, and the Nation.

Because an earlier Supreme Court ruling had held that education was not a fundamental right under the Fourteenth Amendment, *Plyler* was viewed as a major victory for immigrant rights. In spite of the Court's ruling in *Plyler*, however, some states continued to pass laws denying public benefits to undocumented aliens with the hope of driving out existing immigrants and deterring newcomers. Among the most contested of these laws was California's Proposition 187, which its supporters described as "the first giant stride in ultimately ending the ILLEGAL ALIEN (emphasis in original) invasion." Passed by voters in 1994, Proposition 187 excluded undocumented aliens from medical and other public services and denied their children access to public education. It also required that undocumented aliens must be directed in writing to "either obtain legal status or leave the United States," and that government workers, such as police, teachers, and health-care professionals must verify and report the immigration status of all individuals, including children, to the authorities, including the Immigration and Naturalization Service (INS).[24]

Using *Plyler* as a precedent, Proposition 187 was immediately challenged by a coalition of civil rights groups. Several different suits challenged separate provisions of the law, including a suit asserting that to deny the children of undocumented immigrants access to secondary schools was a violation of the right to an equal education guaranteed by the California Constitution. After first issuing a temporary injunction against Proposition 187, in 1998 Federal District Court Judge Mariana Pfaelzer issued a permanent injunction barring its implementation. She held that Proposition 187 violated the Supremacy Clause of the U.S. Constitution, which gives exclusive authority over immigration regulations to the federal government. Judge Pfaelzer also stated that Proposition 187 was illegal because of the Personal Responsibility and Work Opportunity Reconciliation Act, the so-called Welfare Reform Act, passed by Congress in 1996. This act specifically precludes states from establishing laws that are separate and in conflict with federal law on immigration policy and the treatment of immigrants, regardless of the immigrant's legal status.

Judge Pfaelzer's initial injunction led to five years of legal and political debate. This finally ended in July 1999, when a court-approved mediation agreement voided Proposition 187. The agreement confirmed that no child in California would be deprived of an education or stripped of health care due to their place of birth. It also confirmed that the state cannot regulate immigration law, a function the U.S. Constitution clearly assigns to the federal government.[25]

Although these court decisions in Texas and California would seem to make clear that state laws denying public benefits to undocumented aliens are unconstitutional, in November 2004, a similar law, Proposition 200—officially known as the Arizona Taxpayer and Citizen Protection Act—was passed by voters in Arizona. Described by its supporters as being about "protecting the voting process and prohibiting welfare fraud," Proposition 200 requires proof of citizenship when registering to vote (Arizona voters can now vote by mail and on line) and denies illegal immigrants public benefits that are not federally mandated (as are emergency room care and the right of children of illegal aliens to attend public school and to receive vaccinations). It additionally makes it a crime for public employees not to report fraud committed by illegal immigrants to the authorities.[26] Proposition 200 was generated in part by concerns over the fourfold increase in undocumented immigrants from Mexico into Arizona over the past 15 years. It is unlikely to have much impact, however, and was opposed even by those who support immigration reform, along with many state officials, the business community, and unions. Like similar state initiatives elsewhere, it will also undoubtedly be challenged in the courts.

Challenges to immigration practice and policy are not all addressed by political and legal processes, however. Along with anti-immigrant propositions, vigilante groups have also emerged to patrol the Mexican-American border.[27] As increased border patrol is now also viewed as a necessary response to the threat of terrorism post 9/11, immigration policy has again taken on new urgency and again become a subject of national debate.

NOTES

1. Bill Ong Hing, *Defining America Through Immigration Policy* (Philadelphia: Temple University Press, 2004); Christopher Jencks, "Who Should Get In," *New York Review of Books* (November 29, 2001), 57–63; Kathleen M. Moore, "U.S. Immigration Reform and the Meaning of Responsibility," *Studies in Law, Politics, and Society* 20 (2000), 125–155; John Paul Ryan, ed., "Immigration: A Dialogue on Policy, Law, and Values," *Focus on Law Studies* (Spring 1999), 1–15; Jon Gjerde, *Major Problems in American Immigration and Ethnic History.* (Boston: Houghton Mifflin 1998).

2. Jencks, "Who Should Get In?" 57.

3. See, e.g., *Ozawa v. United States,* 260 U.S. 178 (1922); *Yamashita v. Hinkle* 260 U.S. 199 (1922); and *United States v. Bhagat Singh Thind* 262 U.S. 204 (1923).

4. Louise Lamphere, ed., *Structuring Diversity: Ethnographic Perspectives on the New Immigration* (Chicago: University of Chicago Press, 1992), Introduction.

5. Nancy Foner, ed., *American Arrivals: Anthropology Engages the New Immigration* (Santa Fe, NM: School of American Research, 2003).

6. Janet E. Benson, "Undocumented Immigrants and the Meatpacking Industry in the Midwest," in *Illegal Immigration in America: A Reference Handbook,* David W. Haines and Karen E. Rosenblum, eds. (Westport, CT.: Greenwood, 1999) 172–192.

7. Nina Glick-Schiller, Linda Basch, and Christina Szanton-Blanc, eds., *Towards a Transnational Perspective on Migration: Race, Class, Ethnicity and Nationalism Reconsidered* (New York: New York Academy of Sciences, 1992).

8. James Crawford, *Hold Your Tongue: Bilingualism and the Politics of "English Only"* (Reading, MA: Addison-Wesley, 1992).

9. Reynaldo Anaya Valencia, Sonia R. Garcia, Henry Flores, and Jose Roberto Juarez, Jr., *Mexican Americans & the Law: !El Pueblo Unido Jamas Sera Veneido!* (Tucson: The University of Arizona, 2004), 69.

10. *Keyes v. School District No. 1, Denver, Colorado,* 521 F.2d 465 (1975).

11. Jodi Wilgoren, "Divided by a Call for a Common Language," *New York Times,* July 19, 2002, A10.

12. Richard Alba, "Bilingualism Persists, But English Still Dominates," *Migration Information Source* (February 1, 2005), http://www.migrationinformation. org. 1–4; Rachel L. Swarns, "Children of Hispanic Immigrants Continue to Favor English, Study of Census Finds," *New York Times,* December 8, 2004, A 26.

13. Steven W. Bender, *Greasers and Gringos: Latinos, Law, and the American Imagination* (New York: New York University Press, 2003); for critical Reviews of those who warn of dire effects of Latino immigration, such as Samuel P. Huntington, *Who Are We? The Challenges to America's National Identity* (New York: Simon and Schuster, 2004); see Daniel Lazare, "Diversity and its Discontents," *The Nation* (June 14, 2004) and Andrew Hacker, "Patriot Games," *New York Review of Books* (June 24, 2004), 28.

14. Demetrios Papademetriou, "Focusing the Immigration Discussion," *The Hispanic Challenge: What We Know About Latino Immigration,* Philippa Strum and Andrew Selee, eds., (Washington, D.C.: Conference Proceedings, Woodrow Wilson International Center for Scholars, 2004), 5; Alba, "Bilingualism Persists."

15. Alba, "Bilingualism Persists."

16. *United States ex rel. Negron v. State of New York,* 434 F2d 386 (1970).

17. *U.S.A. v. Mospuera et al,* Memorandum and Order, C.R. 92–1228; C.R. 93–0036, U.S. District Court, Eastern District, March 16, 1993, Judge Jack Weinstein, 13.

18. Valencia, *Mexican Americans and the Law,* 115.

19. Valencia, *Mexican Americans and the Law,* 79.

20. *Alva Gutierrez v. Municipal Court of Southeast Judicial District,* 838 F.2d 1031 (9th Cir. 1988), 1063.

21. *Garcia et al v. Spun Steak,* 13 F.3d 296 (1993), 8–9.

22. "California Vote Favors Licenses for Immigrants," *New York Times,* Aug. 28, 2004; "Fight Over Immigrants' Driving Licenses Is Back in Court," *New York Times,* April 7, 2005, Shaila Dewan, "Immigrants in Tennessee Get Certificates to Drive," *New York Times,* May 9, 2005, A12.

23. Jencks, "Who Should Get In?"

24. Stanley Mailman, "California's Proposition 187 and its Lessons," *New York Law Journal,* January 3, 1995, http://www.ssbb.com/article 1.html.

25. "Judge Rules Prop. 187 Unconstitutional, States May Not Make Own Immigration Laws," *ACLU News: The Newspaper of the ACLU of Northern California,* January/February 1998, http://www.aclunc.org/aclunews/news/198/187.html; "CA's Anti-Immigrant Proposition 187 is Voided, Ending State's Five-Year Battle with ACLU, Rights Groups," *Immigrant Rights.* July 29, 1999, http://www.aclu.org/ImmigrantsRights/.

26. Charlie LeDuff, "Immigration Measure Taps Frustrations in Arizona," *New York Times,* Oct. 22, 2004, A14; "Vote Yes on Proposition 200: The Arizona Taxpayer and Citizen Protection Act," http:/yesonprop200.com/articles/articles.html.

27. David Holthouse, "Arizona Showdown," *Intelligence Report* (Southern Poverty Law Center) Summer, 2005, No. 118, 16–31; Ken Ellingwood, *Hard Line: Life and Death on the U.S.-Mexico Border* (NY: Pantheon 2004).

PART II

Religion

CHAPTER 5

Religious Belief and Practice: The Mormons

The Church of Jesus Christ of Latter-day Saints, commonly known as Mormons, is one of the wealthiest and politically most well connected groups in the United States. This could be expected given the Mormons' stress on thrift and personal industry but it might well not have occurred because of the early history of persecution of Mormons in many American communities.

Mormonism originated in the religious experience of a young man named Joseph Smith, who lived in western New York State during the great religious revival of the 1820s. At the age of 14, Smith experienced his first revelation, and three years later, through divine direction, discovered and later translated new scriptures called the Book of Mormon. This large, complex text describes the dispersion of the Israelites, some time after 600 B.C., to North America where Jesus appeared to the deserving, taught, and established his church. A central theme of the Book of Mormon is the cycle of good and evil, human pride, and divine forgiveness.

Soon after his revelation, Smith was attacked because of his extravagant claims of seeing God and angels, which were denounced as heresy by more-established Christian sects. Smith and his growing number of believers, among whom was Brigham Young, were continually harassed as they moved westward to escape persecution and arrest. They first settled in Missouri and then moved to a place on the banks of the Mississippi that Smith named Nauvoo, where they were initially welcomed and set up an autonomous religious community. At Nauvoo Smith claimed to have received a revelation sanctioning polygyny, a form of marriage in which a man is permitted to have more than one wife. Indeed, this practice, generally called polygamy, was demanded by the new religion and put into practice by Smith and a few trusted Mormon leaders, although it led to a schism within the Mormon community.

Smith viewed polygamy as the restoration of the sacred and binding marriage patterns of Abraham, Isaac, and Jacob, and therefore as central to the Mormon religion. Polygamy strengthened the patriarchal nature of Mormon marriage and enhanced the status of the exclusively male priesthood through the new patterns of family networks created by plural marriage. Plural unions, whose earthly purpose was procreation, also reinforced the Mormon emphasis on community, family, and stability over individualism. Marriage, however, was also critical to the entrance of the faithful into the kingdom of God after this life: "Celestial marriage" bound husbands and wives for time and all eternity in an endless union, providing both parties lived by the covenants. The "sealing" of a union in a Mormon temple was the final way by which the Mormon faithful could obtain glory and exaltation in the celestial kingdom of God, and polygamy became a form of "celestial marriage." Joseph Smith paid a heavy price for his revelation: it ultimately led to Smith's arrest and jailhouse murder by an anti-Mormon mob in 1844.[1]

As a result of internal division and ongoing persecution by non-Mormons, in 1847 Brigham Young and Herbert Kimbal decided to lead an advance group of 150 Mormons out of the several thousand at Nauvoo even father west, establishing a colony, which they called Deseret, in the Great Salt Lake Valley. Under Young's vigorous leadership, the Mormons set up a communitarian economy and a highly controlled theocracy, which prospered, aided in part by the immigration of thousands of English working men converted by Mormon missionaries. When Congress organized Deseret as the Utah Territory in 1850, Young was appointed the territorial governor.

This early recognition of Mormon legitimacy soon foundered on the political, economic, and cultural differences between the Mormons and the rest of the United States. The Mormon communalistic economy conflicted with the dominant American value of capitalism, and Mormon theocracy explicitly contravened the First Amendment's "no establishment of religion" clause. The Mormons had thought that by fleeing to the Great Salt Lake Basin, which was, at the time, Mexican territory and therefore beyond the reach of federal administration, they could escape the Constitution, the criminal laws, and the hostile culture of the United States. But just two years after the founding of Deseret, Mormon troubles began again.

The United States feared the Mormon theocracy as a threat to its own expanding sovereignty. Hostility toward the Mormons, who engaged in secret ceremonies and recruited converts abroad, drew upon the larger anti-Masonic, anti-alien, and anti-Catholic spirit in America of the time. The presence of Mormon communities in the West also renewed earlier concerns about Mormon bloc voting. Although most Saints (as they sometimes call themselves) did not practice polygamy, and in many ways lived like other Western pioneers, Mormons were identified as having rejected important American cultural tenets, such as secularism, monogamy, and individualism.

As their difficult and dangerous flight westward had demonstrated, Mormons were tenaciously committed to their own social, religious, and cultural institutions, a commitment perhaps strengthened by persistent opposition. Popular outrage against Mormons grew, fueled by newspaper stories about polygamy and incendiary public pronouncements by the new Republican Party, which equated polygamy with slavery as the "twin relics of barbarism." American officials regarded polygamists as criminals and looked upon the plural wife as a concubine and her children as illegitimate in a "civilized" society. In 1857, President Buchanan sent 2,000 troops West to occupy the Salt Lake Valley, intending to replace Brigham Young with a non-Mormon governor.

In 1862 Congress attempted to eradicate polygamy through the Morrill Antibigamy Act, which failed in its aims for lack of effective enforcement measures. In the early 1870s, interest in the economic resources of the Utah Territory and continued outrage at polygamy revived federal determination to undermine the power of the Mormon Church. Using a legal strategy, the U.S. government began a 20-year campaign against the religious, economic, and political activities of the Saints. This new assault began with the Poland Act of 1874, establishing federal control over the courts and juries of the Utah Territory, which—composed as they were largely of Mormons—had been refusing to convict polygamists under the Morrill Antibigamy Act. Then, after a legal challenge by the Mormons in 1879, the Supreme Court, in *Reynolds v. United States* [98 U.S. 146, (1879)], upheld the constitutionality of federal antibigamy legislation. The Court asserted the sanctity of monogamy and its central place in American culture against the Saints' claims that the Morrill Act violated Mormon First Amendment religious rights and that it was an ex post facto law. The centerpiece of the Court's decision rested upon the new belief-action doctrine articulated in the opinion. According to the justices, the First Amendment guaranteed the right to hold whatever religious opinion one wished but not necessarily the right to act according to that belief or faith.

REYNOLDS V. UNITED STATES 98 U.S. 146 (1879)

Chief Justice Waite, who delivered the opinion of the court, began by asking *the* key legal question for the Justices: " ... Should the accused have been acquitted if he marries a second time, because he believed it to be his religious duty?"

Justice Waite acknowledged the defendant's claim that he was a member of the Mormon Church, that polygamy was an accepted doctrine of the church, that it was the duty of male members of the church, circumstances permitting, to practice polygamy, that this duty was enjoined by books that Mormons believed to be of divine origin, including the Holy Bible, and that "the practice of polygamy was directly enjoined upon the male members … by the Almighty God, in a revelation to Joseph Smith, the founder and prophet of said church, [and] that failing or refusing to practice polygamy … would be punished by damnation in the life to come."

Waite then restated the central question: "… whether religious belief can be accepted as a justification of an overt act made criminal by the law of the land?"

In his answer he affirmed the constitutional restriction on Congress from passing a law prohibiting the free exercise of religion. But he then went on to ask "whether the law now under consideration comes within this prohibition?"

Noting that the word religion is not defined in the Constitution, Justice Waite asked, "what is the religious freedom which has been guaranteed?" In answering, he summed up the history of eighteenth-century debate on the nature of religious freedom and quoted the words of Thomas Jefferson that "religion is a matter which lies solely between man and his God; that he owes account to none other for his faith or his worship; that the legislative powers of the government reach actions only, and not opinions … [and that] the Constitution forbids making any law respecting an establishment of religion or prohibiting the free exercise thereof," thus "building a wall of separation between Church and State."

The Chief Justice continued in his own words:

… [this statement by Jefferson] may be accepted almost as an authoritative declaration of the scope and effect of the amendment thus secured. Congress was deprived of all legislative power over mere opinion, but was left free to reach actions which were in violation of social duties or subversive of good order.

Polygamy has always been odious among the northern and western nations of Europe, and, until the establishment of the Mormon Church, was almost exclusively a feature of the life of Asiatic and of African people. At common law, the second marriage was always void and from the earliest history of England polygamy has been treated as an offence against society.

We think it may safely be said there never has been a time in any State of the Union when polygamy has not been an offence against society, cognizable by the civil courts and punishable with more or less severity. In the face of all this evidence, it is impossible to believe that the constitutional guaranty of religious freedom was intended to prohibit legislation in respect to this most important feature of social life. Marriage, while from its very nature a sacred obligation, is nevertheless, in most civilized nations, a civil contract, and usually regulated by law. Upon it society may be said to be built, and out of its fruits spring social relations and social obligations and duties, with which government is necessarily required to deal. In fact, according as monogamous or polygamous marriages are allowed, do we find the principles on which the government of the people, to a greater or lesser extent, rests ... polygamy leads to the patriarchal principle, and which, when applied to large communities, fetters the people in stationary despotism, while that principle cannot long exist in connection with monogamy .... In our opinion, the [antibigamy] statute immediately under consideration is within the legislative power of Congress. It is constitutional and valid as prescribing a rule of action for all those residing in the Territories, and in places over which the United States have exclusive control. This being so, the only question which remains is, whether those who make polygamy a part of their religion are excepted from the operation of the statute. If they are, then those who do not make polygamy a part of their religious belief may be found guilty and punished, while those who do, must be acquitted and go free. This would be introducing a new element into criminal law. Laws are made for the government of actions, and while they cannot interfere with mere religious belief and opinions, they may with practices. Suppose one believed that human sacrifices were a necessary part of religious worship, would it be seriously contended that the civil government under which he lived could not interfere to prevent a sacrifice? Or if a wife religiously believed it was her duty to burn herself upon the funeral pyre of her dead husband, would it be beyond the power of the civil government to prevent her carrying her belief into practice?

So here, as a law of the organization of society under the exclusive dominion of the United States, it is provided that plural marriages shall not be allowed. Can a man excuse his practices to the contrary because of his religious belief? To permit this would be to make the professed doctrines of religious belief superior to the law of the land, and in effect to permit every citizen to become a law unto himself. Government could exist only in name under such circumstances. But when the offence consists of a positive act which is knowingly done, it would be dangerous to hold that the offender might escape punishment because he religiously believed the law which he had broken ought never to have been made. No case, we believe, can be found that has gone so far.

As to that part of the charge which directed the attention of the jury to the consequences of polygamy. The passage complained of is as follows: "I think it not improper, in the discharge of your duties in this case, that you should consider what are to be the consequences to the innocent victims of this delusion. As this contest goes on, they multiply, and there are pure-minded women and there are innocent children, innocent in the sense even beyond the degree of the innocence of childhood itself. These are to be the sufferers; and as jurors fail to do their duty, and as these cases come up in the Territory of Utah, just so do these victims multiply and spread themselves over the land."

Congress, in 1862 saw fit to make bigamy a crime in the Territories. This was done because of the evil consequences that were supposed to flow from plural marriages ... Upon the showing made by the accused himself, he was guilty of a violation of the law under which he had been indicted.

Three years after *Reynolds,* encouraged by various economic interests and moral reformers, Congress again attempted to curb Mormon power through the Edmunds Act, which prohibited polygamy and unlawful cohabitation and established a federal commission to administer test oaths requiring voters to swear they were neither bigamists nor polygamists. Those Mormons who would not take the oath were barred from public service and voting. An Idaho statute compelling a similar oath was aimed at limiting Mormon participation in territorial and county government and eliminating Mormon control of local schools. As a result of the Edmunds Act, in Utah, Arizona, and Idaho, the surveillance, arrest, and imprisonment of polygamous Mormons intensified, and during the 1880s, more than 1,300 Mormons were imprisoned for practicing polygamy. In 1885, a group of Mormons petitioned President Grover Cleveland for an end to this anti-polygamy campaign. The petition described a double standard and family and personal duress:

[In non-Mormon cities] The paramour of mistresses and harlots, secure from prosecution, walks the streets in open day. No United States official puts a spotter on his "trail," or makes an effort to drag his deeds in guilt and shame before a judge and jury ... But [with respect to the Mormon people] "Spotters" and spies dog their footsteps. Delators [informers] thrust themselves into bedchambers and watch at windows. Children are questioned upon the streets as to the marital relations of their parents. Families are dragged before Commissioners and grand juries, and on pain of punishment for contempt, are compelled to testify against their fathers and husbands. Modest women are made to answer shamefully indecent questions as to the sexual relations of men and women. Attempts are made to bribe men to work up cases against their neighbors. Notoriously disreputable characters are employed to spy into men's family relations.[2]

In these years, Mormons also initiated a challenge, ultimately heard by the U.S. Supreme Court, to Idaho's 1885 oath test. In *Davis v. Beason*, Samuel Davis argued that his conviction for obstructing the oath law, in the territorial district court, violated the constitution's Establishment Clause. As in *Reynolds*, The Supreme Court rejected Davis's claim, reiterating the distinction between belief and action and strongly repudiating the "odious" institution of polygamy. Justice Stephen J. Field wrote the opinion for the Court:

DAVIS V. BEASON 133 U.S. 333 (1889)

... Bigamy and polygamy are crimes by the laws of all civilized and Christian countries. They are crimes by the laws of the United States, and they are crimes by the laws of Idaho. They tend to destroy the purity of the marriage relation, to disturb the peace of families, to degrade woman and to debase man. Few crimes are more pernicious to the best interests of society and receive more general or more deserved punishment. To extend exemption from punishment for such crimes would be to shock the moral judgment of the community. To call their advocacy a tenet of religion is to offend the common sense of mankind. If they are crimes, then to teach, advise and counsel their practice is to aid in their commission, and such teaching and counseling are themselves criminal and proper subjects of punishment, as aiding and abetting crime are in all other cases. The term "religion" has reference to one's views of his relations to his Creator, and to the obligations they impose of reverence for his being and character, and of obedience to his will. It is often confounded with the *cultus* or form of worship of a particular sect, but is distinguishable from the latter. The First Amendment to the Constitution, in declaring that Congress shall make no law respecting the establishment of religion, or forbidding the free exercise thereof, was intended to allow everyone under the jurisdiction of the United States to entertain such notions respecting his relations to his Maker and the duties they impose as may be approved by his judgment and conscience, and to exhibit his sentiments in such form of worship as he may think proper, not injurious to the equal rights of others, and to prohibit legislation for the support of any religious tenets, or the modes of worship of any sect. The oppressive measures adopted, and the cruelties and punishments inflicted by the governments of Europe for many ages, to compel parties to conform in their religious beliefs and modes of worship to the views of the most numerous sect, and the folly of attempting in that way to control the mental operations of persons and enforce an outward conformity to a prescribed standard, led to the adoption of the Amendment in question. It was never intended or supposed that the Amendment could be invoked as a protection against legislation for the punishment of acts inimical to the peace, good order and morals of society. With man's relations to his Maker and the obligations he may think they impose, and the manner in which an expression shall be made by him of his belief on those subjects, no interference can be permitted, provided always the laws of society, designed to secure its peace and prosperity, and the morals of its people, are not interfered with. However free the exercise of religion may be, it must be subordinate to the criminal laws of the country, passed with reference to actions regarded by general consent as properly the subjects of punitive legislation. There have been sects which denied as a part of their religious tenets that there should be any marriage tie, and advocated promiscuous intercourse of the sexes as prompted by the passions of their members. And history discloses the fact that the necessity of human sacrifices, on special occasions, has been a tenet of many sects. Should a sect of either of these kinds ever find its way into this country, swift punishment would follow the carrying into effect of its doctrines, and no heed would be given to the pretense that, as religious beliefs, their supporters could be protected in their exercise by the Constitution of the United States. Probably never before in the history of this country has it been seriously contended that the whole punitive power of the government, for acts recognized by the general consent of the Christian world in modern times as proper matters for prohibitory legislation, must be suspended in order that the tenets of a religious sect encouraging crime may be carried out without hindrance ... and in *Murphy v. Ramsey*, referring to the Act of Congress excluding polygamists and bigamists from voting or holding office, the court, speaking by Mr. Justice Matthews, said: "Certainly no legislation can be supposed more wholesome and necessary in the founding of a free, self-governing commonwealth [the state of Utah] ... than that which seeks to establish it on the basis of the idea of the family, as consisting in and springing from the union for life of one man and one woman in the holy estate of matrimony—the sure foundation of all that is stable and noble in our civilization; the best guaranty of that reverent morality which is the source of all beneficent progress in social and political improvement. And to this end no means are more directly and immediately suitable than those provided by this Act, which endeavors to withdraw all political influence from those who are practically hostile to its attainment."

It is assumed by counsel of the petitioner that, because no mode of worship can be established or religious tenets enforced in this country, therefore any form of worship may be followed and any tenets, however destructive of society, may be held and advocated, if asserted to be a part of the religious doctrines of those advocating and practicing them. But nothing is further from the truth. Whilst legislation for the establishment of a religion is forbidden, and its free exercise permitted, it does not follow that everything which may be so called can be tolerated. Crime is not less odious because sanctioned by what any particular sect may designate as religion.

The Mormons did attract some support for their civil rights among Eastern politicians. Congressman Zebulon Vance of North Carolina, for example, referring to Biblical polygamy, wryly observed that, "If alive today, Moses, the great lawgiver, could not be mayor of a crossroads town ... King Solomon in all his glory could not serve a warrant for 50 cents, and King David ... the man after God's own heart, could not serve the warrants. The rabbis of the temple could not sit upon the jury to try the case."[3]

The judicial and congressional efforts to bring Mormon social institutions in line with the dominant American culture were largely ineffective, however, until Congress passed the draconian Edmunds-Tucker Act in 1887. This statute withdrew Mormon and non-Mormon women's suffrage in Utah; disinherited the children of plural marriages; prescribed another test oath for those wanting to vote, hold political office, and serve on juries; stipulated that legal wives could testify against their husbands; vested all political, military, and legal powers in federal appointees; placed all Utah schools under the control of a court-appointed commissioner; required all marriages to be certified in the probate courts; eliminated all existing electoral districts; and dissolved the church militia. The act also disenfranchised Mormons who advocated polygamy even if they did not practice it. In addition, the Edmunds-Tucker Act repealed the charter of the Mormon Church and provided for the confiscation of its most valuable holdings, resulting in a loss of over $1 million in cash and property.[4]

Church leaders immediately challenged the constitutionality of this statute but without success. In 1889, in *Romney v. United States*, the Supreme Court rejected the Mormon arguments. In ruling that the Edmunds-Tucker Act did not violate religious rights guaranteed in the First Amendment, the Court once again asserted the absolute right of the United States to regulate a church committed to polygamy, a practice it called "a crime against the laws, and abhorrent to the sentiments and feelings of the civilized world." The majority opinion written by Justice Joseph Bradley broke little new legal ground, but the impact of the Edmunds-Tucker Act and the *Romney* decision were both significant. In these actions the United States gave clear notice of the scope of government regulation that it would sanction under the belief-action doctrine announced in *Reynolds*, when religious groups did not conform to dominant culture norms or, in the justices' words, "the enlightened sentiments of mankind."

ROMNEY V. UNITED STATES 136 U.S. 1 (1889)

Notwithstanding the stringent laws which have been passed by Congress—notwithstanding all the efforts made to suppress this barbarous practice—the sect or community composing the Church of Latter-Day Saints perseveres, in defiance of law, in preaching, upholding, promoting and defending [polygamy]. It is a matter of public notoriety that its emissaries are engaged in many countries in propagating this nefarious doctrine, and urging its converts to join the community in Utah. The existence of such a propaganda is a blot on our civilization. The organization of a community for the spread and practice of polygamy is, in a measure, a return to barbarism. It is contrary to the spirit of Christianity and of the civilization which Christianity has produced in the Western World. The question, therefore, is whether the promotion of such a nefarious system and practice, so repugnant to our laws and to the principles of civilization, is to be allowed to continue by the sanction of the government itself; and whether the funds accumulated for that purpose shall be restored to the same unlawful uses as heretofore, to the detriment of the true interests of civil society.

It is unnecessary here to refer to the past history of the sect, to their defiance of the government authorities, to their attempt to establish an independent community, to their efforts to drive from the territory all who were not connected with them in communion and sympathy. The tale is one of patience on the part of the American government and people, and of contempt of authority and resistance to law on the part of the Mormons. Whatever persecutions they may have suffered in the early part of their history, in Missouri and Illinois, they have no excuse for their persistent defiance of law under the government of the United States.

One pretense for this obstinate course is, that their belief in the practice of polygamy, or in the right to indulge in it, is a religious belief, and, therefore, under the protection of the constitutional guaranty of religious freedom. This is altogether a sophistical plea. No doubt the Thugs of India imagined that their belief in the right of assassination was a religious belief; but their thinking so did not make it so. The practice of suttee by the Hindu widows may have sprung from a supposed religious conviction. The offering of human sacrifices by our own ancestors in Britain was no doubt sanctioned by an equally conscientious impulse. But no one, on that account, would hesitate to brand these practices, now, as crimes against society, and obnoxious to condemnation and punishment by the civil authority.

The State has the perfect right to prohibit polygamy, and all other open offences against the enlightened sentiment of mankind, notwithstanding the pretense of religious conviction by which they may be advocated and practiced ... and ... finding Church funds without legal ownership ... to cause them to be seized and to be devoted to objects of undoubted charity and usefulness—such for example as the maintenance of schools.

The confiscation of church property divided the Court. Justice Melville Fuller, joined by Justices Lamar and Field, dissented, and wrote that while they agreed with the right of Congress to enact laws against polygamy, they did not consider Congress "authorized under the cover of that power to seize and confiscate the property of persons, individuals, or corporations, without office found, because they may have been guilty of criminal practices." The dissent was far overshadowed, however, by weight of the Supreme Court decisions, which clearly demonstrated the implacable hostility of the United States to the Mormons. By 1891 this hostility included immigration laws adding polygamy to the list of conditions of "moral turpitude" and became a basis for barring both Mormon and Muslim immigrants.[5] While the government's adamant refusal to accommodate Mormon communitarianism, theocracy, and its "peculiar" custom of polygamy was a challenge to the Mormon's religious culture, it was also motivated by political and legal interests.

After losing these important legal battles, Mormon leaders clearly understood that in order to gain statehood, the church would have to renounce polygamy, dissolve the church party, and refashion aspects of its communalistic economy. In October 1890, following the announcement of an instructive revelation received by Mormon leader, Wilford Woodruff, the Church formally repudiated the practice of polygamy and modified other aspects of its original theology to fit more comfortably with the dominant American culture. The Church was assisted in its efforts to adapt by the U.S. government, which having defeated the Mormons in the courts, now extended the glad hand of political fellowship. In the unsettled political climate at the turn of the century, the Republican Party sought Utah's votes in order to control the U.S. Congress. Eastern investors, seeking outlets for their capital, turned toward Utah, where they found a troubled and declining Mormon economy and leaders ready to make alliances. Although these economic partnerships resulted in the loss of Mormon financial control over various business enterprises, these efforts ultimately integrated the Saints into a burgeoning national capitalist economy based on capital accumulation, private ownership of property, and individual profit taking. Many individual Mormons became very wealthy, which increased the wealth of the church through tithing (the religious obligation of individuals to give 10 percent of their income to the Church) and subsequent investments. Today, the Mormon Church ranks among the richest religious organizations in the United States, owning real estate, stocks and bonds, television and radio stations, a newspaper, insurance companies, and other businesses. By the 1950s, Mormons also moved into national political prominence, holding important positions in the federal government, on the White House staff, in federal bureaucracies, and in the U.S. Congress. The Central Intelligence Agency and the Federal Bureau of Investigation find young Mormons particularly attractive candidates because of their foreign missionary experience and strict adherence to conventional morality.[6]

POLYGAMY IN TWENTIETH-CENTURY AMERICA

After the official repudiation of polygamy by the Mormon Church in 1890, and the excommunication of polygamists, polygamous families

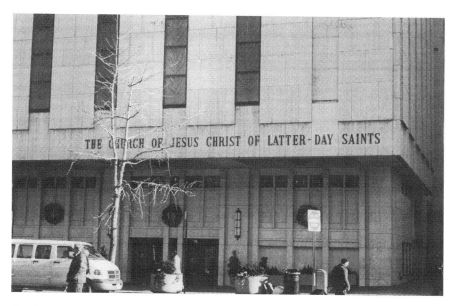

The Mormons, also called Latter-day Saints, grew from a small religious group in upstate New York to one of the wealthiest and most powerful of American religious groups. Their multistory temple, pictured here, is in the heart of the Lincoln Center area, one of the busiest entertainment districts in New York. Photo courtesy of Joan Gregg.

dwindled and scattered. But by the early 1930s, small communities of Mormon fundamentalists who followed "The Principle" (polygamy) had begun to come together in small isolated Western towns as well as at meetings in Salt Lake City and other larger communities. Their growing numbers and visibility were viewed as a threat to civic authorities and to the Mormon Church, and by 1935 arrests of polygamous Mormon men and women began anew. While initially only a handful of people were tried and convicted, the threat of imprisonment revived the practice—common in the 1880s—of polygamous families going into hiding or becoming extraordinarily private in the conduct of their lives.

In early March 1944, federal and local officials declared "war" against the polygamists, conducting massive roundups and criminal prosecutions of polygamous couples on various state and federal charges such as unlawful cohabitation, criminal conspiracy laws, the mailing of obscene literature (their magazine, *Truth,* promoted polygamy), kidnapping, and white slave act violations. Some of these charges were not upheld in court. In 1944, Federal District Court Judge J. Foster Symes, in *United States v. Barlow et al.* (56 F. Supp. 795), dismissed the mailing of obscene materials charge in an opinion sympathetic to the polygamous fundamentalists.

He concluded with the observation made both by earlier Mormon polygamists and by Mormon fundamentalists, that American law and culture
contained an openly double standard and that prosecution of Mormons
was a form of harassment:

[O]ne cannot pick up a national magazine, or go to the theatre or movie without
being confronted with illustrations and advertisements that tend more to incite
sexual desire than do any of the publications in this magazine that have been
called to our attention … In fact sex incitement is a selling point of innumerable
publications and advertisements that pass without comment or prosecution.

A 1946 U.S. Supreme Court decision also supported Mormon fundamentalists by refusing to accept the appropriateness of a federal prosecution under the Federal Kidnapping (Lindbergh) Act. The defendant
had been convicted of kidnapping when he transported a plural wife
across state lines. In the appeal, *Chatwin v. United States* (326 U.S. 455),
Justice Frank Murphy argued for the Court that seizure and detention
had not been involved in the defendant's actions. But ten months later, in
Cleveland v. United States [329 U.S.14 (1946)] in spite of Justice Murphy's
arguments to the contrary, the Supreme Court held that the language of
another federal statute, the Mann ("White Slave Traffic") Act, did cover
the transportation of polygamous wives across state lines. This opinion
reaffirmed the *Reynolds* doctrine that religiously based polygamy did not
have constitutional protection under the First Amendment's free exercise
clause.

In his opinion for the Court, Justice William O. Douglas declined to
place the practice of polygamy in the context of fundamentalist Mormon
religion and culture or Mormon history, calling it "a notorious example of
promiscuity … branded immoral in the law." In a dissent Justice Murphy
rejected the argument that polygamy is "in the same genus" as prostitution
and debauchery and hence covered by the Mann Act simply because the
practice has sexual connotations and has "long been branded as immoral
in the law" of this nation. Justice Murphy added that it was not his intention "to defend the practice of polygamy or to claim that it is morally the
equivalent of monogamy …" But, he continued,

[Polygamy] … was quite common among ancient civilizations and was referred
to many times by the writers of the Old Testament; even today it is to be found
frequently among certain pagan and non-Christian peoples of the world. We must
recognize then, that polygyny, like other forms of marriage, is basically a cultural
institution rooted deeply in the religious beliefs and social mores of those societies
in which it appears. It is equally true that the beliefs and mores of the dominant
culture of the contemporary world condemn the practice as immoral and substitute monogamy in its place. To those beliefs and mores I subscribe, but that does
not alter the fact that polygyny is a form of marriage built upon a set of social and
moral principles. It must be recognized and treated as such.

Justice Murphy's cultural perspective outlined possibly the fairest and most neutral words ever offered by a high court jurist about Mormon polygamy, but this did not save the fundamentalists from criminal conviction under the Mann Act.

As these federal court cases moved forward, Mormon fundamentalists also fought local charges stemming from the police raids, which claimed that the fundamentalists had violated state cohabitation and criminal conspiracy laws. The local trials raised basic issues of fairness as many of the eligible judges and prospective jurors in the tightly knit Mormon communities were members of the Church of Latter-day Saints, which had excommunicated the men whose cases were to be heard. The cases resulting from the 1944 raids also resulted in contradictory judicial decisions by trial and state supreme courts, and in the latter, the cohabitation clause of the state law was held to be impermissibly vague.[7] The law could also present ironies. When one of the 15 convicted fundamentalists challenged a prison rule permitting inmates to send only two one-page letters weekly, officials granted special permission for the man—imprisoned for practicing polygamy—to write six letters a week because he had six wives.[8]

Despite the mixed public response to the 1944 raids, as well as the prosecutors' failure to win convictions in all of the cases against polygamists, raids and court actions continued as a means of stamping out Mormon polygamy. In 1953, the state of Arizona carried out what was to become the last major raid on polygamous communities. In the early morning of Sunday, July 26, state highway patrolmen, deputy sheriffs, national guardsmen, and liquor control agents enlisted for the raid swept down on the rural community of Short Creek. Arrest warrants were served on 36 men and 86 women who were variously charged with rape, statutory rape, carnal knowledge, polygamous living, unlawful and notorious cohabitation, bigamy, and adultery. The state also took 153 of the children of Short Creek into custody, making them wards of the state.

The raid on Short Creek revealed ongoing public revulsion toward polygamy, described by the Arizona governor as "a form of degrading female slavery." In particular, the public was incensed by the marriage of young girls to older fundamentalist men, a charge that continues to bring opprobrium on Mormon fundamentalists today. Local taxpayers were also indignant about the school taxes needed to educate fundamentalist children and the increasing number of fundamentalist mothers with large families who were applying for child welfare. The plight of the children themselves also became a central theme in justifying the raid. Where earlier condemnations of polygamy had focused on its tendency "to destroy the purity of the marriage relation … to degrade woman and to debase man," in its action at Short Creek, the state focused upon the perceived need to save the children of polygamous unions from the immoral socializing influence of their parents.[9] The fact that Short Creek polygamous families were often poor and that the fundamentalists were communal in some of their economic arrangements only enhanced the appeal of a "good Samaritan" operation in which the state would show fundamentalist children how to live a "decent" life.

Several years were required to try the hundreds of cases arising from the Short Creek raid. Most of the arrested polygamous husbands were convicted in the Arizona courts, but many of these convictions were reversed on the grounds that the Arizona legislature had never enacted a statute providing for the prosecution of violations of the state constitution's anti-polygamy clause.

Legal action involving Short Creek's plural wives with dependent children was even more dramatic and complex. Immediately after the raid, the women and children were taken in large groups to Phoenix, almost a day's bus ride away, where the children were placed in government-supported foster homes where "wholesome values" could be learned.[10] In order to be near their children, fundamentalist mothers joined them in the foster homes. Each mother had to argue individually at a juvenile court hearing that she was fit to regain independent custody of her children, a process that lasted for many families from two to four years. Eventually, all of the children were given back to their mothers who promised to—but did not—renounce polygamy.

The Short Creek raid and subsequent prosecutions did not end Mormon fundamentalists' polygamy, which continues to be practiced—as an open secret in communities in Arizona and Utah, especially. Approximately 30,000 to 50,000 polygamous Mormons, calling themselves Fundamentalist Latter Day Saints, or FLDS, still practice polygamy in defiance of the rulings of American courts, state statutes, and mainstream cultural values. Although the Mormon Church condemns polygamy and excommunicates polygamists, the FLDS Mormons continue to consider themselves members of the church of Joseph Smith. They reject the view that polygamy is anti-Christian or that they are promiscuous as charged in *Reynolds*, defending polygamy as a "straighter line to God," and part of the path to eternal life.[11]

After the Short Creek raid, state governments largely dropped their strategy of direct law enforcement and depended more on administrative regulations and state laws regarding cohabitation, and Mormon fundamentalism appeared to drop from the nation's radar screen and the agenda of local area politicians who weighed the political costs of prosecutions. However, in 1984, fundamentalist polygamy again emerged on the legal radar when the murder of a Mormon woman and her 15-month old infant in American Fork, Utah, became a media sensation.[12] Two Mormon fundamentalists and avowed polygamists, Ronald and Daniel Lafferty, admitted to the killing, justifying it as a revelation they had received from God. Dan Lafferty was sentenced to life without parole, while his brother Ron was convicted and sentenced to die by a firing squad. Ron Lafferty adamantly rejected an insanity defense, and his ongoing legal maneuvers and conflicts among various courts as to whether he was competent to stand trial have kept him alive until today.

In spite of the devastating public relations blow to their cause occasioned by the murder, fundamentalists began a slow campaign in the 1980s to win public acceptance. In interviews and appearances on television talk shows, they sought tolerance of their religiously based life style and also explored new ways to challenge statutes, court decisions, and administrative regulations through which the state continued to criminalize polygamy. An HBO television series called "Big Love," about relationships in a polygamous family, was launched in spring 2006 and may expand the debate about polygamy to a wider audience than its supporters ever imagined. Fundamentalists took one step in the legal challenge of *Reynolds* in a late 1980s case involving the right of a polygamous family to adopt children.

Following the decision of a Utah Family Court judge that the polygamous Vaughn Fischer family was not eligible to adopt because the "practice of polygamy is a crime and constitutes immoral conduct," the fundamentalists, joined by the American Civil Liberties Union (ACLU), argued that polygamy should be permitted and asked the Utah Supreme Court to consider whether *Reynolds* was still good law.[13] In a close but important 3–2 decision in this case, the Utah Supreme Court ruled that polygamous families cannot be stripped of civil rights without due process, and that the Fischer family could not automatically be ruled ineligible to adopt because the adults were practicing plural marriage. For the most part, the states have continued to "look the other way," or seek more indirect ways of addressing the continuing practice of polygamy. As Utah's Attorney General observed in 1991, "We all know what's going on. But trying to do anything about it legally would be opening one Pandora's box after another." Reflecting, no doubt, upon the changes in sexual mores of the larger American society, in which so many young couples live together without marrying, he continued, "Once you start going after people for cohabitation, or adultery, where do you stop?"[14]

With the repeal of sodomy laws in the Supreme Court's 2002 opinion in *Lawrence v. Texas* and the acceptance of gay marriage by the Massachusetts State Supreme Court in 2003 (see chapter 10), it may be that Mormon fundamentalists will once again renew efforts in court to overturn the nineteenth-century Supreme Court decisions banning polygamy. In 2004, for example, a man and two women who were denied a marriage license by the Salt Lake County clerk's office filed a lawsuit claiming that they wanted to enter the relationship of marriage without being branded as criminals.[15] They cited the *Lawrence* opinion's protection of private sexual relations as applying to their own case, although in fact, *Lawrence* protects private sexual relations, not marriage. They also charged that the Utah laws against polygamy were targeting Mormons, a violation of the Constitution, which holds that laws banning certain practices must be neutral and not aimed at any particular group. The district court dismissed the case on a technicality, but the reach of *Lawrence* and the impact of gay marriage decisions are clearly viewed by judges, legislatures, and the public, as having a bearing on legal challenges to polygamy.

But the recent publication of several books and media stories documenting historical violence in Mormon communities, as well as providing evidence of incest, child abuse, violence against women, and coerced marriage of teenaged girls to men much older than themselves in fundamentalist Mormon communities, is certain to generate more intense interest in Mormon history, including polygamy.[16] Courts and legislatures have already expressed warnings, as did Justice Scalia, in his dissent in *Lawrence*, that various prohibited forms of marriage, such as polygamy, will certainly be challenged in court following *Lawrence* and state court decisions validating same-sex marriage.[17]

In the current climate of the "defense of marriage," the nineteenth-century Mormon polygamy cases may emerge from their obscurity as a new basis from which to hold fast to the conventional definition of monogamous, heterosexual marriage as a core American value that is of sufficient compelling state interest that it overrides the First Amendment protection of the free (which was never absolutely free) exercise of religion.

NOTES

1. Although Mormons only practice the form of polygamy known as polygyny (multiple wives), we use the term polygamy, which is used in the court cases and popular culture. The discussion of the place of polygamy in the theology of the Church of Jesus Christ of Latter-day Saints draws upon Martha Sonntag Bradley, *Kidnapped from That Land: The Government Raids on the Short Creek Polygamists* (Salt Lake City: University of Utah Press, 1993), 1–3. Although estimates differ, approximately 5 percent of Mormon males and 12 percent of Mormon females have practiced polygyny since the 1850s (ibid., 214). Some historians have argued that contrary to public opinion, polygamy was not especially popular among Mormons and that most men had to be coerced into practicing it. See Maria S. Ellsworth, *Mormon Odyssey: The Story of Ida Hunt Udall, Plural Wife* (Urbana: University of Chicago Press, 1992), 45–46.

2. Merle Wells, *Anti-Mormonism in Idaho, 1872* (Provo, Utah: Brigham Young University Press, 1978), 26.

3. U.S. Congress, Senate, Congressional Record, 51st Cong., 1st Sess., 1890, 51, pt. 7:6833. Quoted in Wells, *Anti-Mormonism in Idaho*, 147.

4. Mark P. Leone, *Roots of Modern Mormonism*. (Cambridge: Harvard University Press, 1979), 151.

5. Kathleen Moore, "Al-mughtaribun: Law and the transformation of Muslim life in North America," (Ph.D. dissertation, University of Massachusetts, Amherst, December 1992), 99–100. Under the Immigration Act of l891 (26 Stat. 1084), Muslim foreigners applying for resident alien status in the United States today must swear they are not polygamists or they will be denied admission.

6. Robert Lindsey, "The Mormons: Growth, Prosperity and Controversy" *New York Times,* January 12, 1986, 19.

7. *State v. Musser et al.,* 175 Pacific Reporter, 2d Series, 724, 734 (1946).

8. Bradley, *Kidnapped from That Land,* 88.

9. Our account of the 1953 raid draws on Bradley, *Kidnapped from That Land,* chapters 8 and 9.

10. Ibid., 153.

11. Timothy Egan, "The Persistence of Polygamy," *New York Times Magazine,* February 28, 1999, 51.

12. Jon Krakauer, *Under the Banner of Heaven: A Story of Violent Faith* (New York: Doubleday, 2003).

13. American Civil Liberties Union, Board Minutes, April 6, 1991.

14. Dirk Johnson, "Polygamists Emerge from Secrecy, Seeking Not Just Peace but Respect," *New York Times,* April 9, 1991, A22.

15. "Lawsuit Uses Repeal of Sodomy Laws to Support Utah Polygamy." *The Advocate,* August 6, 2004, from the Internet: http://www.sodomylaws.org/usa/utah/utnews026.htm.

16. Will Bagley, *Blood of the Prophets: Brigham Young and the Massacre at Mountain Meadows* (Norman: University of Oklahoma Press, 2002).

17. Richard A. Vazquez, "The Practice of Polygamy: Legitimate Free Exercise of Religion or Legitimate Public Menace? Revisiting *Reynolds* in Light of Modern Constitutional Jurisprudence," *New York University Journal of Legislation and Public Policy* 5 (2001/2002), 225–253.

CHAPTER 6

Religious Belief and Practice: The Amish

The Old Order Amish are an Anabaptist religion, which, in 1693, broke with their Swiss Mennonite brethren over matters of theology. The Amish faced severe persecution, even death, for practicing their religious beliefs in Europe, and the opportunity to practice their faith "unmolested and undisturbed" was an important factor in their migration to North America in the early eighteenth century. There are approximately 180,000 Amish in the United States today, mainly living in Ohio, Pennsylvania, and Indiana.

The Amish universe is separated into the "world," which is the non-Amish society, representing vanity, vice, greed, and force, and their own "community of piety." This separation is essential for both the continuity of the Amish as a group and for the salvation of the individual. The Amish are "in the world but not of it," a "congregation of the righteous" and a "peculiar people," organizing their lives around obedience to God, as expressed by conformity to the community's rules.[1] Amish life requires resignation to God's will, yielding to others, self-denial, contentment, and a quiet spirit. These values, modeled after the suffering Jesus who refused to resist his adversaries, clash with the American cultural value that individuals have a legitimate right to exercise force to protect their rights and interests.

The Amish spirit also clashes with the coercive nature of the state, which must sometimes use force to achieve its goals. Thus, though the Amish are enjoined not to "resist, despise, or condemn" the state, they are also not permitted to participate in it.[2] This means that the Amish do not go to court to protect their rights or to force others to comply with contractual obligations, although they do allow themselves to be represented in court by non-Amish attorneys and friendly third parties. The Amish are allowed to vote, though again, in contrast to the Mormons, they are forbidden to hold political office, to serve on juries, or to serve in the armed forces.

Amish religion is woven into the fabric of everyday life. While Amish use the language of religious liberty in their conflicts with the state, these conflicts are also cultural—that of the modern, secular, bureaucratized, technologically complex, individualistic rights-oriented culture of the United States in contrast with that of pietistic Christian religious principles, the importance of the local community, and the simple, nonacquisitive, noncoercive, communal culture of the Amish. Amish separateness is manifest in their speech, dress, social customs, and their agricultural life. The soil has spiritual significance and farming is a moral obligation, not merely a way to make a living, but rather a way to make a life that permits them independence from the surrounding, ungodly world. They reject power machinery, including cars, tractors, electrical tools and appliances, and telephones.

The Amish desire to avoid unnecessary contact with the outside world became more difficult as the U.S. government grew more bureaucratic and regulatory. By the nineteenth century, and throughout the twentieth, the Amish were increasingly drawn into legal conflicts with the state over what they regarded as impermissible intrusions into the exercise of their religion, like mandatory contributions to Social Security, which violated their religious principle of self-sufficiency, or pacifism, which brought them in conflict with local draft boards. On some issues, such as traffic laws, zoning, pollution, and land-use regulations, the Amish negotiated successfully with their local communities, such as in their willingness to use flashing lights on their horse-drawn carriages when required by state law, while on other issues, such as exemptions from Social Security contributions, state and federal governments have accommodated the Amish. Unlike Mormons, the Amish do not proselytize, and this may contribute to their generally favorable popular image. As the Amish expanded into new areas of the United States, however, they often became targets of hostility, particularly because of their wartime pacifism.

One important conflict between the Amish and the government arose over aggressive enforcement of state laws requiring compulsory education until the age of 16, which the Amish view as incompatible with their desire to control their children's interaction with non-Amish. The Amish are not opposed to all formal education. Traditionally, they sent their children to local, one-room schools, whose remoteness permitted the isolation of Amish children from "English" children and teaching a curriculum that did not violate Amish religious tenets. By the mid-twentieth century, however, school organization and curricula reflected the urban and technological developments in the United States and the one-room schoolhouse gave way to larger institutions mixing children from diverse cultural backgrounds; at this time, the age of compulsory education was also extended.

The Amish resisted these educational developments on the grounds that they overexposed Amish children to the outside world and undermined the community's ability to maintain control over its youth. The Amish-controlled "vocational" schools were regarded as academically substandard and not acceptable to the state. The Amish were generally unsuccessful in resisting state education requirements in court, where, represented by non-Amish lawyers, they claimed that such laws violated their free exercise of religion.

Consistent with their religious beliefs, in 1972, three Amish fathers— Jonas Yoder, Wallace Miller, and Adam Yutzy—refused to enroll their 14- and 15-year-old children in a Wisconsin high school. They were charged, tried, and convicted of violating the state's compulsory attendance law and fined $5. This brought the long-simmering controversy between the Amish and the state to the U.S. Supreme Court. In *Wisconsin v. Yoder,* the Court was asked whether the state's interest in universal education up to the age of 16 was more compelling than the Amish First Amendment claim to the right of free exercise of their religion. In its decision the Court held, for the first time in American history, the right of an individual to be exempt from compulsory education laws on the basis of religious freedom.

The Court acknowledged that the Amish respondents sincerely believed that their children's high school attendance was contrary to the Amish religion and way of life, that it would expose them to the danger of the censure of the church community, and that it would endanger their own salvation and that of their children. Expert witnesses in anthropology, religion, and education presented uncontradicted testimony that compulsory high school attendance could adversely affect the continued survival of Amish communities in the United States. Chief Justice Warren Burger wrote the opinion of the court. After describing basic Amish values, the ways in which these values conflict with the larger society, and the problem high school presents both to Amish adolescents and to community solidarity, Justice Burger continued:

WISCONSIN V. YODER 406 U.S. 205 (1972)

.... The Amish do not object to elementary education through the first eight grades ... because they agree that their children must have basic skills in the "three R's" in order to read the Bible, to be good farmers and citizens ... to be able to deal with non-Amish people when necessary in the course of daily affairs ... [and because] it does not significantly expose their children to worldly values or interfere with their development in the Amish community during the crucial adolescent period.... wherever possible [however] they have established their own elementary schools in many respects like the small local schools of the past.... In the Amish belief higher learning tends to develop values they reject as influences that alienate man from God. On the basis of such considerations ... compulsory high school atten- dance could ... result in great psychological harm to Amish children, because of the conflicts it would produce.... the Amish succeed in preparing their high school age children to be productive members of the Amish community. [Their] system of learning through doing the skills directly relevant to their adult roles in the Amish community [is] "ideal" and perhaps superior to ordinary high school education. The evidence also show[s] that the Amish have an excellent record as law-abiding and generally self-sufficient members of society.

There is no doubt as to the power of a State, having a high responsibility for education of its citizens, to impose reasonable regulations for the control and dura- tion of basic education. Providing public schools ranks at the very apex of the function of a State .... [Yet] a State's interest in universal education ... is not totally free from a balancing process when it impinges on fundamental rights and inter- ests, such as those specifically protected by the Free Exercise Clause of the First Amendment, and the traditional interest of parents with respect to the religious upbringing of their children so long as they ... "prepare [them] for additional obli- gations .... " We can accept it as settled, therefore, that, however strong the State's interest in universal compulsory education, it is by no means absolute to the exclu- sion or subordination of all other interests ....

We come then to the quality of the [Amish] claims ... [that Wisconsin's com- pulsory school attendance laws encroach on] their rights and the rights of their children to the free exercise of the[ir] religious beliefs ... In evaluating those claims we must ... determine whether the Amish religious faith and their mode of life are, as they claim, inseparable and interdependent. A way of life, however virtuous and admirable, may not be interposed as a barrier to reasonable state regulation of education if it is based on purely secular considerations; to have the protection of the Religion Clauses, the claims must be rooted in religious belief. Although a determination of what is a "religious" belief or practice entitled to constitutional protection may present a most delicate question, the very concept of ordered lib- erty precludes allowing every person to make his own standards on matters of conduct in which society as a whole has important interests.

....This case abundantly supports the claim that the traditional way of life of the Amish is not merely a matter of personal preference, but one of deep religious conviction, shared by an organized group, and intimately related to daily living.... [This is] shown by the fact that it is in response to their literal interpretation of the Biblical injunction from the Epistle of Paul to the Romans, "be not conformed to this world ..." Moreover, for the Old Order Amish, religion is not simply a mat- ter of theocratic belief ... the Old Order Amish religion pervades and determines virtually their entire way of life ...

... [T]he respondents' religious beliefs and attitude toward life, family, and home have remained constant ... in a period of unparalleled progress in human knowledge generally and great changes in education.... Their way of life ... is ... inherently simple and uncomplicated, albeit difficult to preserve against the pres- sure to conform .... [it does] set them apart from much of contemporary society; these customs are both symbolic and practical. As the society around the Amish has become more populous, urban, industrialized, and complex ... government regu- lation of human affairs has correspondingly become more detailed and pervasive.

The Amish mode of life has thus come into conflict increasingly with requirements of contemporary society exerting a hydraulic insistence on conformity to majoritarian standards .... [In addition] modern compulsory secondary education in rural areas is now largely carried on in a consolidated school, often remote from the student's home and alien to his daily home life .... the values and programs of the modern secondary school are in sharp conflict with the fundamental mode of life mandated by the Amish religion; [and] modern laws requiring compulsory secondary education have accordingly engendered great concern and conflict. The conclusion is inescapable that secondary schooling .... by substantially interfering with the religious development of the Amish child and his integration into the way of life of the Amish faith community at the crucial adolescent stage of development, contravenes the basic religious tenets and practices of the Amish faith, both as to the parent and the child.

The impact of the compulsory-attendance law on respondents' practice of the Amish religion is not only severe, but inescapable, for the Wisconsin law .... compels them, under threat of criminal sanction, to perform acts undeniably at odds with fundamental tenets of their religious beliefs .... the impact of the compulsory-attendance law.... carries with it precisely the kind of objective danger to the free exercise of religion that the First Amendment was designed to prevent....carry[ing] with it a very real threat of undermining the Amish community and religious practice as they exist today; they must either abandon belief and be assimilated into society at large, or be forced to migrate to some other and more tolerant region.

.... [T]he unchallenged testimony of acknowledged experts .... almost 300 years of consistent practice, and strong evidence of a sustained faith pervading and regulating respondents' entire mode of life support the claim that enforcement of the State's requirement of compulsory formal education after the eighth grade would gravely endanger if not destroy the free exercise of respondents' religious beliefs.

Justice Burger then addressed claims by Wisconsin state officials that its interest in universal compulsory formal secondary education to age 16 is so great that it must override Amish claims to the free exercise of their religion:

Wisconsin concedes that under the Religion Clauses religious beliefs are absolutely free from the State's control, but it argues that "actions," even though religiously grounded, are outside the protection of the First Amendment. But our decisions have rejected the idea that religiously grounded conduct is always outside the protection of the Free Exercise Clause. It is true that activities of individuals, even when religiously based, are often subject to regulation by the States in the exercise of their undoubted power to promote the health, safety, and general welfare, or the Federal Government in the exercise of its delegated powers. But to agree that religiously grounded conduct must often be subject to the broad police power of the State is not to deny that there are areas of conduct protected by the Free Exercise Clause of the First Amendment and thus beyond the power of the State to control, even under regulations of general applicability.

.... Nor can this case be disposed of on the grounds that Wisconsin's requirement for school attendance to age 16 applies uniformly to all citizens of the State and does not, on its face, discriminate against religions or a particular religion, or that it is motivated by legitimate secular concerns. A regulation neutral on its face may, in its application, nonetheless offend the constitutional requirement for governmental neutrality if it unduly burdens the free exercise of religion. The Court must not ignore the danger that an exception from a general obligation of citizenship on religious grounds may run afoul of the Establishment Clause, but that danger cannot be allowed to prevent any exception no matter how vital it may be to the protection of values promoted by the right of free exercise.

Justice Burger then addressed Wisconsin's claim that compulsory education is so compelling "that even the established religious practices of the Amish must give way. Where fundamental claims of religious freedom are at stake, however, we cannot accept such a sweeping claim…. " and he insisted that a close examination of the state's two primary arguments in support of compulsory education was demanded.

[The State] notes … that some degree of education is necessary to prepare citizens to participate effectively and intelligently in our open political system if we are to preserve freedom and independence. Further, education prepares individuals to be self-reliant and self-sufficient participants in society. We accept these propositions. However, the evidence …. [persuades us]…. that an additional one or two years of formal high school for Amish children in place of their long-established program of informal vocational education would do little to serve those interests…. the value of all education must be assessed in terms of its capacity to prepare the child for life …. compulsory education for a year or two beyond the eighth grade may be necessary when its goal is the preparation of the child for life in modern society as the majority live, but it is quite another [thing] if the goal of education be viewed as the preparation of the child for life in the separated agrarian community that is the keystone of the Amish faith.

The State attacks respondents' position as one fostering "ignorance" from which the child must be protected by the State. No one can question the State's duty to protect children from ignorance but this argument does not square with the facts…. this record strongly shows that the Amish community has been a highly successful social unit within our society, even if apart from the conventional "mainstream." Its members are productive and very law-abiding members of society; they reject public welfare in any of its usual modern forms … It is neither fair nor correct to suggest that the Amish are opposed to education beyond the eighth grade level. What th[ey] are opposed to [is] conventional formal education of the type provided by a certified high school because it comes at the child's crucial adolescent period of religious development. [One educational expert], for example, testified that their system of learning-by-doing was an "ideal system" of education in terms of preparing Amish children for life as adults in the Amish community, and that "…. they do a better job in this than most of the rest of us do…. it seems to me the self-sufficiency of the community is the best evidence … [that] whatever is being done seems to function well."

…. There can be no assumption that today's majority is "right" and the Amish and others like them are "wrong." A way of life that is odd or even erratic but interferes with no rights or interests of others is not to be condemned because it is different.

The State, however, supports its interest in providing an additional one or two years of compulsory high school education to Amish children because of the possibility that some such children will choose to leave the Amish community, and that if this occurs they will be ill-equipped for life. The State argues that if Amish children leave their church they should not be in the position of making their way in the world without the education available in the one or two additional years the State requires. However, on this record, the argument is highly speculative. There is no specific evidence of the loss of Amish adherents by attrition, nor is there any showing that upon leaving the Amish community Amish children, with their practical agricultural training and habits of industry and self-reliance, would become burdens on society because of educational shortcomings. Indeed, this argument of the State appears to rest primarily on the State's mistaken assumption ... that the Amish do not provide any education for their children beyond the eighth grade, but allow them to grow in "ignorance." To the contrary, not only do the Amish accept the necessity for formal schooling through the eighth grade level, but continue to provide what has been characterized by the undisputed testimony of expert educators as an "ideal" vocational education for their children in the adolescent years.

There is nothing in this record to suggest that the Amish qualities of reliability, self-reliance, and dedication to work would fail to find ready markets in today's society. Absent some contrary evidence supporting the State's position, we are unwilling to assume that persons possessing such valuable vocational skills and habits are doomed to become burdens on society should they determine to leave the Amish faith, nor is there any basis in the record to warrant a finding that an additional one or two years of formal school education beyond the eighth grade would serve to eliminate any such problem that might exist.

Insofar as the State's claim rests on the view that a brief additional period of formal education is imperative to enable the Amish to participate effectively and intelligently in our democratic process, it must fall....

Indeed, the Amish communities singularly parallel and reflect many of the virtues of Jefferson's ideal of the "sturdy yeoman" who would form the basis of what he considered as the ideal of a democratic society. Even their idiosyncratic separateness exemplifies the diversity we profess to admire and encourage ....

The independence and successful social functioning of the Amish community for ... almost three centuries and more than 200 years in this country are strong evidence that there is at best a speculative gain, in terms of meeting the duties of citizenship, from an additional one or two years of compulsory formal education. Against this background it would require a more particularized showing from the State on this point to justify the severe interference with religious freedom such additional compulsory attendance would entail ....

Finally, the State ... argues that a decision exempting Amish children from the State's requirement fails to recognize the substantive right of the Amish child to a secondary education, and fails to give due regard to the power of the State as parens patriae to extend the benefit of secondary education to children .... [But T]his case ... is not one in which any harm to the physical or mental health of the child or to the public safety, peace, order, or welfare has been demonstrated or may be properly inferred. The record is to the contrary, and any reliance on that theory would find no support in the evidence.

The State's argument …. that exemption of Amish parents from the requirements of the compulsory-education law might allow some parents to act contrary to the best interests of their children by foreclosing their opportunity to make an intelligent choice between the Amish way of life and that of the outside world [as argued by Justice Douglas in his dissent] could, of course, be made with respect to all church schools short of college. There is nothing in the record or in the ordinary course of human experience to suggest that non-Amish parents generally consult with children of ages 14–16 if they are placed in a church school of the parents' faith.

Indeed it seems clear that if the State is empowered, as parens patriae to "save" a child from himself or his Amish parents by requiring an additional two years of compulsory formal high school education, the State will in large measure influence, if not determine, the religious future of the child …. therefore this case involves the fundamental interest of parents, as contrasted with that of the State, to guide the religious future and education of their children. The history and culture of Western civilization reflect a strong tradition of parental concern for the nurture and upbringing of their children. This primary role of the parents in the upbringing of their children is now established beyond debate as an enduring American tradition ….

The duty to prepare the child for "additional obligations," referred to [earlier] by the Court, must be read to include the inculcation of moral standards, religious beliefs, and elements of good citizenship…. It is of course, recognized that where nothing more than the general interest of the parent in the nurture and education of his children is involved, it is beyond dispute that the State acts "reasonably" and constitutionally in requiring education to age 16 in some public or private school meeting the standards prescribed by the State. However read, the Court's [earlier] holding[s] stand as a charter of the rights of parents to direct the religious upbringing of their children. And, when the interests of parenthood are combined with a free exercise claim of the nature revealed by this record, more than merely a "reasonable relation to some purpose within the competency of the State" is required to sustain the validity of the State's requirement under the First Amendment. To be sure, the power of the parent, even when linked to a free exercise claim, may be subject to limitation … if it appears that parental decisions will jeopardize the health or safety of the child, or have a potential for significant social burdens. But in this case, the Amish have introduced persuasive evidence undermining the arguments the State has advanced to support its claims in terms of the welfare of the child and society as a whole. The record strongly indicates that accommodating the religious objections of the Amish by forgoing one, or at most two, additional years of compulsory education will not impair the physical or mental health of the child, or result in an inability to be self-supporting or to discharge the duties and responsibilities of citizenship, or in any other way materially detract from the welfare of society.

In the face of our consistent emphasis on the central values underlying the Religion Clauses in our constitutional scheme of government, we cannot accept a parens patriae claim of such all-encompassing scope and with such sweeping potential for broad and unforeseeable application as that urged by the State. For the reasons stated we hold … that the First and Fourteenth Amendments prevent the State from compelling respondents to cause their children to attend formal high school to age 16. It cannot be over-emphasized that we are not dealing with a way of life and mode of education by a group claiming to have recently discovered some "progressive" or more enlightened process for rearing children for modern life. Aided by a history of three centuries as an identifiable religious sect and a long history as a successful and self-sufficient segment of American society, the Amish in this case have convincingly demonstrated the sincerity of their religious beliefs, the interrelationship of belief with their mode of life, the vital role that belief and daily conduct play in the continued survival of Old Order Amish communities and their religious organization, and the hazards presented by the State's enforcement of a statute generally valid as to others. Beyond this, they have carried the even more difficult burden of demonstrating the adequacy of their alternative mode of continuing informal vocational education in terms of precisely those overall interests that the State advances in support of its program of compulsory high school education. In light of this convincing showing, one that probably few other religious groups or sects could make, and weighing the minimal differences between what the State would require and what the Amish already accept, it was incumbent on the State to show with more particularity how its admittedly strong interest in compulsory education would be adversely affected by granting an exemption to the Amish.

Nothing we hold is intended to undermine the general applicability of the State's compulsory school-attendance statutes or to limit the power of the State to promulgate reasonable standards that, while not impairing the free exercise of religion, provide for continuing agricultural vocational education under parental and church guidance by the Old Order Amish or others similarly situated. The States have had a long history of amicable and effective relationships with church-sponsored schools, and there is no basis for assuming that, in this related context, reasonable standards cannot be established concerning the content of the continuing vocational education of Amish children under parental guidance, provided always that state regulations are not inconsistent with what we have said in this opinion.

In a concurring opinion, Justice Byron White, joined by Justices William Brennan and Potter Stewart, reiterated a point he felt the court had insufficiently emphasized in saying:

This would be a very different case for me if respondents' claim were that their religion forbade their children from attending any school at any time and from complying in any way with the educational standards set by the State. Since the Amish children are permitted to acquire the basic tools of literacy to survive in modern society by attending grades one through eight and since the deviation from the State's compulsory-education law is relatively slight, I conclude that respondents' claim must prevail, largely because 'religious freedom—the freedom to believe and to practice strange and, it may be, foreign creeds—has classically been one of the highest values of our society." The importance of the state interest asserted here cannot be denigrated, however. Today, education is perhaps the most important function of state and local governments. Compulsory school attendance laws and the great expenditures for education both demonstrate our recognition of the importance of education to our democratic society....

[R]ecently … the Court re-emphasized the legitimacy of the State's concern for enforcing minimal educational standards [but this] lends no support to the contention that parents may replace state educational requirements with their own idiosyncratic views of what knowledge a child needs to be a productive and happy member of society…. the Court held simply that while a State may posit such standards, it may not pre-empt the educational process by requiring children to attend public schools. In the present case, the State is not concerned with the maintenance of an educational system as an end in itself, it is rather attempting to nurture and develop the human potential of its children whether Amish or non-Amish: to expand their knowledge, broaden their sensibilities, kindle their imagination, foster a spirit of free inquiry, and increase their human understanding and tolerance. It is possible that most Amish children will wish to continue living the rural life of their parents, in which case their training at home will adequately equip them for their future role. Others, however, may wish to become nuclear physicists, ballet dancers, computer programmers, or historians, and for these occupations, formal training will be necessary. There is evidence in the record that many children desert the Amish faith when they come of age. A State has a legitimate interest not only in seeking to develop the latent talents of its children but also in seeking to prepare them for the life style that they may later choose, or at least to provide them with an option other than the life they have led in the past. In the circumstances of this case, although the question is close, I am unable to say that the State has demonstrated that Amish children who leave school in the eighth grade will be intellectually stultified or unable to acquire new academic skills later. The statutory minimum school attendance age set by the State is, after all, only 16.

Decision in cases such as this and the administration of an exemption for Old Order Amish from the State's compulsory school-attendance laws will inevitably involve the kind of close and perhaps repeated scrutiny of religious practices, as is exemplified in today's opinion, which the Court has heretofore been anxious to avoid. But such entanglement does not create a forbidden establishment of religion where it is essential to implement free exercise values threatened by an otherwise neutral program instituted to foster some permissible, nonreligious state objective. I join the Court because the sincerity of the Amish religious policy here is uncontested, because the potentially adverse impact of the state requirement is great, and because the State's valid interest in education has already been largely satisfied by the eight years the children have already spent in school.

In a separate opinion, Justice William Douglas indicated that he joined the decision of the court with respect to reversing the conviction of Jonas Yoder because Yoder's daughter Frieda had testified that she agreed with the decision to withdraw from school on the basis of religious belief. Concerned, however, with the impact of the majority's opinion on those Amish children who might not share the community's view on the unacceptability of education after the eighth grade, Justice Douglas dissented on behalf of the Yutzy and Miller children, who were not called to testify, and whose views were not therefore known, and on behalf of all other Amish children whose views might be contrary to those of their parents:

I agree with the Court that the religious scruples of the Amish are opposed to the education of their children beyond the grade schools, yet I disagree with the Court's conclusion that the matter is within the dispensation of the parents alone....

[N]o analysis of religious-liberty claims can take place in a vacuum. If the parents in this case are allowed a religious exemption, the inevitable effect is to impose the parents' notions of religious duty upon their children. Where the child is mature enough to express potentially conflicting desires, it would be an invasion of the child's rights to permit such an imposition without canvassing his views ... an imposition resulting from this very litigation. As the child has no other effective forum, it is in this litigation that his rights should be considered. And, if an Amish child desires to attend high school, and is mature enough to have that desire respected, the State may well be able to override the parents' religiously motivated objections. Religion is an individual experience. It is not necessary, nor even appropriate, for every Amish child to express his views on the subject in a prosecution of a single adult. Crucial, however, are the views of the child whose parent is the subject of the suit. Frieda Yoder has in fact testified that her own religious views are opposed to high-school education. I therefore join the judgment of the Court as to respondent Jonas Yoder. But Frieda Yoder's views may not be those of Vernon Yutzy or Barbara Miller. I must dissent, therefore, as to respondents Adin Yutzy and Wallace Miller as their motion to dismiss also raised the question of their children's religious liberty.

On this important and vital matter of education, I think the children should be entitled to be heard. While the parents, absent dissent, normally speak for the entire family, the education of the child is a matter on which the child will often have decided views. He may want to be a pianist or an astronaut or an oceanographer. To do so he will have to break from the Amish tradition.

It is the future of the student, not the future of the parents, that is imperiled by today's decision. If a parent keeps his child out of school beyond the grade school, then the child will be forever barred from entry into the new and amazing world of diversity that we have today. The child may decide that that is the preferred course, or he may rebel. It is the student's judgment, not his parents', that is essential if we are to give full meaning to what we have said about the Bill of Rights and of the right of students to be masters of their own destiny. If he is harnessed to the Amish way of life by those in authority over him and if his education is truncated, his entire life may be stunted and deformed. The child, therefore, should be given an opportunity to be heard before the State gives the exemption which we honor today.

Wisconsin v. Yoder resolved an important question of constitutional rights: whether the state's interest in the schooling of young children can be subordinate to the free exercise of religion. Given the acknowledged importance of education in modern societies, it is important to look at the court's reasoning in exempting future generations of Americans from this critical institution of economic and political socialization. The *Yoder* opinion makes clear that the court held for the Amish first, because the Amish only requested exemption from ninth and tenth grades. It also leaves no doubt, however, that factors beyond the constitutional question were involved. The Supreme Court read, accepted, and reasoned from

The image of integrity, honesty, and authenticity central to American views of the Amish gives credibility to the Amish Market's claim to sell fine food with the freshest ingredients, despite the fact that the ownership is non-Amish. Photo courtesy of Joan Gregg.

expert testimony that presented the Amish as self-sufficient, law-abiding, productive, and morally righteous and therefore "deserving" of consideration that, by implication, other groups are not. In his partial dissent Justice Douglas spoke specifically to this point:

I think the emphasis of the Court on the "law and order" record of this Amish group of people is quite irrelevant. A religion is a religion irrespective of what the misdemeanor or felony records of its members might be. I am not at all sure how the Catholics, Episcopalians, the Baptists, Jehovah's Witnesses, the Unitarians, and my own Presbyterians would make out if subjected to such a test.

The weight given by the court majority to the 300-year history of the Amish as a Christian sect, as well as to their contemporary "goodness," raises, as Justice Douglas notes, a central question of constitutional law: whether rights pertain to individuals and groups according to, or regardless of, their law-abidingness, economic success, and social behaviors. When comparing, for example, the Supreme Court's treatment of the Amish, the Mormons, and the Japanese Americans (see chapter 12), the dominant culture's perceptions of the social and economic behaviors of different groups, in different historical periods, do seem to matter. The Mormons, for example, were as self-sufficient as the Amish, but because their self-sufficiency was communal and socialistic, and was allied with such repugnant practices as polygamy, the dominant culture felt the need to repress it. Similarly, the economic self-sufficiency of Japanese-Americans, achieved in part through the use of family labor similar to that of the Amish, was turned against them by large commercial agricultural interests, who portrayed them as "exploitative and un-American," an image not entirely without influence on the Court. The highly positive and even romantic view of the Amish in the larger society is abetted by the nonintrusive, self-contained nature of their religiously based life-style, which conforms to the dominant American sense of what is respectable behavior. The Court's opinion, while making much of the Constitution's ability to accommodate cultural pluralism, in fact, rested more upon the *similarities* between the Amish and the larger society. The Court's sympathy with the Amish is reflected in their letting pass the fact, noted only by Justice Douglas, that the Amish children had not all been heard from. Further, the Court's acceptance of the Amish position that the community did prepare its children adequately for life *within* the community ignored statistics that the Court itself cited that there was significant out-migration of Amish young people.[3] Read in the context of this out-migration, the Court's opinion denies those children who leave the Amish agricultural community the protection of the state in providing adequate educational preparation that is otherwise widely accepted in American law. Unlike the Mormons, the Amish have resisted any major changes in their culture or their theology in order to accommodate the many changes in values and technology in American society. The dominant culture, through social practice and law, has unabashedly accommodated the Amish, supporting the continuation of their subculture, which offers an ideal model of rural, moral, self-sufficient America. This ideal, while fast disappearing in reality, still has an important mythological connection to American identity and history, in contrast to the urban, competitive, materialistic, secular society that we have become.

NOTES

1. John A. Hostetler, *Amish Society,* 4th ed. (Baltimore, MD: Johns Hopkins University Press, 1993).
2. Donald B. Kraybill, ed., *The Amish and the State,* 2nd ed. (Baltimore, MD: Johns Hopkins University Press, 2003).
3. *Wisconsin v. Yoder,* 406 U.S. 205, 240 (1972).

CHAPTER 7

The Culture Wars in American Schools

One of the most important battles over the proper relationship between church and state is taking place today in America's schools. Schools have always been an important battleground in culture clashes in the United States because they are central in reproducing American values and national identity and in assimilating the nation's many culturally different groups.

As part of the contemporary "culture wars," various religious groups are attempting to insert religious belief and practice into public schools and to gain public financing for religious schools.[1] Both these agenda present grave challenges to the establishment clause of the U.S. Constitution, which prohibits the entanglement of government and religion. The establishment clause of the First Amendment of the Constitution was designed by the founding fathers to prevent any religious group from gaining control of state institutions, or from the state favoring one religion over another, or, less explicitly, favoring religion over nonreligion.

The concern of the founding fathers over government entanglement with religion grew out of eighteenth-century Enlightenment values, which rejected religion as the irrefutable and authoritative source of all knowledge. Rather, Enlightenment principles insisted on the right of the individual to subject all areas of knowledge and tradition to historical and scientific scrutiny and to protect individual freedom from government interference.[2]

Applied to education, the establishment clause means that public schools will be free from the establishment of religious principles and practices and that public funds will not be used to support religious (sectarian) schools. With the growing political importance of religious fundamentalism and political conservatism in the United States, challenges to the separation of church and state have emerged with new vigor, however, involving clashes over curriculum, particularly regarding the teaching of evolution; censorship of textbooks and library books; school prayer; sex education; access of religious groups to school sites; and public aid to students in sectarian schools.

In 1971, in *Lemon v. Kurtzman* [403 U.S. 602 (1971)], which involved public aid to religious schools, the U.S. Supreme Court established a three pronged test for evaluating whether legislation or practices regarding public schools violate the establishment clause. The Court held that in order to be constitutional, a statute (1) must have a secular legislative purpose; (2) must not, as its principal or primary effect, advance or inhibit religion; and (3) must not foster an excessive government entanglement with religion. Federal courts have generally used the *Lemon* test to prevent breaches of the establishment clause with regard to schools, but as constitutional scholar Lawrence H. Tribe cautioned, "these [court] decisions take some of the wind out of their [fundamentalist] sails but [they don't] sink the ship."[3] Current political efforts by fundamentalists confirm Tribe's insight. Issues thought settled decades ago, such as the teaching of evolution and the use of public funds for religious schools, have, in the current political climate, taken on new life.[4]

EVOLUTION AND CREATION SCIENCE

The censorship of books and ideas in schools is a staple of the fundamentalist agenda, provoking dramatic confrontations over the teaching of evolution, particularly the origin of the human species. Evolutionary theory, presented in 1858 by Alfred Russell Wallace and Charles Darwin, refutes the literalist biblical view that the world and all its creatures were created *ex nilio* (from nothing) by God in seven days, as described in the book of Genesis. In the early 1920s fundamentalists lobbied state legislators to pass bills prohibiting the teaching of evolution in tax supported schools. Among the states passing such statutes were Mississippi, Arkansas, and Texas. In 1925, Tennessee's passage of an anti-evolution law provoked the famous Scopes "monkey trial," in which two of the nation's most well known lawyers and public figures—William Jennings Bryan and Clarence Darrow—turned a constitutional issue of First Amendment religious freedom into a dramatic courtroom clash opposing science and religion. The Tennessee statute declared it unlawful for any teacher in any public school to teach any theory that denies the story of the divine creation of man as taught in the Bible and to teach instead that man has descended from a lower order of animals."[5] Apprehensive that similar statutes would be widely adopted unless their constitutionality was challenged, the American Civil Liberties

Union (ACLU), along with some local townspeople in Dayton, Tennessee, decided to test the law. John T. Scopes, a young, unmarried, substitute biology teacher in the local high school, who believed it was impossible to teach biology without teaching evolutionary theory, agreed to be arrested so that the issue could be litigated. William Jennings Bryan, a three-time contender for the U.S. presidency, a Southerner and a committed fundamentalist and anti-evolution activist, volunteered to represent the state. Darrow, a Chicago attorney and a well-known supporter of liberal causes, joined with Scopes' local attorney and ACLU lawyers for the defense.

During the trial many scientists testified to the validity of the theory of evolution as an explanation of human origins; some additionally stated that since evolution was itself divinely created, there was no conflict between evolutionary theory and religion. Their statements emphasized, however, that evolutionary theory is not and cannot be consistent with a literal interpretation of the divine creation as narrated in Genesis. In spite of this scientific testimony, local jurors brought in a guilty verdict and Scopes was fined $100. Darrow appealed, and the Tennessee Supreme Court reversed the lower court's decision on a technicality. At the same time the court held, in the face of the contradictory reality, that the literal interpretation of Genesis was not a part of any particular religion and therefore the anti-evolution statute did not violate the establishment clause. The judge opined that while the theory of human evolution could not be taught in Tennessee's public schools, nothing contrary to that theory was required to be taught either.

In a further attempt to pacify the fundamentalists, while also keeping the way open for Tennessee to move into the modern, scientific era, the Tennessee Supreme Court opinions also denied any conflict between a religious viewpoint and modern science, so long as the teaching of evolution did not "deny the story of the divine creation of man as taught in the Bible." While the court hoped that its decision in Scopes would end "this bizarre case … " and bring "peace and dignity" back to Tennessee, its unwillingness to confront the irreconcilable conflict between evolution and fundamentalist theology, left the door open for further legal conflict on the issue.

One result of the Tennessee Court's decision was the passage of a similar anti-evolution law in Arkansas, in 1928, that remained on the books until the 1970s. During this time the issue lay dormant partly because of America's concerns with the Depression and then World War II, and partly because many publishers, ever alert to market considerations, quietly accommodated the fundamentalists by omitting references to Darwin and evolution in their biology textbooks. By the 1960s, however, motivated by the scientific achievements of the Soviet Union in the 1957 launching of the Sputnik satellite, the U.S. government turned its attention to the quality of science teaching in American schools. As part of overhauling science curricula, newly developed textbooks also incorporated the theory of evolution as a major theme.

This post-Sputnik climate led to renewed litigation against anti-evolution statutes. In 1967, Tennessee's "monkey law" was challenged and finally repealed. At this same time, a high school biology teacher in Little Rock, Arkansas, Susan Epperson, challenged Arkansas' anti-evolution statute. New science textbooks purchased by the city included a chapter on evolution, but teaching this material under the 1928 law was a criminal offense. Although Arkansas had never attempted to enforce the law, Epperson was concerned that if fundamentalists pressed for its enforcement, she could be dismissed. She thus instituted legal action, claiming that the Arkansas statute violated her Fourteenth Amendment due process rights because of its vagueness. Epperson sought a declaration that the statute was void and that she could not be dismissed from her job for teaching evolution. Unsuccessful in the lower courts, the case went to the Arkansas State Appeals Court, which upheld the statute in a two-sentence opinion that altogether sidestepped the First Amendment religious issue. Epperson then appealed to the U.S. Supreme Court. Justice Abraham Fortas, writing the majority opinion in *Epperson v. Arkansas* (393 U.S. 97, 1968), spoke directly to the constitutional issue, holding that the anti-evolution statute violated the establishment clause. The Court, however, seemed to view the case as unimportant, noting that "It is possible that the [anti-evolution] statute is presently more of a curiosity than a vital fact of life ..." How wrong that proved to be!

"CREATION SCIENCE" AND EVOLUTION SCIENCE

This misperception of the *Epperson* Court is demonstrated by the subsequent legal battles over evolution. Having failed to get evolution out of the schools, however, fundamentalists now switched their strategy to getting religion in, passing legislation at state and local levels. In the mid-1970s, repackaging Genesis as creationism, these attempts were defeated both in the courts and through the opinions of states' attorneys general. This led the fundamentalists to drop explicit references to Genesis and to substitute the term "Creation Science" for creationism, arguing that this should be taught to "balance" the teaching of evolution.[6]

By 1981, with practically no debate, no hearings and no scientific testimony, the "Creation Science" lobby succeeded in gaining passage of a "balanced treatment" statute in Arkansas, which required creationist views to be presented along with evolution. Barely two months after Act 590, The Balanced Treatment for Creation-Science and Evolution Science Act, became law, two dozen Arkansas citizens and organizations—including many non-fundamentalist religious groups—brought suit in U.S. District Court charging that the Act was nothing more than an attempt to establish religion in the public schools in violation of the Establishment Clause. In *Mclean v. Arkansas* [529 F. Supp. 1255 (1982)], Judge William R. Overton agreed.

In the culture wars over public school curriculum, creationists, and their latest incarnation, supporters of intelligent design, deny the overwhelming scientific evidence supporting the view that humans and the Great Apes evolved from a common ancestor some 14 million years ago. Photo courtesy of Serena Nanda.

Considering the legislative history of Act 590 in the context of the growing fundamentalist subculture and the religious views and motivations of its supporters, Judge Overton characterized this law as one that had "the specific purpose of advancing religion ..." He held that in its major effect of advancing particular religious beliefs and in creating for Arkansas "an excessive and prohibited entanglement with religion," the statute failed all three prongs of the *Lemon* test. Judge Overton reminded the court that "The Establishment Clause ... enshrines two central values: voluntarism and pluralism.... [and that] it is in the area of public schools that these values must be guarded most vigilantly." He noted the resurgence of fundamentalist concerns in the 1960s about the loss of traditional values and their fears of growing secularism in society. He then outlined the origin of "Creation Science" and described fundamentalist attempts to influence public school curricula:

There is an emphasis among current Fundamentalists on the literal interpretation of the Bible and the Book of Genesis as the sole source of knowledge about origins.... In the 1960s and 1970s, several Fundamentalist organizations were formed to promote the idea that the Book of Genesis was supported by scientific data.

The terms "creation science" and "scientific creationism" have been adopted by these Fundamentalists as descriptive of their study of creation and the origins of man..... .

Creationists have adopted the view of Fundamentalists generally that there are only two positions with respect to the origins of the earth and life: belief in the inerrancy of the Genesis story of creation and of a worldwide flood as fact, or belief in what they call evolution....

Judge Overton recapitulated the history of the "creation science" lobby, in which a respiratory therapist named Paul Ellwanger, who was neither trained in law or science, began organizing for the passage of what he hoped would be a model state act, requiring the teaching of creationism as science in opposition to evolution, which he held responsible for abortion, racism, and Nazism, among other social evils. In his opinion, Judge Overton expressed his view that Ellwanger was fully aware that Act 590 was a religious crusade, though he attempted to conceal this purpose. He noted that the introduction of Act 590 to the legislature, by a self-described "born again" Christian Fundamentalist, was "simply and purely an effort to introduce the Biblical version of creation." Every theologian who testified expressed the opinion that the act referred to a "supernatural creation which was performed by God" and was thus clearly religious.

Judge Overton characterized the creationists' attempt to define creationism as science and its claim that it does not involve a supernatural deity as having no evidentiary or rational support. To the contrary, he said,

"creation out of nothing" is a concept unique to Western religions. In traditional Western religious thought, the conception of a creator of the world is a conception of God. Indeed, creation of the world "out of nothing" is the ultimate religious statement because God is the only actor.... the Act refers to one who has the power to bring all the universe into existence from nothing. The only 'one' who has this power is God.

In contrast to the religious and nonscientific nature of "Creation Science," Judge Overton emphasized that science is a "way of knowing." Its essential characteristics are that it is guided by natural law; it is explanatory in terms of natural law; its conclusions are testable against the empirical world and are tentative and falsifiable by further testing. "Creation Science" fails to meet all of these essential criteria, he said. "Creation Science" is not *science*, he said, and added that creation scientists do not think like scientists or work like them: They do not generate theories to be tested; publish articles in scientific journals; reconsider their theories in relation to new data; or keep an open mind about their conclusions. Rather, Judge Overton accurately stated, "[Creation Scientists] take the literal wording of the Book of Genesis and attempt to find scientific support for it. Since "creation science" is not science, Judge Overton went on to say, "the conclusion is inescapable that the only real effect of Act 590 is the advancement of religion." Furthermore, he pointed out, that since Act 590 prohibited instruction

in any religious doctrine or references to religious writings ... [it is also] self-contradictory and compliance is impossible unless the public schools elect to forego significant portions of subjects such as biology, world history, geology, zoology, botany, psychology, anthropology, sociology, philosophy, physics and chemistry. Presently, ... concepts of evolutionary theory ... permeate the public school textbooks. There is no way teachers can teach the Genesis account of creation in a secular manner.

The State Department of Education, through its textbook selection committee, school boards, and school administrators will be required to constantly monitor materials to avoid using religious references. The school boards, administrators and teachers face an impossible task. How is the teacher to respond to questions about a creation suddenly and out of nothing? How will a teacher explain the occurrence of a worldwide flood? How will a teacher explain the concept of a relatively recent age of the earth? The answer is obvious because the only source of this information is ultimately contained in the Book of Genesis ... References to the pervasive nature of religious concepts in creation science texts amply demonstrate why State entanglement with religion is inevitable under Act 590. Involvement of the State in screening texts for impermissible religious references will require State officials to make delicate religious judgments. The need to monitor classroom discussion in order to uphold the Act's prohibition against religious instruction will necessarily involve administrators in questions concerning religion. These continuing involvements of State officials in questions and issues of religion create an excessive and prohibited entanglement with religion ...

Judge Overton also considered the impact of the act upon teachers, who,

rather than teach material in support of creation science which they do not consider academically sound ... will simply forego teaching subjects which might trigger the "balanced treatment" aspects of Act 590 [i.e., evolution] even though they think the subjects are important to a proper presentation of a course. Implementation of Act 590 will have serious and untoward consequences for students, particularly those planning to attend college. Evolution is the cornerstone of modern biology, and ... subject matter relating to such varied topics as the age of the earth, geology, and relationships among living things. Any student who is deprived of instruction as to the prevailing scientific thought on these topics will be denied a significant part of science education. Such a deprivation through the high school level would undoubtedly have an impact upon the quality of education in the State's colleges and universities, especially including the pre-professional and professional programs in the health sciences.

Judge Overton also vigorously rejected the fundamentalist claim that evolution is a religion that infringes upon the student's free exercise rights under the First Amendment and that teaching Creation Science, which is "consistent with some religious beliefs," would provide a needed balance.

He stated that this argument had "no legal merit…. It is clearly established in … law, and perhaps also in common sense, that evolution is not a religion and that teaching evolution does not violate the Establishment Clause…. "

Finally, to the fundamentalists' contention that a majority of Americans believe in a Creator and see nothing wrong in teaching that to school children, Judge Overton reminded the defendants that

The application and content of First Amendment principles are not determined by public opinion polls or by a majority vote. Whether the proponents of Act 590 constitute the majority or the minority is quite irrelevant under a constitutional system of government. No group, no matter how large or small, may use the organs of government, of which the public schools are the most conspicuous and influential, to foist its religious beliefs on others…. [Quoting U.S. Supreme Court Justice Frankfurter] We renew our conviction that 'we have staked the very existence of our country on the faith that complete separation between the state and religion is best for the state and best for religion.' If nowhere else, in the relation between Church and State, 'good fences make good neighbors.'

Simultaneously with the Arkansas challenge, a similar Louisiana statute was also challenged, ultimately reaching the U.S. Supreme Court. In *Edwards v. Aguilar* [55 U.S.L.W. 4860 (1987)], writing for the majority, which found that the statute violated the establishment clause, Justice William Brennan called the Louisiana Act a "sham as to its expressed intention of fostering academic freedom by giving equal time to two competing scientific theories on the origins of man" and characterized the purpose of the act as "advanc[ing] the religious viewpoint that a supernatural being created humankind." Only Justices Antonin Scalia and William Rehnquist dissented, holding that the Court "must accept at face value" the statements of the act's supporters that their intent was not to promote religion, but was to "insure that students would be free to decide for themselves how life began, based upon a fair and balanced presentation of the scientific evidence." Unwilling, or perhaps unable, to see through the transparent efforts of religiously motivated proponents of fundamentalism to use "creation science" in order to evade the constitutional prohibition on government establishment of religion, Justice Scalia accepted Louisiana's view that creation science was empirical inquiry rather than religious belief and thus that it deserved to be taught alongside evolutionary theory.

After *Aguilar* many legal experts believed that fundamentalist attempts to replace the teaching of evolution with religious alternatives in the public schools had been put to rest. They were mistaken: By the 1990s, these efforts intensified and are continuing up to the present. In Kansas, the State Board of Education, having failed to have all references to evolution removed from the state's science curriculum in 1999, pushed through new science standards in 2005 requiring that evolution be challenged in the classroom and removed as a subject on statewide tests. Supported by religious fundamentalists, this was just a first step in introducing religious alternatives to evolution into the classroom.[7]

The Kansas State Board decision is only one of similar actions at the state and local level across the country. Some school districts in Wisconsin and Ohio, like Kansas, hoping to stave off legal challenges, did not specifically ban the teaching of evolution but rather mandated that "various models and theories" of the creation of the earth and the origin of humans be examined, and that Darwinian evolution be subject to "evaluation and criticism" by students. A rural Michigan school board specifically approved the teaching of creationism as an alternative to evolution.

In Dover, Pennsylvania, in 2004, the school board mandated that "Intelligent Design" (ID) be included in the ninth-grade biology curriculum. Intelligent design supporters claim that life is so intricately complex that an architect, or "designer," must be behind it, a view that most of its proponents admit is a religiously motivated belief. In response, eleven parents with children in the school district brought a lawsuit challenging the constitutionality of teaching what they argued was "a religious alternative masquerading as a scientific theory."[8] In his December 2005 decision in this case, *Kitzmiller v. Dover*, federal district court Judge John E. Jones III agreed with the parents, ruling "the secular purposes claimed by the Board amount to a pretext for the Board's real purpose, which was to promote religion in the public school classroom, in violation of the Establishment Clause [of the U.S. Constitution]."[9] In his opinion he criticized school board members for lying "time and again" to cover their religious motives and said Intelligent Design must not be taught in public school science classes.[10] In yet another case, in Georgia, it took a federal judge to declare that anti-evolution stickers in biology textbooks constituted an impermissible violation of the establishment clause by failing to meet the third prong of the *Lemon* test, prohibiting an entanglement of government with religion.[11] The support of President George W. Bush for the teaching of intelligent design has further encouraged religious fundamentalists to continue their assaults on science in the schools as an important part of their strategy in their continuing efforts to break down the separation of church and state.[12]

PUBLIC FUNDING FOR RELIGIOUS SCHOOLS

Another effort by religious communities to erode the "wall of separation between church and state" has been their attempts to use public funds to support religious schools and religious education. While some state laws permitting public aid to parochial schools, where this aid does not directly touch curriculum, have been struck down, political pressure exerted on state legislatures to aid religious schools is more intense than ever.[13] The complex and often logically and legally inconsistent efforts toward this end, as well as the increasing role of state legislatures in supporting such aid, is demonstrated by a case that lasted over 10 years, involving a small, little-known Orthodox Jewish community in New York State called the Satmar Hasidim.[14]

The Satmar Hasidim, like the Amish, are a "community of piety" guided in all aspects of their life by a literalist interpretation of the *Torah* (the first five books of the Hebrew Testament) and the *Talmud* (the interpretive book of Jewish law and tradition). Satmar religion both symbolizes and maintains their separation from the rest of society. Their sexual code requires strict separation of the sexes, except within the immediate family and in the case of children with disabilities. To avoid "impure thoughts" they also maintain strict dress and behavioral codes for males and females.

The Satmar, who strenuously resist interaction with outsiders, speak Yiddish and insulate themselves from English-language media. All Satmar children attend sex-segregated religious schools, where boys study secular academic subjects and Torah while girls learn the basics of homemaking. The community's Rabbi is the ultimate decision maker on all aspects of community life, and any challenge to his religious authority may result in expulsion from the community. The Satmar came to the United States after WW II and originally settled in Brooklyn. As their population expanded they established other communities, one of which was an undeveloped sub-division of the Town of Monroe, in Orange County, New York. As a result of conflicts with Monroe over several issues, such as the town's prohibition on using residences as synagogues and schools, the Satmar legally incorporated as the separate community of Kiryas Joel (Village of Joel, named after their first Rabbi in America), within the Town of Monroe, with boundaries that included only the 320 acres owned and inhabited entirely by Satmars.

The lengthy legal battle involving attempts by Satmar in Kiryas Joel to use public funds to provide special education for their disabled children within a religious, sex-segregated setting, followed a similar case in Brooklyn, in which the Satmar attempted to use public funds to provide remedial education for Satmar girls only, in classrooms separated from the rest of the local public school and closed to other students. In that case, the Satmar stated, "We struggle very hard to maintain our belief and our culture; we want our children separate. The ... heart of the [Jewish] Orthodox tradition ... requires the separation of males and females for every activity, including schooling, and encourages isolation from other cultures. If we have our kids learning with them, they'll be corrupted ... We don't hate these people, but we don't like them. We want to be separate."[15] The courts ruled that Satmar demands violated the establishment clause and so, in their initial litigation in Kiryas Joel, the Satmar changed their strategy, asserting cultural, not religious rights.

All Kiryas Joel children attend the private, religious schools in the village, and the village's handicapped children, pursuant to the federal Individuals with Disabilities Act and New York State Education Law, which entitles handicapped children to a public education "in the least restrictive environment," were educated in special classes at an annex adjacent to and educationally identifiable with the girl's religious school. They were taught by public school teachers whose salaries were paid by public funds allotted to the Monroe-Woodbury Central School District, which includes Kiryas Joel. Children with disabilities from neighboring Hasidic communities also attended the school.

In 1985, however, the U.S. Supreme Court announced two decisions, *Aguilar v. Felton* (473 U.S. 402) and *Grand Rapids v. Ball* (473 U.S. 373), which held that state-financed special education services could only be held on the site of a public school, and not on the site of a religious school. After these decisions, the Monroe-Woodbury public school district announced its intention to cease providing special education services to the Satmar at their private school site and to educate them instead in the district's public schools, where they would be integrated with other children. Monroe-Woodbury was prepared to hire Yiddish-speaking teachers and provide parents with bilingual reports on their children.

Satmar parents refused this offer and went to court. In this initial suit the Satmar did not claim the Monroe law violated their free exercise of religion, but rather that it imposed too great a "traumatic psychological impact" on their children, who would now have to leave their sheltered village environment and would be thrust into a strange environment where their physical appearance, dress, and language would set them apart from the other students. The Satmar claimed that as taxpayers they were entitled to public funds for the cost of special education services and that public support for their private school for disabled children was a legitimate accommodation to the *secular* needs of a culturally distinctive group that "happened" to be of the same religion. Unlike the Amish, then, who claimed that their religion and culture were inseparable, as the Satmar had also claimed in the Brooklyn case, here the Satmar claimed that their religion and culture were separable.

A long, complicated series of legal cases ensued, with the Satmar alternately winning, losing, and appealing at the state level.[16] While the town of Monroe offered to compromise, the New York State Court of Appeals insisted that the only constitutionally acceptable solution was for the Satmar children to be educated within Monroe's public school facilities. Rejecting the Satmar's contention that its culture and religion were separate, the court said, "[P]roviding the educational services in a separate environment addressed parental concerns for Satmar religious and social practices, rather than secular factors such as the children's disability ... and [thereby] violated the Establishment Clause." The court further noted that the distinctive culture of the Satmar was based on their religion, that the "apparent overall goal" of the Satmar was that "children should continue to live by the religious standards of their parents," and that "Satmarer want their school to serve primarily as a bastion against undesirable acculturation."[17] In their appeal, the Satmar switched their claims: Now, citing

Yoder, they based their challenge on the law's infringement of their rights to the free exercise of their religion. The Appeals Court, however, refused to consider this issue, since the Satmar had not raised it in its initial suit.

Politicians now entered the picture: In June 1989, perhaps with Satmar bloc voting in mind, the New York state legislature enacted a new law, Chapter 748, which established a separate public school district co-terminus with the village of Kiryas Joel, for the expressed purpose of providing special education services to the handicapped village children from public funds. As these services would now be offered as part of a public school district, the school was to be entirely nonreligious and subject to all the regulations of the state's public schools. The Monroe-Woodbury Central School district, in an attempt to end the conflict and litigation, supported the bill, and it was signed by then Governor Mario Cuomo.

Though politicians clearly hoped this would resolve the issue, two officials of the state education department, acting as citizen-taxpayers, brought suit against both the Kiryas Joel and Monroe-Woodbury School Districts, challenging the law as a violation of the establishment clause of the United States and New York State Constitutions. The plaintiffs contended that the statute had both the intent and the effect of furthering the Hasidim's religiously based commitment to insulate their children from the larger, diverse society and thus failed the first two prongs of the *Lemon* test. They also contended that the statute violated the third prong of the *Lemon* test because it would require state officials, who would have to monitor the implementation of the statute, to become excessively entangled in religion.

The New York State Supreme Court agreed. Judge Lawrence E. Kahn's opinion noted that, "The legislation is an attempt to camouflage, with secular garments, a religious community as a public school district" and he chided both the legislature and the Satmar for trying to circumvent the First Amendment with constitutionally forbidden legislation, which could "jeopardize the very religious freedom that they now enjoy." Judge Kahn further commented, "The strength of our democracy is that a multitude of religious, ethnic and racial groups can live side by side with respect for each other; and while … the uniqueness of religious values, as observed by the Satmar Sect, is especially to be admired as non-conformity becomes increasingly more difficult to sustain, laws which advance and endorse such parochial needs violate our deep-rooted principle of separation of church and state … "[18]

Subsequent to the rejection of joint appeals by the Kiryas Joel and Monroe School Districts by the courts, Monroe-Woodbury and Kiryas Joel, joined by the Attorney General of the State of New York, appealed to the Supreme Court of the United States. In *The Attorney General of the State of New York et al. v. Louis Grumet and Albert W. Hawk* (512 U.S. 687, 129 L.Ed. 2d 546), heard by the court in 1994, the petitioners' brief reverted to the initial Satmar argument that their religion and culture were separate.

They claimed that the New York Appeals Court's finding that the new law, Chapter 748, violated the establishment clause "evinces a hostility to the group's way of life and a denigration and diminution of their secular concerns, which centered on the emotional trauma of the children and the negative effect on their educational progress." Kiryas Joel claimed that Chapter 748 "was a wholly secular solution to a social problem" and that it exhibited a "tolerance of a minority view, a healthy and constitutional respect for religious diversity," thus preserving the very diversity of society that the respondents claim to champion. The petitioners questioned not only the New York Appeals Court's decision, but also the validity of the *Lemon* test, which they argued was overrestrictive. The Constitution, they claimed, "requires accommodation, not merely tolerance of all religions, and forbids hostility toward any…. callous indifference would violate the idea of free exercise of religion."[19]

The respondents (Grumet and Hawk), supported by many civil liberties organizations, called Chapter 748's "alleged secular purpose … a sham." Noting that the law protected what was unarguably a religious community, they claimed that Chapter 748 failed the *Lemon* test and violated the establishment clause because it was not a law of general applicability, but was enacted expressly to help the Satmar. In addition, they stated that the law ran counter to New York State's goal of "maintain[ing] diversity … and … ensur[ing] that school district boundaries are not drawn in a manner that segregates pupils along ethnic, racial or religious lines." The respondents also claimed that Chapter 748 contravened the standard of separation of church and school established in earlier Supreme Court opinions, which held that "public schools must discharge their public function of training students for citizenship in a heterogeneous democratic society … in an atmosphere free of parochial, divisive, or separatist influences of any sort."[20]

On June 27, 1994, the Supreme Court of the United States affirmed, 6–3, that Chapter 748 violated the establishment clause of the First Amendment. Writing for the majority, Justice David Souter rejected the petitioners' claim that the state law was only the incidental delegation of power to a group who happen to be of the same religion. This, he said, was totally contradicted by the reality of the Satmar community and the history of the litigation.

In light of subsequent events, however, the significance of this case may be found less in the majority opinion than in the concurrences and dissents, in which several Justices raised questions about the continuing validity of the *Lemon* test as the standard for interpreting violations of the establishment clause. In her concurrence, Justice Sandra Day O'Connor questioned whether *Lemon*, as a unitary test for all religious establishment cases, was not due for judicial reconsideration. She asked "What may the government do, consistent with the Establishment Clause, to accommodate people's religious beliefs?" and noted, "there is nothing wrong with the government accommodating a group's deeply held religious belief, so long as it does not discriminate based on sect." Justice Anthony Kennedy, along with Justice O'Connor, also emphasized (as did Justice Antonin Scalia in his dissent) that, "The Establishment Clause does not demand government hostility to religion, religious ideas, religious people, or religious schools" but does demand neutrality. Citing *Oregon v. Smith* (pp. 149–150), Justice Kennedy noted that legislatures may go beyond courts in granting religious accommodations and said that the state law was a perfectly valid accommodation to religion. He did agree with the Court majority, however, that drawing school district lines along the religious lines of the village impermissibly involved the state directly "in accomplishing the religious segregation."

Justice Scalia's dissent, joined by Chief Justice William Rehnquist and Justice Clarence Thomas, accepted the Satmar claim that the state law validly addressed cultural, not religious concerns and held that Chapter 748 had properly addressed the secular concerns of a group that happened also to have a common religion. In this view, the case did not involve public aid to a religiously based private school, but only concerned a public school providing a public secular education to handicapped students. Referring to the Court's majority opinion, Justice Scalia noted an increasing hostility in the Court toward religion in the United States. He sarcastically surmised that "Justice Souter would laud this humanitarian legislation if all of the distinctiveness of Kiryas Joel were attributable to the fact that their parents were nonreligious commune-dwellers, or American Indians, or gypsies … The neutrality demanded by the Religion Clauses require the same indulgence towards cultural characteristics that are accompanied by religious belief. The Establishment Clause does not license government to treat religion and those who teach or practice it as subject to unique disabilities." Justice Scalia agreed with Justices Kennedy and O'Connor on the need to reconsider both *Aquilar* and *Lemon,* which he characterized as "so hostile to our national tradition of accommodation [to religion]."

The Supreme Court's decision did not end attempts by the Satmar and New York State to achieve their goal of public funding for disabled Satmar children in a religious setting. Encouraged by Justices O'Connor's and Kennedy's suggestion that a *general* New York state law would be constitutionally acceptable even if it happened only to benefit the Satmar, the New York legislature crafted two more laws, supposedly neutral on their face, in an attempt to accommodate the Satmar. Each of these laws were struck down by the New York Courts as a violation of the *Lemon* test and the New York State Constitution, which explicitly excludes public funding for "any school … wholly or in part under the control or direction of any religious denomination."[21] Ultimately, however, the Satmar prevailed, as New York State passed yet another law, Chapter 405, which was constructed in a sufficiently general fashion to deter any further constitutional challenges.[22]

The Satmar litigation is significant, not only as an interesting comparison with the Amish, but also because it focused the attention of the U.S. Supreme Court on the value of earlier decisions, like *Lemon* and *Aquilar*, to constrain future decisions on cases involving public funding for religious schools. This reconsideration of establishment doctrine, in the charged political climate of the first decade of the twenty-first century, is an essential context in which to view the recent court decisions on the issue of school vouchers.

SCHOOL VOUCHERS

School vouchers are only one variety of "school-choice" programs that permit state governments to provide public money in the form of tuition rebates to individuals for private school tuition, including sectarian schools. While initially supported across the political spectrum, and particularly by low-income African Americans as a way of improving inner-city public education through competition, vouchers have now become another dimension of attempts by political conservatives to reshape education by expanding public support for religious schools, with the prospect of expanding voucher programs to families at all income levels.

Subsequent to the 1980s "tuition tax credits" promoted by the Reagan administration, by the 1990s the voucher movement was moving forward. In 1990, Milwaukee, Wisconsin, initiated a voucher program through which the state authorized $2,446 for up to 1,000 low-income students to attend nonreligious private schools. By 1994, however, Wisconsin expanded the voucher program to permit enrollment in Catholic schools, with the result that by 1999, state funds allotted for vouchers doubled, public school funding dropped by $28 million, and the numbers of students enrolled in the voucher program increased to almost 6,000.[23]

In 1995, Cleveland, Ohio, enacted a pilot voucher program that gave 2,000 mainly lower-income elementary school children the right to use vouchers in religious and other community schools. A challenge to this law asserted, among other things, that the participating Catholic schools, contrary to the law, were violating the random-admissions requirement by giving preferential admission to Catholics and to siblings of current students. In 1996–97, in a setback for voucher proponents, a trial court in Wisconsin and the appellate court in Ohio declared that because of the inclusion of parochial schools, their state voucher laws violated the state and federal constitution establishment clauses. Subsequently, however, the Wisconsin Supreme Court, in *Jackson vs. Benson* (2002 WI 90) held that the Wisconsin voucher law was constitutional. The U.S. Supreme Court's refusal to hear the case on appeal allowed the Wisconsin Court's decision to stand, which both voucher advocates and legal analysts interpreted as an opening for voucher laws that included religious schools. Subsequently

five states—Florida, Texas, New Mexico, Pennsylvania, and Arizona—
introduced voucher statutes that included religious schools.

The most contested aspect of state voucher programs is the inclusion
of religious schools. Although some of the participating religious schools
permitted students to "opt out" of the school's religious practices or religious education classes, voucher opponents (as well as the schools themselves) emphasize that in most sectarian schools religion is completely
entwined with academic subjects and is the core of the school's mission.
Indeed, some religious schools, such as the Lutheran schools of Milwaukee,
refused to participate in voucher programs if any government oversight
over curriculum and classrooms was included or if students could refuse
to participate in religious instruction.[24]

In 2002, the school voucher issue reached the U.S. Supreme Court. On
June 27, in *Zelman v. Simmons-Harris* (536 U.S. 639), the Court held, 5–
4, that the Cleveland voucher system did not violate the establishment
clause of the Constitution. In his opinion for the majority, Chief Justice
William Rehnquist defended the Court's decision as totally consistent with
past Court decisions on public aid to parochial schools that goes through
private individuals:

The [voucher] program ... was enacted for the valid secular purpose of providing
educational assistance to poor children in a demonstrably failing public school
system ...This Court has always distinguished between government programs
that provide aid directly to religious schools and programs of true private choice,
in which government aid reaches religious schools only as a result of the genuine
and independent choices of private individuals ... we believe that the program
challenged here is a program of true private choice ... and thus constitutional ...
the Ohio program is neutral in all respects toward religion ... the program permits
the participation of all schools within the district, religious or nonreligious.... The
Establishment Clause question is whether Ohio is coercing parents into sending
their children to religious schools, and that question must be answered by evaluating *all* options Ohio provides Cleveland schoolchildren [the program included
magnet schools, community schools and secular private schools in addition to
parochial schools].... [the voucher program] permits ... individuals to exercise
genuine choice among options public and private, secular and religious. The program is therefore a program of true private choice ... and [therefore] does not
offend the establishment clause.

In contrast to the majority opinion, which emphasized intent, the dissenting opinion, written by Justice David Souter joined by Justices Ruth
Bader Ginsburg, Stephen Breyer, and John Paul Stevens, emphasized
impact, noting the many factors that propelled private choice to religious
schools. The dissent rejected the majority's opinion that this case was consistent with Supreme Court precedent in school-establishment cases and
also pointed out that the degree of government oversight that would be
necessary to ensure that the parochial schools were not "teaching religion"

in violation of the establishment clause would require an impermissible entanglement of government with religion:

The applicability of the establishment clause to public funding of benefits to religious schools was settled in *Everson v. Board of Education of Ewing*, which inaugurated the modern era of establishment doctrine. The court stated the principle [with] … no dissent: "no tax in any amount…. can be levied to support any religious … institutions … [in] whatever form they may adopt to teach or practice religion."
   … only by ignoring the meaning of neutrality and private choice [can] the majority even pretend to rest today's decision on those criteria …
   There is … no way to interpret the 96.6 percent of current voucher money going to religious schools as reflecting a free and genuine choice by families that apply for vouchers. [This] percent reflects instead, the fact that too few nonreligious school desks are available and few but religious schools can afford to accept more than a handful of voucher students … Public schools … [do not] have an incentive to participate in the Ohio voucher program, and none has. For the overwhelming number of children in the voucher scheme, the only alternative to the public schools is religious. And it is entirely irrelevant that the state did not deliberately design the network of private schools for the sake of channeling money into religious institutions. The criterion is one of genuinely free choice on the part of the private individuals who choose, [but] a Hobson's choice is not a choice … [and] there is no question that religious schools in Ohio are on the way to becoming bigger businesses … to fit their new stream of tax-raised income.

   The dissent also took up another issue largely ignored by the majority, that of the imposition of religiously based curricula on students:

Religious teaching at taxpayer expense simply cannot be cordoned from taxpayer politics, and every major religion currently espouses social positions that provoke intense opposition. Not all taxpaying Protestant citizens, for example, will be content to underwrite the teaching of the Roman Catholic Church condemning the death penalty. Nor will all of America's Muslims acquiesce in paying for the endorsement of the religious Zionism taught in many religious Jewish schools, … Nor will every secular taxpayer be content to support Muslim views on differential treatment of the sexes, or … to fund the espousal of a wife's obligation of obedience to her husband, presumably taught in [Southern Baptist] schools. Views like these … have been safe in … the sectarian classrooms of this nation … because the free-exercise clause protects them directly, but [also] because the ban on supporting religious establishment has protected free exercise, by keeping it relatively private. With the arrival of vouchers in religious schools, that privacy will go … [The] reality [is] that … in the matter of educational aid the establishment clause has largely been read away… [and] is largely silenced.

   The dissenting opinion then expressed the hope that "a future court will reconsider today's dramatic departure from basic establishment clause principle." One of the problems with establishment clause doctrine is that earlier Supreme Court decisions on public aid to religious education are

136   American Cultural Pluralism and Law

a mélange of contradictory rulings. While in *Everson v. Board of Education of Ewing*, cited in the dissent, the Court held that a voucher-like program was unconstitutional because almost three-quarters of the parents receiving the reimbursements sent their children to church-related schools, over the next two decades the Court handed down several other rulings which appeared to contradict *Ewing*.

Research results do not confirm the claim of voucher proponents that school choice laws, including vouchers, improve education. Furthermore, since none of the voucher laws have accountability clauses and since the private schools involved are not forced to accept all applicants, it is difficult to make any objective comparisons. Voucher opponents note that more than three-quarters of all private schools in the United States, and most of those in low-income neighborhoods, are church affiliated; in addition, the only private schools most poor parents can afford—even with a voucher—are overwhelmingly sectarian. This pushes poor students toward religious institutions, and makes a mockery of the "neutrality" of vouchers. Indeed, it may well be that increasing state funds for vouchers will lead inner-city churches to open parochial schools, once the voucher dollars are there to be used for enrollment.

Subsequent to *Zelman* several court rulings proved a setback for religiously motivated voucher supporters. In February 2004, in a 7–2 decision in *Locke v. Davey* (540 U.S. 712), the U.S. Supreme Court rejected the argument that a state government that subsidizes training for the secular professions, *must also* subsidize, as a matter of the constitutional free exercise of religion, training for divinity students.[25] A month later, a federal judge in Portland, Maine, dismissed a lawsuit filed by two families, citing *Zelman*, who wanted public funds to pay for their children's tuition at a Roman Catholic high school.[26] The judge held that that case *allowed* states to pay religious school tuitions, but did not *require* that they do so. In June 2004, a district court judge in Denver, Colorado, ruled that the state's school voucher program was unconstitutional because it deprived local school boards of their rights in the state constitution to control local schools. In this case, as in others, a coalition of African American groups, teachers, religious groups, and educational organizations opposed the law "as a thinly veiled attempt to direct tax money to private schools motivated by religious ideology."[27] The Colorado decision was followed, in August 2004, by a state appeals court ruling in Florida that its voucher law was unconstitutional because it violates the provision of the Florida constitution that bans the use of tax dollars for religious schools.[28] In spite of some setbacks to vouchers, both in the courts and in state referendums, however, *Zelman* provides support for voucher proponents and others who continue their fight to reinterpret the establishment clause so that it becomes a useful weapon in breaching the wall of separation of church and state in American education.

NOTES

1. Jonathan Zimmerman, *Whose America? Culture Wars in the Public Schools* (Cambridge, MA: Harvard University Press, 2002); Kern Alexander and M. David Alexander, *American Public School Law,* 3rd. ed. (St. Paul, MN: West, 1992), chapter 5.

2. Susan Jacoby, *Freethinkers: A History of American Secularism* (New York: Metropolitan/Holt, 2004); Mark Lilla, "Church Meets State," *New York Times Book Review,* May 15, 2005, 39; Alexander and Alexander, *American Public School Law,* 113–123.

3. William K. Stevens, "Despite Defeats, Fundamentalists Vow to Press Efforts to Reshape Schools," *New York Times,* August 29, 1987, B6.

4. Edward J. Larson, *Summer for the Gods: The Scopes Trial and America's Continuing Debate over Science and Religion* (Cambridge, MA: Harvard University Press, 1998); Daniel J. Kevles, "Darwin in Dayton," *New York Review of Books* (November 18, 1998), 61.

5. *The World's Most Famous Court Trial: State of Tennessee v. John Thomas Scopes.* Complete Stenographic Report of the Court Test of the Tennessee Anti-Evolution Act … Including Speeches and Arguments of Attorneys (New York: Da Capo Press, 1971).

6. Edward J. Larson, *Trial and Error: The American Controversy Over Creation and Evolution,* 3rd ed. (New York: Oxford University Press, 2003).

7. Jodi Wilgoren, "In Kansas, Darwinism Goes on Trial Once More," *New York Times,* May 6, 2005, A18; for an examination of the Kansas decision in the context of contemporary political conservatism, see Thomas Frank, *What's the Matter With Kansas: How Conservatives Won the Heart of America* (New York: Henry Holt/ Metropolitan, 2004).

8. *Kitzmiller, et al. v. Dover Area School District, et al.,* Case No. 04cv2688, Memorandum Opinion, December 20, 2005, Judge John E. Jones III, 49. For a discussion of events leading up to the trial, and the trial, see Margaret Talbot, "Darwin in the Dock," *New Yorker* (December 5, 2005).

9. *Kitzmiller,* 132.

10. *Kitzmiller,* 137.

11. Ariel Hart, "Judge in Georgia Orders Anti-Evolution Stickers Removed from Textbooks," *New York Times,* January 14, 2005, A14.

12. Niall Shanks, *God, the Devil, and Darwin: A Critique of Intelligent Design Theory* (New York: Oxford, 2004); Barbara Forrest and Paul R. Gross, *Creationism's Trojan Horse: The Wedge of Intelligent Design* (New York: Oxford, 2004); Frederick Crews, "Saving Us from Darwin," *New York Review of Books* (October 4, 2001), 24; "Saving Us from Darwin, Pt. II," *New York Review of Books,* 48, no. 16 (October 18, 2001), 51; Laurie Goodstein, "Closing Arguments Made in Trial on Intelligent Design, *New York Times,* Nov. 5, 2005, A14; "Debating Intelligent Design," *Anthropology News,* 46 (December 2005).

13. Alexander and Alexander, *American Public School Law,* 132.

14. Jill Norgren and Serena Nanda, *American Cultural Pluralism and Law,* 2nd ed. (Westport, CT: Praeger, 1996), chapter 7; for a novel exploring the clash of Hasidic communities with the outside world, see Stephen G. Bloom, *Postville: A Clash of Cultures in Heartland America* (New York: Harcourt, 2000).

15. *Parents' Assn. Of P.S. 16 v. Quiñónez* , 803 F.2d , 2d Cir. 1235 (1986), 1236–1238.

16. Norgren and Nanda, chapter 7.

17. *Board of Education of the Monroe-Woodbury CSD v. Wieder*, 72 N.Y.2d 174 (1988).

18. *Louis Grumet et al. v. Board of Education of the Kiryas Joel Village School District et al.*, 187 A.D.2d 16; 592, N.Y.S. 2d 123 (1992).

19. *The Attorney General of the State of New York et al. v. Louis Grumet and Albert W. Hawk*, 512 U.S. 687 (1994), brief for petitioners.

20. *The Attorney General of the State of New York et al. V. Louis Grumet and Albert W. Hawk*, brief for respondents.

21. Joseph Berger, "Judge Rejects 3rd Push to Keep School District of Kiryas Joel," *New York Times*, April 3, 1998, B1.

22. Abby Goodnough, "Ruling Favors Public School in Hasidic Village," *New York Times*, February 20, 2001, B3; Tamar Lewin, "Controversy Over, Enclave Joins School Board Group," *New York Times*, April 20, 2002, B4.

23. Kathy Koch, "School Vouchers," *CQ Researcher* 9, no. 13 (April 9, 1999), 281–304; for a more recent overview see, Kenneth Jost, "School Vouchers Showdown," *CQ Researcher* Vol. 12, no. 6 (February 15, 2002), online.

24. Koch, "School Vouchers," 290.

25. Linda Greenhouse, "Court Says States Need Not Finance Divinity Studies," *New York Times*, February 26, 2004, A1.

26. Robert C. Johnston, "Maine Judge Upholds Ban on Religious-School Vouchers," *Education Week* 23, Issue 29 (March 31, 2004), 20.

27. Jon Sarche, "Public school vouchers unconstitutional, Colorado Supreme Court says," *Associated Press*, June 28, 2004, online.

28. Jackie Hallifax, "Court Rules original school voucher law unconstitutional," *Associated Press*, August 16, 2004, online.

CHAPTER 8

Religion and the Use of Illicit Drugs: The Rastafari and the Native American Church

No issue is better suited to challenge the limits of cultural pluralism in the United States than that of the use of drugs, even in connection with religious practice. The use of substances declared illegal by states and the federal government has put such groups as the Rastafarians and the Native American Church on a collision course with not only their local communities, but with the entire criminal justice system. Religious practices different from those of the mainstream of America have always invited hostility, often leading to government prohibition and prosecution. The widespread scourge of drug use in the late twentieth century intensified the prosecution of drug use, even in religious contexts.

THE SACRAMENTAL USE OF MARIJUANA: THE RASTAFARIANS

An estate on the quiet, exclusive island community of Miami Beach, Florida, 43 Star Island, seems an unlikely setting for a confrontation on the issue of religious use of marijuana, a confrontation whose reverberations drew the attention of politicians in Washington, the venerable national media program *60 Minutes,* and a number of important East Coast lawyers. In the late 1970s, the estate at 43 Star Island, owned by Jacquelyn Renee Town, was used by the Ethiopian Zion Coptic Church as a place of meeting and daily worship. This church is one of the many denominations of the Rastafarians, a religious community that originated in the 1930s on the Caribbean island of Jamaica. Rastafarianism blends elements of Christianity with an African consciousness.

For more than 200 years Jamaica had been colonized by the British. During this period the rise of a white society, built on capitalism and bourgeois respectability, left the black peasantry, descendants of African slaves, in a condition of economic and social oppression. In the 1920s, the teachings of Marcus Garvey, a Jamaican, emphasizing social reform and repatriation to Africa, stirred hopes among this peasantry for a more just life. Attuned to the importance of Africa, an event occurred, in 1934, that mobilized a part of that peasantry. This event, widely reported in the Jamaican press, was the coronation of Ras Tafari as Haile Selassie I, King of Ethiopia. The photographic images of this black African king, whose coronation was attended by European dignitaries, intensified the importance of Africa in the Jamaican black identity. Within a few years, Rastafarian preachers emerged proclaiming the divinity of Haile Selassie, and groups began to form to discuss the connection between Haile Selassie as the messiah and the hopes of black people.

As economic conditions worsened during the Depression of the 1930s, many peasants found themselves landless and moved to Kingston and other cities, where they became part of an urban underclass. The message of the Rastafarian preachers found a wide audience among this group. By the late 1930s, harassment of Rasta leaders began, as the British colonial government realized the revolutionary implications of a spiritual movement

The Rastafarians are a religious group that incorporates Christian symbolism with that of Ethiopian culture, particularly Emperor Haile Selassie. Begun in Jamaica, West Indies, it has diffused throughout the world, sometimes running into conflict with the law over its sacramental use of marijuana. Photo courtesy of Joan Gregg.

that venerated an African king above the British crown, and that rejected the individualistic work ethic of exploitative capitalism.[1]

In spite of hostility from the colonial government, the Rastafarian movement continued to gain followers, and in 1940 Leonard Howell, one of the original Rastafarian prophets, set up a commune called "the Pinnacle." During the 14 years that the commune was in existence, before it was disbanded by Jamaican authorities, the ritual codes and theology of the Rastas were further developed. Many of the central Rastafarian characteristics—the communal sharing of property, the wearing of dreadlocks, sacramental use of marijuana, and particular dietary customs, all of which set the Rastas in opposition to the larger society—developed in this period.

In 1954, after the Pinnacle was disbanded, the Rastas moved again to the cities, and their membership among the urban underclass continued to grow. Shortly afterward, reggae music, which is antiestablishment and inflammatory to authorities, and is popularly associated with the late Bob Marley, became identified with the Rastafari, provoking yet more hostility from the larger society.

Concerned with their growing bad press, in 1960 the Rastas took the initiative and invited scholars from the University of the West Indies to visit their Kingston communes. The positive report from these academic fieldworkers, disseminated through the Jamaican press, did indeed alter the previous negative image of the Rastas as "ganga smoking, good-for-nothing rascals," and the Rastas' relations with the government, now independent from England since 1962, improved for a number of years. In 1972, the People's National Party (PNP) candidate, Michael Manley, successfully campaigned for the post of prime minister on a platform that incorporated Rasta ideals and symbols. He even used reggae music to popularize his reformist economic program. This gave him widespread appeal among the poor. Much of the middle class, however, remained uncomfortable with the Rasta lifestyle, including their use of marijuana, and with the Rasta ideology that so firmly rejected the individualist, profit-oriented basis of emerging Jamaican capitalism.

Throughout the 1970s, the processes of formalization and sectarianism took place within the Rasta movement. Just as the Methodist church, for example, following its prophet, John Wesley, split off from the larger Protestant movement in Europe, so too, did the Ethiopian Zion Coptic Church split off from the other Rastafarian churches, developing a somewhat different ritual and theology. In spite of sectarian differences, however, there is a common core to Rastafarianism: Haile Selassie is the living God, at least of African people, and he is revealed only to true believers; black African people, who are the reincarnation of the ancient Israelites, are considered superior to whites, although individual whites who are able to put aside racist beliefs are accepted into Rasta congregations; Ethiopia, which stands for all of Africa, is Heaven; in opposition stands Babylon,

the corrupt, secular world outside. Enjoined by Haile Selassie to liberate
their own societies from oppression and social injustice, Rastafarians live
"in the white-dominated world, without becoming part of it." Like the
Amish, the Rastafarians engage in a delicate balancing between a life of
opposition to the values and practices of the larger society and the need to
interact with that society.

Like all fundamentalist religious communities, the Rastafarian
theology creates an encompassing, highly structured lifestyle and a
traditional morality. Rastafarian ritual observances are syncretic and
largely based on the Old Testament: They follow the dietary laws of
Leviticus (similar to the kosher practices of orthodox Jews) and, based
on Leviticus 21:5, Rastafarian men do not shave or cut their hair. Following their central belief that Babylon is Hell, Rastas resist the institutions
of Babylon, including marriage, sending their children to public schools,
and the payment of taxes. Women, according to Corinthians 1:4, do not
expose their hair and eschew the use of cosmetics. In both daily life and
religious practices Rasta women engage in different activities and have
different responsibilities than do men. Women do not hold leadership
positions in the religious community and are not permitted in "reasoning sessions."

Reasoning sessions are the heart of Rasta spiritualism. In worship
services that occur mornings, afternoons, and evenings Rastafarian men
recite biblical passages and discuss their "reasonings" or understandings
of them. The smoking of marijuana is essential to these sessions. Cannabis
is described by a Rastafarian as the mystical body and blood of "Jesus."
It enhances enlightenment, permits him to find the spirit of love, unity,
and justice within himself, and serves to bring him closer to God. For the
Rastas, ganja as a sacrament is legitimated by many references to biblical
scripture: from Genesis 1:11–12, "and God said, let the earth bring forth
grass, the herb yielding seed, and ... God saw that it was good." For
Rastas, ganja is the only true sacrament. Rasta theology holds that wine
alcohol is a dead spirit, distilled by corrupted man, the false sacrament
of the white man's Christendom, causing drunkenness and crime and is,
therefore, not the symbol of the body and blood of Christ. Ganja, on the
other hand, is a natural substance, and coming from God directly, must
be good and true.[2] For this reason, Rastafarians challenge the labeling of
ganja as a drug; similarly, they also abjure not only what our society calls
"hard drugs" such as processed heroin and cocaine, but also synthetic and
manufactured medicines.

Although law enforcement agents have characterized the Rastafarians'
use of marijuana as "freewheeling," in part because Rastafarian religious
services do not conform to the scheduled nature of religious services most
Americans are used to, in fact, Rasta religious services, including the use
of ganja, do conform to specific rules and doctrines. The ganja pipes, for
example, are considered holy objects, and ganja use is preceded by specific

prayers. Indeed, the Rastas might easily be ignored as another of the many fundamentalist Christian sects that have frequently emerged in Western history, were it not for their use of ganja. It is the Rastas' practice of using ganja that has joined them in conflict with the government of the United States, despite the ostensible protection of the First Amendment, which holds that "Congress shall make no law ... prohibiting the free exercise [of religion]."

"HOLY SMOKE": LITIGATION AND THE ETHIOPIAN ZION COPTIC CHURCH

The most widely known litigation involving the religious use of marijuana centered on the Rasta congregation that gathered at 43 Star Island, Miami Beach. The beginnings of this litigation actually reach back into the early 1970s when several members of the Ethiopian Zion Coptic Church were arrested in connection with the confiscation of large quantities of marijuana in several locations in central Florida. The Florida locale is not surprising given its proximity to Jamaica, which is both the origin point of the church and a major source of marijuana production. Furthermore, the Star Island congregation had had close links with the Jamaican Rastafarians since the 1960s. During this period, Coptic Church members first found their way to Rasta communes as part of a generation of American counterculture youth searching for more congenial environments in which to practice alternative lifestyles. Of the many young white people who went to Jamaica, a small number professed a sincere conversion to Rastafarianism and were accepted by Jamaican Rastas as part of the community. Some of these people later returned to the United States and established the Ethiopian Zion Coptic Church in Miami, keeping active personal and spiritual relationships with Rasta leaders in Jamaica, among them Keith Gordon, who was to later figure in the litigation.

In the late 1970s, following phone calls by neighbors, Janet Reno, then a prosecutor for the state of Florida, along with officials representing the City of Miami Beach filed a complaint against the members of the Ethiopian Zion Coptic Church, charging them with a violation of local zoning ordinances that prevent a religious congregation from holding services in a residential neighborhood. The complaint against them also charged the illegal use of marijuana in violation of Florida public nuisance statutes. These charges, minor as they might seem, became part of a strategy by state and local law enforcement agents to rid Florida of a group that officials saw as a drug enterprise and not as a genuine religion. According to *Miami Herald* reporter Joe Oglesby's informant, "The idea is to put [the Coptics] out of business."[3]

The trial and appeals courts found, however, that the Coptic Church was a bona fide religion of long standing, and that the use of marijuana was a genuine religious sacrament essential to religious practice. In this aspect of the case, the courts did not lend support to the government strategy to close down the church. However, both courts ultimately ruled against church members on the public nuisance charge because the ganja sacrament was offered to children and to adult nonmembers. The judges also pointed out that Coptics used cannabis throughout the day and did not limit its use to the church facility.

On the zoning issue, too, the courts found against the Coptics. While the trial judge had offered what undoubtedly seemed to him the compromise that the owner, Renee Town, could worship at 43 Star Island with her family and friends, both local and appeals courts nevertheless held that the property could not be used for church meetings.

What would have happened after the Supreme Court of Florida upheld the trial court's injunction against the Coptics, and the U.S. Supreme Court refused to hear the case on appeal, became a moot question when, on October 28, 1979, the television news show *60 Minutes* aired a feature piece entitled "Holy Smoke," describing the 43 Star Island Coptic community. The prime time, nationwide broadcast, showing the open and frequent use of marijuana by the Coptics, prompted Florida Governor Robert Graham to urge the U.S. government to bring a "massive" federal case—one that would revive the earlier smuggling and possession and use charges—against the Coptics. The U.S. Justice Department agreed to explore this possibility and subsequently instructed the U.S. attorney in Miami to bring a case.

As a result, in the early hours of the morning, three weeks after the *60 Minutes* broadcast, federal and local police raided the 43 Star Island compound. In an attempt to obtain evidence of large caches of marijuana, a Drug Enforcement Administration tow truck, accompanied by armed agents, rammed the gates, interrupting the morning prayer service. Although no marijuana was found, a six-count indictment was issued charging 19 members of the Coptic church with conspiracy to violate the federal Controlled Substance Act. In addition, Keith Gordon, the Coptic spiritual leader from Jamaica, and two members of the Star Island community—Thomas Reilly, known as "brother Louv," and Clifton Middleton—were charged with conducting a criminal enterprise. The government alleged that the street value of marijuana seized in previous raids involving Coptics totaled $80 to $100 million. As one of the lawyers for the Coptics, Milton M. Ferrell Jr. later explained, the U.S. attorney's office was able to construct the case that Governor Graham wanted by stringing together all the previous Florida cases, which had been up to now unsuccessfully prosecuted, as a federal conspiracy case.

The defense mounted by attorneys for the Coptics in this federal prosecution pursued a dual strategy. Offering evidence from a number of internists, psychiatrists, nutritionists, and anthropologists, the defense claimed that the classification of marijuana as a harmful and dangerous drug was arbitrary and irrational and therefore violated Fifth Amendment due process and equal protection guarantees. But the lawyers for the Coptics also argued that since marijuana was an indispensable part of the Coptic religion, prohibiting its use violated the First Amendment free exercise rights of church members.

Attempting to prove the irrationality of the classification of marijuana as harmful and dangerous, defense witnesses, on the basis of prior research as well as clinical examinations of both Jamaican and American Coptics, testified that they found no physically or psychologically harmful effects of marijuana use, even among persons who had been using it for a long time.

Dr. Lester Grinspoon, a psychiatrist from the Harvard Medical School and Director of the Massachusetts Mental Health Center, testified that the effects of marijuana use are "limited and mild," that they disappear when the high is over, and that they "are not medically harmful to the user."[4] He and a medical colleague further testified that the allegedly harmful effects of long-term use of marijuana—that it leads to addiction, causes crime and other aggressive behavior, and leads to brain damage—are all "myths ... without any valid empirical foundation."[5]

In challenging the classification of marijuana as a dangerous drug, still other witnesses pointed to the empirical evidence that marijuana has therapeutic properties in the treatment of glaucoma, neurological disorders, and nausea induced by chemotherapy.[6] Indeed, Dr. Grinspoon capped his testimony with the provocative statement that "the single greatest danger encountered by the marijuana user is that of being arrested by law enforcement personnel."[7]

The defense strategy did not work. And despite earlier court findings that the Coptics were a sincere and long-established religious group, the jury found all but one of the defendants guilty as charged. Four months later, U.S. District Judge William Hoeveler imposed sentences ranging from 7 to 15 years. With nine of the Coptics in jail, and ten others fugitives from the law, Florida officials got their wish to put this Coptic Church out of business. In this case, the constitutional issue of free exercise of religion could not withstand the determination of the government to prosecute the Coptic Church on a drug conspiracy charge.

THE PEYOTE WAY AND AMERICAN JUSTICE

American courts have not responded in the same way to all groups that use controlled substances in their religious rituals. Much depends upon the period in which a case comes before the judiciary, prevailing judicial philosophies, and the particular group involved, as well as the specific nature of the ritual and the substance in question. In the 1964 California case *People v. Woody* (61 Cal. 2d 716), for example, Native Americans successfully litigated the right to use peyote in Native American Church ritual.

The sacramental use of peyote by indigenous peoples in North America dates back thousands of years. Spanish explorers in the 1600s observed the religious use of peyote by Native Americans in Mexico and the American Southwest.[8] The peyote cactus grew in abundance south of the Rio Grande and was used as a sacrament by native priests for inducing visions. In the nineteenth century, unorganized and varied forms of this peyote religion spread to some North American tribes from the Southwest as far as California and Oklahoma, although at the same time, Spanish priests attempted to suppress it, fearing it would inhibit conversion to Catholicism.[9] Because peyote induces visions, it was branded by the Spanish as an evil that would impair both the physical and mental health of the Indians. Despite this attempted suppression of native religion, peyotism continued to travel north where it again provoked hostility among Catholic and Protestant missionaries, as well as agents of the U.S. Bureau of Indian Affairs.

Denouncing it as a "heathenish" practice, the U.S. government and missionaries attempted to prohibit peyotism as part of an explicit assimilationist policy on the part of the United States intended to transform Native Americans into good democrats, Christians, and farmers. While penalties were both threatened and inflicted upon Native Americans who engaged in peyote rituals, it was not until 1899 that a statute was enacted, in the territory of Oklahoma, specifically controlling the use of peyote.[10] Subsequently, over several decades a number of states passed statutes criminalizing the use of peyote even in religious rituals. At the national level, despite more than a half century of lobbying, antipeyotists did not win congressional approval for legislation making peyote illegal until passage of the Drug Abuse Control Act of 1965.

During the period of antipeyotist harassment in the early twentieth century, it became clear to peyotists and their supporters that gaining protection under the First Amendment would be easier if they organized as a legally incorporated church with a recognized name, officials, and established rules. And so, in 1918, in Oklahoma, a group of peyotists met and signed articles of incorporation as the Native American Church (NAC). Their church charter clearly acknowledged the importance of Christianity in belief and practice: "The purpose for which this corporation is formed is to foster and promote the religious belief of the several tribes of Indians in the State of Oklahoma, in the Christian religion with the practice of the Peyote Sacrament as commonly understood and used among the adherents of this religion in the several tribes ... and to teach the Christian religion with morality, sobriety, industry, kindly charity and right living and to cultivate a spirit of self-respect and brotherly union among the members of the Native Race of Indians."[11] This incorporation of Christian elements proved critical in the *Woody* case.

Peyote is a non-habit-forming, hallucinogenic drug derived from a small, spineless cactus growing principally in northern Mexico and southern

Texas. Peyote buttons, which are generally dried and then eaten, are extremely bitter and often produce vomiting. Peyote has psychedelic properties that produce feelings of friendliness, pleasant euphoria, relaxation, timelessness, and visual images of bright and kaleidoscopic colors or scenes involving animals or humans. In some cases it produces hallucinatory symptoms similar to those observed in paranoiac schizophrenia.[12]

The cornerstone of the peyote religion is a ceremony that is marked by the sacramental use of peyote. The ceremony is usually led by men; traditionally women were excluded, but today they may participate. The ritual usually lasts from sundown Saturday night to dawn on Sunday. A church member will sponsor a meeting to give thanks for past good fortune, to find guidance for future conduct, or because he is worried about his own or a family member's ill health. Although peyotism infuses the daily life of peyotists in the form of singing and the possession of household ritual paraphernalia (peyote rattle and drum), the monthly meetings are especially important and attract peyotists from long distances, specially and carefully dressed for the occasion. During the ten-hour ceremony, peyote buttons are passed and eaten; much of the night is spent in singing and prayer. The meeting sponsor supervises the ceremony, deciding the order of events and the amount of peyote to be consumed.

Peyotists believe that peyote is a divine plant revealed to the Native Americans and capable of working miracles; the ceremonial taking of peyote establishes communion with God or the spiritual world in general. Unlike marijuana for the Rastafarians, peyote is more than a sacrament; it is itself an object of worship, and prayers are directed to it. Also in contrast to marijuana use among Rastafarians, peyote use outside the ritual meeting is considered sacrilegious.

PSYCHEDELIC BUTTONS: THE NATIVE AMERICAN CHURCH AND THE COURTS

On April 28, 1962, a group of Navajo Native American Church members met in a hogan (a Navajo dwelling made of earth supported by timbers) in the desert near Needles, California. As with the Rastafarians, local law enforcement officials were aware of drug use during religious ceremonies and had the hogan under surveillance. Members of the congregation, who were participating in a peyote ceremony, were arrested and subsequently convicted of violating the California Health and Safety Code, which prohibits the unauthorized use of peyote. Unlike many other states, and the federal government, California, at the time of this arrest, did not grant a religious exemption for peyote use.

The convicted NAC members appealed to the California Supreme Court, arguing that since peyote is an integral part of their religious faith, invoking the Code against them abridged their right to free exercise of religion and was, therefore, unconstitutional. The California Supreme

Court agreed and overturned the lower court conviction on the grounds that criminalizing the use of peyote would remove the "theological heart" of the religion.

In his opinion in *People v. Woody,* California Supreme Court Justice Matthew Tobriner first acknowledged that for many people strict enforcement of drug laws was more important than "carv[ing] out an ... exception for a few believers in a strange faith," as peyotism has been described in the attorney general's brief for the state. But, Tobriner argued, the religious use of peyote posed little danger to the state, and the state's interest in its prohibition was, therefore, outweighed by the First Amendment interest in religious freedom held by NAC members.

In affirming the religious rights of this subculture, Justice Tobriner wrote, "In a mass society, which presses at every point toward conformity, the protection of self-expression, however unique, of the individual and the group becomes ever more important. The varying currents of the subcultures that flow into the mainstream of our national life give it depth and beauty. We preserve a greater value than an ancient tradition when we protect the rights of the Indians who honestly practiced an old religion in using peyote one night at a meeting in a desert Hogan near Needles, California."

These widely quoted and inspiring words require close examination and raise the question of the degree to which Judge Tobriner's opinion was a significant voice for American multiculturalism. First, peyotism was not, in fact, the "strange faith" the state attorney general claimed. As Judge Tobriner himself noted in his opinion, the NAC incorporated many familiar elements of Christianity; indeed, in their articles of incorporation they explicitly referred to themselves as a Christian church. Second, at the time of this decision—1964—the drug culture that would so concern American courts at a later time was not yet perceived by the nation as a major problem. Third, the qualities of peyote—which include extreme bitterness and a strong tendency to induce vomiting—would appear to place limits on its widespread use as a recreational drug.

Finally, the NAC has no political or social agenda perceived as threatening to the dominant American culture. Unlike the Indian Ghost Dance of the late nineteenth century, and some other Native American revitalization movements, peyotism does not emphasize a change in the social order. Although it is an attempt to continue significant aspects of native religion, it is not informed by a vision of whites disappearing and the land once again in possession of Native Americans. Unlike the mass energy released through the Ghost Dance, peyotism is quietistic, with each individual seeking his own road of enlightenment and self-awareness.

On balance, then, the Tobriner decision yielded, at best, a narrow point. Religious exemption for use of a drug would be permitted where the ritual was highly controlled and for the most part limited to a small, quietistic Christian subculture—little enough danger in all this. Thus, the case of

People v. Woody, although hailed as an important affirmation of cultural pluralism, can, in retrospect, only be regarded as a partial victory.

Although *Woody* was a state supreme court decision, it was widely cited and influential in state and federal courts addressing issues of First Amendment free exercise rights. Native Americans considered the issue of religious use of peyote by NAC members a settled matter of law. They were wrong. In the 1990 case of *Oregon v. Smith* (494 U.S. 872), the U.S. Supreme Court ruled that the First Amendment did not protect NAC members engaged in peyote ritual. The case involved two NAC members in Oregon, both of whom were fired from their jobs and denied unemployment benefits after participating in a sacramental peyote rite. Oregon state law disqualified employees discharged for work-related "misconduct" from receiving compensation. The men argued that the "misconduct" was, in fact, constitutionally protected religious activity. After several rounds of technical legal skirmishes, the state of Oregon sought to resolve the case in the U.S. Supreme Court. Given the large number of states (23), along with the federal government, that exempted religious peyote use from criminalization, and the principles expounded in *Woody,* no one was prepared for the Supreme Court decision, which, finding against the Native American Church members, considerably curtailed religious freedom in general and ritual use of peyote in particular.

Justice Antonin Scalia's opinion for the Court held that constitutional protection for religious rights only prevents government from coercing religious beliefs and does not compel it to support all religious practice. So-called "neutral" laws that regulate conduct, but not belief, may, he wrote, be applied to religious persons. His opinion broke new ground by abandoning the use of the compelling state interest test by which government is required to demonstrate the most significant of reasons to deny First Amendment religious rights. Scalia argued that the compelling interest test offered too much protection for religious liberty and that, in particular, the religious diversity found in the United States was a luxury that the nation could not afford.

Following this legal reasoning, the Scalia decision narrowed constitutional protection for religious conduct that would otherwise be punishable under criminal law. Critically, the opinion left to state legislatures the decision of what religious conduct would be permitted. Under Scalia's interpretation, these legislatures could, if they wished, exempt otherwise proscribed conduct—such as religious drug use—but Scalia's opinion did not hold that there was a constitutional requirement that they do so.

Anticipating that his opinion would throw religious groups upon the mercies of majoritarian legislatures, Scalia acknowledged that "leaving accommodation to the political process will place at a relative disadvantage those religious practices that are not widely engaged in." He defended this position—which seemed to many as utterly contrary to the very rights that the First Amendment was designed to protect—by writing, "[this] unavoidable consequence of democratic government must be preferred to a system in which each conscience is a law unto itself or in which judges weigh the social importance of all laws against the centrality of all religious beliefs." Such an interpretation, Scalia wrote, would "be courting anarchy, [a] danger which increases in direct proportion to the society's diversity of religious beliefs."

Justice Sandra Day O'Connor, while joining in the result of the majority, strongly disagreed with Scalia's reasoning, in particular abandoning the compelling interest test. Acknowledging that no right is absolute, she nevertheless underscored the Supreme Court's long-standing commitment to the preferred position of religious rights even when the exercise of these rights conflicts with other laws, unless such laws are "required by clear and compelling governmental interests 'of the highest order.'"

The dissenting justices—Harry Blackmun, William Brennan and Thurgood Marshall—took strong exception to the result and opinion of the court as diminishing religious rights. In several revealing comments, however, the dissenters also made clear that their openness to the religious use of peyote by members of the Native American Church specifically would not extend to religious use of marijuana by members of the Ethiopian Zion Coptic Church. These justices cited several reasons for distinguishing religious peyote use from other drugs, including marijuana: They believed that the unpleasant physiological qualities of peyote made it "self limiting" and discouraged casual, social use; they noted that drug trafficking in substances such as marijuana and heroin involved "greed and violence" and was far more extensive than peyote (the total amount of illegal peyote seized by federal authorities between 1980 and 1987 was 19.4 pounds, in contrast to the more than 15 million pounds of marijuana seized in that same period); and they distinguished between the restricted "ceremonial context" of peyote use in the Native American Church and the teaching of the Ethiopian Zion Church that "marijuana is properly smoked 'continually all day.'"

In both the *Oregon v. Smith* majority opinion and dissent, a strong signal was given to the Ethiopian Zion Coptic Church and other groups that seek to use marijuana openly in their religious life that such religious conduct will not be protected. In *Oregon v. Smith*, it is implicit that the state of Oregon, as well as the majority of the court, accepted the Federal Drug Enforcement's classification of marijuana with the most dangerous drugs, for example, heroin and LSD. And while the dissenting justices did forcefully challenge the similar classification of peyote, which they claim "rests on no evidentiary foundation at all," even they did not extend this challenge to marijuana. Thus, these dissenting justices also implicitly accepted the government's view that marijuana is harmful and dangerous.

Justice Scalia's opinion produced a firestorm of anger and reaction. Working through members of Congress, the Native American Church in coalition with the nation's major religious denominations, human rights groups, and Native American tribes and national organizations successfully lobbied for two corrective laws.[13] The first, the 1993 Religious Freedom Restoration Act (RFRA) (107 Stat. 1488), restored the pre-*Smith* compelling-government interest test. Shortly thereafter, President Bill Clinton signed additional legislation specifically granting Native Americans the right to use peyote for religious purposes (42 U.S.C. 1996a).

In 1997, however, the U.S. Supreme Court ruled, in the case of *City of Boerne v. Flores* (521 U.S. 507), that the Religious Freedom Restoration Act, which provided a higher standard of protection for religious rights than those outlined by the Court in *Smith,* could not be applied to states. Following a pattern of decision making repeated frequently by the Rehnquist Court, a majority found that, in enacting the law, Congress had exceeded its power under Section 5 of the Fourteenth Amendment. The outcome was a victory for states' rights. The decision in *Boerne* left open the question of the applicability of the RFRA with respect to the federal government. That issue was addressed in November 2005 when attorneys from the U.S. Justice Department and lawyers for the small O Centra Espirita Beneficiente Uniao Do Vegetal religious sect (UDV) appeared before the justices of the Supreme Court to argue the future of the Religious Freedom Restoration Act and, by extension, the rights of religious groups that use controlled substances in religious services.

The UDV is a very small religious group, founded in 1963 in Brazil. Its beliefs draw upon Christian theology and indigenous spirituality. UDV ceremonies include the bimonthly use of a hallucinogenic—*hoasca*—described in one court opinion as a "liquid, tea-like mixture." The plants from which it is made are listed on Schedule I of the Controlled Substances Act as well as international conventions regulating drug trafficking. In 1999 the American chapter of the UDV ran afoul of federal customs agents who seized a quantity of "tea extract" intended for ceremonial use. In response, the group sought injunctive relief in federal court to prohibit the government from restricting its "importation, possession, and use of the hallucinogenic tea" for religious purposes. A decision of the Tenth Circuit granted an injunction and appeared to hold that the RFRA protected the UDV's right to use the tea in legitimate religious ceremonies [389 F.3d 973 (2004)]. The Bush administration appealed this decision and the U.S. Supreme Court heard argument on November 1, 2005.

Although the comments of the justices during oral argument are not necessarily a reliable clue as to the outcome of a case, when the Court heard the case several justices expressed views suggesting that the Religious Freedom Restoration Act might survive this challenge and that the rights of the UDV, under that statute, might also be upheld. Justice Ruth Bader Ginsburg pointed to the exemption that Congress had granted to recognized Native American tribes wishing to make religious use of peyote, citing it as an example of the government being able to make exceptions to general laws such as the Controlled Substance Act.[14] Interestingly, Justice Scalia agreed with her, telling the government's lawyer that the peyote exception demonstrates, "you can make an exemption without the sky falling." Chief Justice John Roberts, on the bench for only a month, also seemed anxious to carve out a place for the religious use of *hoasca* tea, commenting that an exemption need not be "a once-and-for-all determination" should it later turn out that the group abused or sold the tea.

In this case the justices' comments did predict the Court's final decision. With no dissent, they agreed that the federal government's actions had, with respect to the rights of O Centro members, substantially burdened the free exercise of religion in violation of the Religious Freedom Act. Writing for the Court, Chief Justice Roberts avoided the ratification of an absolute constitutional right instead arguing that it was well within the capacity of courts to make "case-by-case consideration of religious exemptions to generally applicable rules."[15] This approach promises protection for the UDV as well as the Native American Church. It seems unlikely, however, that the Ethiopian Coptic Church will fare as well under American law. As cited in the Florida decisions, the willingness of the Coptic Church to offer the marijuana sacrament to children and to adult nonmembers inhibits courts from granting them the right to a religious exemption from the drug laws, even as the courts acknowledge the centrality of the marijuana sacrament to their religion. Rastafarian dress and hairstyle distance them from a majority of the American population as does the perception of Rastas as a group that condemns wage labor. The Rastafarians' very open, and frequent, use of marijuana, as well as their willingness to sell it, also militates against their success in gaining further religious rights. Marijuana use is viewed by a number of experts as a possible "slippery slope" ending in heroin or cocaine addiction, and continues to be stigmatized as a drug of choice for those who reject the values of the dominant culture. These opinions have repeatedly found powerful expression in the refusal of federal officials to permit the use of marijuana even for proven medical purposes such as mitigating the negative side affects of chemotherapy or aiding individuals with glaucoma.[16]

Members of religious groups who claim the right to use controlled substances in religious ritual assert one of the most cherished American values: that of the free exercise of religion. In particular, they raise the question of whether religious practices that are not widely engaged in and are perceived as threatening to the dominant culture can find protection under the First Amendment.

Justice Scalia's view, in *Smith,* that majoritarian legislatures are the proper arena in which religious groups must seek to win their rights—in these cases, to win a religious exemption for drug use—imposes a heavy burden on groups that are often small and outside the mainstream. Members of the Native American Church finally succeeded, in part because the impact of the Scalia opinion reached far beyond the NAC, into the heart of American religion and, in part because of the special legal relationship between Native Americans and the government of the United States. For the moment, it appears that the Supreme Court will engage in individual assessments of the right to use drugs in religious ceremonies in which both the particular drug, and the cultural values of church members, will be subject to judicial judgment.

NOTES

1. See Leonard E. Barrett Sr., *The Rastafarians: Sounds of Cultural Dissonance* (Boston: Beacon Press, 1988) and William F. Lewis, *Soul Rebels* (Prospect Heights, IL: Waveland Press, 1993).

2. *Town v. Florida ex rel. Reno*, Brief for the Appellant to the Supreme Court of the United States (March 31, 1980), 13a.

3. Joe Oglesby, "Probe Aims at Shutting Down Coptics," *Miami Herald*, December 6, 1978.

4. *United States v. Morison*, Motion to Dismiss the Indictment (Case No. 79–379-CR-WMH), 3.

5. Ibid., 10.

6. *New York Times*, May 1, 1991, B22.

7. *United States v. Morison*, Motion to Dismiss, 6.

8. Native American Rights Fund, *Legal Review* 20 (Winter/Spring 1995), 7.

9. Alice Beck Kehoe, *The Ghost Dance: Ethnohistory and Revitalization* (Fort Worth: Holt, Rinehart, 1989), 108.

10. Omar Stewart, *Peyote Religion* (Norman: University of Oklahoma Press, 1987), 130–31.

11. Ibid., 224.

12. Ibid., 3.

13. Native American Rights Fund, *Legal Review*, 19.

14. Linda Greenhouse, "Justices Weighing Narcotics Policy Against Needs of a Church," *New York Times*, November 2, 2005, A26. Subsequent quotes in this paragraph are also from this article.

15. *Gonzales, Attorney General v. O Centro Espirita Beneficente Uniao Do Vegetal*, 546 U.S.___ (2006).

16. The case of *Gonzales v. Raich* [545 U.S. ___ (2005)] raised the question of whether states could permit their residents to use marijuana to relieve their illnesses without violating the federal Controlled Substance Act. In a 6–3 decision the Court ruled no.

PART III

Gender

CHAPTER 9

Women's Nature, Women's Lives, Women's Rights

American law has been based on gender stereotypes defining the woman's world as that of home and hearth. Constrained by the view of women as made by nature for childbirth and childcare, women's lives were shaped into a subculture whose sole criterion was gender, though this was modified by race and class. The myth of women as fragile, dependent, childlike creatures formed the basis of laws that created and maintained a reality in which women, often under the guise of protective law, were denied access to political power and economic resources.

LIMITS ON CIVIC PARTICIPATION

The image of woman as a child or an appendage of her husband eased the way for a broad denial of her political rights. Although the franchise has been regarded as fundamental to a democratic republic throughout the nineteenth century, armed with these images, lawmakers denied women a constitutionally guaranteed right to vote.

In 1872 Virginia Minor sued the state of Missouri, claiming that the actions of its officials, prohibiting her and other women from voting in state and federal elections, violated the "privileges and immunities of citizenship" granted by the recently adopted Fourteenth Amendment. In this case, *Minor v. Happersett* [21 Wall. 162 (1875)], the U.S. Supreme Court held that the right to vote was not necessarily one of the privileges or immunities of citizenship, and specifically that suffrage was not coextensive with citizenship.

The heart of the Court's reasoning in this extraordinary decision lay in two conclusions: First, that since virtually all women in all jurisdictions had historically been denied the right to vote, it was not inappropriate, nor indeed unconstitutional, for state governments to continue that which they had always done, even in light of this new civil rights amendment. Chief Justice Morrison Waite wrote that given the long history of women's political exclusion, "it is certainly now too late to contend that a government is not republican within the meaning of this guaranty in the Constitution, because women are not made voters." Despite the plaintiff's accusation that the denial of the vote to women was an egregious violation of the spirit of the Republic, the Court also concluded that sex was merely another perfectly reasonable criterion, along with age, property-holding status, being of "quiet and reasonable behavior," and length of residence, by which states might grant or withhold the right to vote. After *Minor, w*omen activists intensified efforts to win the vote through a federal constitutional amendment or more enlightened state laws. In 1884 Belva Lockwood, a lawyer living in Washington, D.C., drew attention to women's exclusion from the political process by running a full campaign for the office of president. She said, "I cannot vote but I can be voted for." Women only won the constitutional right to vote in 1920 with the ratification of the Nineteenth Amendment.

Consistent with the view that a woman's domain was home and children, virtually all local governments similarly exempted women from jury duty, unless they specifically volunteered. This was a double burden; it not only excluded women from full participation in the civic culture, but it also denied women plaintiffs and defendants a jury of their peers. The U.S. Supreme Court upheld this practice until 1975 when it struck down, citing the Sixth Amendment, a jury registration statute that permitted but did not obligate women to serve on juries. In this case, *Taylor v. Louisiana* (419 U.S. 522), the justices reasoned that, "Restricting jury service to only special groups or excluding identifiable segments playing major roles in the community cannot be squared with the constitutional concept of jury trial.

While the issues of women's right to vote and sex discrimination in jury duty have been resolved, women's full participation in the service of their country is still circumscribed by national law. National policy obligates men but not women to register for a military draft and has long prohibited women from serving in combat positions. The 1980 Supreme Court decision in *Rostker v. Goldberg* [453 U.S. 57 (1981)] upheld the constitutional authority of Congress to exclude women from even having to *register* for any future military draft. Writing for the majority, Justice William Rehnquist stressed judicial deference to congressional authority over matters of national defense and military affairs. His opinion accepted the congressional view, rejected by a lower federal court, that since the "purpose of military registration was to prepare for a draft of *combat troops*," registering women was not worth the effort.

Belva Lockwood, one of the first women lawyers in the United States, ran for the presidency in 1884 to draw attention to women's struggle for suffrage. This *Puck Magazine* cartoon was one of many publicizing her campaign. Photo from the collection of Jill Norgren.

Rejection of women for combat service reinforces the stereotype of women as physically weak and in need of male protection. The successful performance of women in the Persian Gulf and Iraq wars, however, has encouraged Defense Department officials to review longstanding restrictions on women in combat positions and to create new mixed-sex "forward support companies." Women have, de facto, been operating in combat areas. Opinion in Congress remains sharply divided on whether to lift the prohibition, although members understand that barring women from "direct" combat duty limits their promotion to senior ranks. In upholding restrictions on women's full participation in the military, American lawmakers fail to consider whether such limitations hinder the ability of women to change their status in society, sending the message, according to Congresswoman Loretta Sanchez, "that women can't do this job."[1]

LEGAL LIMITS ON EDUCATION AND EMPLOYMENT

Many people argue that the burdens of second-class citizenship are balanced by the high regard in which wives and mothers are held in American cultural ideology. This high—even noble—regard does not, unfortunately, translate into fair and equal economic currency. This is true for women in the domestic sphere, and even more so when they seek participation in the public sphere.

Economically the formal laws and informal practices discriminating against women have been countless. The view of women as "only" wives and mothers, and less capable by their nature of intellectual reasoning, meant that they did not require higher education. Women were consistently kept out of educational institutions necessary for economic success. Only recently have such educational opportunities for women in colleges and professional schools opened up to them in relation to their numbers in the population. Even so, studies as recent as the 1990s demonstrated that school was a place of unequal opportunity for girls and women, with teachers, for example, calling on girls less frequently in class and offering them less constructive criticism, damaging their chances of obtaining scholarships, getting into college, and doing well while there.[2] Moreover, although Title IX of the 1972 Higher Education Amendments barred sex discrimination in schools and colleges that receive federal aid, the Supreme Court's 1984 decision in *Grove City College v. Bell* (465 U.S. 555) limited the scope of that legislation. In response, in 1988 Congress passed the Civil Rights Restoration Act, legislation intended to clarify the application of Title IX and, thus, lessen the future impact of the *Grove City* decision. Debate continues about gender rights in the classroom and in school-sponsored athletic training where funding has historically favored boy's and men's sports teams.[3]

Perhaps the most closely watched case of recent years involving sex discrimination in the classroom was decided in 1996. In *U.S. v. Virginia* (518 U.S. 515) the Supreme Court was asked to determine if the males-only admission policy of the state-supported Virginia Military Institute (VMI), a school dedicated to producing "citizen-soldiers," violated the Fourteenth Amendment's Equal Protection Clause. Answering for the Court, Justice Ruth Bader Ginsburg wrote that VMI had failed to demonstrate "exceedingly persuasive justification" for its gender-based, single-sex policy: "However 'liberally' this plan serves the State's sons, it makes no provision whatever for her daughters. That is not equal protection." Ginsburg pointed to the successful entry of women into the federal military academies and their subsequent careers in the nation's military as evidence that Virginia's fears for the future of VMI "may not be solidly grounded." She concluded that "[T]here is no reason to believe that the admission of women capable of all activities required of VMI cadets would destroy the Institute rather than enhance its capacity to serve the 'more perfect Union.'" It remains to be seen, particularly in elementary and secondary education, whether Ginsburg's opinion, one that appears to accept single-sex schooling where genuinely equal conditions, both tangible and intangible, exist, will encourage gender-segregated teaching (see Detroit's male academy, chapter 3).

Even as women have overcome the formidable obstacles to higher education, informal hiring practices and formal law often prevented them from practicing their professions and establishing professional status equal to that of men. Women educated as lawyers in the nineteenth century, for example, were told by the Supreme Court that it was not a violation of their Fourteenth Amendment rights to be barred from practice by state law.

In 1872, Mrs. Myra Bradwell, a resident of Illinois, was refused a license to practice law on the grounds that "as a married women [she] would be bound neither by her express contracts nor by those implied contracts which it is the policy of law to create between attorney and client." The U.S. Supreme Court held in *Bradwell v. Illinois* [83 U.S. 130 (1873)] that although not expressly excluded, it was never the intention of the Illinois legislature to allow women to practice law. Writing for the majority in *Bradwell*, Justice Samuel Miller, who asserted that "God designed the sexes to occupy different spheres of action," emphasized the right of state governments to control and regulate professional licenses. Justice Joseph Bradley, in a famous concurring opinion, took up the theme of "women's place" and the economic limitations properly imposed upon them:

... the civil law, as well as nature herself, has always recognized a wide difference in the respective spheres and destinies of man and women. Man is, or should be, woman's protector and defender. The natural and proper timidity and delicacy which belongs to the female sex evidently unfits it for many of the occupations of civil life. The constitution of the family organization, which is founded in the divine ordinance, as well as in the nature of things, indicates the domestic sphere as that which properly belongs to the domain and functions of womanhood. The harmony, not to say identity, of interests and views which belong, or should belong, to the family institution is repugnant to the idea of a woman adopting a distinct and independent career from that of her husband. So firmly fixed was this sentiment in the founders of the common law that it became a maxim of that system of jurisprudence that a woman had no legal existence separate from her husband, who was regarded as her head and representative in the social state ...

In nonprofessional occupations, it was accepted that women would be workers, as indeed they were, in many unskilled and semiskilled positions. At the beginning of the twentieth century, a growing reform movement resulted in legislation that improved conditions of all workers.

However, to the extent that some of these protective labor laws were directed specifically at women, exempting them, for example, from certain hazardous or strenuous work, these laws reinforced the stereotypes of women as weaker and less capable than men, and resulted in excluding them from a wide range of blue-collar work.

In 1903 the Oregon state legislature passed an act limiting the number of hours women could be employed "in any mechanical establishment, or factory, or laundry" to ten hours during any one day. This protective legislation was resisted by employers. One disgruntled laundry owner— Curt Muller—after having been convicted of violating the law, brought suit, charging that the law, by restricting the right to contract, violated the Fourteenth Amendment due process and equal protection rights of employers and employees.

Mr. Muller undoubtedly expected a sympathetic hearing from the U.S. Supreme Court that had, only two years before, in *Lochner v. New York* [198 U.S. 45 (1905)], invalidated a New York law regulating the number of hours that any worker, male or female, could be required to work in bakeries. The Court's reasoning was that the law was not a legitimate exercise of state police power, but "an unreasonable, unnecessary and arbitrary interference with the right and liberty of the individual to contract in relation to his labor," and thus unconstitutional. In *Muller v. Oregon* [208 U.S. 412 (1908)], however, the Court found that the difference between the sexes was sufficient legal reason to uphold the state's use of its regulatory powers. Its reasoning paved the way for a variety of sex-based discriminatory laws. In *Muller* Justice David Brewer wrote:

… [that] woman's physical structure and the performance of maternal functions place her at a disadvantage in the struggle for subsistence is obvious. This is especially true when the burdens of motherhood are upon her. Even when they are not, by abundant testimony of the medical fraternity continuance for a long time on her feet at work, repeating this from day to day, tends to injurious effects upon the body, and, as healthy mothers are essential to vigorous offspring, the physical well-being of woman becomes an object of public interest and care in order to preserve the strength and vigor of the race … history discloses the fact that woman has always been dependent upon man. He established his control at the outset by superior physical strength, and this control in various forms, with diminishing intensity, has continued to the present …. Differentiated by these matters from the other sex, she is properly placed in a class by herself, and legislation designed for her protection may be sustained, even when like legislation is not necessary for men, and could not be sustained.

While today the language in *Muller* stands as a remnant of the Victorian age, the ideas expressed in this decision persisted well into the twentieth century, affecting women's employment opportunities. As late as 1948, in the case of *Goesaert v. Cleary* [335 U.S. 464 (1948)], the U.S. Supreme Court upheld a Michigan law forbidding any female to act as a bartender unless she was the wife or daughter of a male owner. Justice Felix Frankfurter, in his opinion for the majority, dismissed in a humorous aside, what many, including Justices Rutledge, Douglas, and Murphy, in their dissent, held as central—the notion that the Michigan law was nothing more than a veiled attempt to limit a profitable occupation to men.

The lack of a highly organized women's movement during the 1950s and early 1960s resulted in few significant changes in the legal view of women's employment rights. For example, courts upheld local laws and regulations that mandated that women, even in the earliest stages of pregnancy, resign positions as schoolteachers and, until litigated in the late 1960s and early 1970s, that women airline stewardesses were not allowed to continue their jobs past the age of 35 or if they got married. In many occupations women, of course, were never or barely considered at all, relegated, for example, to the lower-status and lower-paying jobs of nurse rather than physician, matron rather than police officer, secretary rather than corporate executive, and waitress rather than bartender.

National legislative efforts to provide redress and prevent further discrimination against women in employment—reinforced by state and local initiatives—finally met success when Congress passed the Equal Pay Act of 1963 forbidding sex discrimination in wages and Title VII of the 1964 Civil Rights Act barring an employer from discriminating against any employee because of sex (as well as race, religion, and national origin) in hiring, firing, promoting, compensating, or in any other aspects of employment. Title VII did not specifically address questions of employment discrimination arising from pregnancy. Thus, in 1978, to overturn the effects of the Supreme Court's ruling in *General Electric Co. v. Gilbert* [429 U.S. 125 (1976)], stating that discrimination on the basis of pregnancy was not sex discrimination under Title VII, Congress passed the Pregnancy Discrimination Act (PDA). This law amends Title VII by prohibiting employment discrimination against pregnant women, for example, firing a woman because she has become pregnant.

An important test of the Pregnancy Discrimination Act, and California civil rights law, occurred several years later. This case, *California Federal Savings and Loan v. Guerra* [479 U.S. 272 (1987)], expressed women's concern that pregnancy, which fulfills critical personal and societal needs, not impede women's careers. The litigation also demonstrated a major division within the women's movement. On one side were women's organizations that argued that women have special biological needs that should receive special treatment in law such as pregnancy leave. Other feminist groups, however, contended that preferential treatment, harkening back to the era of *Muller*, leads to job segregation, lower wages, and the stereotyping of women as childbearers. These feminists insisted that all laws must be sex-neutral and that such neutrality was the intent of Congress in passing Title VII.

In *Guerra* the U.S. Supreme Court ruled that requiring an employer to provide unpaid pregnancy leave, and to guarantee a comparable job upon return to the workplace did not violate Title VII's antidiscrimination mandate because Congress intended that the Pregnancy Discrimination Act amend Title VII.

The critical role of Congress in helping women, and men, balance family responsibilities with the demands of employment was again demonstrated when, in 1993, national lawmakers passed the much-debated Family and Medical Leave Act (FMLA). This legislation mandates that companies with more than fifty employees provide up to twelve weeks unpaid leave for workers to care for a newborn or adopted child, or a critically ill family member.

Even with the passage of these many acts, it has become clear that the mere passage of legislation demanding equal treatment in employment for women, as in the case of racial minorities, was not sufficient to overcome widely held and deeply ingrained attitudes that kept women out of many occupations or prevented women from receiving equal or comparable pay.[4] Armed with legislation, executive orders, and the Constitution itself, women followed the lead of the African American civil rights movement in pressing for affirmative plans in both public and private employment that would incorporate them into the labor force at all levels consistent with their numbers in the population and with their skills and training.

By the 1980s men began responding to affirmative action for women, as they had to affirmative action claims on behalf of African Americans, by taking their grievances to court. Holding that such affirmative-action plans violated both the equal protection provisions of the Constitution and the intent to bar all discrimination expressed in Title VII, Paul E. Johnson, a transportation worker passed over in favor of a woman for promotion to the position of road dispatcher with the Santa Clara, California Transportation Agency as a result of a voluntary affirmative-action plan, sued the agency. The U.S. Supreme Court decided against Mr. Johnson. In the 1987 ruling in *Johnson v. Santa Clara County Transportation Agency* (480 U.S. 616), the Court upheld voluntary affirmative-action plans instituted by employers, including employers who had not previously been cited in court for discriminating against women, as long as these plans were flexible, gradual, and limited in their adverse effects on other groups. In its decision, the Court made clear that qualified individuals *could* benefit from such affirmative-action plans even where they could not prove that they were personally victims of past discrimination.

A scathing dissent written by Justice Antonin Scalia, joined by Chief Justice William Rehnquist and Justice Byron White, attacked the decision as "converting [Title VII] from a guarantee that race or sex will not be the basis for employment determinations, to a guarantee that it often will … we [now] effectively replace the goal of a discrimination-free society with the quite incompatible goal of proportionate representation by … sex in the workplace." Justice Scalia held that the traditional absence of women in road-maintenance jobs was due primarily to "[the absence] of women eager to shoulder pick and shovel," and stated that he found it unacceptable to use Title VII to overcome the effect of "societal attitudes that have limited the entry of ... a particular sex, into certain jobs." Ignoring the historical facts of past discrimination in employment against women, Justice Scalia added that "the only losers [by this decision] ... are the Johnsons of the country."

Sixteen years later, however, Chief Justice Rehnquist surprised court watchers when he authored the majority opinion in *Nevada v. Hibbs* [538 U.S. (2003)] upholding the right of state employees to sue in federal courts for money damages under the enforcement provisions of the Family and Medical Leave Act. For many years Rehnquist had led the Court in efforts to protect states' rights (see *City of Boerne v. Flores,* chapter 8 and *Alabama v. Garrett,* chapter 11). In this instance, however, he agreed that William Hibbs, who had been fired by the state of Nevada while on leave caring for his injured wife, had suffered discrimination barred by the FMLA and that Congress had clearly stated its intention in the language of the statute to permit lawsuits for damages in federal courts.

The Chief Justice began by pointing out that government action to address and prevent gender discrimination is subject to heightened judicial scrutiny. Gender-based classifications must serve "important governmental objectives" [*Craig v. Boren,* 429 U.S. 190 (1976)]. He wrote that the record of state laws discriminating on the basis of sex as evidenced by *Bradwell, Mueller,* and *Goesaert,* was "weighty enough to justify the enactment of prophylactic ... legislation [FMLA]." The act survived heightened scrutiny because its provisions were narrowly related to the congressional objective of addressing gender discrimination. In ruling for Mr. Hibbs, Rehnquist noted that the FMLA "attacks the formerly state-sanctioned stereotype that only women are responsible for family caregiving."[5]

MARRIAGE, MONEY, AND THE LAW

Discrimination in employment has not meant, of course, that women do not, and have not, worked. But in addition to being limited in the choice of occupations, law and social custom have supported the male view that women could not and should not be relied upon for family economic security, that they are secondary wage earners appropriately given less salary, responsibility, and benefits. The idea of the male as major breadwinner has dominated, serving as a rationale for discrimination against women who would compete for jobs and promotions, even where they were, in fact, head of household. This became an issue in lawsuits involving national chains such as Sears and Lucky Stores.[6]

As a result of the efforts of the women's movement since the 1970s, there have been major changes in virtually all aspects of the laws and practices formerly used to discriminate against women in the economic sphere.

Fighting the assumption that the family is dependent only upon male earnings and benefits, women attacked administrative practices and social security laws that denied them equal benefits. In *Frontiero v. Richardson* [411 U.S. 677 (1973)], the U.S. Supreme Court ruled that the Army's regulations permitting males in the armed services an automatic dependency allowance for their wives but requiring servicewomen to prove that their husbands were dependent violated women's equal protection rights.[7]

In the subsequent cases of *Weinberger v. Wiesenfeld* [420 U.S. 636 (1975)] and *Califano v. Goldfarb* [430 U.S. 199 (1977)], the Supreme Court struck down social security laws, which the justices argued were based on a traditional way of thinking about females as dependents. Private-sector pension plans and payment schemes that discriminate against women have also been successfully challenged in the courts.

Law has not only differentiated married men from married women with respect to employment benefits, such as pensions, but, for much of U.S. history, undermined women's economic independence by limiting a married woman's property rights. Until the last of these state laws was abolished in the 1970s, husbands could control a wife's property, wages, if she earned any, and her legal responsibilities and identity.[8]

Divorce, inadequate and unpaid alimony and child support, domestic violence, teen pregnancy, inadequate education, physical and mental illness, chronic disability, widowhood, and immigration are among the personal situations, along with economic downturns and natural disasters, that leave women and their children in need of public assistance. In 1996, during the administration of Democratic president Bill Clinton, in a bipartisan move to "end welfare as we know it," Congress enacted major changes in the federal welfare law. The 60-year-old Aid to Families with Dependent Children (AFDC) policy was "scrapped," replaced by the Temporary Assistance for Needy Families (TANF) program.[9] Using a block grant rather than a matching-grant funding approach, TANF gave the states extensive authority to operate programs of their own design. Work-participation requirements were established and a lifetime limit imposed on participation in TANF. Restrictive provisions were imposed on recent legal immigrants. Professor Dorothy Roberts has said that TANF 'brought both an end to the federal guarantee of assistance to poor children and an increasing emphasis on marriage as the solution to poverty."[10]

TANF has reduced welfare caseloads and made welfare offices seem like employment agencies, but in 2000, according to a report by the National Association of Social Workers, "nearly 40 percent of former welfare recipients continued to live below the federal poverty line," while the percentage of families living in deep poverty grew.[11] Nearly 50 percent of female-headed households with children under five were living below the poverty level versus 15 percent of families with two adults.[12] Law professor Martha Davis suggests that, in the face of these statistics, "the question is how to change the debate about poverty and welfare so the fact that women are disproportionately poor [as compared with men] is recognized as a key factor rather than being viewed as irrelevant or accidental."[13] She has proposed that activists focus on litigation strategies designed to keep the facts of the unequal economic situation of women and their children before the public. She also suggests that advocates for women focus on state constitutions and laws because TANF has increased the significance of state policy.

THE STRUGGLE FOR REPRODUCTIVE AUTONOMY

The creation and maintenance of a subculture of female dependency and powerlessness have been both expressed and furthered by laws criminalizing birth control and abortion, which denied women control over their own bodies. Understanding that the cultural definition of woman's nature as childbearer and nurturer restricted her opportunities in the larger society, in recent years many women were eager to unburden themselves of the laws criminalizing birth control and abortion, laws that not only denied women the right to make these important personal decisions for themselves, without the aid of the state, but also resulted in unwanted pregnancies.

Early litigation in the line of cases brought to establish women's reproductive freedom included that of *Poe v. Ullman* [367 U.S. 497 (1961)], challenging the constitutionality of the Connecticut statute providing that, "Any person who uses any drug, medicinal article or instrument for the purpose of preventing conception shall be fined not less than fifty dollars or imprisoned not less than sixty days ... and that [a]ny person who assists, abets, counsels, causes, hires or commands another to commit any offense may be prosecuted and punished as if he were the principal offender." Although the majority opinion of the Court dismissed the appeal because of "the lack of immediacy" of any threat of prosecution, Justice William Brennan, in his concurrence, pointed to the central but unspoken issue in the case: "The true controversy in this case is over the opening of birth-control clinics on a large scale; it is that which the State has prevented in the past, not the use of contraceptives by isolated and individual married couples." The Connecticut prohibition fell disproportionately on poor women, as it was generally acknowledged that middle-class women received birth-control information and could purchase birth-control supplies in Connecticut.

Leaving aside for the moment this issue of class equity, and returning to the main issue of reproductive freedom, the extensive dissents in *Poe*, introduced by Justices William O. Douglas and John M. Harlan, advanced much of the reasoning subsequently used in *Griswold v. Connecticut* [381 U.S. 479 (1965)], which, four years later, struck down the contested Connecticut statute. Specifically, in *Poe*, Douglas and Harlan spoke of a zone of privacy that protected the *marital* bedroom from state intrusion regarding the use of birth control:

The regulation as applied in this case touches the relationship between man and wife. It reaches into the intimacies of the marriage relationship. If we imagine a regime of full enforcement of the law in the manner of an Anthony Comstock, we would reach the point where search warrants issued and officers appeared in bedrooms to find out what went on. It is said that this is not that case. And so it is not. But when the State makes "use" a crime and applies the criminal sanction to man and wife, the State has entered the innermost sanctum of the home. If it can make this law, it can enforce it. And proof of its violation necessarily involves an inquiry into the relations between man and wife.

That is an invasion of the privacy that is implicit in a free society.

Justice Harlan continued with the theme of the relationship of privacy to the home, arguing that a woman's right to privacy in the use of birth control derives not from her status as woman, but as householder. His opinion outlines a right of privacy that not only protects the physical integrity of the home, as generally understood in Fourth Amendment litigation, but that must include "the life which characteristically has its place in the home."

This theme, the right to privacy inhering in the marital relationship, became the basis for the opinion of the Court in *Griswold*. It is striking that in terms of *women's* rights neither Douglas's opinion for the Court nor the three concurring opinions vest the right to be free of state regulation in matters expressed as a "right to privacy," in the status of being a woman. Rather, this right is vested in the marital *relationship*. Seven years later, in another birth-control case (involving distribution of birth control to a single woman), *Eisenstadt v. Baird* [405 U.S. 438 (1972)], the Supreme Court moved a step closer to giving constitutional support to the comprehensive right to reproductive autonomy, by holding that "if the right to privacy means anything, it is the right of the *individual*, married or single, to be free from unwarranted governmental intrusion into matters so fundamentally affecting a person as the decision whether to bear or beget a child."

The now famous 1973 U.S. Supreme Court decision decriminalizing abortion, *Roe v. Wade* (410 U.S. 113), extends the doctrine outlined in the birth-control cases that "the right to privacy grounded in the concept of personal liberty encompasses the woman's right to decide whether to terminate her pregnancy." The Court noted that laws criminalizing abortion are "not of ancient, or even of common-law origin, but rather gain momentum only in the latter half of the nineteenth century." Acknowledging the special relationship women have to childbirth, the Court said:

This right of privacy ... is broad enough to encompass a woman's decision whether or not to terminate her pregnancy. The detriment that the State would impose upon the pregnant woman by denying this choice altogether is apparent. Specific and direct harm medically diagnosable even in early pregnancy may be involved. Maternity, or additional offspring, may force upon the woman a distressful life and future. Psychological harm may be imminent. Mental and physical health may be taxed by child care. There is also the distress, for all concerned, associated with the unwanted child, and there is the problem of bringing a child into a family already unable, psychologically and otherwise, to care for it. In other cases, as in this one, the additional difficulties and continuing stigma of unwed motherhood may be involved.

Reluctant to give the woman full autonomy, however, the *Roe* Court specified that any decision should be made by a woman "in consultation with her physician." In striking down state antiabortion statutes as unconstitutional, in other ways the justices held that this fundamental right of personal liberty was not unqualified. The right of women, they said, must be considered against "compelling" state interests, including the state's right to protect maternal and prenatal life. The Court ruled that in the second and third trimesters of pregnancy, states could regulate or even prohibit abortion:

With respect to the State's important and legitimate interest in the health of the mother, the "compelling" point ... is at approximately the end of the first trimester ... from and after this point, a State may regulate the abortion procedure to the extent that the regulation reasonably relates to the preservation and protection of maternal health. Examples of permissible state regulation in this area are requirements as to the qualifications of the person who is to perform the abortion ... [and] the facility in which the procedure is to be performed.

With respect to the State's ... interest in potential life, the "compelling" point is at viability ... If the State is interested in protecting fetal life after viability, it may go so far as to proscribe abortion during that period, except when it is necessary to preserve the life or health of the mother.

Immediately following the *Roe* decision, right-to-life groups, unhappy with the outcome of the litigation, initiated a highly organized lobby effort addressed to Congress, state legislatures, local city councils, and the media. Although their long-range aims were to reverse the Supreme Court decision through constitutional amendment or a new case overturning *Roe,* for the immediate future they concentrated on weakening the decision by urging legislatures to withhold public funding of abortions, and in other ways to create obstacles for women who wished to have abortions. An early antiabortion movement success came with respect to the issue of funding: In 1980, in the case of *Harris v. McRae* (448 U.S. 297), the U.S. Supreme Court upheld the so-called Hyde Amendment by which Congress had limited federal funding of abortions under the Medicaid program to those necessary to save the life of the mother. Subsequently, in *Webster v. Reproductive Health Services* [492 U.S. 490 (1989)], the Court challenged *Roe*'s trimester formulation by upholding the legality of viability tests on a fetus thought to be at least of 20 weeks gestation, and ruled that states may further limit government involvement in the provision of abortion services by prohibiting the use of public facilities or public employees.

In the 1980s and 1990s the movement to overturn *Roe* became highly political and sometimes physically violent. Both Ronald Reagan and

George H. Bush campaigned for the presidency on antiabortion plat-forms; Bill Clinton was elected to the presidency on a pro-choice platform. Each president influenced the direction of Justice Department policy in abortion litigation, the nominations made for federal judgeships—in particular, the Supreme Court—and the nature of encouragement given to pro- and antiabortion groups. During the Reagan and George H. Bush administrations, Justice Department lawyers asked the Supreme Court to overturn *Roe* in six separate cases.

Increasingly in these years, antichoice demonstrations at the site of reproductive health clinics resulted in confrontation and physical injuries to clients and clinic staff. In 1994 Congress enacted, and President Clinton signed into law, legislation intended to provide safe access to reproduc-tive health clinics. The Freedom of Access to Clinic Entrances Act (FACE), passed over the objections of antiabortion groups concerned about infringement upon First Amendment rights, makes it a federal crime to block access to clinics that provide reproductive services. In a number of states, however, this has become a moot issue as the number of abortion providers has decreased by 11 percent from 1996 to 2000 and 87 percent of U.S. counties have no abortion provider.[14]

The appointment, in the Reagan-Bush years, of several Supreme Court justices thought to disagree with the *Roe* decision led to speculation that the Supreme Court's narrowing of *Roe*'s protections would ultimately result in the decision being overturned. A critical test occurred in the 1992 case *Planned Parenthood v. Casey* (505 U.S. 833). In *Casey*, a divided Court reaf-firmed the constitutional right to abortion, opening its opinion with the words, "Liberty finds no refuge in a jurisprudence of doubt…. The essen-tial holding of *Roe v. Wade* should be retained and once again reaffirmed." But, using Justice Sandra Day O'Connor's new judicial test—whether a state abortion regulation has the purpose or effect of imposing an "undue burden"—the Court upheld the right of states to try to persuade a woman not to have an abortion, to impose a 24-hour waiting period prior to an abortion, and to require teenagers to have the consent of one parent or a judge before the procedure. The "undue burden" test does not require strict judicial scrutiny, opening the way for greater state and federal of regulation of abortion. In *Casey*, however, the majority did strike down one regulation, a rule requiring that a wife notify her husband before an abortion. The justices reasoned that, "A state may not give to a man the kind of dominion over his wife that parents exercise over their children." The Court also chose to bar the regulation on the grounds that such notifi-cation might result in physical or psychological abuse against the wife.

With the composition of the U.S. Supreme Court changing, new chal-lenges to *Roe* are occurring as the struggle to control women's bodies continues.[15] The Court's continuing endorsement of *Casey*'s "undue burden" test, most recently in *Stenberg v. Carhart* [530 U.S. 914 (2000)], a contentious test of partial-birth abortion, affirms that the basic right established in *Roe* remains, although greatly modified by regulations involving notification, informed consent, waiting periods, and place of service, and affected by ability to pay. The Food and Drug Administration's approval in 1997 of Plan B Emergency Contraception may further reduce the demand for abortion; it may also prompt new litigation as proponents and opponents contest, for example, whether the drug must be obtained by prescription or purchased over the counter.

The new world of biomedical technology has also prompted legal debate about a range of reproductive issues barely considered—outside the pages of science fiction—until recent years. The capacity to store eggs, sperm, and embryos raises questions about an individual's right to have—or not to have—a child in an entirely new context. The use of a deceased relative's stored sperm for artificial insemination has been contested in courts, and divorced husbands have sued former wives to bar the implantation of frozen embryos. The federal government has refused to acknowledge the survivorship rights of a child conceived with frozen sperm after the death of the father. This "brave new world" compels the law to address issues of reproduction that remain central to the human condition but about which society has little experience.

HARASSMENT AND VIOLENCE AGAINST WOMEN

Gender-based violence in the United States has been described as an "epidemic" by many experts.[16] Despite living in a culture that calls upon men to honor and protect them, women find that they are frequently the victims of physical and sexual assault. Historically, domestic violence and harassment at the workplace and school were considered private matters, often neither criminalized by law nor penalized by civil action. For many years rape laws required corroboration from a third party, a standard that defeated most rape convictions.

Advocates for women have long been concerned about America's culture of violence expressed as a gender war. At the turn of the twentieth century reformers advocated against the poverty that forced some women into prostitution, a profession that often exposes women to violence. Later, Andrea Dworkin and Catherine MacKinnon led a movement in which they argued that "pornography is sex discrimination which degrades women, portrays them as appropriate and deserving targets for sexual violence, [and] denies them equal opportunities."[17] As the modern women's movement organized, specific sites of gender violence were identified and remedies for its alleviation, or punishment, proposed. In addition to the shadowy worlds of pornography and prostitution, the everyday worlds of home and workplace were marked as places where women experience harassment and assault.

Opponents of sexual harassment, behavior described both as "the assertion of power by men over women perceived to be in a vulnerable position with respect to male authority" and unlawful discrimination, have armed themselves with the provisions of the 1964 Civil Rights Act's Title VII banning discrimination in employment and the Education Amendment Act's Title IX prohibiting discrimination in educational programs, as well as standards established by the EEOC (the Equal Employment Opportunity Commission).[18] Women have been urged to file complaints with the EEOC. Statistics show that while men claim harassment at the workplace, women are overwhelmingly the victims of this discriminatory behavior. In 2004 the EEOC received 13,136 charges of sexual harassment; 85 percent of these charges were filed by women.[19]

Along with the EEOC, courts at every level have been important arbiters of what will be considered unlawful sexual harassment, although initially, in the 1970s, judges rarely agreed that it affected the conditions of work for women much less issues of pay and promotion.[20] Among the questions put to judges were whether a company or organization must pay money damages for the harassing actions of an employee; whether victims had to prove that the claimed harassing behavior was "unwelcome"; whether evidence of a victim's dress, manner, and speech could be introduced at trial to argue that she had invited attention; whether there must be proven injury, or tangible loss, rather than a feeling of annoyance or distress; whether courts should use a "reasonable woman," or victim, rather than "reasonable person" test through which to interpret the law; and whether same-sex claims of harassment could be successfully asserted under Title VII.

In an important breakthrough, in 1986, the Supreme Court found that a hostile work environment, in which there was explicit sexual talk or pictures, even with no "quid pro quo" demands for sexual favors, should be considered unlawful harassment. Writing for the Court in *Meritor Savings Bank v. Vinson* (477 U.S. 57) Justice Rehnquist said that the creation of such circumstances was prohibited by law when it was "sufficiently severe or pervasive 'to alter the conditions of [the victim's] employment and create an abusive working environment.'" He wrote that "employees have a right to work in an environment free from discriminatory intimations, ridicule and insult" and that Mechelle Vinson was correct in asserting that unwelcome sexual advances create an offensive environment in violation of Title VII.

Five years after *Meritor* a federal appeals court addressed the critical question of whose "perspective" or standards should be used in the determination of whether conduct constitutes unlawful sexual harassment. In *Ellison v. Brady* [924 F.2d 872 (9th Cir. 1991)] Circuit Judge Robert Beezer wrote,

... we believe that in evaluating the severity and pervasiveness of sexual harassment, we should focus on the perspective of the victim. If we only examined whether a reasonable person would engage in allegedly harassing conduct, we would run the risk of reinforcing the prevailing level of discrimination. Harassers could continue to harass merely because a particularly discriminatory practice was common, and victims of harassment would have no remedy ... We adopt the perspective of a reasonable woman primarily because we believe that a sex-blind reasonable person standard tends to be male-biased and tends to systematically ignore the experiences of women.

This new standard caused a firestorm of discussion and was rejected, in favor of the reasonable person test, by the U.S. Supreme Court in *Harris v. Forklift Systems, Inc.* [510 U.S. 17 (1993)]. In this decision, a unanimous Court also adopted a "middle path" on the question of how much of a tangible psychological injury must be sustained to make harassment actionable. Justice O'Connor wrote, bluntly, "Title VII comes into play before the harassing conduct leads to a nervous breakdown."

More recently, while continuing to address the question of under what circumstances employers are liable, under Title VII and Title IX, for the actions of employees, the Court has ruled that the protections of Title VII apply to same-sex harassment. In *Oncale v. Sundowner Offshore Services* [523 U.S. 75 (1998)] Justice Scalia, who often writes that Congress must be explicit in establishing a cause of action, reasoned for a unanimous Court:

We see no justification in the statutory language or our precedents for a categorical rule excluding same-sex harassment claims for the coverage of Title VII. As some courts have observed, male-on-male sexual harassment in the workplace was assuredly not the principal evil Congress was concerned with when it enacted Title VII. But statutory prohibitions often go beyond the principal evil to cover reasonably comparable evils, and it is ultimately the provisions of our laws rather than the principal concerns of our legislators by which we are governed.

EEOC statistics demonstrate that despite an increased willingness of courts to see sexual harassment as an unlawful form of conduct, girls and women continue to suffer disproportionately from hostile school and work environments where they are subjected to unwanted and unwelcome harassment that affects their performance and well-being. Girls and women also find that the outside world is not the only place where they experience violence. Shamefully, physical and sexual assault also occur, in large numbers, within the home and other places thought "safe." The perpetrators are not brutes hiding in alleys, but members of family, and friends.

The Violence Against Women Act of 1994 (VAWA) has been called "the most ambitious federal legislation ever enacted to deal with the epidemic of violence against women in this country."[21] It contains dozens of provisions designed to protect women and according to law professor Sally Goldfarb "reconceptualized violence against women as part of a social pattern rather than merely as an isolated crime or personal injury ... [recognizing that] gender-motivated violence is a collective injury, a social wrong carried out on an individual level."[22] VAWA makes it a federal crime to cross state lines in order to commit domestic violence or violate an order of protection and requires that each state honor protection orders issued by other states. The original legislation and its renewal authorized funding for battered women's shelters, victim services agencies, criminal justice personnel, and record keeping.

However, much to the disappointment of the reformers and legislators who wrote VAWA, one of its most important provisions has not survived judicial scrutiny. In 2000, in *U.S. v. Morrison* (529 U.S. 598), in a 5–4 vote, the Supreme Court struck down as unconstitutional the section of VAWA by which Congress sought to provide victims of gender-motivated violence a federal civil remedy, that is, the right to sue their attackers under federal law.

Even before *Morrison* many judges had gone on record as opposing the civil remedy, according to one activist, "on the ground that it would force the federal courts to deal with domestic relations matters that [the judges] considered to be beneath their notice," and that they felt should be resolved by state rather than federal law.[23] Writing for the majority in *Morrison,* Chief Justice Rehnquist affirmed this view and struck down the civil remedies provision, arguing that Congress had exceeded its authority under the commerce clause and Section 5 of the Fourteenth Amendment. Ignoring evidence that many states refused to address domestic violence in law and did not prosecute attackers, he reasoned that the Framers of the Constitution had "carefully crafted [a] balance of power between the States and the National Government," and that gender-based violence properly fell within the police powers of the states. Dissenting, Justice David Souter wrote that violence against women has profound economic consequences, citing evidence offered at congressional hearings about loss of employment due to physical and psychological battering and abuse, loss of homes (and, therefore, homelessness), and medical expenses. Offering support that a federal civil remedies action would not be abused, he also stated that "less than 1 percent of all [rape] victims have collected damages." He also noted that Congress had "followed procedures to protect the federalism values at stake" and that, in response, attorneys general in 38 states expressed support for VAWA. Responding to the majority's decision, one activist concluded that the loss of the civil remedies provision would considerably slow the social change necessary to end violence against women.[24]

CAN THERE BE A CULTURAL DEFENSE FOR THE USE OF VIOLENCE?

One of the areas in which violence against women has attracted attention is that of the cultural defense as this relates to people from other cultures who claim as a defense in their violence against women that their culture sanctions such violence under certain circumstances. Because of the drama of some of these cases, a national debate has emerged over the degree to which American law can and should be modified to take into account foreign cultural practices, or what is called the cultural defense.

A cultural defense holds that persons socialized in a minority or foreign culture, who regularly conduct themselves in accordance with their own culture's norms, should not be held fully accountable for conduct that violates official U.S. law, if those individuals' conduct conforms to the prescriptions of their own culture. The intention of a cultural defense in a criminal case is to negate or mitigate criminal responsibility where acts are committed under a reasonable, good-faith belief in their propriety, based upon the actor's cultural heritage or tradition.

Because the American legal system is based on a view of the individual as having an ability to reason and to understand the law, a cultural defense is incompatible with our most basic legal values. American law does recognize mitigation, but addresses the gap between legal fault and moral fault in ways consistent with our own central cultural value of individual responsibility. American courts formally recognize different degrees of moral culpability in considering intention, knowledge, recklessness, and negligence. Consistent with this American value of individualized justice, various defenses involving diminished mental capacity, such as the insanity defense and more recently the "battered-wife" defense, have been officially recognized by some American courts. While American courts reject the official use of the cultural defense, it has succeeded in a number of cases involving violence (even murder) against women. Basic to the culture defense is the social scientific assumption that culture and the institutions of socialization—class, family, schools, religion—play a preeminent part in "determining" (or at the very least influencing, conditioning, shaping, or channeling) personality, values, and behavior.

Yet American courts, while generally having been hostile to the cultural defense mounted as an independent, substantive defense in criminal trials, do sometimes use cultural evidence as relevant in explaining the state of mind underlying the criminal actions taken by a person from a foreign culture in reducing charges, and thus in mitigating the severity of punishment.[25] In homicide cases, cultural factors may be introduced as evidence of diminished capacity as a result of extreme emotional disturbance, for example, the extreme rage experienced by men from some cultures who react violently to perceived threats or attacks on their honor.

In *People v. Moua* (No. 328106–0, Fresno Superior Ct. 1985), cultural evidence played a central role. Kong Moua was a Hmong immigrant from the isolated mountain areas of Laos. Hmong have patrilineal clans, and male elders adjudicate disputes, a cultural practice they continue in the United States. A traditional Hmong marriage practice is called *zij poj niam*, which is actually similar to elopement, though it is translated into English as "marriage by capture." *Zij poj niam* begins with a ritualized flirtation to which a woman acquiesces by giving the man some token item. The man then takes the woman to his family's home to consummate the union. To demonstrate her virtue, the woman must ritually protest this by saying, "No, no, I'm not ready," and by weeping and moaning. To demonstrate his masculinity, the man must ignore these protests and firmly lead the woman to the bedroom, where they consummate the marriage. Thereafter, the woman is considered unmarriageable by other Hmong men. If the woman does not protest sufficiently she is considered unchaste, and if the man does not assert himself, he is considered weak.

In this case, Kong Moua followed Hmong custom, claiming that both he and his "wife," Xeng Xiong, who was an "Americanized" 19-year-old working in a local college, had observed the traditional ritual by flirting and exchanging tokens of affection.[26] Kong Moua claimed that he sincerely believed that Xeng Xiong wanted to marry him, but Xeng Xiong's parents called the police and filed rape and kidnapping charges against him. Because a conviction for rape requires intent, and a defendant who reasonably and honestly believes that the female's lack of resistance communicated her consent can be acquitted, the prosecutor and judge had to determine whether Moua was in fact sincere, and whether the woman's protests were authentic or merely ritualistic. Based on anthropological literature documenting Hmong marital customs as well as interviews with Moua and Xiong introduced in the pretrial negotiations, the judge and prosecutor decided that Moua was sincere, but also that Xiong had not consented. After conferring with Hmong clan elders, Moua was allowed to plead guilty to a lesser charge of false imprisonment and was sentenced to 120 days in jail and fined $1,200, of which $900 went to Xiong's parents as reparations.[27]

Where the cultural defense has involved spousal homicide following accusations of infidelity, courts have acted inconsistently. In one case, occurring in 1982 in New York, a Laotian man murdered his wife, claiming that the "shame" brought on by her alleged relationship with another man drove him into "extreme emotional stress." The trial judge refused to permit cultural evidence regarding the stress and disorientation encountered by Laotian refugees in attempting to assimilate into American culture before the jury, and the defendant, who was convicted of second degree murder, was sentenced to 15 years to life at Attica. The defendant appealed and the New York Court of Appeals ruled in his favor, stating that the cultural evidence regarding the shame brought on the defendant and his family by his wife's display of affection for another man was relevant in that it was sufficient to trigger the defendant's loss of control.[28]

A similar case, New York v. Chen, received wide national criticism, with particular censure of the judge's decision from the Chinese-American community.[29] On the morning of September 7, 1987, Dong Lu Chen, a recent immigrant from Hong Kong, originally from the People's Republic of China, had an argument with his wife of 23 years, Jian Wan Chen, in their Brooklyn apartment. Mr. Chen suspected his wife of an affair and just prior to the murder, he stated, Mrs. Chen refused to sleep with him, reportedly saying that "this need was being taken care of elsewhere." Chen took this to mean that his wife admitted having an affair. He became so enraged that he went from the bedroom, where they were arguing, into the living room, picked up a claw hammer lying in a corner, returned to the bedroom and struck his wife eight times on the head, which resulted in her death. The couple's son entered the apartment just after the killing and called the police. Chen had admitted the killing to his son, and did so again, speaking through the interpreter on a video tape at the police station.

Mr. Chen had been in the United States for a little more than a year prior to the killing, employed most recently as a dishwasher in Maryland where he lived much of the time while his wife and two teenaged children remained in New York City. Chen lived in a Chinese-speaking community and appeared to have known little beyond its cultural walls. There was also some suggestion in his records of a learning disability. Mr. Chen's court-appointed lawyer mounted a cultural defense, drawing on the expertise of an anthropologist whose specialty was Taiwanese and Chinese culture. The anthropologist testified that Chen felt enormous humiliation and shame at the thought of his wife's (alleged) adultery, a condition that made him subject to, at minimum, extreme emotional distress. The anthropologist also testified that the shame and dishonor that falls upon a man if his wife's infidelity becomes known within the Chinese community is so great that he could not hope to marry again if he divorced his wife. This shame, combined with the absence of a community that in China would have offered intervention and prevented the killing, led to Chen's attack on his wife. Repeatedly, the anthropological expert sought to explain to the presiding judge the great extent to which Mr. Chen's actions were dictated by cultural factors so deeply ingrained in him that Chen could not—as an individual—resist them.

Judge Edward Pincus was persuaded by the cultural defense. He ruled that because Chen "took all his Chinese culture with him to the United States, he was not entirely responsible for his actions ... he was the product of his culture." Although Pincus stated that, "The culture was never an excuse," he went on to say that "it was something that made Chen crack more easily."[30] Judge Pincus found Chen guilty of second-degree manslaughter (the prosecutor had originally planned a charge of second-degree murder) and sentenced him to five years' probation, less time already served, and mandated psychiatric help. Judge Pincus defended his light sentence by noting that Chen's children and other relatives in New York offered Chen a home with them. In addition, Judge Pincus noted that during the one and one-half years Chen had already served in jail he had been greatly harassed because he did not speak English, and that his chances for rehabilitation in prison seemed nonexistent.[31]

Chen's sentence was strongly protested by women's groups, Asian-American groups, the district attorney's office, legal scholars, and the press. On hearing the sentence, then Brooklyn District Attorney Elizabeth Holtzman was "enraged," arguing that "anyone who comes to this country must be prepared to live by and obey the laws of this country. There should be one standard of justice, not one that depends on the cultural background of the defendant," Holtzman said.[32]

The connections between culturally rooted concepts of honor, shame, patriarchy, the treatment of women as property, and gender violence pose a dilemma for American courts, which find themselves having to mediate the contradictions between serving justice in a culturally diverse society and adhering to the requirements of a single standard of law. Cultural sensitivity is reasonable, and even necessary, in a multicultural society like our own, and yet these sensitivities are sometimes clearly at odds with other powerful necessities, for example, the need to protect women from violence.

The conflict experienced in American courts as they try to steer a course between respecting cultural differences and protecting women's rights has international legal dimensions. The U.N. Universal Declaration of Human Rights proclaims that all humans have equal and inalienable rights to liberty, dignity, and the security of their persons. A conflict has arisen between universal women's rights and cultural values over the appropriate legal responses to the various African cultural practices of female circumcision that, as a result of increasing immigration from Africa, are now occurring in the United States.

In February 1994, in Portland, Oregon, deportation proceedings were held in the case of a Nigerian citizen, Lydia Omowunmi Oluloro, who was an illegal resident in the United States. Ms. Oluloro, who had two daughters, sought asylum in the United States because she claimed that if she were to return to Nigeria with her two daughters, they would be forcibly circumcised, as she had been as a child, and that her opposition and resistance to this cultural practice for her daughters would result in ostracism, abuse, or even jailing. Evidence on the issue of female genital mutilation was central in this case. In her first deportation hearing, the immigration judge recognized the potential dilemma raised by the conflict between universal human rights and specific cultural practices: "Initially, with all due respect to foreign cultures, the Court agrees with the respondent that the custom of Female Genital Mutilation is reprehensible, unfair, and disgusting, notwithstanding its long history and numerous faithful adherents. While uncritical multiculturalists might argue that it is improper to pass judgment on long-established mores and customs of other cultures, this Court will note that torture and other forms of barbarity … are traditional in many cultures today, and cannot be condoned."[33] He nevertheless turned down her request for asylum. However, in a second hearing, where the same issue was central to her defense, an immigration judge found in her favor. He noted that "although this court attempts to respect the traditions and cultures of other societies, as to this practice of female genital mutilation, the court concludes that it is cruel and serves no known medical purpose. While it could possibly have had some purpose in ancient cultures, whatever the utility the practice might ever have had, it no longer exists." He concluded that the forcible circumcision of Ms. Oluloro's daughters was likely if she returned to Nigeria and that this constituted a sufficiently "extreme hardship" to permit her to remain in the United States.[34]

Debate over the cultural defense grows out of the increasingly multicultural nature of our society and ambivalence over the issue of local cultural autonomy if the nation-state is to survive. Those favoring a cultural defense argue that one standard of justice is too rigid in a diverse society. Those who reject it contend that a major function of law is to lay down a common set of values necessary to maintaining social order, and a body of positive law that compels the obedience of all regardless of individual notions of morality.[35] This discussion, carried out in the context of cultural defense, in fact, expresses a fundamental issue of American life—the continuing tension between states' rights and national law. Local culture can greatly affect the nature and degree of any citizen's rights. This is particularly true for women because state-to-state differences in law and politics shape outcomes in divorce, welfare, prevention and punishment of domestic violence and rape, workplace discrimination, and access to reproductive health services. Women's rights often result from changes in national law but they continue to be profoundly affected by the decisions of state and local communities.

NOTES

1. Ann Scott Tyson, "Panel Votes to Ban Women from Combat," *Washington Post*, May 12, 2005, AO8.

2. American Association of University Women Educational Foundation, *How Schools Shortchange Women* (Washington, DC: AAUW, 1992).

3. For example, see *Cohen v. Brown University* [101 F. 3d 155 (1st Circuit, 1996)]. In 1997 the U.S. Supreme Court declined to hear Brown's appeal that it had not violated Title IX and discriminated on the basis of sex when it eliminated certain varsity sports teams.

4. On the continuing wage gap between men and women, see Francine D. Blau and Lawrence M. Kahn, "Gender Differences in Pay," *Journal of Economic Perspectives 14* (Fall 2000) and Jenny Strasburg, "Equity: Losing Ground," *San Francisco Chronicle,* January 9, 2005, 14; on comparable pay, see *Washington v. American Federation of State, County, and Municipal Employees,* 770 F. 2d 1401 (9th Cir. 1985).

5. One expert reports that 42 percent of the people who have taken family leave under the FMLA are men who use it for their own serious health conditions, or to care for a spouse or parent. Sheila Thomas in *Women's Rights in Theory and Practice* (Washington, D.C.: Woodrow Wilson Center for International Scholars, 2002, 23)

6. *EEOC v. Sears,* 628 F. Supp. 1264 (N.D. Ill. 1986), aff'd 839 F.2d 302 (7th Cir. 1988); *Stender v. Lucky Stores, Inc.,* 803 F. Supp. ILL. 259 (N.D. Cal. 1992). Each case

raised the question of whether women aspire to the same positions and promotions as do men.

7. *Frontiero* might be considered a cultural victory but a strategic legal defeat as attorneys failed to convince the Supreme Court that sex-based classifications, like those based on race, were suspect, triggering strict judicial scrutiny. In *Craig v. Boren* the Court established heightened scrutiny as the standard for gender-based classifications.

8. Barbara Sinclair Deckard, *The Women's Movement* (New York: Harper and Row, 1983), 157–58.

9. Nancy Duff Campbell in *Women's Rights in Theory and Practice,* 72, summarizing TANF's provisions.

10. Ibid., 68.

11. http://www.naswdc.org/advocacy/welfare/legislation/recommend.pdf: "Recommendations for the Reauthorization of [TANF]," November 30, 2001, 2; also, Olivia Golden, *Assessing New Federalism—Eight Years Later* (Washington, DC: Urban Institute, 2005), http://www.urban.org/ANF_EightYearsLater.pdf.

12. http://www.prcdc.org/summaries/poverty/poverty.html. Where parents are separated, child support becomes critical to household finances. Welfare reform, according to the Center for Law and Social Policy, "has given states sweeping new enforcement tools and automated interstate data bases." As a result, the performance of child-support programs began to improve in the late 1990s, with collection rates rising from 18 percent in the mid-1990s to 51 percent in 2004. http://www.clasp.org/publications/backing_away_on_child_support.pdf

13. Davis, in *Women's Rights in Theory and Practice,* 76.

14. Lawrence B. Finer and Stanley K. Henshaw, "Abortion Incidence and Services in the United States in 2000," *Perspectives on Sexual and Reproductive Health* 35 (January/February 2003), 1.

15. See *International Union, U.A.W. v. Johnson Controls,* 499 U.S. 187 (1991); *Hill v. Colorado,* 530 U.S. 703 (2000); *Ferguson v. Charleston, S.C.,* 532 U.S. 67 (2001); and, most recently, one of many local prosecutions involving fetal endangerment due to maternal drug use, *State of Hawai'i v. Tayshea Aiwohi,* FC. CR. No. 03-1-0036.

16. Natalie J. Sokoloff, ed., *Domestic Violence at the Margins* (New Brunswick: Rutgers University Press, 2005), xvi.

17. Joel B. Grossman, "The First Amendment and the New Anti-Pornography Statutes," *News for Teachers for Political Science* (Spring 1985), 1. For a fuller discussion of the history and legal cases involved in female sexuality and commerce, see the second edition of *American Cultural Pluralism and Law.*

18. Susan Gluck Mezey, *Elusive Equality* (Boulder: Lynne Rienner, 2003), 129; EEOC website, http://www.eeoc.gov/types/sexual_harassment.html.

19. EEOC website.

20. The 2005 film, *North Country,* presents a fictionalized account of the lawsuit brought by women miners at the Eveleth Mines who claimed sexual harassment.

21. Goldfarb in *Women's Rights in Theory and Practice,* 52.

22. Ibid., 53.

23. Goldfarb in *Women's Rights in Theory and Practice,* 53–4.

24. Goldfarb in *Women's Rights in Theory and Practice,* 55.

25. Alison Dundes Renteln, *The Cultural Defense* (New York: Oxford University Press, 2004), 32–35.

26. Alison Dundes Renteln, "Culture and Culpability," in Renteln and Alan Dundes, eds. *Folk Law* (New York: Garland, 1994), 866.

27. Paul J. Mangarella, "Justice in a Culturally Pluralistic Society," *Journal of Ethnic Studies* 19(1991), 70.

28. *People v. Aphaylath*, 510 N.Y.S. 2d 83 (Ct. App. 1986).

29. *New York v. Chen*, Indictment No. 7774/87, NYS Sup. Ct., Kings County, December 2, 1988 (trial transcript).

30. Celestine Bohlen, "Holtzman May Appeal Probation in the Killing of a Chinese Woman," *New York Times*, April 5, 1989, B3.

31. *New York v. Chen*, 352–63.

32. Bohlen, "Holtzman," B3.

33. *In re Lydia Omowunmi Oluloro*, Trial Memorandum, No. A72147491, U.S. Department of Justice, Portland, Oregon, February 7, 1994.

34. *In re Lydia Omowunmi Oluloro*, Oral Decision, U.S. Department of Justice, Executive Office for Immigration Review, Seattle, Washington, March 23, 1994.

35. Julia P. Sams, "The Availability of the 'Cultural Defense' as an Excuse for Criminal Behavior," *Georgia Journal of International & Comparative Law* 16 (Spring 1986), 335.

CHAPTER 10

Family Values: Gays and Marriage

A significant social change in American society since the 1960s is the emergence of homosexual men and women into the public and political life of the nation. While intimate same-sex relationships have always been part of the Western cultural experience, they have often been disparaged, stigmatized, and punished by law, though this varied in different historical periods. The ancient Greeks considered homosexuality as natural as heterosexuality, but the Hebrew and Christian Testaments condemn same-sex relationships as sinful and unnatural. Anti-sodomy laws (criminalizing oral and anal sex) that applied to both heterosexuals and homosexuals were incorporated into English common law and subsequently incorporated into American law, with a few states enacting antisodomy laws that only applied to homosexuals.

As the result of the widespread social disapproval of homosexuality expressed in law, religious injunction, and social discrimination in the United States, these relationships were often invisible. By the early twentieth century, with increasing urbanization, an incipient male homosexual subculture and later a lesbian subculture developed in the United States. By the 1950s, and particularly in the 1960s, changing social norms and increased political activism by many minorities paved the way for the emergence of these previously underground homosexual subcultures. Today, the existence of gay male and lesbian communities supporting distinctive subcultures, the open assertion of homosexual identities, and an activist political agenda calling for the removal of legal and social barriers against homosexuals is an important part of a larger civil and human rights movement in the United States and internationally.

Since the 1970s, the gay civil rights agenda has included legal challenges to state antisodomy laws as well as efforts to have the U.S. Supreme Court declare such statutes unconstitutional. Antisodomy statutes symbolically denigrate and criminalize activities at the heart of same-sex relationships. Although such statutes were seldom enforced, their existence made every homosexual potentially subject to criminal sanctions and provided a basis for discriminatory exclusion, for example, in the United States military.[1] Even when state sodomy laws included heterosexuals, as many did, such laws were primarily enforced against homosexuals.

An early Supreme Court case, *Doe v. Richmond* [425 U.S. 901 (1976)], affirmed a Virginia court's decision that the state's antisodomy laws were constitutionally valid. Plaintiffs had challenged the Virginia statute, contending that it deprived adult males engaging in "regular homosexual relations consensually and in private," of their constitutional rights to freedom of expression, privacy, and due process. In stressing the regular, consensual, and private nature of homosexual relationships, Doe sought to have them accepted as equal to marriage and therefore accorded the same privacy rights the Supreme Court had granted to married couples in *Griswold*.[2] The Virginia court rejected the plaintiffs' argument, holding that "the Constitution only condemns State legislation that trespasses upon the privacy of … marriage, upon the sanctity of the home, or upon the nature of family life." It concluded that *Griswold* applied only to marital rights of heterosexual couples.

Gays continued their challenges, however. In 1986, Michael Hardwick brought suit against the Georgia antisodomy law (which applied to both homosexuals and heterosexuals), claiming that his homosexual activity, which took place in his home, was a private and intimate association beyond the reach of state regulation, and that the Georgia law violated his constitutional rights of privacy.[3] The case reached the U.S. Supreme Court, which rejected Hardwick's claim in a 5–4 decision. The majority opinion, written by Justice Byron White, framed the central issue not as the right to privacy, but rather " … whether the Federal Constitution confers a fundamental right upon homosexuals to engage in sodomy and hence invalidates the laws of the many States that still make such conduct illegal and have done so for a very long time."

BOWERS V. HARDWICK 478 U.S. 186 (1986)

… We first register our disagreement with … respondent that the Court's prior cases [e.g., *Griswold*] have construed the Constitution to confer a right of privacy that extends to homosexual sodomy … we think … that none of the rights announced in those cases bears any resemblance to the claimed constitutional right of homosexuals to engage in acts of sodomy that is asserted in this case. No connection between family, marriage, or procreation on the one hand and homosexual activity on the other has been demonstrated, either by the [Georgia]Court of Appeals or by respondent ... any claim that these cases ... stand for the proposition that any kind of private sexual conduct between consenting adults is constitutionally insulated from state proscription is unsupportable.

... [the] respondent would have us announce ... a fundamental right to engage in homosexual sodomy. This we are quite unwilling to do ... the Court has sought to identify the nature of the rights qualifying for heightened judicial protection ... this category includes those fundamental liberties that are "implicit in the concept of ordered liberty," such that "neither liberty nor justice would exist if [they] were sacrificed" [and] those liberties that are "deeply rooted in this Nation's history and tradition."

It is obvious to us that neither of these formulations would extend a fundamental right to homosexuals to engage in acts of consensual sodomy. Proscriptions against that conduct have ancient roots. Sodomy was a criminal offense at common law and was forbidden by the laws of the original thirteen States when they ratified the Bill of Rights ... until 1961, all 50 States outlawed sodomy, and today, 24 States and the District of Columbia continue to [do so] ... Against this background, to claim that a right to engage in such conduct is "deeply rooted in this Nation's history and tradition" or "implicit in the concept of ordered liberty" is, at best, facetious.

Even if th[is] conduct is not a fundamental right, respondent asserts that there must be a rational basis for the law and that there is none in this case other than the presumed belief of a majority of the electorate in Georgia that homosexual sodomy is immoral and unacceptable. This is said to be an inadequate rationale to support the law. The law, however, is constantly based on notions of morality, and if all laws representing essentially moral choices are to be invalidated under the Due Process Clause, the courts will be very busy indeed. [Still, the respondent] insists that majority sentiments about the morality of homosexuality should be declared inadequate. We do not agree, and are unpersuaded that the sodomy laws of some 25 States should be invalidated on this basis.

In a separate, concurring opinion, Chief Justice Warren Burger underscored his view that "in constitutional terms there is no such thing as a fundamental right to commit homosexual sodomy" and emphasized that "The proscriptions against sodomy have very ancient roots ... hav[ing] been subject to state intervention throughout the history of Western Civilization. Condemnation of those practices is firmly rooted in Judeo-Christian moral and ethical standards ... To hold that the act of homosexual sodomy is somehow protected as a fundamental right would be to cast aside millennia of moral teaching."

Justice Lewis Powell's concurring opinion did however, question the severity of the Georgia statute's penalty—potential imprisonment of up to twenty years—as possibly creating a serious Eighth Amendment (cruel and unusual punishment) issue. Since Hardwick had not, however, been tried and sentenced, that issue was not before the court.

Justice Harry Blackmun wrote an eloquent dissent, which subsequently became the basis for the reversal of *Bowers* in *Lawrence v. Texas* (see below).

He argued, first, that the majority was incorrect in analyzing the rights at issue in the narrow terms of homosexuality:

... This case is not about "a fundamental right to engage in homosexual sodomy, as the Court purports to declare ... [but rather] was about the most comprehensive of rights and the right most valued by civilized men ... the right to be let alone. [Georgia's statute] denies individuals the right to decide for themselves whether to engage in particular forms of private, consensual sexual activity. The Court concludes that the statute is valid essentially because "the laws of many States still make such conduct illegal and have done so for a very long time ... But the fact that the moral judgments expressed by these statutes may be 'natural and familiar' ought not to conclude our judgment upon the question whether [they] conflict with the Constitution ... Like Justice Holmes, I believe that 'it is revolting to have no better reason for a rule of law than that so it was laid down in the time of Henry IV.' It is still more revolting if the grounds upon which it was laid down have vanished long since, and the rule simply persists from blind imitation of the past ... I believe we must analyze respondent's claim in the light of the values that underlie the constitutional right to privacy. If that means anything, it means that, before Georgia can prosecute its citizens for making choices about the most intimate aspects of their lives, it must do more than assert that the choice they have made is an 'abominable crime not fit to be named among Christians'.... In its haste to ... hold that the Constitution does not 'confer a fundamental right upon homosexuals to engage in sodomy,' ... the majority has distorted the question this case presents ... The Court's cramped reading of the issue ... makes for a short opinion, but it does little to make for a persuasive one.

Justice Blackmun noted that the protection of marriage and the family articulated in earlier court decisions [e.g., *Griswold*] rested not on the contributions marriage and family make to society, but on the fact that,

they form so central a part of an individual's life.... "[T]he concept of privacy embodies the 'moral fact that a person belongs to himself and not others nor to society as a whole' " ...

Only the most willful blindness could obscure the fact that sexual intimacy is "a sensitive, key relationship of human existence, central to family life, community welfare, and the development of human personality." The fact that individuals define themselves in a significant way through their intimate sexual relationships with others suggests, in a Nation as diverse as ours, that there may be many "right" ways of conducting those relationships, and that much of the richness of a relationship will come from the freedom an individual has to choose the form and nature of these intensely personal bonds.

Justice Blackmun then turned to a religious freedom case, quoting the Court's opinion in *Yoder* (see chapter 6),

"There can be no assumption that today's majority is 'right' and the Amish and others like them are 'wrong.' A way of life that is odd or even erratic but interferes with no rights or interests of others is not to be condemned because it is different."

The Court claims that its decision today merely refuses to recognize a fundamental right to engage in homosexual sodomy; what the Court really has refused to recognize is the fundamental interest all individuals have in controlling the nature of their intimate associations with others.

... "[T]he essence of a Fourth Amendment violation is ... 'the invasion of [an individual's] indefensible right of personal security, personal liberty and private property ...' " Indeed, the right of an individual to conduct intimate relationships in the intimacy of his or her own home seems to me to be the heart of the Constitution's protection of privacy.

Justice Blackmun dismissed the Court's opinion that the long history of laws against sodomy and the proscription on homosexuality by "traditional Judeo-Christian values" were sufficient to violate Hardwick's right to privacy. Citing *West Virginia Board of Education v. Barnette,* he said:

"we apply the limitations of the Constitution with no fear that freedom to be intellectually and spiritually diverse or even contrary will disintegrate the social organization ... [F]reedom to differ is not limited to things that do not matter much. That would be a mere shadow of freedom. The test of its substance is the right to differ as to things that touch the heart of the existing order." It is precisely because the issue raised by this case touches the heart of what makes individuals what they are that we should be especially sensitive to the rights of those whose choices upset the majority.

Justice Blackmun stated that just because some religious groups condemned homosexuality this did not give the State a

license to impose their judgments on the entire citizenry. The legitimacy of secular legislation depends instead on whether the State can advance some justification for its law beyond its conformity to religious doctrine ... "[m]ere public intolerance or animosity cannot constitutionally justify the deprivation of a person's physical liberty."

Justice Blackmun also emphasized that while acts in public places may come under state prohibitions, "intimate behavior that occurs in intimate places" cannot:

This case involves no real interference with the rights of others, for the mere knowledge that other individuals do not adhere to one's value system cannot be a legally cognizable interest, let alone an interest that can justify invading the houses, hearts, and minds of citizens who choose to live their lives differently.

He reminded the court that they had changed their minds before and hoped that it would also "reconsider its analysis [here] and conclude that depriving individuals of the right to choose for themselves how to conduct their intimate relationships poses a far greater threat to the values most deeply rooted in our Nation's history than tolerance of nonconformity could ever do. Because I think the Court today betrays those values, I dissent."

In another dissent, Justice John Paul Stevens held that a law which included heterosexuals could not be differentially enforced against homosexuals: "Every free citizen," he said,

has the same interest in "liberty" that the members of the majority share ... the homosexual and the heterosexual have the same interest in deciding how he will live his own life, and ... how he will conduct himself in his personal and voluntary associations with his companions. State intrusion into the private conduct of either is equally burdensome ... A policy of selective application [against homosexuals] must be supported by a neutral and legitimate interest—something more substantial than a habitual dislike for, or ignorance about, the disfavored group ...

Justice Powell originally planned to join Justice Blackmun's dissent, but then changed his mind; he did not completely agree with Justice Blackmun's sweeping arguments about the right to privacy, though he did believe that sodomy laws were unenforced, unenforceable, and generally useless. Four years after *Bowers*, Justice Powell expressed second thoughts about his vote: "I think I probably made a mistake," he said. Looking back, he viewed the *Bowers* decision as inconsistent with *Roe v. Wade*, a case in which he had joined the majority in holding that the right to privacy embedded in liberty gave women a constitutional right to obtain abortions. [4]

Within a year of the *Bowers* decision, Justice Powell retired and Antonin Scalia and Anthony Kennedy and later, Clarence Thomas joined the Court. In 2002, a new sodomy case, *Lawrence v. Texas* came before the Supreme Court; unlike the Georgia statute, however, the Texas antisodomy law only applied to homosexuals. In *Lawrence*, the Court reversed *Bowers*, finding that the Texas antisodomy law violated the Due Process Clause of the United States Constitution. The majority opinion, written by Justice Kennedy, drew heavily on Justice Blackmun's dissent in *Bowers*, while Justices Scalia and Thomas's dissents reiterated the majority opinion in *Bowers*.

LAWRENCE V. TEXAS 539 U.S. 558(2003)

The question before the Court is the validity of a Texas statute making it a crime for two persons of the same sex to engage in certain intimate sexual conduct ... [In this case] we consider.... Whether ... the Texas "homosexual conduct" law—which criminalizes sexual intimacy by same-sex couples—violate[s] the Fourteenth Amendment guarantee of equal protection of laws? ... Whether Petitioners' criminal convictions for adult consensual sexual intimacy in the home violates their vital interests in liberty and privacy protected by the Due Process Clause of the Fourteenth Amendment [and].... Whether *Bowers v. Hardwick* should be overruled?

We conclude the case should be resolved by determining whether the petitioners were free as adults to engage in the private conduct in the exercise of their liberty under the Due Process Clause of the Fourteenth Amendment to the Constitution. For this inquiry we deem it necessary to reconsider the Court's holding in *Bowers*.

Justice Anthony Kennedy, looking at earlier Supreme Court cases involving the substantive reach of liberty under the Due Process Clause, noted that while in *Griswold* the Court affirmed the right to privacy in the context of marriage and "the protected space of the marital bedroom," in subsequent cases (e.g., *Eisenstadt v. Baird* invalidating a state law prohibiting distribution of contraceptives to unmarried persons) the Court extended the right to make certain decisions regarding sexual conduct beyond the marital relationship. Justice Kennedy criticized the Court's framing of *Bowers* as incorrect, and as a failure "to appreciate the extent of the liberty at stake." He went on to say that

... the [antisodomy] laws ... have far-reaching consequences, touching upon the most private human conduct, sexual behavior, and in the most private of places, the home. The statutes ... seek to control a personal relationship that, whether or not entitled to formal recognition in the law, is within the liberty of persons to choose without being punished as criminals.

This, as a general rule, should counsel against attempts by the State, or a court, to define the meaning of the relationship or to set its boundaries absent injury to a person or abuse of an institution the law protects. It suffices for us to acknowledge that adults may choose to enter upon this relationship in the confines of their homes and their own private lives and still retain their dignity as free persons. When sexuality finds overt expression in intimate conduct with another person, the conduct can be but one element in a personal bond that is more enduring. The liberty protected by the Constitution allows homosexual persons the right to make this choice.

... there is no longstanding history in this country of laws directed at homosexual conduct as a distinct matter ... [early American sodomy laws] were directed at both heterosexual and homosexuals and sought to prohibit non-procreative sexual activity more generally ... the concept of the homosexual as a distinct category of person did not emerge until the late 19th century ... [and while] the sodomy laws of general application did not "suggest approval of homosexual conduct," they were not generally enforced against consenting adults acting in private ... [rather] many of the sodomy prosecutions involved acts carried out without consent, as in the case of a minor or the victim of an assault.

Justice Kennedy further noted that American laws targeting same-sex couples did not develop until the 1970s; that only nine states have such laws; and that in the last twenty years many of these states have moved toward abolishing those laws. In summary, he said, "the historical premises relied upon in *Bowers* are not without doubt and, at the very least, are overstated." He then expanded on this point:

It must be acknowledged, of course, that the Court in *Bowers* was making the broader point that for centuries there have powerful voices to condemn homosexual conduct as immoral. The condemnation has been shaped by religious beliefs, conceptions of right and acceptable behavior, and respect for the traditional family. For many persons these are ... profound and deep convictions accepted as ethical and moral principles ... These considerations do not answer the question before us, however. The issue is whether the majority may use the power of the State to enforce these views on the whole society through the operation of the criminal law. [Citing an earlier privacy case he said] "Our obligation is to define the liberty of all, not to mandate our own moral code."

Justice Kennedy criticized Justice Burger's view in *Bowers* that private homosexual conduct between consenting adults was subject to state intervention throughout the history of Western Civilization, citing evidence in European countries and the European Court of Human Rights to the contrary. In any case, he emphasized, it was American law over the past 50 years that was most relevant. These laws, he said, "show an emerging awareness that liberty gives substantial protection to adult persons in deciding how to conduct their private lives in matters pertaining to sex."

He then cited the Supreme Court decision in *Planned Parenthood of Southeast Pa. v. Casey* [505 U.S. 933(1992)], that threw the principles of the *Bowers* decision into doubt. Here the Court confirmed that

the substantive force of the liberty protected by the Due Process Clause ... afford[s] constitutional protection to personal decisions relating to marriage, procreation, contraception, family relationships, child rearing, and education.... These matters ... are central to the liberty protected by the Fourteenth Amendment. At the heart of liberty is the right to define one's own concept of existence, of meaning, of the universe, and of the mystery of human life. Beliefs about these matters could not define the attributes of personhood were they formed under compulsion of the State ... Persons in a homosexual relationship may seek autonomy for these purposes, just as heterosexual persons do. The decision in *Bowers* would deny them this right.

Justice Kennedy acknowledged that while subsequent to *Bowers* the court had also struck down legislation targeting homosexuals as a violation of the Equal Protection Clause rather than on Fourth Amendment violation of privacy grounds, e.g., *Romer v. Evans* [517 U.S. 620 (1996)], it was essential for the Court to "address whether *Bowers* itself has continuing validity." To leave the basic finding in *Bowers* "unexamined," he said, is to allow "its continuance as precedent [that] demeans the lives of homosexual persons" and that a criminal conviction, however minor the crime, had important consequences for an individual.

Citing Justice Stevens's dissent in *Bowers,* Justice Kennedy emphasized that precedent alone was not a sufficient reason for sustaining the opinion in *Bowers:*

... The fact that the governing majority in a State has traditionally viewed a particular practice as immoral is not a sufficient reason for upholding a law prohibiting the practice; [referring to *Loving v. Virginia,* striking down a law criminalizing interracial marriage] neither history nor tradition could save a law prohibiting miscegenation from constitutional attack ... individual decisions by married persons, concerning the intimacies of their physical relationship, even when not intended to produce offspring, are a form of "liberty" protected by the Due Process Clause of the Fourteenth Amendment. Moreover, this protection extends to intimate choices by unmarried as well as married persons.

Justice Stevens' analysis, in our view, should have been controlling in *Bowers* and should control here. *Bowers* was not correct when it was decided, and it is not correct today. It ought not to remain binding precedent. *Bowers v. Hardwick* should be and is now overruled.

The present case does not involve whether the government must give formal recognition to any relationship that homosexual persons seek to enter. The case does involve two adults who, with full and mutual consent from each other, engaged in sexual practices common to a homosexual lifestyle. The petitioners are entitled to respect for their private lives. The State cannot demean their existence or control their destiny by making their private sexual conduct a crime. Their right to liberty under the Due Process Clause gives them the full right to engage in their conduct without intervention of the government ... The Texas statute [which was defended on the basis of "promoting morality"] furthers no legitimate state interest which can justify its intrusion into the personal and private life of the individual. [Those who ratified the Due Process Clause and the Fourteenth Amendment] knew times can blind us to certain truths and later generations can see that laws once thought necessary and proper in fact serve only to oppress. As the Constitution endures, persons in every generation can invoke its principles in their own search for greater freedom.

Justice Sandra Day O'Connor voted with the Court majority in holding the Texas law unconstitutional, but based her opinion on the Fourteenth Amendment's Equal Protection Clause rather than on the Due Process Clause, saying that the Texas law made "homosexuals unequal in the eyes of the law by making particular conduct—and only that conduct [homosexual sodomy] subject to criminal offense." She emphasized that "the law's effect ... is not limited to just those convicted but brands all homosexuals as criminals ... making it more difficult for homosexuals to be treated in the same manner as everyone else."

In rejecting Texas's claim that "moral disapproval is a legitimate state interest to justify by itself a statute that bans homosexual sodomy, but not heterosexual sodomy," Justice O'Connor held that " ... Moral disapproval of a group (without any other state interest) is not sufficient to justify a law that discriminates." She also dismissed the state's argument that "the law [only] affected conduct, not (homosexual) persons, noting that "the conduct targeted by this law is conduct that is closely correlated with being homosexual … it is thus directed toward gay persons as a class." Justice O'Connor stated that it was not necessary to decide the case on the basis of substantive due process [liberty and privacy issues regarding personal relationships and sex-related behavior] because, she was confident, "if the state anti-sodomy laws were rewritten to apply to hetero and homosexuals, they would not long stand." She concluded, however, that other laws that distinguished between homosexuals and heterosexuals might not necessarily fail if they were related to "any legitimate state interest … such as national security or preserving the traditional institution of marriage. Unlike the moral disapproval of same-sex relations—the asserted state interest in this case—other reasons exist to promote the institution of marriage beyond mere moral disapproval of an excluded group. A law branding one class of persons as criminal solely based on the State's moral disapproval of that class and the conduct associated with that class runs contrary to the values of the Constitution and the Equal Protection Clause … "

Chief Justice Rehnquist and Justice Thomas joined in a dissent, authored by Justice Scalia, which persisted in viewing both *Bowers* and *Lawrence* as asking the Court to declare that homosexual sodomy was a "fundamental right" under the Due Process Clause of the Constitution. The dissent stated that there was no such right, repeating majority arguments in *Bowers* about the long history of disapproval of homosexual sodomy expressed in the religions and laws of Western civilization generally and the United States in particular. Justice Scalia criticized the Court's willingness to overturn *Bowers* for what he viewed as an overreaction to the widespread opposition it generated in legal journals and society at large.

Justice Scalia reminded the Court that its past decisions had permitted the government to abridge or abrogate individual rights and liberties if these were not "fundamental," "traditionally protected by our society," or "privileges long recognized at common law as essential to the orderly pursuit of happiness by free men" if the government had a legitimate state interest in doing so. He reiterated the Court's conclusion in *Bowers* that "a right to engage in homosexual sodomy was not 'deeply rooted in this Nation's history and tradition'" and noted with some sharpness that the Court's decision in *Lawrence* had not in fact explicitly overruled *Bowers* in this respect.

Justice Scalia vehemently dissented from the Court's opinion that the Texas antisodomy law had no rational basis or "legitimate state interest which can justify its intrusion into the personal and private life of the individual. To the contrary," he said, "the Court had previously validated many state laws based on a substantial government interest in protecting order and morality … State laws against bigamy, same-sex marriage, adult incest, prostitution, masturbation, adultery, fornication, bestiality, and obscenity are likewise sustainable only in light of *Bowers'* validation of laws based on moral choices." He viewed the Court's overruling of *Bowers* as entailing "a massive disruption of the current social order ... " and criticized what he called the Court's embrace of the declaration that "the fact that the governing majority in a State has traditionally viewed a particular practice as immoral is not a sufficient reason for upholding a law prohibiting the practice." "This," Justice Scalia said, "effectively decrees the end of all morals legislation."

Anticipating future cases claiming a right to gay marriage, Justice Scalia criticized Justice O'Connor's concurrence on the grounds of equal protection. He assigned to her the view that laws exhibiting "a ... desire to harm a politically unpopular group, are invalid *even though* there may be a conceivable rational basis to support them." He added that "This reasoning leaves on pretty shaky grounds state laws limiting marriage to opposite-sex couples" though he acknowledged that "Justice O'Connor seeks to preserve these laws by her conclusory statement that 'preserving the traditional institution of marriage' is a legitimate state interest." Justice Scalia rejected Justice O'Connor's statement as "illogical," asking, "isn't 'preserving the traditional institution of marriage' ... just a kinder way of describing the State's *moral disapproval* (Scalia's emphasis) of same-sex couples?"

Justice Scalia continued:

Today's opinion is the product of a Court, which is the product of a law-profession culture, that has largely signed on to the so-called homosexual agenda ... promoted by some homosexual activists directed at eliminating the moral opprobrium that has traditionally attached to homosexual conduct....

One of the most revealing statements in today's opinion is the Court's grim warning that the criminalization of homosexual conduct is "an invitation to subject homosexual persons to discrimination in both the public and in the private spheres." It is clear from this that the Court has taken sides in the culture war, departing from its role of assuring, as neutral observer, that the democratic rules of engagement are observed. Many Americans do not want persons who openly engage in homosexual conduct as partners in their business, as scoutmasters for their children, as teachers in their children's schools, or as boarders in their home. They view this as protecting themselves and their families from a lifestyle that they believe to be immoral and destructive. The Court views it as "discrimination" which it is the function of our judgments to deter. So imbued is the Court with the law profession's anti-anti-homosexual culture, that it is seemingly unaware that the attitudes of that culture are not obviously "mainstream"; that in most States what the Court calls "discrimination" against those who engage in homosexual acts is perfectly legal; that proposals to ban such "discrimination" under Title VII have repeatedly been rejected by Congress; that in some cases such "discrimination" is *mandated* by federal statute [e.g., the discharge from the armed forces of any service member who engages in or intends to engage in homosexual acts]; and that in some cases such "discrimination" is a constitutional right [e.g., *Boy Scouts of America v. Dale*].

Justice Scalia then asserted,

I have nothing against homosexuals, or any other group, promoting their agenda through normal democratic means ... every group has the right to persuade its fellow citizens that its view of such matters is the best.... But persuading one's fellow citizens is one thing, and imposing one's views in absence of democratic majority will is something else. I would no more *require* a State to criminalize homosexual acts ... than I would *forbid* it to do so. What Texas has chosen to do is well within the range of traditional democratic action, and its hand should not be stayed through the invention of a brand-new "constitutional right" by a Court that is impatient of democratic change.... But it is the premise of our system that those judgments are to be made by the people, and not imposed by a governing caste [e.g., the Courts] that knows best.

.... The people may feel that their disapprobation of homosexual conduct is strong enough to disallow homosexual marriage, but not strong enough to criminalize private homosexual acts—and may legislate accordingly. The Court today pretends that it possesses a similar freedom of action, so that we need not fear judicial imposition of homosexual marriage, as has recently occurred in Canada ... the Court says that the present case "does not involve whether the government must give formal recognition to any relationship that homosexual persons seek to enter." Do not believe it. More illuminating than this bald, unreasoned disclaimer is the progression of thought displayed by an earlier passage in the Court's opinion, which notes the constitutional protections afforded to "personal decisions relating to *marriage* (his emphasis) procreation, contraception, family relationships, child rearing and education," and then declares that "persons in a homosexual relationship may seek autonomy for these purposes, just as heterosexual persons do." Today's opinion dismantles the structure of constitutional law that has permitted a distinction to be made between heterosexual and homosexual unions, insofar as formal recognition of marriage is considered. If moral disapprobation of homosexual conduct is "no legitimate state interest" for purposes of proscribing that conduct, and if, as the Court coos (casting aside all pretense of neutrality), "[w]hen sexuality finds overt expression in intimate conduct with another person, the conduct can be but one element in a personal bond that is more enduring," what justification could there possibly be for denying the benefits of marriage to homosexual couples exercising "[t]he liberty protected by the Constitution"? Surely not the encouragement of procreation, since the sterile and the elderly are allowed to marry. This case "does not involve [as the Court said] the issue of homosexual marriage" only if one entertains the belief that principle and logic have nothing to do with the decisions of this Court. Many will hope that, as the Court comfortingly assures us, this is so.

The matters appropriate for this Court's resolution are only three: Texas's prohibition of sodomy neither infringes a "fundamental right" (which the Court does not dispute), nor is unsupported by a rational relation to what the Constitution considers a legitimate state interest, nor denies the equal protection of the laws. I dissent.

The *Lawrence* decision was hailed as a great victory for gay civil rights; as legal scholar Suzanne Goldberg said, *Lawrence* profoundly changed the landscape for gay men and lesbians because sodomy laws, even if not often enforced, effectively labeled gays as "criminals who deserved unequal treatment." One subsequent activist effort certainly influenced by *Lawrence,* as Justice Scalia anticipated, was the issue of gay marriage.[5]

GAY MARRIAGE

Challenges to antisodomy statutes, including the Supreme Court decision in *Lawrence* succeeded in removing criminal sanctions from homosexual relationships with important symbolic and practical effects and logically opened the way for gay marriage. Prior to *Lawrence,* several challenges to state laws defining marriage as a union between a man and a woman had been initiated, without success. In 1971, a homosexual couple denied a marriage license by a county district court in Minnesota brought suit, but the Minnesota Supreme Court, in *Baker v. Nelson* (191 N.W.2d 185), rejected their claim. The Court held that an absence of a specific ban on homosexual marriage in Minnesota state law could not reasonably be interpreted to mean that the legislature intended to authorize such marriages. The judge stated that marriage was a term commonly used to mean "the state of union between persons of the opposite sex [and that] [T]he institution of marriage as a union of man and woman, uniquely involving the procreation and rearing of children within a family, is as old as the book of Genesis." He dismissed the view that the U.S. Supreme Court's decision (e.g., *Loving v. Virginia*) invalidating statutes forbidding interracial marriage was a basis for affirming homosexual marriage. While agreeing that "[M]arriage is one of the basic civil rights of man," the court held that "in commonsense and in a constitutional sense, there is a clear distinction between a marital restriction based merely upon race and one based upon the fundamental difference in sex."

While the *Bowers* decision set back the case for same-sex marriage, throughout the 1990s there were several challenges to state constitutions that defined marriage as a union only between a man and a woman. Many of these challenges failed, however, as most courts, like that in Minnesota, reaffirmed the right of the state legislature to define marriage as valid only between persons of the opposite sex. But in 1993, a court challenge in Hawaii catapulted the issue of gay marriage into the center of public awareness. When three gay couples were refused marriage licenses, they sued, claiming that the state constitution's ban on same-sex marriage violated their rights to privacy and unlawfully discriminated against gays and lesbians. The Supreme Court of Hawaii, in *Baehr v. Lewin* [852 P.2d 44 (1993)], rejected these arguments but did find that the ban violated explicit state constitutional prohibitions on gender discrimination and therefore probably violated the Equal Protection Clause of the Hawaiian Constitution. In spite of what was initially viewed as a favorable finding, ultimately the court's decision had a negative impact, as it was subsequently overruled by a voter-approved amendment to the Hawaiian Constitution banning same sex-marriage.[6]

The ruling in *Baehr* also generated anti-gay-marriage activism by social conservatives who were concerned that if gay marriage were permitted in Hawaii, it would have to be recognized by other states. One result of this political pressure was congressional approval, by an overwhelming majority, of the Federal Defense of Marriage Act (DOMA), which was signed into law by President Bill Clinton in 1996. DOMA limits federal recognition of marriage to unions between a man and a woman. It thus prevents same-sex couples from receiving any of the federal rights or benefits of marriage, such as filing joint income tax or obtaining any spousal benefits under Social Security or other federal programs, even if a state eventually allows same-sex marriage. DOMA also declared that states were not obligated to recognize any same-sex marriages that might be legally sanctioned in other states. This would appear to violate the Full Faith and Credit Clause of the Constitution that guarantees that states will honor each other's legal acts and contracts and for which no categorical exceptions are specified or authorized. Only the federal courts can change this law, unless it is repealed, but to date, the law has not been challenged in court.

But in 2000, several important and prominent court decisions gave new momentum to the gay marriage legal agenda. In *Baker v. State* [744 A.2d 864, 886 (1999)], the Vermont State Supreme Court held that same-sex couples were entitled to "obtain the same benefits and protections afforded by Vermont Law to married opposite-sex couples." The Court did not decree a particular remedy, but sent the issue to the state legislature to construct appropriate legislation to implement its decision. The legislature responded by creating a new status open to same-sex couples called "Civil Unions." This status included all of the legal benefits of marriage, such as the right to receive maintenance and support from a partner; access to state courts and rules for division of property and child custody upon divorce; priority of inheritance if a partner dies without a will; the right to adopt children together and to become the legal guardian of their partner's children; the right to qualify for family health insurance; visitation and notice rights when a partner is hospitalized; and many other benefits. While many opponents of gay marriage felt Vermont had gone too far in accommodating gay relationships, many gays viewed Vermont as a defeat because it withheld the status of marriage.[7]

In 2001, Massachusetts went where Vermont had feared to tread. On April 11, seven gay and lesbian couples filed same-sex marriage suits in the trial court in Boston. The couples stressed the practical problems resulting from being unable to marry, such as obstacles to visiting rights when a partner was ill, covering a partner's child with health insurance, or being burdened with taxes in selling their home that would not be applied to married couples. "Unequal treatment is inconsistent with the Constitution," their attorney said, "[All] these couples seek is equality." The Massachusetts suit resulted in an outcry in "defense of marriage" by politicians in Massachusetts and elsewhere, who viewed marriage as an important American institution that should be limited to heterosexual couples. And indeed, the Boston trial court rejected the suit. Judge Thomas Connolly relied on what he called the "centuries-old" definition of marriage and the "central" role of procreation in marriage. "Recognizing that procreation is marriage's central purpose, it is rational for the legislature to limit marriage to opposite-sex couples who, theoretically, are capable of procreation," Connolly wrote. He directed the plaintiffs (as did Justice Scalia in his dissent in *Lawrence*) to take their plea to the legislature, not to the courts.[8]

The plaintiffs appealed and the case, *Goodridge v. Massachusetts Department of Public Health* ([440 Mass. 309 (2003)], reached the Massachusetts Supreme Judicial Court on March 4, 2003. On November 19, this Court reversed the lower court's decision, holding that same-sex couples have a state constitutional right to the "protections, benefits, and obligations of civil marriage." As a state ruling, the *Goodridge* decision was not compelled by the *Lawrence* decision, nor, given its basis in state law, can it be appealed to the Supreme Court. *Lawrence* was clearly influential, however, as Chief Justice Margaret Marshall quoted from its majority opinion, stating that "Our obligation is to define the liberty of all, not to mandate our own moral code." The Massachusetts court considered and rejected the various rationales put forward by the state to defend its opposition to same-sex marriage, including providing a "favorable setting for procreation" and childrearing and defending the institution of marriage. To these points, Chief Justice Marshall responded that, "It is the exclusive and permanent commitment of the marriage partners to one another, not the begetting of children, that is the *sine qua non* of civil marriage." She noted that the plaintiffs "seek only to be married, not to undermine the institution of civil marriage ... The marriage ban works a deep and scarring hardship on a very real segment of the community for no rational reason."

The gay challengers to the Massachusetts law had claimed that "civil unions" would not satisfy the requirements of the Massachusetts Constitution " ... for when it comes to marriage, there really is no such thing as separating the word 'marriage' from the protections it provides. The reason for that is that one of the most important protections of marriage is the word, because the word is what conveys the status that everyone understands as the ultimate expression of love and commitment ... To follow Vermont by creating a separate system, just for gay people, simply perpetuates the stigma of exclusion that we now face because it would essentially be branding gay people and our relationships as unworthy of this civil institution of marriage."[9]

And the Court agreed. Despite the Massachusetts governor's attempt to block implementation of the court's mandate, and despite an attempt in the Massachusetts legislature to substitute a civil unions bill for marriage, the Massachusetts Court held firm that civil unions were not an acceptable

Opponents of gay marriage say that it undermines the American family, but supporters of gay marriage assert that denying gay marriage legal recognition deprives gays of the right to express the same commitment to family ties allowed to other Americans. Photo courtesy of Joan Gregg.

implementation of its ruling. Indeed, the court's response to the legislature was a simple, "No," and it characterized the civil unions bill as "an attempt to circumvent the court's decision." The court acknowledged that its ruling conflicted with the federal DOMA, but said that withholding the term "marriage" from gay relationships "assigned same sex … couples to second class status," which is a violation of the Massachusetts Constitution which forbids "group classifications based on unsupportable distinctions." And so, gay marriage became legal in Massachusetts.

WHAT NEXT AFTER MASSACHUSETTS?

Court decisions on gay marriage are complicated by the intense politicization of this issue. Although the Massachusetts Supreme Judicial Court, in its final decision legalizing gay marriage, specifically said its ruling was a matter of constitutional law, not social policy, just after the Court's decision, the Massachusetts legislature passed an amendment to invalidate it. This amendment cannot take effect for several years, however, as it requires ratification in the 2005–2006 legislative session and in a public referendum.[10] Meanwhile, President George Bush, with an eye on the upcoming national elections, and perhaps anticipating that the federal

DOMA might not withstand constitutional scrutiny, called for an amendment to the U.S. Constitution to limit marriage to a union between a man and a woman. Though this initiative failed, it did serve the conservatives' political agenda, which hoped to make same-sex marriage a wedge issue in the national election; eleven states put same-sex marriage ban amendments to state constitutions on the ballot, and all passed. This is in addition to the 37 states that had already enacted similar laws after the 1996 passage of the federal DOMA statute.[11]

Partly as a result of the 2004 national election and the success of the state referenda, soon after the election gay activists began shaping their agenda for the future.[12] Some, like Evan Wolfson, Executive Director of Freedom to Marry, are totally committed to pursuing a litigation strategy accepting nothing less than gay marriage, confident that eventually the courts will decide that anti-gay marriage bans violate the Constitution.[13] Wolfson notes that marriage issues—divorce, interracial marriage, use of contraception among married couples, property and other rights for married women—have always generated intense debate in the United States and that eventually these battles were won in the courts and subsequently in the arena of public opinion and legislation. Other gay activists agree, arguing that gay marriage is now the central issue for the gay community.[14]

Other gay groups, such as the Human Rights Campaign, are following a different direction, putting their energies into fighting for benefits like those secured by civil unions or domestic partnerships, rather than litigating for gay marriage. The strategy of these groups is to educate the public about the lives of gay people through personal contacts in community organizations, with the aim of defusing the hostility and even hatred engendered by gay marriage litigation and its legislative fall-out.[15]

Conservative Justices, like Antonin Scalia, persist in framing gay rights as social issues that should be fought in legislatures, rather than in courts. But many gay activists are adamant that the legal struggle must continue because gay marriage is an issue of basic civil rights, not to be decided by majority votes in state referendums or state legislatures, as Justice Scalia recommended in his dissent. The Supreme Court's decision in *Lawrence* would seem to confirm this view.

GENDER NON-CONFORMITY AND MARRIAGE

Although the issue of gay marriage has attracted the most attention from politicians, the public, and the media, another important civil rights issue involves the rights of gender non-conformists, sometimes called transsexuals or transgendered people.[16] Transsexuals and transgendered persons have, as well as homosexuals, challenged state marriage laws, challenging courts to consider new concepts of sex and gender developing in the medical and social sciences, instead of relying only on "traditional" or even dictionary definitions of man and woman, male and female. Court cases involving the rights of transsexuals in marriage essentially raise the question of whether a transsexual is to be legally defined in terms of the sex at birth, or the sex/gender identity after sex-reassignment surgery.

One such case, *In the Matter of the Estate of Marshall G. Gardiner, Deceased,* [273 Kan. 191; 42 P.3d 120 (2002)] reached the Supreme Court of Kansas. J'Noel Ball and Marshall Gardiner were married in Kansas. J'Noel was a transsexual; she was born a male and had been undergoing the physiological transformation to become a female for several years. In August 1994 J'Noel underwent sex-reassignment surgery involving the removal of his penis and the construction of a vagina and vaginal canal. The doctor performing the surgery stated that J'Noel should now be considered a "functioning, anatomical female." After the surgery J'Noel petitioned the Circuit Court of Outagamie County, Wisconsin, where she was born, for a new birth certificate that would reflect her new name as J'Noel Ball and her sex as female. The court ordered the state registrar to make these changes, permissible under Wisconsin law. J'Noel also had her driver's license, passport, health documents, and her student identification at two universities changed to reflect this new sex/gender transformation.

While a student J'Noel Ball met and married Marshall Gardiner in Kansas in 1998. In August 1999 Gardiner died without leaving a will. His son Joe, by a previous marriage, went to court to oppose J'Noel's receiving a spousal share of his father's estate. Joe Gardiner claimed that J'Noel's marriage to his father was void because J'Noel remained a male for the purpose of the "opposite sex" requirement of Kansas law, which recognizes "only the traditional marriage between two parties who are of the opposite sex." The district court upheld Joe Gardiner's claim and J'Noel appealed to the state's Supreme Court, with the support of the American Civil Liberties Union and other civil rights groups.

The Kansas Supreme Court upheld the district court's finding. The court acknowledged that both science and the courts are divided on whether transsexuals are more appropriately defined in terms of their birth sex status or their post-operative sex/gender status. But the Kansas court held that, while "through surgery and hormones, a transsexual can be made to look like a woman ... the sex assignment surgery does not create the internal sexual organs of a woman .... There is no womb, cervix or ovaries in the post-operative transsexual female." The Court acknowledged that, "J'Noel, born male, wants and believes herself to be a woman. She has made every conceivable effort to make herself a female ... her female anatomy, however, is still all man-made. The body J'Noel inhabits is a male body in all aspects other than what the physicians have supplied.... From that the Court has to conclude, that ... as a matter of law, J'Noel is a male."

The Court held that the Kansas legislature had clearly intended to sanction marriage only between a male and a female, and that these words "in everyday understanding do not encompass transsexuals. The common, ordinary meaning of 'persons of the opposite sex' contemplates what is commonly understood to be a biological man and a biological woman. A post-operative male-to-female transsexual does not fit the common definition of a female. A traditional marriage is the legal relationship between a biological man and a biological woman ... whose relationship is founded on the distinction of sex. The stated purpose of [the Kansas law] is to recognize that only traditional marriages are valid in this state. A post-operative male-to-female transsexual is not a woman within the meaning of the statutes and cannot validly marry another man." Thus, the Court held the marriage between J'Noel and Marshall Gardiner to be void. This Kansas decision, while breaking no new legal ground, illustrates the complex issues state courts and legislatures will have to consider in evaluating the legal validity of various kinds of marriages, particularly in light of court decisions on gay marriage.

NOTES

1. Jill Norgren and Serena Nanda, *American Cultural Pluralism and Law,* 2nd ed. (Westport, CT: Praeger, 1996), chapter 9; David F. Burrelli and Charles Dale, "Homosexuals and U.S. Military Policy: Current Issues." CRS Report for Congress (Washington, D.C.: The Library of Congress, updated May 27, 2005); for treatment of gay rights in federal and state appellate courts, see Daniel Pinello, *Gay Rights and American Law* (New York: Cambridge, 2003).

2. *Griswold v. Connecticut* [381 U.S. 479 (1965)].

3. Peter Irons, *The Courage of Their Convictions: Sixteen Americans who Fought Their Way to the Supreme Court* (New York: The Free Press, 1988), chapter 16, "Michael Hardwick v. Michael Bowers."

4. *Roe v. Wade* [410 U.S. 113 (1973)]; Linda Greenhouse, "When Second Thoughts Come Too Late," *New York Times,* November 5, 1990, A14.

5. Linda Greenhouse, "Same-sex Marriage: The Context; Supreme Court Paved Way for Marriage Ruling with Sodomy Law Decision." *New York Times,* Nov. 19, 2003, A24.

6. For overviews of gay marriage as a civil right, see Jonathan Goldberg-Hiller, *The Limits to Union: Same-Sex Marriage and the Politics of Civil Rights* (Ann Arbor: The University of Michigan Press, 2002); Jo Ann Citron, Review of *Equality Practice: Civil Unions and the Future of Gay Rights,* by William N. Eskridge, *The Women's Review of Books,* 20 (January 2003), 7; Evan Gerstmann, *Same Sex Marriage and the Constitution* (New York: Cambridge, 2004).

7. David Moats, *Civil Wars: A Battle for Gay Marriage,* (Orlando: Harcourt, 2004).

8. David Garrow, "Toward a More Perfect Union," *New York Times Magazine,* May 9, 2004, 52.

9. Garrow, "Toward a More Perfect Union," 55.

10. Pam Belluck, "Massachusetts Plans to Revisit Amendment on Gay Marriage," *New York Times,* May 10, 2005, A13; Pam Belluck, "Effort to Undo Gay Marriage Ruling Fails, for Moment," *New York Times,* February 12, 2004, A26; Pam Belluck, "Setback is Dealt to Gay Marriage," *New York Times,* March 30, 2004, A1.

11. Katharine Q. Seelye, "Moral Values Cited as a Defining Issue of the Election," *New York Times*, November 4, 2004, A4; Adam Liptak, "Caution in Court for Gay Rights Groups," *New York Times*, November 12, 2004, A16; includes map indicating status of same-sex marriage by state.

12. "Lambda Legal Issues Analysis/Advisory on Antigay Amendments to State Constitutions Passed by Voters," http://www.lambdalegal.org/; for a detailed history of judicial, legislative, and political responses to the attempts of gay people to marry, see Martin Dupuis, *Same-Sex Marriage, Legal Mobilization, and the Politics of Rights* (New York: Peter Lang, 2002).

13. Evan Wolfson, *Why Marriage Matters: America, Equality, and Gay People's Right to Marry,* (New York: Simon and Schuster, 2004).

14. Richard Goldstein, "The Radical Case for Gay Marriage: Why Progressives Must Join this Fight," *Village Voice*, September 3–9, 2003, 32–34; Evan Gerstmann, *Same-Sex Marriage and the Constitution* (Cambridge: Cambridge University Press, 2004).

15. Kate Zernike, "Groups Vow Not to Let Losses Dash Gay Rights," *New York Times*, November 14, 2004, A30; John M. Broder, "Groups Debate Slower Strategy on Gay Rights," *New York Times*, December 8, 2004, A1.

16. Transgender Law and Policy Institute, http://www.transgenderlaw.org/; Paisley Currah, "Defending Genders: Sex and Gender Non-Conformity: the Civil Rights Strategies of Sexual Minorities, *Hastings Law Journal*, 48 (August 1997), 1363–85; Arthur S. Leonard, *Sexuality and the Law: An Encyclopedia of Major Legal Cases* (New York: Garland, 1993).

PART IV

Community and Citizenship

CHAPTER 11

Fighting Prejudice: Persons with Disabilities and Homeless Persons

Persons with disabilities and homeless persons fight against prejudice and discrimination arising from a culture that worships self-reliance and pays only modest lip service to the idea that "no man is an island unto himself." Members of each group are engaged in a struggle that tests the willingness of our affluent and democratic society to validate their humanity and acknowledge their contributions. In the twentieth century each group benefited from the efforts of activists who attacked societal prejudice while asserting the equal rights of group members. In particular, over the past 30 years strong new social movements have been formed by each group as both disabled and homeless persons seized the power to define themselves and to use the media and courts to challenge the many forms of discrimination that they encounter. The resulting dialogue has greatly expanded the public's understanding of the obstacles faced by members of these two groups. It has also provoked a sometimes angry examination of what is meant by equal rights and reasonable accommodation in a culture obsessed with individual achievement.

AMERICANS WITH DISABILITIES

Individuals with disabilities, writes social scientist Ruth O'Brien, "have physical and mental impairments as a result of birth, an injury, or an illness."[1] Activists acknowledge, however, that the term "disability" is sometimes too broad to have useful meaning. Writer Nancy Mairs, a quadriplegic, has pointed out that her life with multiple sclerosis bore "little resemblance" to that of her 91-year-old mother-in-law, "still physically robust but increasingly confused," or her 33-year-old niece "who has no eyes, and none of the three of us has much in common with the ... man mumbling and shambling down the street in front of my house."[2] And the lives of these people are distinctly different from the quadriplegic rugby players whose fierce, full-contact wheelchair competition is documented in the film *Murderball*.

Advocates for disability rights do agree that they are fighting the widespread tendency to view individuals with impairments as "the other" and to think of them as "a symbol of failure, frailty, and ... a counterpoint to normality."[3] In all societies attitudes toward the disabled are shaped by cultural values. In the United States, broadly speaking, this pits norms of self-reliance and competition against social and religious ideas of compassion, diversity, and the ethic of care.

In the United States in the late nineteenth century, and for much of the twentieth century, families, supplemented by institutional care providers, looked after the disabled. After the Civil War, "homes" for veterans were established, financed by public revenue including the newly expanded pension benefits given to injured soldiers. Asylums warehoused adults, and children, with physical and mental impairments. Laura Bridgman, blind and deaf, lived at Boston's Perkins Institution for the Blind from the age of seven.[4] But Helen Keller, a person of greater economic privilege, lived in the home of her parents, her friend and teacher Anne Sullivan and, later in life, her own house.[5]

In the first half of the twentieth century, as the power of physicians and the importance of science increased, disabilities came to be viewed as a medical condition. Treatment and care followed from this perspective. But in the early 1970s as individuals with disabilities began to build a social movement in which they would have greater say, assumptions changed. The fundamental tenet of the movement is now that "'disability' is a social construction rather than a medical condition." This is not, activists argue, to look away from medical realities but "to emphasize that such realities are not intrinsically disabling; they become so only when society is constructed, whether deliberately or heedlessly, so that it fails to take into account the full range of human capabilities."[6]

In 1990, with considerable bipartisan fanfare, Congress enacted, and the first President Bush signed, the Americans with Disabilities Act (ADA) (104 Stat. 327). In celebrating the new law the president said it signaled "the end to the unjustified segregation and exclusion of persons with disabilities from the mainstream of American life."[7] Supporters also applauded the ADA as landmark legislation that would address the problems of earlier federal laws, in particular the 1973 Rehabilitation Act, whose overly broad language left it open to judicial attack and did not protect individuals with disabilities from private sector discrimination.

According to the ADA's preamble, persons with disabilities constituted a "discrete and insular minority who have been faced with restrictions and limitations, subjected to a history of purposeful unequal treatment, and relegated to a position of political powerlessness ... resulting from stereotypic assumptions not truly indicative ... of individual ability ... to participate in, and contribute to society."[8] The legislation expressed, in concrete terms, a new disability policy framework, one that was grounded in equal rights law, with the goals of inclusion, empowerment, and economic opportunity. One activist called it a "declaration of independence and equity for people with disabilities."[9]

The Americans with Disabilities Act prohibits discrimination against individuals with disabilities in employment, transportation, public accommodations, and communications. Its provisions cover the actions of the federal, state, and local governments as well as private employers with as few as 15 employees. At the workplace, the law requires nondiscriminatory application procedures, qualification standards, and selection criteria. Employers must make "reasonable accommodation to the known limitations of a qualified applicant or employee unless to do so would cause an undue hardship." Individuals with a contagious disease and people who illegally used drugs or alcohol are excluded from the bill's protection.

The law also requires that providers of public and private transportation purchase or lease buses and railroad cars that are accessible to individuals with disabilities. Barriers to access in terminals are outlawed. The comprehensive nature of the legislation is further expressed in Title III, the public accommodations section, which prohibits discrimination by private owners of hotels, theaters, restaurants, shopping malls, stores, and office buildings. Like private businessmen and women, state and local governments were told that public facilities, services, and communications must be accessible to the disabled.

The years since passage of the ADA have seen important changes benefiting individuals with disabilities and the general public. Access to public transportation and to sidewalks, public buildings, and private businesses has improved. Some studies show that employment has risen among people with work limitations, although other analyses have found that the ADA's "accommodation mandates" have diminished employment opportunities for persons with disabilities.[10] Critically, through individual writing and use of the media, the disability rights community has laid out a blunt and honest appraisal of issues and solutions. In personal narratives they describe how they have, and have not, used the ADA to address discrimination. And they show how difficult it is to change the public's views about persons with disabilities, citing, for example, the columnist Ruth Shalit who wrote that the ADA had created a "lifelong buffet of perks, special breaks and procedural protections" for people with questionable disabilities.[11]

While Congress and some state and local governments have responded positively to the modern disability rights campaign, the federal judiciary, in the short time since enactment of the ADA, has proven to be significant

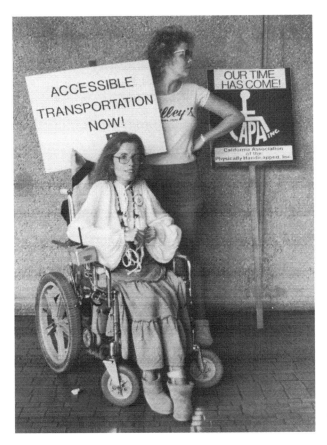

Transportation, critical for employment as well as quality of life, has been an important issue for the disability rights movement. Access to mass transportation is addressed in the 1990 Americans with Disabilities Act. Photo courtesy of Tom Olin.

obstacle. Federal judges have interpreted the act narrowly, "enfeebl[ing]" and "gutting," in particular, the provisions adopted to prevent discrimination in employment.[12] Early in its deliberations, the U.S. Supreme Court sent a clear message in *Bradgon v. Abbott* [524 U.S. 624(1998)]. The justices indicated that *defining* disability would constitute a significant part of their decision making, and that the determination of who had a disability must be made on a case-by-case basis.

Activists speak of the 1999 *Sutton v. United Air Lines* case (527 U.S. 471) as a stark indication of the high court's willingness to gut the employment protections of the ADA. The controversy in *Sutton* began when twin sisters, with severe but completely correctable visual acuity of 20/200, sued

United Air Lines, which had rejected their applications for employment as pilots because they did not meet its minimum requirements of uncorrected vision. The sisters, Karen Sutton and Kimberly Hinton, already worked as pilots for regional airlines and met federal vision standards for global airline pilots. They filed suit under the ADA arguing that they were being impermissibly discriminated against because of their physical impairment.

In a 7–2 decision, upholding two lower federal courts, the Supreme Court ruled that the airline was within its rights under the ADA in refusing to hire Sutton and Hinton. In her majority opinion, referring to *Bragdon*, Sandra Day O'Connor made it clear that, unlike members of racial or gender groups, individuals claiming to belong to the category *disabled* have to *prove* membership. To do so an individual must show that a physical or mental impairment substantially limits one or more major life activities, that there is a record of such impairment, or that he or she is regarded as having such an impairment.

O'Connor then went on to state, in a shattering interpretation of the ADA, that under Title I an individual does not have a disability if her condition could be mitigated, or corrected, with medication or equipment. In other words, an individual may not prove a disability by being examined in her uncorrected state, that is, for example, without a needed prosthetic limb, eyeglasses, or antipsychotic medicine. Congress, O'Connor wrote, did not intend "to include all persons with corrected physical limitations among those covered by the Act."

Justices John Paul Stevens, joined by Justice Stephen Breyer, dissented. Stevens opened his opinion by calling for the Court to "give it [the ADA] a generous, rather than a miserly, construction," an interpretation that admits an individual into the category *disabled* "without regard to mitigation." He found that congressional reports filed prior to passage of the legislation were "replete with references to the understanding that the act's protected class includes individuals with various medical conditions that ordinarily are perfectly 'correctable' with medication or treatment." He also argued that executive branch agencies have "consistently interpreted the act as mandating that the presence of disability turns on an individual's uncorrected state." Further, he said, the majority had been "cowed by [the airline's] persistent argument that viewing all individuals in their unmitigated state will lead to a tidal wave of lawsuits."

Addressing what he saw both as the flaw in the Court's reasoning and a bitter irony, he suggested that "if United regards [Sutton and Hinton] as unqualified because they cannot see well without glasses, it seems eminently fair for a court also to use uncorrected vision as the basis for evaluating [their] life activity of seeing."

A year later the Supreme Court cemented its narrow reading of the ADA in another workplace case, *Toyota v. Williams* (534 U.S. 184). Again determined to limit the number of individuals entitled to the basic assurances of the law, a unanimous Court ruled against assembly line worker Ella Williams, who had contested Toyota's right to terminate her employment after failing to accommodate her needs as a worker who had developed bilateral carpal tunnel syndrome. Writing the Court's opinion, Justice O'Connor reaffirmed that *individualized assessments* of the effect of an impairment must govern the determination of who qualified as disabled. "It is insufficient," she wrote, "for individuals attempting to prove disability status under this test to merely submit evidence of a medical diagnosis of an impairment." Instead, she argued, a claimant must prove a disability "by offering evidence that the extent of the limitation ... *in terms of their own experience* ... is substantial" (emphasis added). Using this approach the Court found that Ella Williams, who was able to perform certain personal hygiene and household chores, was not substantially limited in the major life activity, manual tasks, and need not, therefore, be accommodated by her employer who, no longer wishing to assign her to a modified inspection job, terminated her employment. In other words, because Ella Williams was able to brush her teeth twice a day and help with certain household tasks, the Court found that she was not sufficiently impaired to require accommodation for eight hours of repetitive work gripping tools with hands and arms extended. Toyota was within its rights in firing her for refusing to do so.

While decisions like *Sutton* and *Toyota* sharply disappointed the disability rights community, a challenge brought under the ADA's Title II, prohibiting discrimination in the provision of public services, has been hailed as a partial victory. In *Olmstead, Commissioner, Georgia Department of Human Resources v. L. C.*, [527 U.S. 581 (1999)], the justices concluded, albeit with a "qualified yes," that the ADA requires states to place persons with mental disabilities in community settings rather than in institutions. Writing for a divided Court Justice Ruth Bader Ginsburg said that, "when the State's treatment professionals have determined that community placement is appropriate [and] the transfer from institutional care to a less restrictive setting is not opposed by the affected individual," such action is in order. She added, however, the caveat that "the placement ... tak[es] into account the resources available to the State and the needs of others with mental disabilities."

Consistent with the Court's general approach to disability law, Ginsburg refused to discuss the issues presented in terms of constitutional rights, insisting that the courts below had been correct in resolving the case "solely on statutory grounds," rather than the Fourteenth Amendment due process claims (the right to be free from undue restraint). Yet Ginsburg's opinion did hold that unjustified isolation is "properly regarded as discrimination based on disability."

In a lengthy concurring opinion Justice Anthony Kennedy addressed the question of deinstitutionalization, a now many-decades long debate in medical and political communities. He stated that, "depopulation of state mental hospitals has its dark side," and quoted an expert who had concluded that for a substantial minority of mentally ill persons "deinstitutionalization has been a psychiatric *Titanic*." Kennedy warned that it "would be unreasonable, it would be a tragic event, then, were the ... ADA to be interpreted so that States had some incentive, for fear of litigation, to drive those in need of medical care and treatment out of appropriate care and into settings with too little assistance and supervision." He also cautioned, reflecting the Rehnquist Court's deference to federalism and Georgia's cost-based defense, that "[G]rave constitutional concerns are raised when a federal court is given the authority to review the State's choices in basic matters such as establishing or declining to establish new [mental health] programs." In his dissent, Justice Clarence Thomas echoed this concern, writing that "the majority's approach imposes significant federalism costs, directing States how to make decisions about their delivery of public services."

At least one activist, however, disagrees with Thomas, arguing that while *Olmstead* provides a very important recognition of the right to live outside institutions, states "can ... cry poverty to avoid doing anything meaningful to implement the decision," so that implementation has been spotty at best with "many states hav[ing] a very cynical attitude about what's required of them."[13]

Lawsuits under the ADA have continued unabated since these early cases. The range of issues addressed has been broad and the judicial decisions mixed. In one closely watched case Patricia Garrett, a registered nurse employed by the University of Alabama, sued under provisions of the ADA claiming that her treatment and recovery needs as a breast cancer patient had not been properly accommodated by the university. The U.S. Supreme Court ruled against her in *University of Alabama v. Garrett* [531 U.S. 356 (2001)], agreeing with Alabama that Garrett's money damages lawsuit, in a federal court, was barred by Eleventh Amendment (state) sovereign immunity. In another case, however, Casey Martin, a professional golfer who suffers from a congenital degenerative circulatory disorder that makes it dangerous for him to walk for long periods, succeeded in arguing that, under the ADA, he must be allowed to use a cart on the PGA tour; and in a 2005 case, the Court agreed that even cruise ships sailing under foreign flag which call at American ports must make some (but not complete) accommodation for passengers with disabilities.

In addition to the Rehnquist Court's use of individual assessment in the determination of who qualified as disabled under the ADA, its deference to federalism emerged as a defining theme in its jurisprudence. For this reason, and after Alabama's victory in the *Garrett* case, the disability community waited tensely for the outcome of *Tennessee v. Lane* (541 U.S. 509), which was decided by the Supreme Court in May 2004.

In *Lane* the justices were asked to decide whether Congress had the power under the Fourteenth Amendment's Section 5 to legislate, through the ADA, the enforcement of the constitutional right of physical access to courts. The case arose when George Lane, a paraplegic who uses a wheel-chair, had to crawl up two flights of stairs to get into a Tennessee court-room where he was facing criminal charges. When the state and county failed to provide access, he sought damages and equitable relief, citing the ADA's Title II, which prohibits discrimination in public services.

In *Garrett* the justices had decided that the ADA's Title I employment provisions did not "validly abrogate" state sovereign immunity. They had not, however, addressed this question with respect to the ADA's Title II, public services. In *Lane,* in a 5–4 decision, they decided that "the funda-mental right of access to courts, constitutes a valid exercise of Congress' [Section] 5 authority to enforce guarantees of the Fourteenth Amendment [here due process access to the courthouse]," rejecting the state's assertion of a sovereign immunity from suit. Writing for the Court, Justice Stevens argued that "the unequal treatment of disabled persons in the administra-tion of judicial services has a long history." Congress, he said, "was justi-fied in concluding that this 'difficult and intractable proble[m]' warranted 'added prophylactic measures in response,'" including the abrogation of state sovereign immunity.

The disability rights community celebrated the *Lane* opinion, hoping it would be the opening wedge for the greater use of the ADA's access to public services provisions. In contrast to the line of ADA cases involv-ing the workplace, many of which have been decided on narrow grounds providing limited, or even no, protection against discrimination, *Lane* augurs the possibility of a more sweeping judicial endorsement of rights for disabled persons seeking equal and fair access to public services and programs. In *Lane* Justice Stevens took pains to note how disabled persons had often been shut out of civic life for reasons of access. Looking at *Lane,* on the one hand, and *Garrett* on the other, one legal commentator argues that there appears "an enduring lesson … [T]he government has more leeway … when it is trying to promote access to legislatures and court-rooms [than employment]."[14] A subsequent but inconclusive test of Title II occurred in 2005 in the case of wheelchair-bound prisoner Tony Goodman (*Goodman v. Georgia*), leaving observers uncertain whether, under the new leadership of Chief Justice John G. Roberts, the Court will continue or end the "enfeebling" of the ADA.

We turn now to a case study of a second group that has used the law to end the effects of prejudice and discrimination. Like the movement to establish the rights of persons with disabilities, political and legal action on behalf of individuals who are homeless presents fundamental ques-tions concerning the willingness of our society to support changes through which people can live more humane lives. In the next part of this chapter we examine the social and legal situation of homeless persons, one that is additionally burdened by the too-common public view that they are mor-ally responsible for their own failures because they reject important core values of American culture.

HOMELESS MEN

Homeless persons include many different groups—single men and women, families, the mentally and physically ill, working and middle-class people down on their luck, and many others. We focus here upon single men, a group that has given rise to many legal cases that have asserted the rights of homeless individuals.

The link between stable residence and social order has a long history in the United States. Often, transient strangers were not welcomed in American communities, which using a variety of laws, such as vagrancy laws, kept transients "moving on."[15] With increasing immigration, internal migration, expanding transportation, and the expansion of industrialization, which required a stable, cheap, and docile labor force, however, worker movement in the United States increased greatly and communities became less able to defend their boundaries and insulate themselves from working men on the move. In spite of this great movement, however, these men on the move were viewed as potential criminals and parasites, people who shared few values of settled family life. Historically, and today, these men viewed the police as "the guardian angels of organized society." Whether vigilant, as in small towns, or more lenient, as in big cities, in enforcing vagrancy laws, the police and the courts presented a major obstacle to those men without stable homes in the community.[16]

American cultural images of men on the move reflect our ambivalence about the dual values of freedom and responsibility: on the one hand, the romance of the hero-cowboy living in male company without family only marginally attached to the larger society, and on the other, the attributes of failure, dependency, lack of self-control, unpredictability, and excessive drinking that attach to those we label "the homeless."

The desire of government to control those perceived as alienated from or in opposition to dominant cultural values of docile wage labor, home and property ownership, and social mobility and respectability may be seen in the many laws passed by local communities—against vagrancy, public drunkenness, and begging—that were, and are, employed to control these "dangerous classes." Because homeless men often drink to excess, they are particularly vulnerable to laws against public drunkenness, a major way that government penalizes a lifestyle so opposed to mainstream American values.[17] Although jail time has proven practically useless in rehabilitating individuals who drink too much, from a cultural perspective, laws against public intoxication express the American belief that uncontrollable drinking symbolizes a moral defect and a threatening detachment from the American values that underlie our economic and political system: achievement orientation, consumerism, willingness to submit to the discipline of wage labor, and commitment to the nuclear family. We suggest that it is, then, not excessive drinking but the opposition of homeless persons to American values that is at the heart of legal actions denying them the right to be different.

LIVING IN PUBLIC SPACES

Prior to the 1960s, many male urban transients either had intermittent housing or were homeless only because they were on the move. Beginning in the late 1960s, however, the number of individuals labeled as homeless increased rapidly and their character changed significantly. In many cities, urban redevelopment programs claimed many of the areas that had previously housed Skid Row inhabitants in single-room occupancy hotels, mission lodgings, and shantytowns. With the exception of the elderly, who were not perceived as threatening, most of the men and, now, increasingly women who had found shelter in these areas were literally on the street. Because little new, low-income public housing was built after the 1960s, these individuals, like an increasing number of poor people, were displaced with nowhere to go. In addition, with the decriminalization of vagrancy and public drunkenness during these years, many of the homeless men who might have been jailed were now on the street.

Two other social phenomena during this time added to the homeless population. One was the deinstitutionalization of the mentally ill, which was the result of some states' policies of closing their large psychiatric facilities, combined with the lack of community halfway houses. The other was the destruction of inexpensive Single Room Occupancy (SRO) housing as real estate developers were given tax incentives to gentrify urban neighborhoods. At the same time, the rapid expansion of drug use throughout the United States both brought many other dependent persons to cities and increased the numbers of urban residents who, because of addiction, drifted down the ladder of poverty and joined other populations of homeless living in public spaces.

Given the cultural importance of a home in American society, individuals who live in public spaces are often seen as alien and threatening. Further, in a nation whose dominant cultural myth is that "all people can make it if they really want to and work hard," anyone who lives on the street is easily stamped as a self-made failure deserving very little sympathy. In our culture, where social status and respectability are largely expressed by home and neighborhood, people who have achieved statuses of which they are proud resist sharing their space with homeless persons. It is difficult for many Americans to be sympathetic to homeless persons, who must create a life for themselves under the constraints of extreme poverty and often the liabilities of drug addiction, mental illness, physical disability, or alcoholism.

In addition, partly because facilities for washing, changing clothes, and sleeping are not easily available to homeless people, they must perform many private acts of personal hygiene in public. And finally, not only are homeless persons not usually considered part of a community despite their presence, in addition, the presence of mental illness or drug addiction makes them appear unpredictable and therefore

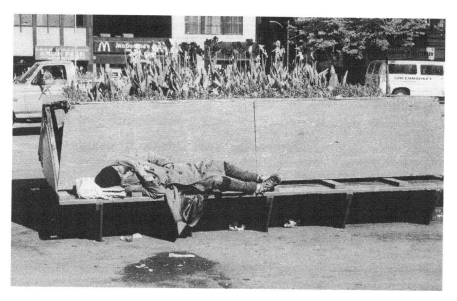

An increase in poverty and a decline in government-funded affordable housing mean that many more Americans are without shelter, seeking to survive on the streets as best they can in the face of laws against begging and inappropriate use of public spaces. Photo courtesy of Serena Nanda.

dangerous. For all these reasons the demand on the part of homeless people that they have unfettered access to public space goes beyond that which many Americans today are willing to accommodate. As a result, in the cities and suburbs of America laws and regulations are being both invoked and newly created in order to restrict the use of public places by homeless individuals.[18]

Many of the issues about the rights of homeless persons to use public space emerged dramatically in a case involving the quiet suburban town of Morristown, New Jersey, in the late 1980s.[19] Richard Kreimer, a longtime resident of the town, had become homeless, and he, like many other homeless persons around the country, frequented the reading room of the public library. Other library users and the librarians objected to Kreimer's presence because he often stared at other patrons and because his body and clothes smelled offensively. In a specific effort to keep Mr. Kreimer out of the library, the library adopted a set of written rules that permitted library staff broad latitude to eject patrons who were not engaged "in activities associated with use of a public library;" patrons who engaged in behaviors that harassed and annoyed other individuals in the library; and patrons "whose bodily hygiene is so offensive as to constitute a nuisance to other persons." Based on these regulations, Kreimer was ejected from the library by six police officers.

Kreimer sued the police, library officials, and the township in federal court, claiming a violation of his First Amendment rights. In a very sympathetic opinion, issued in May 1991, federal district court Judge H. Lee Sarokin struck down the Morristown library rules that had been used to eject Mr. Kreimer.[20] First, in holding that the library regulations violated Kreimer's First Amendment right to participate in free expressive activities, Judge Sarokin noted that "[T]he public library is one of our great symbols of democracy. It is a living embodiment of the First Amendment because it includes voices of dissent. It tolerates that which is offensive … [and] … provides access to books, newspapers and magazines." Stating that the library was the "quintessential" traditional public forum for the communication of ideas, Judge Sarokin argued that any government attempt to restrict access to such forums must be justified by a significant government interest and be "narrowly tailored to serve that interest, and the government must leave open alternative channels of communication." He defined the permissible purposes of the library very broadly, including that of "quiet contemplation" as well as reading. While acknowledging that "[L]ibraries cannot and should not be transformed into hotels or kitchens, even for the needy," and that library governing boards had the right and obligation to assure that the library was used for its intended purposes, Judge Sarokin was also firm in stating that such regulations must be specific, neutral, and nondiscriminatory in their enforcement.

Judge Sarokin was also sensitive to the social-class bias raised in this case. He characterized the bodily hygiene rule as a "smell test" that was also really a "wealth" test, with a disparate impact on the poor, and particularly on homeless individuals like Mr. Kreimer who had no access to a shower. Noting that Mr. Kreimer could not afford newspapers and books, Judge Sarokin admonished society that "[I]f we wish to shield our eyes and noses from the homeless, we should revoke their condition, not their library cards." Judge Sarokin then went on to say that the greatness of our country lies in its tolerance of a wide diversity of people, even those whom we may find repulsive, and particularly when the "cause of our revulsion may be of our own making."

Nearly a year later, a federal appeals court reversed Judge Sarokin's decision, holding that the Morristown library rules were consistent with the nature of a library; that a library was only a limited public forum; and that a person with offensive bodily hygiene illegitimately interfered with other patrons' rights and could be ejected.[21]

THE RIGHT TO PRIVACY

"The wind may enter, the rain may enter, the sun may enter, but the King may not enter." This quote from English common law is the foundation of one of America's most cherished rights, that to be free from the intrusion of government in one's home, articulated in the Fourth Amendment's command that people hold the right against government "to be secure in their persons, houses, papers, and effects, against unreasonable searches and seizures" without probable cause. One question raised by occupation of public spaces by individuals who are homeless is whether they enjoy that same protection.

In 1991, a case before the Connecticut Supreme Court explicitly raised this issue. In August 1987, David Mooney had been arrested for robbery and murder based on information provided by an accomplice hoping to plea bargain. Seeking evidence, local police went to an area under a high-way bridge abutment where Mooney had been living at the time of his arrest. There they found a closed duffel bag and a closed cardboard box containing personal belongings. Although they did not have a warrant, the police searched these containers and found evidence linking Mooney to the robbery and murder for which he was arrested, and subsequently convicted.[22]

On appeal, Mooney's court-appointed lawyer argued that the trial court should have suppressed evidence seized by the police from under his highway bridge abutment home. Mooney claimed that the police had violated his Fourth Amendment rights "by invading his home without a warrant" and that the police had further violated those rights when they seized and then searched his belongings including the closed duffel bag and cardboard box. Mooney argued that the abutment was his home: He had been living there for one month, he was the only person living in that place, he had no other residence during this period, and when he left the area during the day, he attempted to secure all of his belongings and to place them out of public view. His belongings included a blanket used as a mattress, a rolled-up sleeping bag, a place for trash, and several closed containers.

Reversing the decision of the trial court, the Connecticut Appeals Court accepted that as Mooney had attempted to establish and protect the privacy of his belongings in his "home" by placing them in closed containers out of public view, evidence seized from these containers could not be used by the prosecution. The court majority opinion argued that it would be contrary to American "values and notions of custom and civility" to deny Mooney his "last shred of privacy from the prying eyes of outsiders" to permit search of his belongings without a legal warrant. The court made clear, however, that it was not deciding whether the Fourth Amendment protects the belongings of all homeless persons regardless of specific cir-cumstances.[23]

In a sharply worded dissent, three of the judges argued that as Mooney's belongings were "knowingly exposed to the public," they could be legally considered abandoned, and thus Mooney could have no reasonable expec-tation of privacy. The dissent insisted that homeless individuals should not have greater privacy rights in public places—even if they considered them their homes—than members of the general public. In a telling conclusion the dissenting judges criticized the majority, accusing them of "allowing the current publicity and plight of the homeless to create an empathy that in turn has created bad Fourth Amendment law."

ECONOMIC RIGHTS OF HOMELESS PERSONS

Courts have also affected the ability of homeless persons to survive through adjudicating issues involving their rights to make a living. A very important way that homeless individuals survive today is by returning bottles and cans to retail food stores to claim deposits. In 1983, the New York State legislature enacted the Returnable Container Act, which required retailers to redeem bottles and cans of products carried by that store, during business hours, with no proof of purchase. This law was intended to discourage litter and to protect the environment by contributing to the state's recycling program. Under this legislation, consumers were required to pay an additional five cents on each bottle or can to encourage the return of containers rather than their casual disposal.

In urban areas such as New York City, the Returnable Container Act had the additional consequence of providing an important source of income for homeless persons. The law permitted an individual to return up to 240 cans or bottles at any one store per day. Many stores, however, contrary to the law, only accepted 10 to 20 bottles and cans at a time, severely affecting the income of homeless persons. In 1988 the Legal Action Center for the Homeless in New York City took this issue to court.

These advocates for homeless people fashioned a class action suit, charging that "the homeless relied heavily on the refunds on cans for their daily bread and board" and that the supermarkets' refusal to accept 240 cans "constituted a special injury against the homeless." The Legal Action Center filed for damages, civil penalties, and injunctive relief. Lawyers for the six supermarkets cited in the litigation responded that the law imposed an unfair burden on their clients: The stores incurred costs of labor and processing the refunds, they had to pay rent for the storage of empties, they received more empties than they sold, and they claimed that distributors often "balked" at picking up the empties. In addition, the stores received complaints from customers about the unpleasant appearance and smell of the homeless persons and the clogging of entranceways by homeless people waiting to redeem their cans and bottles. They did not add that supermarket management would prefer that containers not be redeemed at all so that the store could keep the five-cent deposit. In fact, since nowhere near all redeemable containers are returned, stores do already get to keep much of the deposit, which they could use to cover their costs in redeeming containers.

In July 1989, *Conway Farmer v. D'Agostino* was heard in New York County Supreme Court by Judge Beverly S. Cohen, who granted a preliminary injunction that ordered the supermarkets to obey the state law and accept 240 cans at a time from any one individual. Judge Cohen wrote that she understood the reluctance of the markets to extend themselves to help the homeless: " … there is not much incentive to the supermarkets to welcome numbers of the poor and homeless onto their premises to engage in an activity which brings no profit" and which brings problems to them. However, she also reminded the supermarkets that "[H]ardship resulting from obeying the law" cannot be taken into account.[24] Judge Cohen agreed that homeless people suffered irreparable economic harm from not being permitted to redeem their full quota of containers. She noted that the economic position of homeless people is precarious, and therefore rejected the claim of the supermarket lawyers that homeless individuals are no different from other people who receive money from returning cans and bottles. Quoting Anatole France, that "[T]he Law in its majestic equality forbids all men, the rich as well as the poor, to sleep under bridges, to beg in the streets and to steal bread," Judge Cohen said that to treat homeless people the same as others, would be, "acting blindly to ignore the huge disparity in economic position between the homeless and others in our city."[25]

That homeless persons are indeed different from other people is clearly seen in the case of begging in public spaces. Much of the public's hostility to panhandlers grows out of their perception that panhandlers could work if they wanted to. Panhandlers are aware of this and in their pitches for money often attempt to persuade the public that they prefer work to begging, but are unable to work.[26] Many homeless persons in fact cannot work because of mental illness, physical disability, or drug and alcohol addiction. While this might not preclude needy homeless individuals from doing irregular simple labor, these conditions do prevent them from holding regular, even unskilled jobs.

In cities with large pedestrian populations and heavily used mass transit, such as New York City, panhandlers are found in great numbers, especially since the 1980s, no longer confined to skid rows, but in more affluent sections of the city and on mass transit. In 1989, the management of the New York City Transit Authority (TA) and other public transit operations commenced "Operation Enforcement," a program designed to enforce a long-standing prohibition on panhandling that already existed in the city's subways. Claiming that passengers waiting for trains and buses, and subway riders, felt "harassed and intimidated" by panhandlers whose demands for money included "unwanted touching, detaining, impeding and intimidating," the TA distributed a million and a half pamphlets summarizing their rules, including "No panhandling or begging." These rules, also displayed on thousands of posters throughout the subway system, warned violators that they would be subject to arrest, fines, and removal.

Soon after this enforcement campaign began, the Legal Action Center for the Homeless brought a class action suit in federal district court, on behalf of all needy homeless persons who lived in the state of New York and "would be asking or soliciting others for charity for their own benefit" in train, bus, and other places of public transport. In *Young v. NYTA*, these advocates for homeless persons argued that begging was a form of political and social communication protected by the First Amendment right to free speech and that the TA prohibitions were thus a violation of the Constitution.[27] In defense of their position, the Center claimed that in view of the current economic and political situation in New York, begging was a vital political speech because each destitute person who begs is communicating the uncomfortable, disturbing idea of extreme poverty in the midst of staggering wealth. Evicting beggars from the subways thus cuts off one of their most effective channels of communication.

Federal district court Judge Leonard B. Sand agreed that begging is communicative conduct, deserving of First Amendment protection. He noted the testimony of two homeless plaintiffs who said that their begging often led to questions from passersby interested in knowing what it was like to be homeless and soliciting their opinions on public programs for the homeless. The plaintiffs described these conversations as opportunities for them to be advocates for the homeless. Judge Sand also pointed out that the "simple request for money by a beggar cannot but remind the passerby that people in the city live in poverty and often lack the essentials for survival." For Judge Sand, begging was a form of communication that was both "unmistakably informative and persuasive" about a major public policy issue. He held that transportation terminals were public forums where individuals were entitled to practice free speech, and suggested the TA regulate this activity rather than imposing a total ban.[28]

The Transit Authority appealed and the federal court of appeals overturned Sand's decision.[29] Appeals Court Judge Frank X. Altimari expressed the court's "grave doubt as to whether begging and panhandling in the subway are sufficiently imbued with a communicative character to justify constitutional protection." This court held that begging was "expressive conduct" rather than "pure speech" and was therefore entitled to less First Amendment protection. Central to the appeal court's argument was the view that "most individuals who beg are not doing so to convey any social or political message. Rather they beg to collect money." In addition, the court stated that whatever possible social or political message was intended by panhandling, most passengers were unlikely to discern the message and in any case were more likely to experience a sense of threat, harassment, or intimidation than a political message.

In upholding the "substantial government interests" of the TA regulations, Judge Altimari pointed out that "[T]he subway is not a domain of the privileged and powerful but the primary means of transportation for literally millions of people of modest means, including hardworking men and women, students and elderly pensioners … [and] begging and panhandling often involve 'unwanted touching and detaining of passengers.'" He implied that panhandling is often very close to extortion: "Begging is 'inherently aggressive' to passengers who are 'captive' in the subway ... [and whether intended or not] begging in the subway often amounts to nothing less than assault, creating in the passengers the apprehension of imminent danger, and thus raises legitimate concerns about public safety." Based upon this reasoning, the appeals court reversed the district court, which it said, "... reflected undue deference 'to the alleged individual rights of beggars and panhandlers' and 'amounts to nothing less than a menace to the common good.'"[30] The judges said that while they were sympathetic to the homeless, "it is not the role of this court to resolve all the problems of the homeless" and on balance, they found the TA prohibition on begging was reasonable.

In this and other similar opinions, courts argued strongly that because beggars are not licensed and, therefore, presumptively screened by the state, they represent an "unknown element" insofar as their character, honesty, and intention.[31] In *Young v. NYTA,* Judge Altimari specifically stated that "government clearly has an interest in protecting the general public from being approached for money by potentially disruptive or intimidating sources," and these court opinions view begging as a menace to the common good. On this point, none of these court opinions compared individual begging with the possible psychological intimidation, harassment, or inconvenience of other forms of constitutionally protected solicitation, such as telephone solicitation or door-to-door charitable solicitation, which also raise the issue of a "captive" audience in a potentially dangerous way.

A RIGHT TO BE HOMELESS

The ambivalence of American culture toward homeless people is reflected in the varied legal positions taken by state and federal courts. Similar to other groups seeking rights through the courts, an important factor explaining legal outcomes of cases involving homeless persons is the degree to which the group in question is perceived as culturally and morally distant from the larger American society. Judges sympathetic to the claims of homeless persons are aware of this and have explicitly rejected cultural distance as a reason to deny rights. Judge Sarokin made this point in criticizing the Morristown library officials who, he said, "suffer from the discriminatory assumption that poverty is a proxy for 'moral pestilence;'" he also called the library's "hygiene test" an "irrational and unreasonable wealth classification with a disparate impact on the poor."[32] Cultural or moral distance was also invoked in those court opinions rejecting the claims of homeless people, emphasizing instead the threat, fright, and intimidation that the ordinary subway rider experiences from homeless panhandlers.

While homeless persons have always been among us, what is new is their willingness to challenge government actions that curtail their most fundamental rights, like those of privacy, access to public spaces, and the right to earn a living. The increased rights consciousness of the 1960s and the emergence of public interest law groups (for example, the New York Coalition for the Homeless and the New York Legal Action Center for the Homeless) and private pro bono legal advocacy have been critical in the ability of individuals who are homeless to claim their rights. At the same time that some of these rights are being upheld, however, across the nation increasing hostility by local officials and some segments of the public toward homeless persons is demonstrated by increasing numbers of local ordinances that target or fall unequally on them. Many of these ordinances give the police wide discretion in enforcement, including arrest, "moving them along," confiscating their personal property, and destroying their makeshift shelters."[33]

Advocates for homeless persons charge that the "knee jerk response of criminalizing the symptoms of homelessness" is both inhumane and ineffective. Successful litigation reminds the public that homeless persons have rights, but it is costly and does not solve the problem of homelessness. Tolerance and more humane treatment, rather than law, may be a better solution. James Spradley's anthropological study of "urban nomads" in Seattle, reminds us that there are men who will always be tramps and transients.[34] He asks, "Is American society large enough to tolerate and even welcome such diversity?"

NOTES

1. Ruth O'Brien, *Crippled Justice: The History of Modern Disability Policy in the Workplace* (Chicago: University of Chicago Press, 2001), 1.
2. Nancy Mairs, "Disability/gender Bifocals," *The Women's Review of Books* (June 2004), 16.
3. O'Brien, *Crippled Justice*, 1.
4. Elisabeth Gitter, *The Imprisoned Guest* (New York: Farrar, Straus and Giroux, 2001).
5. Dorothy Herrmann, *Helen Keller: A Life* (New York: Knopf, 1998).
6. Mairs, "Disability," 16.
7. President George Herbert Walker Bush, ADA Signing Statement (July 26, 1990).
8. 42 U.S. C. Section 12101 (a)(7).
9. O'Brien, *Crippled Justice*, 162.
10. Douglas Kruse and Lisa Schur, "Employment of People with Disabilities Following ADA," *Industrial Relations* 42 (2003); Peter Blanck, "Justice for All?: Stories About Americans with Disabilities and Their Civil Rights," *Journal of Gender, Race, & Justice* 8 (2004); Ruth Colker, *The Disability Pendulum* (New York: New York University Press, 2005), chapter 3.
11. Ruth Shalit, "Defining Disability Down," *New Republic* (April 25, 1997), 16; Colker, *Disability Pendulum*, 6–7.
12. O'Brien, *Crippled Justice*, 5; Ruth O'Brien, *Bodies in Revolt* (New York: Routledge, 2005), ix.
13. Personal communication to authors (September 29, 2005).

14. Vikram David Amar, "The Supreme Court Hands Down a Key Federalism/ Disability Law Decision, And Surprises Some Observers with its Results," *Writ* (May 27, 2004), http://writ.news.findlaw.com/amar/20040527.html.

15. David J. Rothman, *The Discovery of the Asylum: Social Order and Disorder in the New Republic* (Boston: Little, Brown, 1971).

16. Sidney L. Harring, "Class Conflict and the Suppression of Tramps in Buffalo, 1892–1894," *Law and Society Review* 11 (Summer 1977); Nels Anderson, *The Hobo: The Sociology of the Homeless Man* (Chicago: University of Chicago Press, 1923; 1965).

17. *Powell v. Texas*, 392 U.S. 514, 538–39, (1968).

18. *The Right to Remain Nowhere: A Report on Anti-Homeless Laws and Litigation in 16 United States Cities* (Washington, DC: National Law Center on Homelessness and Poverty, December 1993).

19. Robert Hanley, "Suing, A Homeless Man Refuses to Yield," *New York Times*, October 10, 1991, B1; Robert Hanley, "Homeless Man Has Deal in 2nd Suit in Morristown," *New York Times*, March 3, 1992, B7; Robert Hanley, "Library Wins in Homeless Man Case," *New York Times*, March 26, 1992, B8.

20. *Kreimer v. Bureau of Police for Town of Morristown*, 765 F. Supp. 181 (D.J.N. 1991), 182–84.

21. *Joint Free Public Library of Morristown and Morristown Township v. Kreimer*, 958 F. 2d. 1242 (1992).

22. "A Homeless Person's Cave Is His or Her Castle," *New York Times*, December 4, 1990, A30.

23. *State of Connecticut v. Mooney*, 218 Conn. 85 (1991).

24. *Conway Farmer v. D'Agostino Supermarkets, Inc.*, Supreme Court: New York County, IAS Part 31, Index No. 11170/89. Opinion, Beverly S. Cohen, Judge, July 20, 1989.

25. Ibid., 7.

26. Brackette F. Williams, "Homework on Homelessness and Begging in Two U.S. Cities," *Current Anthropology* 36(1), February 1995.

27. *Young v. New York City Transit Authority*, 729 Supp. 341 (S.D.N.Y., 1990).

28. Ibid., 352.

29. *Young v. NYTA*, 903 F. 2d 146 (2nd Cir. 1990).

30. Ibid., 149–58.

31. *Walley v. NYTA*, Supp. Ct. State of NY, Kings County, Decision, Index No. 177/91, June 3, 1991. Opinion, Judge Jules L. Spodek.

32. *Kreimer v. Morristown* (1991), 196.

33. *The Right to Remain Nowhere*, 5.

34. James P. Spradley, *You Owe Yourself a Drunk: An Ethnography of Urban Nomads* (Boston: Little, Brown, 1970), 261–62.

100 Percent American: Who Qualifies in a National Emergency? Japanese Americans and the Law

The tolerance, appreciation, and legitimization of cultural differences vary with the historical period. In times of war, rights accorded cultural minorities often become restricted. In the United States this issue was clearly raised in the experiences of Japanese Americans during World War II. The wartime experiences of Japanese Americans, put under curfew and forcibly evacuated to detention camps, demonstrate the extent to which officials were prepared to go to protect the national security from what many in the government perceived as a dire threat from a portion of the citizenry within its own borders. Upwards of 120,000 Japanese Americans, 70,000 of whom were American citizens and the rest of whom were resident aliens, were imprisoned for several years during World War II.

By 1941 relations between Japan and the United States had deteriorated, strained by Japan's expansionist policies toward China and Southeast Asia. On December 7 the Japanese attacked the American naval base at Pearl Harbor, Hawaii. The next day the United States declared war on Japan and several days later entered the European war against Fascist Germany and Italy.

In response to Pearl Harbor, and reflecting a longstanding antagonism toward Asians in the western United States, popular and official sentiment pressed for action to be taken against the perceived threat of sabotage and espionage posed by Americans of Japanese ancestry, including Japanese American citizens, on the West Coast.

Two months later, in February 1942, President Roosevelt announced Executive Order No. 9066. This executive act authorized the secretary of war "to prescribe military areas ... from which any or all persons may be

The attack on the U.S. naval base at Pearl Harbor by the Japanese in World War II is memorialized in Honolulu, Hawaii. The alleged need to protect California from its Japanese American residents, fueled by economic interests wishing to dispossess Japanese Americans of their farms and businesses, led American courts to uphold Japanese American internment, despite the absence of any evidence of their disloyalty. Photo courtesy of Joan Gregg.

excluded, and ... subject[ed] to whatever restrictions the Secretary of War ... may impose.... " In language that created a smokescreen for the government's actions, the secretary of war was further authorized to provide for residents excluded from restricted areas "such transportation, food, shelter, and other accommodations as may be necessary" to implement the order. President Roosevelt's justification for this measure rested on the assertion that "the successful prosecution of the war requires every possible protection against espionage and ... sabotage."

Lt. General J. L. DeWitt, military commander of the Western Defense Command, became the central figure in implementing the executive order with regard to imposing a curfew and evacuating, relocating, and interning Americans of Japanese ancestry from the Pacific Coast of the United States, which he believed was especially vulnerable to acts of espionage and to attack because of its geographical location. Under Executive Order 9066, DeWitt was given authority to "provide for the removal from designated areas of persons whose removal is necessary in the interests of national security" and for their relocation, maintenance, and supervision. In March 1942 Congress enacted legislation ratifying this presidential order and imposing criminal sanctions on those who would not comply.

The attack on Pearl Harbor was the catalyst for transforming longstanding antagonism, even hatred, of the Japanese by whites living on the West Coast into new measures of legally sanctioned discrimination. Legally approved discrimination against Asian immigrants and Asian Americans stretched back into the nineteenth century and was never solely the product of attitudes on the West Coast. Indeed, in spirit and often in wording, legal disabilities applied to Asian immigrants drew upon colonial and early-Republic-era laws intended to limit the political and social rights of Native Americans and African Americans. One of the earliest acts of Congress, for example, the 1790 Naturalization Act, restricted American citizenship to "a free white person." This eighteenth-century legislation—elaborated upon by the Naturalization Act of 1870—continued to be an integral part of national policy against the naturalization of persons of Asian ancestry until the 1952 McCarran-Walter Act.[1]

Various nineteenth-century state laws singled out Asians in other ways. Legislation prohibited Asian immigrants and Asian Americans from testifying against a white person, purchasing land, or marrying a Caucasian. Asian heritage defendants were treated more harshly in criminal courts.[2] The national Homestead Act of 1862 tied eligibility for land to citizenship, which thus excluded Asian immigrants. And, in 1882, the desire to limit labor competition from Chinese workers and to insulate American society from new cultural influences led Congress to enact draconian anti-Asian legislation. Through the 1882 Chinese Exclusion Act, the federal government barred all Chinese laborers from entering the United States for ten years, specifically prohibited the naturalization of Chinese in the United States for citizenship while requiring them to carry identity papers, and denied entry to the United States to the wives of Chinese laborers already in the country.[3]

Exclusion legislation was extended in the 1917 Immigration Act. In this statute Congress enumerated more than 30 classes of people who were prohibited from entering the United States, including those who were residents of the geographic area designated the Asiatic Barred Zone (India, Afghanistan, Burma, Thailand, most of the Polynesian islands, the area then known as Indochina, Indonesia, Malaysia, and the Asiatic parts of Russia).[4] Exclusion legislation applicable to Japanese was enacted in the Immigration Restriction Act of 1924.[5] The rationale given for barring Asian persons was that they were unwilling to assimilate and would work for low wages. Americans did not stop to consider how American xenophobia, anti-miscegenation, and school segregation laws directed toward Asians, and court decisions preventing Asian naturalization, prevented assimilation.[6]

At the time of the bombing of Pearl Harbor, two groups of people of Japanese ancestry lived in the United States. The first consisted of resident aliens who had qualified as legal immigrants prior to the restrictive 1924 Immigration Act. A second group included Japanese Americans who were citizens because they had been born in the United States. In implementing Executive Order 9066, Lt. General DeWitt officially named "all persons of Japanese ancestry, both alien and non-alien" as the subject of his security measures. The discriminatory nature of these orders is revealed in the fact that they applied to Japanese-heritage American citizens solely on the basis of their identity and that *no* incidents of espionage or sabotage in the months prior to these orders involved Japanese resident aliens. Indeed, both the Federal Bureau of Investigation (FBI) and the Federal Communications Commission (FCC) stated that no such security threat existed and that the military measures proposed by DeWitt were unnecessary.

Dewitt, however, argued otherwise in a February 1942 report to the secretary of war: "The Japanese race is an enemy race and while many second and third generation Japanese born on U.S. soil, possessed of U.S. citizenship, have become 'Americanized,' the racial strains are undiluted." DeWitt concluded his observations with an extraordinary act of reasoning: "The very fact that no [Japanese American] sabotage has taken place to date is a disturbing and confirming indication that such action will be taken."[7]

The discriminatory treatment of Japanese Americans is further underscored by contrasting their treatment with that of German and Italian American citizens and aliens living in the United States at the outbreak of the war. While some German and Italian Americans and aliens were evacuated and imprisoned, there was no systematic internment *by group* of German or Italian Americans. German and Italian Americans subject to evacuation or internment, unlike Japanese Americans, were nearly all afforded prompt loyalty hearings. By late 1942, when most Japanese Americans on the West Coast were beginning a three year incarceration, German and Italian Americans had benefited from loyalty proceedings and were free to live where they pleased. The contrasting treatment is all the more remarkable in light of organized pro-German rallies in the late 1930s, the discovery of several German spy rings at the beginning of the war, and reports by the U.S. government that the Nazis conducted "devastating naval warfare ... along the East Coast" perhaps with aid from people on shore.[8] Despite these facts, the wartime curfew, evacuation, and internment measures as they targeted an entire community on the basis of racial identity fell only on Japanese Americans and resident alien Japanese.

These measures did not go unchallenged. Between 1942 and 1944 four legal appeals testing the constitutionality of the military's regulations as they applied to Japanese Americans and aliens were initiated and reached the U.S. Supreme Court. In the first case to be heard by the Court, *Hirabayashi v. United States* (1943), Japanese American plaintiffs challenged the legality of both the curfew and the evacuation orders. The justices of the Supreme Court avoided the issue of evacuation and addressed only the question of curfew orders, unanimously upholding them. The Court did not question the government's assertion that Japanese Americans maintained their attachment to Japan or that they posed a serious security threat. The justices reasoned that war powers were sufficiently broad to justify the government's actions. On the same day the court also upheld curfew regulations in *Yasui v. United States* [320 U.S. 115 (1943)]. Six months later a divided court upheld the exclusion order challenged in *Korematsu v. United States*, while refusing to consider the legality of detention. In *Korematsu*, Justice Hugo Black wrote, "hardships are a part of war ... and ... all citizens ... feel the impact of war in greater or lesser measure." With these words Black—otherwise a noted civil libertarian—expressed the willingness of the Court, and the country, to impose this burden exclusively on those of Japanese ancestry—both citizens and non-citizens—despite undisputed findings that greater security risks existed within the German and Italian communities in the United States.

HIRABAYASHI V. UNITED STATES 320 U.S. 81 (1943)

Chief Justice Stone delivered the opinion of the Court.

Appellant, an American citizen of Japanese ancestry, was convicted in the district court of violating the Act of Congress of March 21, 1942, which makes it a misdemeanor knowingly to disregard restrictions made applicable by a military commander to persons in a military area prescribed by him as such, all as authorized by an Executive Order of the President.

The questions for our decision are whether the particular restriction violated, namely that all persons of Japanese ancestry residing in such an area be within their place of residence daily between the hours of 8:00 p.m. and 6:00 a.m., was adopted by the military commander in the exercise of an unconstitutional delegation by Congress of its legislative power, and whether the restriction un-constitutionally discriminated between citizens of Japanese ancestry and those of other ancestries in violation of the Fifth Amendment.

The indictment is in two counts. The second charges that appellant, being a person of Japanese ancestry, had on a specified date, contrary to a restriction promulgated by the military commander ... failed to remain in his place of residence in the designated military area between the hours of 8:00 o'clock p.m. and

6:00 a.m. The first count charges that appellant, on May 11 and 12, 1942, had, contrary to a Civilian Exclusion Order ... failed to report to the Civil Control Station within the designated area, it appearing that appellant's required presence there was a preliminary step to the exclusion from that area of persons of Japanese ancestry ....

[A]ppellant asserted that the indictment should be dismissed because he was an American citizen who had never been a subject of and had never borne allegiance to the Empire of Japan, and also because the Act of March 21, 1942, was an unconstitutional delegation of Congressional power. On the trial to a jury it appeared that the appellant was born in Seattle in 1918, of Japanese parents who had come from Japan to the United States, and who had never afterward returned to Japan; that he was educated in the Washington public schools and at the time of his arrest was a senior in the University of Washington; that he had never been in Japan or had any association with Japanese residing there.

The evidence showed that appellant had failed to report to the Civil Control Station ... He admitted failure to do so, and stated it had at all times been his belief that he would be waiving his rights as an American citizen by so doing.

We conclude that it was within the constitutional power of Congress and the executive arm of the Government to prescribe this curfew order for the period under consideration and that its promulgation by the military commander involved no unlawful delegation of legislative power.

The war power of the national government is "the power to wage war successfully." ... The power is not restricted to the winning of victories in the field and the repulse of enemy forces. It embraces every phase of the national defense ...

That reasonably prudent men charged with the responsibility of our national defense had ample ground for concluding that they must face the danger of invasion, take measures against it, and in making the choice of measures consider our internal situation, cannot be doubted.

As the curfew was made applicable to citizens residing in the area only if they were of Japanese ancestry, our inquiry must be whether in the light of all the facts and circumstances there was any substantial basis for the conclusion, in which Congress and the military commander united, that the curfew as applied was a protective measure necessary to meet the threat of sabotage and espionage which would substantially affect the war effort and which might reasonably be expected to aid a threatened enemy invasion. The alternative which appellant insists must be accepted is for the military authorities to impose the curfew on all citizens within the military area, or on none. In a case of threatened danger requiring prompt action, it is a choice between inflicting obviously needless hardship on the many, or sitting passive and unresisting in the presence of the threat. We think that constitutional government, in time of war, is not so powerless and does not compel so hard a choice if those charged with the responsibility of our national defense have reasonable ground for believing that the threat is real.

When the orders were promulgated there was a vast concentration, within Military Areas Nos. 1 and 2, of installations and facilities for the production of military equipment, especially ships and airplanes. Important Army and Navy bases were located in California and Washington. Approximately one-fourth of the total value of the major aircraft contracts then let by Government procurement officers were to be performed in the State of California. California ranked second, and Washington fifth, of all the states of the Union with respect to the value of shipbuilding contracts to be performed.

At a time of threatened Japanese attack upon this country, the nature of our inhabitants' attachments to the Japanese enemy was consequently a matter of grave concern. Of the 126,000 persons of Japanese descent in the United States, citizens and non-citizens, approximately 112,000 resided in California, Oregon and Washington at the time of the adoption of the military regulations. Of these approximately two-thirds are citizens because born in the United States ...

There is support for the view that social, economic and political conditions which have prevailed since the close of the last century, when the Japanese began to come to this country in substantial numbers, have intensified their solidarity and have in large measure prevented their assimilation as an integral part of the white population.

In addition, large numbers of children of Japanese parentage are sent to Japanese language schools outside the regular hours of public schools in the locality. Some of these schools are generally believed to be sources of Japanese nationalistic propaganda, cultivating allegiance to Japan. Considerable numbers, estimated to be approximately 10,000, of American-born children of Japanese parentage have been sent to Japan for all or a part of their education.

Congress and the Executive, including the military commander, could have attributed special significance, in its bearing on the loyalties of persons of Japanese descent, to the maintenance by Japan of its system of dual citizenship. Children born in the United States of alien Japanese parents, and especially those children born before December 1, 1924, are under many circumstances deemed, by Japanese law, to be citizens of Japan.

The large number of resident alien Japanese, approximately one-third of all Japanese inhabitants of the country, are of mature years and occupy positions of influence in Japanese communities. The association of influential Japanese residents with Japanese Consulates has been deemed a ready means for the dissemination of propaganda and for the maintenance of the influence of the Japanese Government with the Japanese population in this country.

As a result of all these conditions affecting the life of the Japanese, both aliens and citizens, in the Pacific Coast area, there has been relatively little social intercourse between them and the white population. The restrictions, both practical and legal, affecting the privileges and opportunities afforded to persons of Japanese extraction residing in the United States, have been sources of irritation and may well have tended to increase their isolation, and in many instances their attachments to Japan and its institutions.

Appellant does not deny that, given the danger, a curfew was an appropriate measure against sabotage.

But appellant insists that the exercise of the power is inappropriate and unconstitutional because it discriminates against citizens of Japanese ancestry, in violation of the Fifth Amendment.

Distinctions between citizens solely because of their ancestry are by their very nature odious to a free people whose institutions are founded upon the doctrine of equality. For that reason, legislative classification or discriminations based on race alone has often been held to be a denial of equal protection. We may assume that these considerations would be controlling here were it not for the fact that the danger of espionage and sabotage, in time of war and of threatened invasion, calls upon the military authorities to scrutinize every relevant fact bearing on the loyalty of populations in the danger areas. Because racial discriminations are in most circumstances irrelevant and therefore prohibited, it by no means follows that, in dealing with the perils of war, Congress and the Executive are wholly precluded from taking into account those facts and circumstances which are relevant to measures for our national defense and for the successful prosecution of the war, and which may in fact place citizens of one ancestry in a different category from others .... We cannot close our eyes to the fact, demonstrated by experience, that in time of war residents having ethnic affiliations with an invading enemy may be a greater source of danger than those of a different ancestry ... In this case it is enough that circumstances within the knowledge of those charged with the responsibility for maintaining the national defense afforded a rational basis for the decision which they made.

   Though the opinion of the Court, which employed a rational relation test, was ultimately unanimous, in the preliminary voting Justice Frank Murphy had dissented. Under strong pressure from Justice Felix Frankfurter, Murphy agreed to change his vote and to side with the majority.[9] He wrote a concurring opinion, however, that barely veiled his distaste for the court's holding:

... It does not follow, however, that the broad guarantees of the Bill of Rights and other provisions of the Constitution protecting essential liberties are suspended by the mere existence of a state of war. It has been frequently stated and recognized by this Court that the war power, like the other great substantive powers of government, is subject to the limitations of the Constitution.
   Distinctions based on color and ancestry are utterly inconsistent with our traditions and ideals. They are at variance with the principles for which we are now waging war. We cannot close our eyes to the fact that for centuries the Old World has been torn by racial and religious conflicts and has suffered the worst kind of anguish because of inequality of treatment for different groups ... Nothing is written more firmly into our law than the compact of the Plymouth voyagers to have just and equal law. To say that any group cannot be assimilated is to admit that the great American experiment has failed, that our way of life has failed when confronted with the normal attachment of certain groups to the lands of their forefathers. As a nation we embrace many groups, some of them among the oldest settlements in our midst, which have isolated themselves for religious and cultural reasons.
   Today is the first time, so far as I am aware, that we have sustained a substantial restriction of the personal liberty of citizens of the United States based upon the accident of race or ancestry. Under the curfew order here challenged no less than 70,000 American citizens have been placed under a special ban and deprived of their liberty because of their particular racial inheritance. In this sense it bears a melancholy resemblance to the treatment accorded to members of the Jewish race in Germany and in other parts of Europe. The result is the creation in this country of two classes of citizens for the purposes of a critical and perilous hour—to

sanction discrimination between groups of United States citizens on the basis of ancestry. In my opinion this goes to the very brink of constitutional power.

Except under conditions of great emergency a regulation of this kind applicable solely to citizens of a particular racial extraction would not be regarded as in accord with the requirement of due process of law contained in the Fifth Amendment. We have consistently held that attempts to apply regulatory action to particular groups solely on the basis of racial distinction or classification is not in accordance with due process of law as prescribed by the Fifth and Fourteenth Amendments.

In the *Hirabayashi* case, the court sidestepped the issue of the exclusion of Japanese Americans from their residential communities, now designated military areas. The constitutionality of these orders was finally taken up in *Korematsu v. United States.* In its decision the justices established that the use of racial classifications by government is suspect and, when legally challenged, must be subject to "the most rigid" judicial scrutiny. Employing this standard, a majority of the high court's members nevertheless concluded that "pressing public necessity" justified the racial classification used to evacuate Japanese Americans from their homes. Justice Black delivered the opinion of the majority:

KOREMATSU V. UNITED STATES 323 U.S. 214 (1944)

The petitioner, an American of Japanese descent, was convicted in a federal district court for remaining in San Leandro, California, a "Military Area," contrary to Civilian Exclusion Order No. 34 … of the U.S. Army, which directed that after May 9, 1942, all persons of Japanese ancestry should be excluded from that area. No question was raised as to petitioner's loyalty to the United States.

It should be noted, to begin with, that all legal restrictions which curtail the civil rights of a single racial group are immediately suspect. That is not to say that all restrictions are unconstitutional. It is to say that courts must subject them to the most rigid scrutiny. Pressing public necessity may sometimes justify the existence of such restrictions; racial antagonism never can.

In the light of the principles we announced in the *Hirabayashi* case, we are unable to conclude that it was beyond the war power of Congress and the Executive to exclude those of Japanese ancestry from the West Coast war area at the time they did…. [E]xclusion from a threatened area, no less than curfew, has a definite and close relationship to the prevention of espionage and sabotage.

In this case the petitioner challenges the assumptions upon which we rested our conclusions in the *Hirabayashi* case. He also urges that by May 1942, when Order No. 34 was promulgated, all danger of Japanese invasion of the West Coast had disappeared. After careful consideration of these contentions we are compelled to reject them.

In doing so, we are not unmindful of the hardships imposed by it upon a large group of American citizens. But hardships are part of war, and war is an aggregation of hardships. All citizens alike, both in and out of uniform, feel the impact of war in greater or lesser measure. Citizenship has its responsibilities as well as its privileges, and in time of war the burden is always heavier. Compulsory exclusion of large groups of citizens from their homes, except under circumstances of direst emergency and peril, is inconsistent with our basic governmental institutions. But when under conditions of modern warfare our shores are threatened by hostile forces, the power to protect must be commensurate with the threatened danger....

It is said that we are dealing here with the case of imprisonment of a citizen in a concentration camp solely because of his ancestry, without evidence or inquiry concerning his loyalty and good disposition towards the United States. Our task would be simple, our duty clear, were this a case involving the imprisonment of a loyal citizen in a concentration camp because of racial prejudice. Regardless of the true nature of the assembly and relocation centers—and we deem it unjustifiable to call them concentration camps with all the ugly connotations that term implies—we are dealing specifically with nothing but an exclusion order. To cast this case into outlines of racial prejudice, without reference to the real military dangers which were presented, merely confuses the issue. Korematsu was not excluded from the Military Area because of hostility to him or his race. He *was* excluded because we are at war with the Japanese Empire, because the properly constituted military authorities feared an invasion ... because they decided that the military urgency of the situation demanded that all citizens of Japanese ancestry be segregated from the West Coast temporarily, and finally, because Congress, reposing its confidence in this time of war in our military leaders—as inevitably it must—determined that they should have the power to do just this. There was evidence of disloyalty on the part of some, the military authorities considered that the need for action was great, and time was short. We cannot—by availing ourselves of the calm perspective of hindsight—now say that at that time these actions were unjustified.

Despite the pressures of wartime, or, perhaps, because an Allied victory was beginning to appear likely, three of the justices dissented from the opinion of the majority in *Korematsu*. Justice Owen Roberts wrote of a "clear violation of constitutional rights" in which a citizen was convicted "for not submitting to imprisonment in a concentration camp, based on his ancestry ... without evidence or inquiry concerning his loyalty ... toward the United States." Justice Robert Jackson, too, dissented, arguing:

Korematsu was born on our soil, of parents born in Japan. The Constitution makes him a citizen of the United States by nativity and a citizen of California by residence. No claim is made that he is not loyal to this country.

A citizen's presence in the locality, however, was made a crime only if his parents were of Japanese birth. Had Korematsu been one of four—the others say, a German alien enemy, an Italian enemy alien, and a citizen of American-born ancestors, convicted of treason but out on parole—only Korematsu's presence would have violated the order. The difference between their innocence and his crime would result, not from anything he did, said, or thought, different than they, but only in that he was born of different racial stock.

Now, if any fundamental assumption underlies our system, it is that guilt is personal and not inheritable. Even if all of one's antecedents had been convicted of treason, the Constitution forbids its penalties to be visited upon him, for it provides that "no attainder of treason shall work corruption of blood, or forfeiture except during the life of the person attained." But here is an attempt to make an otherwise innocent act a crime merely because this prisoner is the son of parents as to whom he had no choice, and belongs to a race from which there is no way to resign.

Much is said of the danger to liberty from the Army program for deporting and detaining these citizens of Japanese extraction. But a judicial construction of the due process clause that will sustain this order is a far more subtle blow to liberty than the promulgation of the order itself. A military order, however, unconstitutional, is not apt to last longer than the military emergency ... But once a judicial opinion rationalizes such an order to show that it conforms to the Constitution, or rather rationalizes the Constitution to show that the Constitution sanctions such an order, the Court for all time has validated the principle of racial discrimination in criminal procedure and of transplanting American citizens. The principle then lies about like a loaded weapon ready for the hand of any authority that can bring forward a plausible claim of an urgent need.

Even more than Jackson, Justice Murphy's dissent confronted the racial issue head on, arguing that, under judicial standards set by the Court, the evacuation order failed to justify itself:

This exclusion of "all persons of Japanese ancestry, both alien and non-alien" goes over "the very brink of constitutional power" and falls into the ugly abyss of racism.

In dealing with matters relating to the prosecution and progress of a war, we must accord great respect and consideration to the judgments of the military authorities.

At the same time, however, it is essential that there be definite limits to military discretion, especially where martial law has not been declared. Individuals must not be left impoverished of their constitutional rights on a plea of military necessity that has neither substance nor support ...

Being an obvious racial discrimination, the order deprives all those within its scope of the equal protection of the laws as guaranteed by the Fifth Amendment. It further deprives these individuals of their constitutional rights to live and work where they will, to establish a home where they choose and move about freely. In excommunicating them without benefit of hearings, this order also deprives them of all their constitutional rights to procedural due process.

It must be conceded that the military and naval situation in the spring of 1942 was such as to generate a very real fear of invasion of the Pacific Coast, accompanied by fears of sabotage and espionage in that area ... [I]t is necessary only that the action have some reasonable relation to the removal of the dangers of invasion, sabotage and espionage. But the exclusion, either temporarily or permanently, of all persons with Japanese blood in their veins has no such reasonable relation. And that relation is lacking because the exclusion order necessarily must rely for its reasonableness upon the assumption that *all* persons of Japanese ancestry may have a dangerous tendency to commit sabotage and espionage ... That this forced exclusion was the result in good measure of this erroneous assumption of racial guilt rather than bona fide military necessity is evidenced by the Commanding General's Final Report on the evacuation from the Pacific Coast area. In it he refers to all individuals of Japanese descent as "subversive," as belonging to "an enemy race" whose "racial strains are undiluted," and as constituting "over 112,000 potential enemies ... at large today" along the Pacific Coast. In support of this blanket condemnation of all persons of Japanese descent, however, no reliable evidence is cited to show that such individuals were generally disloyal ... Individuals of Japanese ancestry are condemned because they are said to be "a large, unassimilated, tightly knit racial group, bound to an enemy nation by strong ties of race, culture, custom and religion." They are claimed to be given to "emperor worshipping ceremonies" and to "dual citizenship." Japanese language schools and allegedly pro-Japanese organizations are cited as evidence of possible group disloyalty ... charged or proved, that persons of Japanese ancestry were responsible for three minor isolated shellings and bombings of the Pacific Coast area, as well as for unidentified radio transmissions and night signaling.

The main reasons relied upon by those responsible for the forced evacuation, therefore, do not prove a reasonable relation between the group characteristics of Japanese Americans and the dangers of invasion, sabotage, and espionage. The reasons appear, instead, to be largely an accumulation of much of the misinformation, half-truths and insinuations that for years have been directed against Japanese Americans by people with racial and economic prejudices—the same people who have been among the foremost advocates of the evacuation. A military judgment based upon such racial and sociological considerations is not entitled to the great weight ordinarily given the judgments based upon strictly military considerations.... [T]o infer that examples of individual disloyalty prove group disloyalty and justify discriminatory action against the entire group is to deny that under our system of law individual guilt is the sole basis for deprivation of rights. Moreover, this inference, which is at the very heart of the evacuation orders, has been used in support of the abhorrent and despicable treatment of minority groups by the dictatorial tyrannies which this nation is now pledged to destroy. To give constitutional sanction to that inference in this case, however well-intentioned may have been the military command on the Pacific Coast, is to adopt one of the cruelest of the rationales used by our enemies to destroy the dignity of the individual and to encourage and open the door to discriminatory actions against other minority groups in the passions of tomorrow.

I dissent, therefore, from this legalization of racism. Racial discrimination in any form and in any degree has no justifiable part whatever in our democratic way of life. It is unattractive in any setting but it is utterly revolting among a free people who have embraced the principles set forth in the Constitution of the United States. All residents of this nation are kin in some way by blood or culture to a foreign land. Yet they are primarily and necessarily a part of the new and distinct civilization of the United States. They must accordingly be treated at all times as the heirs of the American experiment and as entitled to all the rights and freedoms guaranteed by the Constitution.

On the same day that the Supreme Court handed down its opinion in the *Korematsu* case, the justices announced their decision in the fourth major challenge to the denial of constitutional rights of Japanese

Americans. This case was *Ex parte Endo* [323 U.S. 283 (1944)]. For the first and only time in this sequence of litigation the Court conceded wartime rights of Japanese Americans, agreeing that a concededly loyal American of Japanese ancestry could not be detained beyond the period needed to determine her loyalty. The decision in *Endo*, unanimously authorizing a writ of habeas corpus, was a hollow victory given the court's prior ruling in *Korematsu*. While free to leave the detention center, Ms. Endo was not permitted, under the *Korematsu* decision (upholding evacuation), to return to her home in California, which the Army still classified as a restricted military zone and thus off limits to Japanese Americans. As in *Korematsu*, it was again Justice Murphy, in his concurrence, who most forcefully took issue with the government's unconstitutional use of racial classification in these cases: "Detention in Relocation Centers of persons of Japanese ancestry regardless of loyalty is not only unauthorized by Congress or the Executive but is another example of the unconstitutional resort to racism inherent in the entire evacuation program …. Racial discrimination of this nature bears no reasonable relation to military necessity and is utterly foreign to the ideals and traditions of the American people."

In historical perspective, it is difficult to see how the Court upheld the use of this racial classification, a classification which, in the Court's own words, is suspect and demands the most rigid scrutiny. It is also difficult to understand how, given the flimsiness of the evidence presented by the military and disputed by other government agencies like the FBI, the Court justified its decisions as ones grounded in "military necessity." For example, the justices appeared to accept without question DeWitt's contention that internment of Japanese Americans was necessary because there was no efficient way to "separate out the loyal from the disloyal," in spite of the widespread knowledge that the British had successfully carried out such a clearance program and that the United States had employed loyalty hearings for German and Italian Americans as early as 1942.

The inescapable conclusion is that these Supreme Court decisions must be understood in the context of extreme anti-Asian racial prejudice, exacerbated by economic competition on the West Coast as well as national wartime concerns. Japanese Americans were included in the general prejudice against Asians, beginning with the immigration of Chinese laborers in the mid-nineteenth century. The Japanese, in fact, came to supplant the Chinese as targets of racial hatred after the Chinese Exclusion Act, as the number of Japanese on the West Coast increased and their economic position improved.

Although the Japanese never exceeded 2 percent of California's population, and although during the period in which anti-Japanese sentiment grew, farms owned by Japanese occupied only 1 percent of cultivated land in California, their considerable economic success was perceived as threatening to Caucasian Californians, increasingly reluctant to share the wealth made possible by irrigation and an ever-expanding population.

The ability of Japanese farmers in California to produce farm goods whose value far exceeded that of white farmers, along with the more general race prejudice, led to an organized movement on the part of California farm interests to pass laws limiting Japanese land ownership and even excluding them altogether.

Despite anti-Asian and specifically anti-Japanese legislation, such as the 1924 Immigration Restriction Act, the fears of Caucasians on the West Coast did not diminish. With the attack on Pearl Harbor, representatives from white business organizations, such as the Farm Growers Association, renewed their anti-Japanese lobbying. As Austin Anson, managing secretary of the Salinas Vegetable Grower-Shipper Association frankly admitted:

We are charged with wanting to get rid of the Japs for selfish reasons … We do. It's a question of whether the white man lives on the Pacific Coast or the brown men. They came into this valley to work, and they stayed to take over … They undersell the white man in the markets … they work their women and children while the white farmer has to pay wages for his help. If all the Japs were removed tomorrow, we'd never miss them in two weeks, because the white farmer can take over and produce everything the Jap does. And we don't want them back when the war ends, either.[10]

Wartime fears about the loyalty of Japanese Americans and their subsequent internment provided an ideal opportunity for Anglo farmers to remove competition and to buy some of the best farmland in California at less than fair market value.

In addition to the prejudice against the Japanese based on economic competition, the belief that Japanese Americans resisted assimilation intensified discrimination against them. DeWitt's final report asserted that mechanisms for maintaining Japanese American ethnic identity—native language schools, voluntary ethnic associations, and dual citizenship— posed permanent and insoluble problems of national security; he did not feel that similar mechanisms among Germans and Italians posed the same threat. The undocumented and unfair nature of this allegation was commented upon by Justice Murphy, as he correctly noted that "where assimilation is a problem, it is largely the result of certain social customs and laws of the American general public." Justice Murphy further pointed out that the retention of ethnic customs "by some persons" was not evidence of disloyalty. The charge of disloyalty based on dual citizenship, he wrote, reflects a misunderstanding of the true situation, in which Japan claimed as her citizens all persons born of Japanese nationals wherever located. By World War II, Japan had modified this doctrine, and allowed all Japanese born in the United States to renounce any claim of dual citizenship and released her political claim to all those born in the United States after 1925.[11]

The belief that Japanese Americans did not assimilate fed widespread fear in the months after Pearl Harbor that they were disloyal and would engage in espionage and sabotage. The United States did not give Japanese Americans the opportunity to prove their loyalty through government hearings prior to incarceration in detention centers. Justice Jackson focuses upon this issue of due process in his *Korematsu* dissent, arguing that, given the extremely important constitutional questions involved, and the severe consequences of incarceration for the Japanese Americans, such hearings could and should have been ordered by government leaders.

The pervasive belief that these wartime cases represented an egregious denial of due process and equal protection, in violation of constitutional guarantees, prompted an immediate protesting of these decisions. After the war, this opposition coalesced into action for redress to which Congress made only the most minimal response. In 1948 that body passed the Japanese American Claims Act, giving persons of Japanese ancestry the right to claim from the government real and personal property losses (e.g., for homes, land, store leases, and stock), but not income. The Act required such elaborate proof, however, that the resulting awards totaled only $37 million (out of $131 million claimed) which was far below what would have been full and fair compensation for actual economic losses.[12] Executive Order 9066 itself was not, in fact, repealed until 1976 when President Gerald R. Ford publicly acknowledged Japanese American wartime loyalty.

THE MODERN REDRESS MOVEMENT

The modern redress movement began in the late 1970s, taking shape slowly, with members of the Japanese American community disagreeing on the nature of an appropriate response from the national government. Some individuals argued that the United States need only offer a formal apology for its discriminatory wartime policies, while other activists insisted upon monetary reparations, an antidiscrimination education campaign, and the vacating (to annul or to void) of wartime criminal convictions of Japanese Americans who had resisted curfew and evacuation. This modern movement has focused its efforts upon legislative and judicial forums and has been driven, in part, by the discovery that the White House and the military had suppressed evidence and made false statements in its legal briefs in *Hirabayashi* and *Korematsu*.

In 1980 Congress took a step toward meeting demands for redress when it established the Commission on the Wartime Relocation and Internment of Civilians (CWRIC), a body empowered to determine whether any wrong was committed against those American citizens and permanent resident aliens affected by Executive Order 9066, and if so, to recommend to Congress appropriate remedies. In its 1983 report, *Personal Justice Denied*, the members of this government commission concluded that the detention of the Japanese Americans was not justified by military necessity and that "the broad historical causes which shaped these decisions were race prejudice, war hysteria and a failure of political leadership."[13] The CWRIC characterized the incarceration as a "grave injustice." The commission subsequently recommended offering a national apology to the victims of Executive Order 9066, a presidential pardon of persons convicted of disobeying this order, favorable review by executive agencies of applications by Japanese Americans for restitution of "positions, status or entitlements, lost as a consequence of the order," an appropriation of 1.5 billion dollars to provide compensatory payments of $20,000 to each surviving victim, and support for a foundation for social education on issues of civil liberties.[14]

In the summer of 1988 Congress passed the "Civil Liberties Act," also known as "The Japanese Reparations Act" (Public Law 100–383). This legislation enacted the commission's 1983 recommendations. President Ronald Reagan, who had previously opposed government sponsored redress, signed the bill on August 10, opening the way for the Department of Justice to establish the administrative mechanism for certification of the $20,000 compensatory payment to survivors of the internment camps. The first reparation checks were issued in October 1990. The Office of Redress Administration reported that, by the end of 1994, 79,515 individuals had qualified for the $20,000 payment.[15]

In the courts, modern redress litigation originally took two directions: The original wartime plaintiffs, Yasui, Korematsu, and Hirabayashi, sought to have their convictions vacated thereby clearing their names. The three men argued that the evidence suppressed by the executive branch in 1943 and 1944 tainted the government's arguments before the Supreme Court and that it was possible, under the common law writ of error *coram nobis*, to reopen their cases in the federal courts in which they had first been heard.[16] In another quite different case, 19 named Japanese Americans plaintiffs filed suit in *Hohri v. United States* on behalf of a potential class of 120,000 victims. They sought billions of dollars in monetary damages for confiscation of property and deprivation of liberty during the war for all who were incarcerated, or their heirs.

A federal judge first dismissed the *Hohri* suit in May 1984 holding that the six-year statute of limitations for actions against the United States barred hearing the case. In his opinion, Judge Louis Oberdorfer wrote that the plaintiffs had circumstantial evidence that internment was not justified by "military necessity" as early as 1949 and should have brought legal action against the United States in the 1950s. Plaintiff William Hohri responded: "We had just come out from behind barbed wire and had been intimidated by losing four major cases in the Supreme Court based on what we now recognize as fraudulent evidence of 'military necessity.' Given those problems, the political climate of the early 1950s, and the need to start rebuilding our broken lives, how could we have been expected to mount a major lawsuit of this kind?"[17] Appeals in the *Hohri* case, which continued to turn on technical issues of jurisdiction and statute of limitations, proceeded for much of the 1980s until, in October 1988, the U.S. Supreme Court denied the last writ of certiorari.[18]

Litigation in the 1980s to clear the names of Yasui, Korematsu, and Hirabayashi proceeded with more success. Korematsu's conviction was rendered void and a finding was made of misconduct on the part of the government. Yasui won a vacating of his conviction, but did not get a finding of governmental misconduct. He appealed this as a civil suit and lost the appeal on a technicality. When he died, in November 1986, the court ruled that the case could not continue. Gordon Hirabayashi also saw his wartime conviction vacated. Quietly, many Japanese Americans and civil libertarians had hoped that at least one of the *Yasui, Korematsu,* or *Hirabayashi* appeals would go to U.S. Supreme Court. Had this happened, the justices might have considered whether *Korematsu* should be overruled "to assure that in a comparable future emergency, the balance between individual rights and perceived national security would not again be struck as it was during World War II."[19] None of the appeals did go to the Supreme Court thus preventing this outcome.

The most recent legal action connected to the redress movement has been a challenge, on the part of a number of individuals, to the federal government's denial of certification for the $20,000 compensatory payments. Claims have been filed, for example, by Japanese Americans who as children were neither taken to nor born in the internment camps, but who state that they were "deprived of liberty or property" as the result of wartime "racial prejudice, wartime hysteria, and a failure of political leadership."[20] These children, it is argued in legal briefs, "solely because of their Japanese ancestry, were involuntarily excluded from their homes and forbidden to return during the war by federal law."[21] They moved with their families, who sold their belongings and left their jobs, to regions outside the designated military areas, at the urging of the government and as an involuntary alternative to internment. Most families suffered severe economic hardships trading skilled jobs and professions for irregular minimum-wage work. They were, it is claimed, in exile in their native country. Courts have issued conflicting decisions in these cases.[22] Years of appeals will determine whether Congress intended to benefit a broad class of victims or, as lawyers for the U.S. Department of Justice contend, only those "most directly affected" by the evacuation and internment orders.

Japanese Americans, as a racially visible group, have long experienced social, economic, and political discrimination in the United States. At the national level this has been expressed by exclusionary immigration and naturalization legislation and wartime actions that were based on their visibility. Historically, at a local level Japanese Americans, particularly on the West Coast, have been the victims of newspaper propaganda, economic discrimination, and organized lobbying designed to undermine their status as Americans and even to remove them from American soil. While the justification for these actions was often rationalized by the so-called cultural differences and "clannishness" of the Japanese Americans, in fact, members of this community have demonstrated a consistent willingness to assimilate. And indeed, many of the cultural values maintained by Americans of Japanese heritage, especially patterns of hard work, saving, achievement orientation, lawfulness, family solidarity, and personal discipline, are time-honored values of the dominant American culture. Yet, in a country where racial differences have always mattered, powerful government and economic interests were able to use wartime concerns to manipulate this prejudice and to cast Japanese Americans into an unchosen status as outsiders from which, during the war, even the highest court of the land would not rescue them.

Subsequent legislative and judicial actions suggest that at least partial redress is possible. But while reparations have been paid and convictions made void, *Hirabayashi* and *Korematsu* have not been overruled. This suggests that, in wartime, military necessity might again be argued to supersede individual due process and equal protection rights.[23] Thus, the final test of the Supreme Court's decision in *Endo,* and congressional intent in enacting the 1988 Civil Liberties Act, will be whether the United States will prohibit racial and ethnic prejudice when promulgating policies justified as necessary for wartime military security. This question again came before the country in the starkest terms after the attacks carried out by Muslim terrorists on September 11, 2001. We turn, therefore, to a discussion of the legal issues raised by President George W. Bush's post-9/11 "war on terror" and its effects, in particular, on American Muslims, minority group members who, like Japanese Americans during World War II, are little understood by the dominant culture.

NOTES

1. Hyung-chan Kim, *A Legal History of Asian Americans, 1790-1990* (Westport, Ct.: Greenwood Press, 1994), 33. The right of the United States, on the basis of this legislation, to deny Asian Americans the right of naturalization was upheld by the U.S. Supreme Court in *Ozawa v. United States,* 260 U.S. 178 (1922). The McCarran-Walter Act, an otherwise conservative legislative initiative, ended earlier restrictive immigration and naturalization laws that targeted Asians.

2. John R. Wunder, "The Chinese and the Courts in the Pacific Northwest: Justice Denied?" *Pacific Historical Review* 52 (1983), 191–211.

3. 22 Stat. 58. In 1892 Congress extended the period of exclusion for an additional ten years. 27 Stat. 25. Merchants and teachers were permitted to settle. Legal restriction upon Japanese immigration to the United States was initiated in the so-called "Gentleman's Agreement of 1908" signed by the governments of the United States and Japan.

4. Kim, *A Legal History of Asian Americans,* 105; 39 Stat. 874.

5. 43 Stat. 153.

6. See, e.g., *Ozawa v. United States,* 260 U.S. 178 (1922); *Yamashita v. Hinkle,* 260 U.S. 199 (1922); and *United States v. Bhagat Singh Thind,* 262 U.S. 204 (1923).

7. Lt. General John L. DeWitt, *Final Recommendation of the Commanding General, Western Defense Command and Fourth Army, to the Secretary of War* (February 14, 1942) (Final Recommendation) (Joint Appendix), 109–10.

8. "Raskin Replies," *The Nation* (April 1, 1991), 398; also, Joel B. Grossman, Shirley Castelnuovo, and Randal Boe, "*Korematsu* after 40 Years: Can It Happen Again?" Paper presented at the Midwest Political Science Association Meeting (Chicago: April 18, 1985).

9. Grossman, "*Korematsu* after 40 Years," 17ff.

10. *Korematsu v. United States,* 323 U.S. 214, 239 (1944). Interned Japanese Americans were permitted to leave the camps if they could demonstrate that they had the ability to support themselves outside of the military exclusion zones. For example, more than 2,000 interned Japanese Americans were released to work in one of the country's largest vegetable processing plants in Seabrook, New Jersey, which was experiencing a wartime labor shortage. Jon Nordheimer, "Remembering a Haven from Shame," *New York Times,* July 20, 1994, B1.

11. *Korematsu v. U.S.,* 323 U.S. 214, 237.

12. Philip Tajitsu Nash, "Moving for Redress," *Yale Law Journal* 94 (January 1985), 747.

13. Ibid., 749.

14. Nash, "Moving for Redress, 749–50.

15. Phone interview with staff, Office of Redress Administration, December 1994.

16. Roger Daniels, *Prisoners without Trial* (New York: Hill and Wang, 1993), 99.

17. Nash, "Moving for Redress," 751.

18. *Hohri v. United States,* 586 F. Supp. 796 (1984) and *Hohri v. United States,* 782 F.2d 227 (D.C. Cir. 1986).

19. Grossman, "*Korematsu* after 40 Years," 9.

20. Appellant's Brief in the United States Court of Appeals for the Federal Circuit at 5, 7, *Ishida v. United States,* 94–5151 (December 15, 1994).

21. Brief for Amicus Curiae, National Coalition for Redress and Reparations in the United States Court of Appeals for the Federal Circuit, *Ishida v. United States* (December 5, 1994), 1.

22. *Ishida v. United States,* 31 Fed. Cl. 280 (1994) and *Consolo v. United States,* 31 Fed. Cl. 447 (1994).

23. Mark Tushnet, ed., *The Constitution in Wartime: Beyond Alarmism and Complacency* (Durham, NC: Duke University Press, 2005).

CHAPTER 13

Cultural Pluralism and the Rule of Law Post-9/11

On a beautiful Tuesday morning, September 11, 2001, at 8:46 A.M., and at 9:03 A.M., suicide highjackers deliberately crashed two commercial airliners into the twin towers of the World Trade Center in New York City. Several minutes later other hijackers crashed another airliner into the Pentagon, and a fourth plane, heading for Washington, D.C., crashed in a Pennsylvania field. Altogether almost 3,000 people were killed.[1] The United States, including the president, went into shock. Investigators identified the attackers as members of Al Qaeda, a terrorist network controlled and organized by Osama bin Laden, a Saudi Arabian national operating out of Afghanistan under the sanctions of the Taliban government.[2]

In response, President George Bush declared "a new kind of war," a global "war on terror," and with various approvals by Congress, soon after initiated a series of laws and actions as part of his strategy to eliminate the terrorist threat from abroad and at home. By October 2, 2001, the president approved plans to order American troops into Afghanistan to force the Taliban government to give up Osama bin Laden, believed to be hiding in the mountains along the Afghanistan/Pakistan border.[3] In addition, members of the president's administration began a series of secret policy discussions, including proposals for the treatment of those captured on the battlefield, aimed at protecting the security of the nation.

Emerging from the Bush administration's "war on terror" was an increased military and police presence throughout the nation as armed personnel inside the United States were redeployed with new and greater force. Across the country, airports, bridges, tunnels, train and bus stations, and American landmarks were given permanent guards. The argument presented for this increased militarism was that of national security. Given the horrendous acts of 9/11, little popular opposition emerged.[4] This intensified emphasis on national security also witnessed the emergence of a new legal culture by the Bush Administration, leading to several initiatives, particularly regarding detention of alleged terrorists, that were ultimately challenged, in legislatures and in courts, as violating the U.S. Constitution and international laws and treaties, such as the Geneva Convention, to which the United States was a signatory.

This new legal culture included the passage of the so-called Patriot Act; the detention, registration, regulation, and deportation of Muslim/ Arab citizens and alien immigrants in the United States; and the detention of "enemy combatants" at the American naval base at Guantánamo Bay, Cuba. With the invasion and occupation of Iraq, the maltreatment and torture of Iraqi prisoners, as well as those at other U.S. detention, centers not only raised questions about the legality of such acts, but called attention to the ways in which these acts singled out Islamic cultural patterns as part of a pattern of prisoner humiliation and abuse.

Reminiscent of the response to the Pearl Harbor attack, in the trauma and grief following the attack by Muslim terrorists on the World Trade Center in New York City on September 11, 2001, government measures to curtail constitutional protections affected all Americans, but fell hardest on American Arabs and Muslims. Photo courtesy of Joan Gregg.

TREATMENT OF MUSLIMS/ARABS IN THE UNITED STATES: ETHNIC PROFILING

An estimated 6 million Muslims live in the United States, of whom about 68 percent were born elsewhere, in over 80 different countries.[5] The largest group, over 30 percent, are from India, Pakistan, and Bangladesh; 26 percent are from Arab nations; while 17 percent are African Americans. American Muslims tend to be better educated and economically better off than many other immigrant groups, and are well integrated in local civil institutions, such as PTAs and Interfaith Councils. On a national level they tend to favor government programs to promote health, decrease poverty, and protect the environment, but they are more conservative on social issues, such as rights for women.

There is great religious, ideological, and cultural diversity among Muslim communities in the United States and, as with other immigrant groups, their self-identity involves the interplay of several factors, such as national origin, religion, the environment of the host country, the United States, and the length of time they have been here. Since 60 percent of the Muslim immigrants come from countries in which Muslims are a majority and that operate under Muslim (sharia) law, accommodation to a secular, culturally pluralistic society in which they are a minority, poses certain difficulties in integration. On the other hand, despite the fact that most Muslim immigration to the United States has taken place in the last 20 years, Muslims today are now increasingly integrating into the civil and political life of the nation, following the process experienced by other immigrant groups.[6]

The horrific tragedy of 9/11 thus had a particular impact on American Arab/Muslims who were not only challenged to reflect on their place in the United States, but who were also particularly targeted by post-9/11 security measures and increasingly regarded with suspicion by the larger society.[7]

As our chapter on Japanese American internment demonstrates, in times of national insecurity, immigrants, both resident aliens and citizens, are always politically vulnerable. This is particularly true when their appearance and/or culture or religion are different from the majority, and also when the larger society has little knowledge about or great sympathy for their community. In another parallel between the Japanese internment cases and Muslim Americans post-9/11, history clearly demonstrates that when a democratic government seeks a balance between security and liberty, targeting aliens from a nation or ethnic group defined as the enemy raises little public resistance. Consistent with past history, almost immediately after 9/11 the government targeted Muslim/Arab immigrants in the United States for regulation, detention, and deportation.[8]

With President Bush's declaration of a "war on terror" after 9/11, one, he claimed that may go on indefinitely, the U.S. government immediately began to curtail domestic civil liberties, as part of a domestic "war on terror" that selectively focused on Muslim/Arab aliens. Thousands were detained in secret, under newly created immigration laws by the INS (Immigration Service); refused trials or hearings for months; interrogated under highly coercive conditions; held incommunicado and without access to lawyers; deported for wholly innocent political associations with disfavored groups; and detained indefinitely solely on Attorney General John Ashcroft's "say-so." In public, Arab/Muslims (and others, such as Sikhs, mis-identified as Arabs or Muslims) were verbally and physically abused and discriminated against at work, in airports, and in an enormously increased rate of hate crimes.[9] Media bias and defamation, in both print and television, as well as racist statements by some politicians and religious leaders, helped fan the flames of popular hostility.[10] Islamic advocacy groups reported 1,658 cases of discrimination, profiling harassment and physical assaults against persons of Arab/Muslim appearance by January 2002, three times the number of the previous year.[11] After 9/11, public opinion polls indicated that 60 percent of Americans favored ethnic profiling of Arabs/Muslims, and that the only group Americans disapproved of more than Muslims/Arabs was atheists.[12]

Post-9/11 government actions affected not only the individual subjects of the government's initiatives, but also their families. As many Arabs/Muslims were deported or voluntarily left the United States out of fear, their communities lost population and Arab/Muslim businesses consequently suffered.[13] While President Bush and Attorney General Ashcroft explicitly rejected Muslim/Arab "ethnic profiling," it was also clear that this was the targeted group that would be most affected by the government's domestic antiterrorism strategy which the attorney general defined as "taking suspected terrorists in violation of the law off the streets and keeping them locked up."[14]

Six weeks after 9/11 over 1,000 individuals had been rounded up in a mass preventive detention. On October 31, 2001, the attorney general created the Foreign Terrorist Tracking Force (FTTF) to institutionalize his detention strategy, aimed at "enhanc[ing] our ability to protect the United States from the threat of terrorist *aliens.*" The strategy's centerpiece was to use the INS and U.S. immigration law to "detain individuals who pose a national security risk for any violations of criminal or immigration laws." Technical violations of immigration law were used as a pretext for the FBI to seize Muslim/Arab men who were on an FBI "suspicious" list, holding them in custody, and only then interrogating them about activities related to terrorism. This strategy, which detained persons solely on the basis of their ethnic origins in the absence of "probable cause" or any evidence of "overt acts," which are required for conspiracy charges, violated Constitutional protections under American criminal law, which apply to aliens as well as U.S. citizens.[15]

Because many areas of the American economy depend on undocumented immigrants, the nation has long tolerated the presence of millions of noncitizens who have violated some immigration rule. And because immigration law imposes a wide range of technical obligations on all foreign nationals, INS laws are particularly useful as pretexts for holding "suspicious" persons without meeting the constitutional requirements that ordinarily apply to preventive detention. Any immigrant community targeted by the INS will inevitably include many visa violators, hence the impact on Muslim/Arab communities.

Additionally, in the winter of 2001–2, the Justice Department officially selected 5,000 young immigrant men for interviews *not* on the basis of any specific information regarding possible links to terrorist activities, but solely on the basis of their age, date of arrival in the United States, and country of origin, most of which were Muslim/Arab countries where Al Qaeda support was supposed to exist. A new 25-day waiting period was established for U.S. visas for men between 16 and 45 from selected Arab/Muslim countries. On September 11, 2002, the Justice Department launched another program, requiring foreign nationals from Arab/Muslim nations to register and submit to fingerprinting and photographs at entry, at regular intervals during their stay, and at exit, with criminal penalties for failure to comply. Subsequently, the government extended similar requirements to male foreign nationals above 16 years old from 25 Muslim/Arab countries who were not permanent residents and were already living in the United States.[16]

By May 2003, almost 2,500 foreign nationals had been detained under an Absconder Apprehension Initiative, which expressly targeted for prioritized deportation 6,000 Arabs/Muslims among the more than 300,000 foreign nationals with outstanding deportation orders. Also in May 2003, another 2,747 noncitizens were detained in connection with a Special Registration program also directed at Arabs and Muslims. Citing national security interests, the Attorney General demanded secrecy regarding these detentions. He sent a memo to all immigration judges not only to keep the hearings secret, with only the alien and his attorney present, but also to refuse to confirm or deny that such detentions were taking place. This exclusion of the public, the press, legal observers, and even members of the immigrant's family is contrary to due process protections, which require a public trial unless the government can make an individualized showing for the need for confidentiality, which it at no time attempted to do. Indeed, although the government justified the secrecy of the detentions by claiming the need to prevent Al Qaeda from knowing who was being detained and to protect the privacy of the detainees, several of the detentions received wide publicity, and many detainees declared they did not want their arrests kept secret.[17]

Several human rights groups attempted to uncover information about the detentions, some of which were challenged in court. After several courts held the secrecy claims unconstitutional, the Justice Department agreed to "rethink" its policy. As one judge said, "[d]emocracies die behind closed doors"; another said, "Secret arrests are a concept odious to a democratic society ... the first priority of the judicial branch must be to ensure that our Government always operates within the statutory and constitutional constraints which distinguish a democracy from a dictatorship."[18] And in June 2003, a report by the Justice Department's own inspector general criticized the whole alien detention operation, noting that of the 738 foreign nationals detained within the first year after 9/11, not one was charged with any terrorist crime; virtually all were cleared of any connection to terrorism by the FBI; all were arrested on flimsy reasons and presumptively treated as terrorists, denied bond, and held for months until receiving FBI clearance or being deported; and many were held incommunicado in maximum security conditions and subject to physical and verbal abuse. Of the more than 5,500 domestic detentions implemented under the various government initiatives, not one person was actually charged with a crime, and the government had been singularly unsuccessful in its prosecution of the few suspected terrorists that had been arrested.[19]

Ethnic profiling rests on a *generalization* about people in a particular group (in contrast to a description containing ethnic factors that is related to the search for a specific perpetrator in a specific crime situation) and breaches constitutional guarantees to equal protection. As noted in *Plyler* (see chapter 4), a case involving the provision of services to undocumented immigrants, the U.S. Constitution states that political and religious freedom rights and due process and equal protection apply to all "persons" subject to our laws, not just to citizens. Challenges to this differentiation between alien and citizen soon found their way into court, regarding not only domestic detainees, but also those being detained as "enemy combatants."

"ENEMY COMBATANTS" AND RIGHTS OF HABEAS CORPUS

The right to habeas corpus refers to the constitutionally based right to have a hearing in court on the facts of a charge or detention. The abrogation of this right became a critical legal issue for persons captured on the battlefields in Afghanistan or several arrested in the United States for their supposed connections to Al Qaeda. Thousands of persons captured in Afghanistan were declared "enemy combatants" by President Bush and detained in military custody, without being charged of any crime, at the U.S. naval base at Guantánamo Bay, Cuba, potentially for the duration of the war on terror, which the government acknowledged might last indefinitely.

The Bush administration claimed that in order to prevent further terrorist attacks and prevent these persons from returning to the battlefield, the executive had the power to declare such persons, whether foreign nationals or U.S. citizens, "enemy combatants"; to arrest and hold them for an indefinite period without bringing charges; and to deny them a hearing in federal court or access to a lawyer. The president claimed that "enemy combatants" were not entitled to the protections accorded prisoners of war, which under international law, including the Geneva Conventions, require certain minimum standards of humane treatment.[20] The Bush administration also claimed that because the Guantánamo military installation was in Cuba, it was not under the sovereign power of the United States and therefore the detainees had no rights to challenge their detentions under federal law.

These detentions and other related Justice Department actions generated widespread protests in the United States and abroad both by human rights groups and by other governments. The American Civil Liberties Union and the Center for Constitutional Law began habeas corpus suits in federal court on behalf of some of the detainees and persons arrested on suspicion of terror-related activities. In April 2004, three of these suits reached the U.S. Supreme Court. These cases raised important questions about the constitutional rights of citizens and non-citizens in wartime conditions, as well as about the scope of executive power. This relationship, between the reach of executive power and the targeting of those who are different, again highlights the comparison between the treatment of Muslims, both aliens and citizens, and that of the Japanese during World War II, a comparison remarked on repeatedly in the media and the court opinions. Significantly, one of those filing a brief against the government was Fred Korematsu, then 82 years old, who had challenged the Japanese internment cases (see chapter 12).

These cases, which raised the issue of the constitutionally mandated separation of powers and the limits on the executive, were the first review of presidential war powers in over 50 years. They required the courts and the nation to deeply examine how the delicate balance between individual liberty and national security would operate in the modern age of terrorism. Each case examined whether, or how, legal precedents from World War II, especially the Geneva Conventions and subsequent acts of Congress regarding detention and treatment of prisoners of war, might apply to post-9/11 anti-terrorism efforts and to President Bush's designated "enemy combatants." The more than 60 briefs filed by legal and military analysts, international political figures, former prisoners of war, and civil rights groups against the government testifies to the importance of these cases in their consequences for upholding the rule of law in the United States.

Rumsfeld v. Padilla

The case of *Rumsfeld v. Padilla* [542 U.S., 507 (2004)] concerned Jose Padilla, an American citizen and convert to Islam, who was arrested on a federal warrant in Chicago as a material witness in connection with terrorist activities and initially sent to a federal prison in New York. When his court-appointed lawyer challenged his arrest, the government withdrew its claim that he was a material witness and declared him an "enemy combatant." Padilla was then transferred to a military base in South Carolina where he was held for over two years incommunicado, subject to intensive interrogation, with no access to a lawyer. In June 2004, the Supreme Court dismissed Padilla's case in a 5–4 decision on narrow procedural grounds relating to proper jurisdiction. The Court declared that Padilla's case had been brought in the "wrong forum" and required his lawyers to begin their case again in South Carolina.[21]

In a brief but eloquent dissent, Justice John Stevens, joined by Justices David Souter, Ruth Ginsburg, and Stephen Breyer, rebuked the Court for focusing on the narrow jurisdictional issue, and "failing to deal meaningfully with the questions of profound importance to the nation." Regarding what they held was the real issue, that is, the question of whether Padilla was entitled to a hearing on the justification of his detention, Justice Stevens wrote,

At stake in this case is nothing less than the essence of a free society. Even more important than the method of selecting the people's rulers and their successors is the character of the constraints imposed on the Executive by the rule of law.

Unconstrained Executive detention for the purpose of investigating and preventing subversive activity is the hallmark of the Star Chamber. Access to counsel for the purpose of protecting the citizen from official mistakes and mistreatment is the hallmark of due process ....

Executive detention of subversive citizens ... may not be justified by the naked interest in using unlawful procedures to extract information. Incommunicado detention for months on end is such a procedure .... For if this nation is to remain true to the ideals symbolized by its flag, it must not wield the tools of tyrants even to resist an assault by the forces of tyranny.

As a follow up to this decision, Padilla's lawyers did indeed "begin again," and in September, 2005, a federal appeals court panel ruled unanimously that the president did have the authority to detain Padilla as an enemy combatant, overruling the trial court opinion in South Carolina that the president had overstepped his bounds by detaining Padilla for three years.[22]

Hamdi v. Rumsfeld

A second case, *Hamdi v. Rumsfeld*, raised the question of whether a U.S. citizen, captured overseas during military operations connected to the "global war on terror," can be detained without access to American courts. The plaintiff, Yasir Esam Hamdi, was an American citizen, born in Louisiana, who lived for most of his 24 years in Saudi Arabia. The government claimed that he was captured while fighting for the Taliban in

Afghanistan in 2001, and he was detained at the Guantánamo naval base. When interrogators there discovered he was an American citizen, Hamdi was transferred to a naval brig in South Carolina, where he remained incommunicado for more than two years.

In June 2002, Hamdi's father brought a habeas corpus petition on his son's behalf in Federal District Court in Virginia; his petition alleged that Hamdi was not fighting alongside the Taliban but had gone to Afghanistan as a volunteer relief worker and got trapped when the Americans invaded Afghanistan. The army responded to Hamdi's demand that the government justify his detention by offering the so-called "Mobbs memorandum," constructed by Michael Mobbs, a minor Defense Department official, which declared, without supporting evidence, that Hamdi was with a Taliban unit and was captured with a Kalashnikov rifle in his possession when that unit surrendered to the Northern Alliance, who later turned him over to the American military.

After a series of decisions and appeals in the federal courts, Hamdi's case reached the U.S. Supreme Court, where the government essentially argued that it was critical to national security that the president be given unimpeded support as commander in chief in times of armed conflict " ... largely unencumbered by the deliberative process of the Congress or the evidentiary burdens imposed by the judiciary ... " The government further claimed that affording Hamdi a habeas corpus hearing failed to give proper deference to the president's authority, under Article II of the Constitution, to conduct military affairs, and that any effort by the courts to "second-guess" the president's military decision to detain Hamdi would undermine the constitutionally based separation of powers and substantially weaken the executive's authority to provide for the common defense in time of war.

Hamdi's lawyers argued that the administration had gone too far in its quest for unchecked power, abandoning the American tradition of fairness to prisoners and devotion to the rule of law, and that a victory for the administration would mean that the president could have indefinite latitude to lock up people, contrary to our system of laws which "does not entrust any one person, including the president, with such unbridled power to abridge individual liberty."[23]

The Supreme Court ruled 8–1 in favor of Hamdi's petition. Justice Sandra Day O'Connor wrote the opinion for the Court, holding that Hamdi did have the right to use American courts to argue that he is being held illegally and that the military cannot keep a U.S. citizen, seized overseas during military operations, in indefinite custody without access to federal courts to challenge the basis for his designation as an enemy combatant. The Court also, not unsurprisingly, and quite firmly, rejected the government's claim that for a court to "interfere" with the actions of the president in his role as commander in chief violated the constitutionally mandated separation of powers.

HAMDI V. RUMSFELD 542 U.S. 507 [JUNE 2004]

We hold that … due process demands that a citizen held in the United States as an enemy combatant be given a meaningful opportunity to contest the factual basis for that detention before a neutral decisionmaker ….

In June 2002, Hamdi's father, Esam Fouad Hamdi, filed the present petition for a writ of habeas corpus … arguing that "[a]s an American citizen, … Hamdi enjoys the full protections of the Constitution," and that Hamdi's detention in the United States without charges, access to an impartial tribunal, or assistance of counsel "violated and continue[s] to violate the Fifth and Fourteenth Amendments to the U.S. Constitution." The habeas petition asks that the court, among other things … [to] appoint counsel for Hamdi; … order respondents to cease interrogating him … declare that he is being held in violation of the Fifth and Fourteenth Amendments … schedule an evidentiary hearing, at which Petitioners may adduce proof in support of their allegations" … [and] order that Hamdi be released from his "unlawful custody."

The threshold question before us is whether the Executive has the authority to detain citizens who qualify as "enemy combatants …. [that is] part of or supporting forces hostile to the United States or coalition partners" in Afghanistan and who "engaged in an armed conflict against the United States" there. We therefore answer only the narrow question before us: whether the detention of citizens falling within that definition is authorized …."

The Court then rejected Hamdi's argument that his son's detention was not legally authorized; it agreed with the government that the Authorization of the Use of Military Force did provide legal authorization for detaining Hamdi, that it appropriately applied to individuals who fought against the United States in Afghanistan as part of the Taliban, and that it applied to citizens as well as aliens, who pose the same kind of threat of returning to the battlefield if released.

Justice O'Connor continued …

Hamdi objects … that Congress has not authorized the *indefinite* detention to which he is now subject …. We take Hamdi's objection to be not to the lack of certainty regarding the date on which the conflict will end, but to the substantial prospect of perpetual detention. We recognize that the national security underpinnings of the "war on terror," although crucially important, are broad and malleable …. The prospect Hamdi raises is therefore not far-fetched. If the Government does not consider this unconventional war won for two generations, and if it maintains during that time that Hamdi might, if released, rejoin forces fighting against the United States, then the position it has taken throughout the litigation of this case suggests that Hamdi's detention could last for the rest of his life ….

It is a clearly established principle of the law of war that detention may last no longer than active hostilities … and … we agree that indefinite detention for the purpose of interrogation is not authorized based on longstanding law-of-war principles ….

Even in cases in which the detention of enemy combatants is legally autho-rized [however], there remains the question of what process is constitutionally due to a citizen who disputes his enemy-combatant status. Hamdi argues that he is owed a meaningful and timely hearing and that "extra-judicial detention [that] begins and ends with the submission of an affidavit based on third-hand hearsay" [i.e., the Mobbs declaration] does not comport with the Fifth and Four-teenth Amendments. The Government counters that any more process than was provided below would be both unworkable and "constitutionally intolerable."

The Court then went on to examine the issues of habeas corpus and due process. Justice O'Connor noted that habeas corpus is available to every person in the United States, unless it is suspended, and that it is a "critical check on the Executive, ensuring that it does not detain individu-als except in accordance with law .... Thus, it is undisputed that Hamdi was properly before [the federal court] to challenge his detention..." and to hear and challenge the evidence of the government's case. The Court recognized some need for flexibility in such hearings but did not accept the government's view that such flexibility meant the Court must accept the statements in the Mobbs Declaration as final. Indeed, the Court rejected the Fourth Circuit's decision that Hamdi's seizure was "undisputed," noting that Hamdi did not concede the allegations and was not permit-ted to speak for himself nor through a lawyer, and that the declaration itself was ambiguous as to whether Hamdi "resided" in Afghanistan, was "captured" on the battlefield, or was "engaged in an armed conflict."

The Court then closely considered the question of what level of defer-ence courts owe the executive in wartime. While it rejected the govern-ment's position that any hearings to challenge the "facts" of Hamdi's detention violated the separation of powers mandated by the Constitu-tion, it also did not go as far as the District Court in claiming that anything less than the full protections of a criminal trial would violate Hamdi's constitutional rights. Justice O'Connor continued, addressing

... the tension that often exists between the autonomy that the Government asserts is necessary in order to pursue effectively a particular goal and the process that a citizen contends he is due before he is deprived of a constitutional right. The ordinary mechanism that we use for balancing such serious competing interests, and for determining the procedures that are necessary to ensure that a citizen is not "deprived of life, liberty, or property, without due process of law," dictates that the process due in any given instance is determined by weighing "the private interest that will be affected by the official action" against the Government's asserted inter-est ... and the burdens the Government would face in providing greater process. [This] calculus then contemplates a judicious balancing of these concerns....

It is beyond question that substantial interests lie on both sides of the scale in this case. Hamdi's "private interest ... affected by the official action," is the most elemental of liberty interests—the interest in being free from physical detention by one's own government.

Nor is the weight on this side of the ... scale offset by the circumstances of war or the accusation of treasonous behavior, for "[i]t is clear that commitment for *any* purpose constitutes a significant deprivation of liberty that requires due process protection ..." and at this stage in the ... calculus, we consider the interest of the *erroneously* detained individual ... Indeed ... the risk of erroneous deprivation of a citizen's liberty in the absence of sufficient process here is very real ... Moreover, as critical as the Government's interest may be in detaining those who actually pose an immediate threat to the national security of the United States during ongoing international conflict, history and common sense teach us that an unchecked system of detention carries the potential to become a means for oppression and abuse of others who do not present that sort of threat ... [O]ur starting point for th[is] analysis is unaltered by the allegations surrounding the particular detainee or the organizations with which he is alleged to have associated. We reaffirm today the fundamental nature of a citizen's right to be free from involuntary confinement by his own government without due process of law, and we weigh the opposing governmental interests against the curtailment of liberty that such confinement entails.

Justice O'Connor then weighed the citizen's interest against those of the government, particularly the interest in ensuring that those who have fought with the enemy during a war do not return to battle against the United States, but also the practical difficulties that would ensue if military officers engaged in battle were "unnecessarily and dangerously distracted by litigation half a world away."

Striking the proper constitutional balance here is of great importance to the Nation during this period of ongoing combat. But it is equally vital that our calculus not give short shrift to the values that this country holds dear or to the privilege that is American citizenship. It is during our most challenging and uncertain moments that our Nation's commitment to due process is most severely tested; and it is in those times that we must preserve our commitment at home to the principles for which we fight abroad ... With due recognition of these competing concerns ... we therefore hold that a citizen-detainee seeking to challenge his classification as an enemy combatant must receive notice of the factual basis for his classification, and a fair opportunity to rebut the Government's factual assertions before a neutral decision maker ... These essential constitutional promises may not be eroded ....

At the same time ... enemy combatant proceedings may be tailored to alleviate their uncommon potential to burden the Executive at a time of ongoing military conflict [i.e., the possible acceptance of hearsay and fair opportunities for rebuttal of charges where the Government puts forth credible evidence that the habeas petitioner meets the enemy-combatant criteria at which time] ... [and] the onus could shift to the petitioner to rebut that evidence with more persuasive evidence that he falls outside the criteria. A burden-shifting scheme of this sort ... would sufficiently address the "risk of erroneous deprivation" of a detainee's liberty interest while eliminating certain procedures that have questionable additional value.

While we accord the greatest respect and consideration to the judgments of military authorities in matters relating to the actual prosecution of a war, and recognize that the scope of that discretion necessarily is wide, it does not infringe on the core role of the military for the courts to exercise their own time-honored and constitutionally mandated roles of reviewing and resolving claims like those presented here.

In sum…the threats to military operations posed by a basic system of independent review are not so weighty as to trump a citizen's core rights to challenge meaningfully the Government's case and to be heard by an impartial adjudicator.

In so holding, we necessarily reject the Government's assertion that separation of powers principles mandate a heavily circumscribed role for the courts in such circumstances. Indeed, the position that the courts must forgo any examination of the individual case and focus exclusively on the legality of the broader detention scheme cannot be mandated by any reasonable view of separation of powers, as this approach serves only to *condense* power into a single branch of government. We have long since made clear that a state of war is not a blank check for the President when it comes to the rights of the Nation's citizens. Whatever power the U.S. Constitution envisions for the Executive in its exchanges with other nations or with enemy organizations in times of conflict, it most assuredly envisions a role for all three branches when individual liberties are at stake …. Likewise, we have made clear that, unless Congress acts to suspend it, the Great Writ of habeas corpus allows the Judicial Branch to play a necessary role in maintaining this delicate balance of governance, serving as an important judicial check on the Executive's discretion in the realm of detentions …. Thus, while we do not question that our due process assessment must pay keen attention to the particular burdens faced by the Executive in the context of military action, it would turn our system of checks and balances on its head to suggest that a citizen could not make his way to court with a challenge to the factual basis for his detention by his government, simply because the Executive opposes making available such a challenge. Absent suspension of the writ by Congress, a citizen detained as an enemy combatant is entitled to this process.

Plainly, the "process" Hamdi has received is not that to which he is entitled under the Due Process Clause.

Justice O'Connor's opinion raised the possibility that the standards the Court would find minimally acceptable could be met by military tribunals, to which the government subsequently agreed, though these were not to be full military trials.[24] In the absence of such tribunals, Justice O'Connor held, it is the responsibility of courts to ensure that habeas corpus petitions from "enemy combatant" detainees provide the constitutionally mandated protections. The Supreme Court then vacated the Fourth Circuit judgment and remanded the case back to the District Court to structure an equitable hearing situation.

Subsequent to this Supreme Court decision, however, the U.S. government decided to engage in negotiations with Hamdi's lawyers, rather than continue a legal battle. Hamdi was permitted to return to Saudi Arabia under a contracted agreement to renounce his American citizenship; never to travel to Afghanistan, Iraq, Pakistan, Syria, the West Bank, or the Gaza Strip; not to travel anywhere outside Saudi Arabia for the next five years; not to seek permission to travel to the United States for the next ten years; to release the United States from any legal liability for his detention; and to surrender the right to challenge any terms of the agreement in court. Hamdi was never charged with a crime and on his departure from the United States, a Pentagon spokesman said "Hamdi was no longer considered a threat…and did not possess any further intelligence value."[25]

In a second habeas corpus case, *Rasul v. Bush* (542 U.S. 466 [June 28, 2004]), brought by 14 Guantánamo detainees, the Supreme Court held, in a 6–3 decision, that the more than 600 foreign nationals detained at Guantánamo Bay under "enemy combatant" status were entitled to habeas corpus hearings in American federal courts, reversing earlier decisions in federal district and appeals courts.[26]

The Court's majority rejected the Bush administration's claim that habeas corpus hearings were not required for the Guantánamo detainees because the Guantánamo Naval Base was located in a place not under the sovereign power of the United States. The Court did not rule on the detainees' claims of having been wrongly confined but ruled only that they have a right to have their claims heard in federal court and sent the case back to the district court with instructions to begin considering them. On Feb. 1, 2005, lawyers for the detainees won an important decision in the Federal District Court in Washington, which ruled that Guantánamo detainees *were* entitled to a hearing in federal courts to determine whether they had been unlawfully detained. Judge Joyce Green also ruled that the military tribunals under which the government had proposed to try the detainees were unconstitutional because the detainees could not, in most cases, see the evidence against them. Additionally, she also questioned whether some of the information used against the detainees had been obtained by torture and was thus unreliable, raising that question for the first but undoubtedly not the last time.[27]

TORTURE AND THE U.S. WAR AGAINST TERROR

The Geneva Conventions are a system of international humanitarian law that limits the ways in which wars may be fought, including the protections that must be accorded to individuals during hostilities. Meant to control the evils of war, the Conventions protect people who do not take part in the fighting (civilians, medics, chaplains, and relief workers) and those who can no longer fight (wounded and sick enemy soldiers as well as prisoners of war). Many countries of the world, including the United States, have become signatories to this international law and have agreed not to use torture in war. When Judge Green questioned whether information was obtained through torture she certainly had in mind the legal obligation of U.S. authorities to treat enemies according both to the antitorture provisions of the Geneva Conventions and the requirements of the U.S. Uniform Code of Military Justice and the U.S. Army Field Manual on Intelligence Interrogation, regulations taught to our soldiers and military police that also prohibit torture.

After President George W. Bush declared the "war on terror," members of his administration began to argue for expanded executive branch powers to counter the threat posed by international terrorists and the governments that supported them. Memoranda written by officials at the Department of Justice as early as September 25, 2001, not only spelled out broad presidential power to order military and intelligence operations in response to the 9/11 attacks but also, in keeping with the new post-9/11 legal culture, they proposed a substantial downsizing of U.S. obligations under the Geneva Conventions.

These officials, joined by attorneys at the Office of White House Counsel, urged new standards of conduct for interrogation under international and U.S. law. Their analysis, subsequently famous as the "so-called torture memo," redefined the operative definition of torture governing the actions of American intelligence and military operatives. It did so by distinguishing torture from acceptable "cruel, inhuman, and degrading treatment." According to the administration's new definition there must be "specific intent to inflict severe pain, the infliction of such pain must be the ... precise objective [with] the victim experience[ing] intense pain or suffering of the kind that is equivalent to the pain that would be associated with serious physical injury so severe that death, organ failure, or permanent damage resulting in a loss of significant body function will result."[28] Scholars writing about the change in standards have said that the government's intent was to limit the charge of torture to "extreme acts."[29]

As the United States pursued terrorists in Afghanistan in 2002, President Bush accepted his advisors' legal opinions that the Geneva Conventions, with its human rights protections, did not apply to Al Qaeda, nor for the most part to the Taliban. Instead, using generalities, he directed that the armed forces were to treat any detainees "humanely" and where possible "in a manner consistent with the principles of Geneva."[30] This directive, supplemented by other legal interpretations and orders, governed the actions of our soldiers in Afghanistan, where there was no declared war, as well as interrogators at Guantánamo Bay, Cuba. Journalist Seymour Hersh has argued that the use of torture began in Afghanistan, "where Pentagon civilians sought to transform what they viewed as an 'overly cautious' military culture."[31] It was subsequently argued by members of the armed forces, scholars, and reporters, including Hersh, that there was a direct "road" from the permission given by the president to ignore the antitorture provisions of the Geneva Conventions in Afghanistan and Guantánamo to the widespread use of torture in Iraq, where officials were desperate for "actionable intelligence," but where we were engaged in a declared war, with the actions of U.S. troops covered by the Geneva Conventions as well as U.S. civil and military law.

Americans awoke to the undeniable realization that American troops were engaged in the use of torture both unleashed and unchecked by high government officials with the release of photographs from Abu Ghraib prison in Iraq. The image of a hooded man, "tottering on a box, supplicant arms outstretched, wires trailing from his fingers" led the morning and evening news along with pornographic photographs of a naked prisoner wearing only a leather collar "at the feet of [an] American female in camouflage pants."[32] Although President Bush denounced the conduct as "disgraceful," limited to a few "bad apples," and "not represent[ing] America," it soon became clear, through investigations of the Red Cross, Human Rights Watch, and the Army's own Taguba Report, that abuses were widespread.[33] In Iraq, prisoners were beaten, cuffed in stressful positions for long hours, forced to remain naked, hooded for extended periods, sexually abused, and "waterboarded" (while tied to a tilt board, the prisoner's head is repeatedly forced into foul liquid, often a mixture of water and urine, causing loss of breath and vomiting). Most critically, evidence mounted that the "genesis" of abusive interrogation procedures as well as the routine use of violence against prisoners prior to interrogation to soften them could be found not only in Iraq but in Afghanistan and Guantánamo, "and ultimately in decisions made by high officials in Washington to redefine the meaning of torture."[34]

American servicemen and women stationed in Iraq testified to the abuse and their confusion on the proper application of the Geneva Conventions in the treatment of wartime prisoners. They described uncertainty as to the precise meaning of President Bush's "humane treatment" directive.[35] Their firsthand accounts provided evidence of "the routine use of physical and mental torture as a means of intelligence gathering" as well as "stress relief" by scared, bored, and undertrained troops.[36] One soldier confirmed that discipline was sufficiently loose that on their days off "people would show up [at the prisoners' tent] ... to work out [their] frustration ... In a way it was sport ... One day a sergeant show[ed] up ... and broke [a prisoner's] leg with a mini Louisville Slugger that was a metal bat. He was a f`... cook. He shouldn't be with no [prisoners].[37]

In 2005 Republican Senator John McCain, a Navy veteran who spent 5 years as a prisoner of war in Hanoi, introduced in Congress an antitorture amendment. The senator's purpose was to clarify what interrogation techniques were permissible for U.S. armed forces as well as interrogators from the Department of Defense (DOD) and the CIA. Senator McCain's intent was to overturn Bush administration policy, to now prohibit "cruel, inhuman, or degrading treatment or punishment," and to hold soldiers and agents to the provisions of the Army Field Manual. Pointing to the effects of the Bush administration's new legal culture, one of the 29 retired military officers who signed a letter in support of the amendment wrote:

It is now apparent that the abuse of prisoners in Abu Ghraib, Guantánamo and elsewhere took place in part because our men and women in uniform were given ambiguous instructions, which in some cases authorized treatment that went beyond what was allowed by the Army Field Manual. Administration officials confused matters further by declaring that U.S. personnel are not bound by long-standing prohibitions of cruel treatment when interrogating non-U.S. citizens on foreign soil. As a result, we suddenly had one set of rules for interrogating prisoners of war, and another for "enemy combatants;" one set for Guantánamo, and another for Iraq; one set for our military, and another for the CIA. Our service members were denied clear guidance, and left to take the blame when things went wrong. They deserve better than that.[38]

Senator McCain and his supporters did not, however, draw specific attention to a particularly troubling aspect of the abuse, namely, the ways in which U.S. soldiers and interrogators singled out Islamic culture in their efforts to humiliate and mistreat prisoners.

Late in 2005 veteran journalist Joseph Lelyveld wrote that "[I]t's asking a lot of the individual military policeman … to draw a fine line between the war on terror and a war on Islam."[39] Clearly, from the testimony of prisoners and U.S. service personnel, many soldiers and interrogators were not able to or chose not to distinguish between stopping terrorism and attacking Islam. The experiences of U.S. Captain James Yee, a West Point graduate and convert to Islam, offer compelling evidence of how, throughout the post-9/11 period, antagonism toward prisoners, and efforts to break them, have rested upon the debasement of Muslim practices and religious items. Yee, an Army chaplain assigned to Guantánamo's Camp Delta, observed such practices repeatedly: unnecessarily confrontational methods of handling the Koran during cell searches; removing detainees in shackles for interrogation just as the time arrived for prayer; wrapping Muslim prisoners in the Israeli flag; and drowning out a recording of verses of the Koran with cacophonous rock music.[40]

At Camp Delta, treatment of the Koran, placed in every Muslim prisoner's cell or cage, became the focal point of a struggle between the detainees and the camp's commanding officer, a man reported to have "sought counseling from a chaplain to deal with the anger he felt against 'those Muslims' responsible for the attack [on the Pentagon in which friends had died]."[41] After an interrogator threw a detainee's Koran on the floor, "stepped on it, and kicked it across the room" the prisoners went on a strike of silence, waiting for an apology from the commander.[42] His failure to offer one led to a series of suicide attempts by the detainees. Equally disturbing, after Yee was removed as Camp Delta's Muslim chaplain, in part for speaking up about these abuses, the position was left unfilled. The detainees went without access to a spiritual advisor who, among other responsibilities, would have discussed the religious needs of these men with the camp's commanding officer.

Attacks on Islamic beliefs meant to inflame, offend, and humiliate were not unique to Guantánamo. The Pentagon confirmed that American soldiers in Afghanistan burned and desecrated the bodies of two Taliban fighters, publicly placing their corpses "facing west," in an apparent, deliberate mocking of the Islamic requirement to face Mecca during prayer.[43] Elsewhere, female soldiers have been used to humiliate detainees by touching them and by making them undress, most famously at Abu Ghraib but also at Guantánamo, where declassified accounts describe the use of sexually provocative tactics on the part of female interrogators meant to violate Muslim taboos about contact between the sexes and religious purity.[44]

The case against the abuse of prisoners of war and detainees, including the use of torture, rests upon several facts and arguments. Political realists insist simply that such acts are not in the national interest. They contend that torture and abuse on our part will, in the future, jeopardize our troops, and that the intelligence gained through torture is unreliable. For other Americans, however, moral considerations frame the argument against the use of torture. They believe that all human beings are members of a moral community, entitled to basic rights.

Strategic self-interest as well as moral argument caused the United States to sign the Geneva Conventions and to establish federal and military law and regulations concerning the lawful treatment of prisoners in wartime. The obligation, and the tension, of holding to the law has been a theme of this book. We have examined the extent to which cultural differences can be tolerated while maintaining the integrity of our nation-state. Nothing has more starkly posed this question than the legal and political response to the terrorist attacks of 9/11, especially as these actions involve Arab and Muslim Americans and Islam itself—long viewed by the West in terms of tension, conflict, and stereotype. Our long-standing respect for law and courts suggests that fundamental human rights will ultimately define who we are and how we aspire to interact with societies around the world.

NOTES

1. *The 9/11 Commission Report: Final Report of the National Commission on Terrorist Attacks Upon the United States* (New York: W.W. Norton, 2004).

2. Steve Coll, *Ghost Wars: the Secret History of the CIA, Afghanistan, and bin Laden, from the Soviet Invasion to September 10, 2001* (New York: Penguin, 2004).

3. *9/11 Report*, 330–44.

4. Avram Bornstein, "Antiterrorist Policing in New York City after 9/11: Comparing Perspectives on a Complex Process," *Human Organization* 64 (1), 2005, 52–53; Christopher E. Smith, *Constitutional Rights: Myths and Realities* (Belmont, CA. Wadsworth, 2004), Ch. 10.

5. Zahid H. Bukhar, "Demography, Identity, Space: Defining American Muslims," in Philippa Strum and Danielle Tarantolo, eds., *Muslims in the United States: Demography, Beliefs, Institutions* (Washington , D.C.: Woodrow Wilson International Center for Scholars, Division of United States Studies, 2003), 7–20.

6. Mohamed Nimer, "Social and Political Institutions of American Muslims: Liberty and Civic Responsibility," in Strum and Tarantolo, *Muslims in the United States*, 45–61.

7. Kathleen Moore, "'United We Stand': American Attitudes toward (Muslim) Immigration Post-September 11th." *Muslim World* 92 (1 & 2), Spring 2002, pp.S39–58 (available on line); Andrew Shryock, "New Images of Arab Detroit: Seeing Otherness and Identity Through the Lens of September 11," *American Anthropologist* 104 (3), September 2002, 917–22.

8. David Cole, *Enemy Aliens: Double Standards and Constitutional Freedoms in the War on Terrorism* (New York: The New Press, 2003); Tram Nguyen, *We Are All Suspects Now: Untold Stories from Immigrant Communities after 9/11* (Boston: Beacon Press, 2005).

9. Cole, *Enemy Aliens*, 5; Nguyen, *We Are All Suspects Now*.

10. *Report on Hate Crimes & Discrimination Against Arab Americans: the Post-September 11 Backlash, September 11, 2001 to October 11, 2002* (Washington, D.C.: American-Arab Anti-Discrimination Committee Research Institute, 2003).

11. Cole, *Enemy Aliens*, 47; Nguyen, *We Are All Suspects Now*, xxii.

12. Scott Keeter and Andrew Kohut, "American Public Opinion About Muslims in the U.S. and Abroad," in Strum and Tarantolo, *Muslims in the United States*, 185–202, 186.

13. *Worlds Apart: How Deporting Immigrants After 9/11 Tore Families Apart and Shattered Communities* (New York: American Civil Liberties Union, December 2004).

14. Cole, *Enemy Aliens*, 22.

15. Cole, *Enemy Aliens*, 190–91; Nguyen, *We Are All Suspects Now*, "A timeline of major events and policies affecting immigrants and civil liberties," 159–75.

16. Cole, *Enemy Aliens*, 28.

17. Ibid., 47.

18. Cited in Cole, *Enemy Aliens*, 28–29.

19. Rachel L. Swarns, "Program's Value in Dispute as a Tool to Fight Terrorism," *New York Times*, December 21, 2004, A26; David Cole, "Ashcroft: 0 for 5,000." *The Nation* (October 4, 2004), 6; Matthew Purdy and Lowell Bergman, "Where the Trail Led: Between Evidence and Suspicion: An Unclear Danger: Inside the Investigation of Terror in Lackawanna," *New York Times*, October 12, 2003, A35.

20. Ronald Dworkin, "What the Court Really Said," *New York Review of Books*, (August 12, 2004), 26.

21. Dworkin, ibid., 27; as of December, 2005, the Bush administration decided not to continue holding Padilla as an enemy combatant in the military brig and said it would instead try him in a criminal court on narrower charges. Eric Lichtblau, "In Legal Shift, U.S. Charges Detainee in Terrorism Case," *New York Times*, November 23, 2005, A1.

22. Neil Lewis, "Court Gives Bush Right to Detain U.S. Combatant," *New York Times*, September 10, 2005, A1. However, on December 21, 2005, that same court handed the Bush administration a significant defeat when it rejected the government's motion to transfer Padilla from military custody to federal civilian law enforcement authorities. In a strongly worded opinion the three-judge panel

said the Department of Justice request gave the appearance that the government was trying to avoid Supreme Court review of an issue of "national importance" *Padilla v. C. T. Hanft, U.S.N.*, U.S. Court of Appeals, 4th Cir., No. 05–6396 (CA-04–2221–26AJ), 2.

23. Joan Biskupic, "Prisoners test legal limits of war on terror," *USA Today*, April 19, 2004, 13A, citing brief from the ACLU.

24. For an examination of the government's position and an evaluation of military tribunals, see Louis Fisher, *Military Tribunals and Presidential Power: American Revolution to the War on Terrorism* (Lawrence: University Press of Kansas, 2005).

25. Philip Shenon, "U.S. Signals End to Legal Fight Over an 'Enemy Combatant,'" *New York Times*, August 12, 2004, A10; Joel Brinkley, "From Afghanistan to Saudi Arabia, via Guantánamo," *New York Times*, October 16, 2004, A4.

26. Dworkin, "What the Court Really Said"; Linda Greenhouse, "Supreme Court Affirms Legal Rights of Those Deemed 'Enemy Combatants,'" *New York Times*, June 29, 2004, A1, A14.

27. Neil A. Lewis, "Judge Extends Legal Rights for Guantánamo Detainees," *New York Times*, February 1, 2005, A12; "In Rising Numbers, Lawyers Head for Guantánamo Bay," *New York Times*, May 30, 2005, A10. As of December, 2005, Congress is debating the passage of a measure that would override the Supreme Court decision and deny noncitizens held in Guantánamo the right to challenge their detentions and to know what they are charged with. Eric Schmitt, "Senate Approves Limiting Rights of U.S. Detainees," *New York Times*, November 10, 2005, A1.

28. Karen J. Greenberg and Joshua L. Dratel, eds. *The Torture Papers: The Road to Abu Ghraib* (New York: Cambridge University Press, 2005), 174, 183.

29. Ibid., 183.

30. Presidential Directive, February 7, 2002.

31. Lisa Hajjar, "In the Penal Colony," *The Nation* (February 5, 2005), 23; Seymour Hersh, *Chain of Command: The Road from 9/11 to Abu Ghraib* (New York: Harper Collins, 2004).

32. Mark Danner, "Abu Ghraib: The Hidden Story," *New York Review of Books* (October 7, 2004), 44.

33. Maj. General Antonio M. Taguba, *The Taguba Report*, http://news.findlaw.com/hdocs/docs/iraq/tagubarpt.html, accessed December 9, 2005.

34. Ibid., 44.

35. *Taguba Report*, 67.

36. "Torture in Iraq: A Report by Human Rights Watch," *New York Review of Books* (November 3, 2005), 67.

37. Ibid., 70.

38. R.S.K. *"Wash. Times* Editorial on McCain Anti-Torture Amendment Minimized its Effects on Detainee Policy," Media Matters for America, November 14, 2005, http://mediamatters.org/items/200511140009, accessed December 9, 2005.

39. Joseph Lelyveld, "The Strange Case of Chaplain Yee," *New York Review of Books* (December 15, 2005), 8.

40. Lelyveld, "The Strange Case," 8–9, reviewing *For God and Country: Faith and Patriotism Under Fire* (New York: Public Affairs, 2005), Yee's autobiographi-

cal account of his time in the armed forces, his arrest, exoneration, and honorable discharge.

41. Ibid., 12.

42. Ibid., 10.

43. Eric Schmitt, "Army Examining Report of Abuse," *New York Times,* October 20, 2005, A1.

44. Carol D. Leonnig and Dana Priest, "Detainees Accuse Female Interrogators," *Washington* Post, February 10, 2005, AO1; Jane Mayer, "The Experiment," *New Yorker* (July 11 & 18, 2005), p. 65.

Selected Bibliography

INTRODUCTION: *E PLURIBUS UNUM?*

Deveaux, Monique. *Cultural Pluralism and Dilemmas of Justice.* Ithaca, New York: Cornell University Press, 2000.

Keyssar, Alexander. *The Right to Vote: The Contested History of Democracy in the United States.* New York: Basic Books, 2000.

Shweder, Richard A., Martha Minow, and Hazel Rose Markus, eds. *Engaging Cultural Differences: The Multicultural Challenge in Liberal Democracies.* New York: Russell Sage Foundation, 2002.

Smith, Christopher E. *Constitutional Rights: Myths and Realities.* Belmont, CA: Wadsworth, 2004.

CHAPTER 1: NATIVE AMERICANS, LAND, AND LAW

Cramer, Renée Ann. *Cash, Color, and Colonialism: The Politics of Tribal Acknowledgment.* Norman: University of Oklahoma Press, 2005.

Harring, Sidney. *Crow Dog's Case.* New York: Cambridge University Press, 1994.

Norgren, Jill. *The Cherokee Cases.* Norman: University of Oklahoma Press, 2004.

Robertson, Lindsay G. *Conquest by Law: How the Discovery of America Dispossessed Indigenous Peoples of Their Lands.* New York: Oxford University Press, 2005.

Wilkins, David E. and K. Tsianina Lomawaima. *Uneven Ground: American Indian Sovereignty and Federal Law.* Norman: University of Oklahoma Press, 2001.

The Snowbird Cherokees. Film. Director Rich Panter. VHS color. 60 min. SCE-TV Marketing Department, 1-800-553-7752.

CHAPTER 2: TROUBLE IN PARADISE: NATIVE HAWAIIAN AND PUERTO RICAN SOVEREIGNTY

Malavet, Pedro A. *America's Possessive Colony: The Political and Cultural Conflict between the United States and Puerto Rico.* New York: New York University Press, 2004.
Merry, Sally. *Colonizing Hawai'i: the Cultural Power of Law.* Princeton, NJ: Princeton University Press, 2000.
Silva, Noenoe K. *Aloha Betrayed: Native Hawaiian Resistance to American Colonialism.* Durham, NC: Duke University Press, 2004.
Stannard, David E. *Honor Killing: How the Infamous "Massie Affair" Transformed Hawai'i.* New York: Viking, 2005.
Trask, Haunani. *From a Native Daughter: Colonialism and Sovereignty in Hawaii.* Monroe, MA: Common Courage Press, 1993.
Act of War: The Overthrow of the Hawaiian Nation. 1993. Film. VHS color. 58 min. Center for Hawaiian Studies, Contact Na Maka o ka 'Aina, General Delivery, Na'alehu, Hawai'i 96772; 1-800-WAR-1811.
The Tribunal: Peoples' International Tribunal Hawai'i 1993. Film. Contact Na Maka o ka'Aina General Delivery, Na'alehu, Hawai'i 96772; 1 800 WAR-1811.

CHAPTER 3: AFRICAN AMERICANS: THE FIGHT FOR JUSTICE AND EQUALITY

Anderson, Terry H. *The Pursuit of Fairness: A History of Affirmative Action.* New York: Oxford University Press, 2004.
Bell, Derrick. *Faces at the Bottom of the Well: The Permanence of Racism.* New York: Basic Books, 1992.
Berry, Mary Francis. *Black Resistance/White Law: A History of Constitutional Racism in America.* Rev. ed. New York: Penguin, 1994.
Klarman, Michael J. *From Jim Crow to Civil Rights: The Supreme Court and the Struggle for Racial Equality.* New York: Oxford University Press, 2004.
Lopez, Ian. *White by Law: The Legal Construction of Race.* New York: New York University Press, 1997.
Yarbrough, Tinsley E. *Race and Redistricting: The Shaw-Cromartie Cases.* Lawrence: University Press of Kansas, 2002.

CHAPTER 4: IMMIGRATION: LATINOS AND LAW

Bender, Steven W. *Greasers and Gringos: Latinos, Law, and the American Imagination.* New York: New York University Press, 2003.
Ellingwood, Ken. *Hard Line: Life and Death on the U.S.-Mexico Border.* New York: Pantheon, 2004.
Foner, Nancy, ed. *American Arrivals: Anthropology Engages the New Immigration.* Santa Fe, NM: School of American Research, 2003.
Magduk, Ron. *Democracy for All : Restoring Immigrant Voting in the United States* New York: Routledge, 2006.

Valencia, Reynoldo Anaya, Sonia R. García, Henry Flores, and José Roberto Juárez Jr. *Mexican Americans and the Law.* Tucson: University of Arizona Press, 2004.
Farmingville. 2003. Film. 78 min. Color. In English and Spanish with English subtitles. VHS and DVD. Available from Docurama, 126 Fifth Avenue (15th floor), New York, New York 10011 or www.docurama.com.

CHAPTER 5: RELIGIOUS BELIEF AND PRACTICE: THE MORMONS

Altman, Irwin and Joseph Ginat. *Polygamous Families in Contemporary Society.* New York: Cambridge University Press, 1996.
Brodie, Fawn. *No Man Knows My History: The Life of Joseph Smith, the Mormon Prophet.* 2nd ed. New York: Knopf, 1971.
Krakauer, Jon. *Under The Banner of Heaven: A Story of Violent Faith.* New York: Doubleday, 2003.
Ostling, Richard and Joan K. Ostling. *Mormon America: The Power and the Promise.* San Francisco, CA: HarperSanFrancisco, 1999.

CHAPTER 6: RELIGIOUS BELIEF AND PRACTICE: THE AMISH

Fisher, Sara E. and Rachel K. Stahl. *The Amish School.* Intercourse, PA: Good Books, 1986.
Jones, Darryl. *Amish Life: Living Plainly and Serving God.* Bloomington: Indiana University Press, 2005.
Kraybill, Donald B., ed. *The Amish and the State.* 2nd ed. Baltimore, MD: Johns Hopkins University Press, 2003.
Peters, Shawn Francis. *The Yoder Case: Religious Freedom, Education, and Parental Rights.* Lawrence: University Press of Kansas, 2003.
Devil's Playground. 2002. Film. 77 min. Color. In English and occasional German with English subtitles. Available in VHS; DVD for U.S. and Canada only. Wellspring Home Video, 419 Park Avenue South, New York, New York 10016. (212) 686–0387.

CHAPTER 7: THE CULTURE WARS IN AMERICAN SCHOOLS

Frank, Thomas. *What's The Matter with Kansas: How Conservatives Won The Heart of America.* New York: Henry Holt, 2004.
Larson, Edward J. *Summer for the Gods: the Scopes Trial and America's Continuing Debate Over Science and Religion.* Cambridge, MA: Harvard University Press, 1998.
Moe, Terry M. *Schools, Vouchers, and the American Public.* Washington, DC: Brookings, 2001.
Zimmerman, Jonathan. *Whose America? Culture Wars in the Public Schools.* Cambridge, MA: Harvard University Press, 2002.

CHAPTER 8: RELIGION AND THE USE OF ILLICIT DRUGS: THE RASTAFARI AND THE NATIVE AMERICAN CHURCH

Grinspoon, Lester and James B. Bakalar. *Marihuana, the Forbidden Medicine.* Rev. and exp. ed. New Haven: Yale University Press, 1997.

Lewis, William F. *Soul Rebels: The Rastafari.* Prospect Heights, IL: Waveland Press, 1993.

Long, Carolyn. *Religious Freedom and Indian Rights: The Case of Oregon v. Smith.* Lawrence: University Press of Kansas, 2000.

Steinmetz, Paul B. *Pipe, Bible, and Peyote among the Oglala Lakota: A Study in Religious Identity.* Syracuse, NY: Syracuse University Press, 1998.

Stewart, Omer C. *Peyote Religion: A History.* Norman: University of Oklahoma Press, 1987.

CHAPTER 9: WOMEN'S NATURE, WOMEN'S LIVES, WOMEN'S RIGHTS

Cochan, Augustus B. *Sexual Harassment and the Law: The Mechelle Vinson Case.* Lawrence: University Press of Kansas, 2004.

Gordon, Linda. *The Moral Property of Women: A History of Birth Control Politics in America.* Urbana: University of Illinois Press, 2002.

Sokoloff, Natalie J., ed. *Domestic Violence at the Margins: Readings on Race, Class, Gender and Culture.* New Brunswick: Rutgers University Press, 2005.

Solinger, Rickie. *Pregnancy and Power: A Short History of Reproductive Politics in America.* New York: New York University Press, 2005.

Strum, Philippa. *Women in the Barracks: The VMI Case and Equal Rights.* Lawrence: University Press of Kansas, 2002.

CHAPTER 10: FAMILY VALUES: GAYS AND MARRIAGE

Gerstmann, Evan. *Same-Sex Marriage and the Constitution.* New York: Cambridge University Press, 2004.

Mello, Michael. *Legalizing Gay Marriage.* Philadelphia: Temple University Press, 2004.

Moats, David. *Civil Wars: The Battle for Gay Marriage.* Orlando, FL: Harcourt, 2004.

Pinello, Daniel. *America's Struggle for Same-Sex Marriage.* New York: Cambridge University Press, 2006.

CHAPTER 11: FIGHTING PREJUDICE: PERSONS WITH DISABILITIES AND HOMELESS PERSONS

Colker, Ruth. *The Disability Pendulum: The First Decade of the Americans with Disabilities Act.* New York: New York University Press, 2005.

Desjarlais, Robert. *Shelter Blues: Sanity and Selfhood among the Homeless.* Philadelphia: University of Pennsylvania Press, 1997.

Feldman, Leonard C. *Citizens without Shelter: Homelessness, Democracy, and Political Exclusion.* Ithaca, NY: Cornell University Press, 2004.

Kusmer, Kenneth. *Down and Out, On the Road: The Homeless in American History.* New York: Oxford University Press, 2003.

Lyon-Callo, Vincent. *Inequality, Poverty, and Neoliberal Governance: Activist Ethnography in the Homeless Sheltering Industry.* Toronto: Broadview Press, 2004.

Mezey, Susan Gluck. *Disabling Interpretations: The Americans with Disabilities Act in Federal Court.* Pittsburgh: University of Pittsburgh Press, 2005.

O'Brien, Ruth, ed. *Voices from the Edge: Narratives about the Americans with Disabilities Act.* New York: Oxford University Press, 2004.

CHAPTER 12: 100 PERCENT AMERICAN: WHO QUALIFIES IN A NATIONAL EMERGENCY? JAPANESE AMERICANS AND THE LAW

Daniels, Roger. *Prisoners without Trial: Japanese Americans in World War II.* Rev. ed. New York: Hill and Wang, 2004.

Irons, Peter. *Justice at War: The Story of the Japanese American Internment Cases.* Berkeley: University of California Press, 1993.

Pfaelzer, Jean. *Driven Out! Ethnic Cleansing in the American West: Roundups and Resistance of Chinese Americans.* New York: Random House, in press.

Tateishi, John. *And Justice for All: An Oral History of Japanese American Detention Camps.* Seattle: University of Washington Press, 1999.

CHAPTER 13: CULTURAL PLURALISM AND THE RULE OF LAW POST–9/11

Cole, David. *Enemy Aliens: Double Standards and Constitutional Freedoms in the War on Terrorism.* New York: New Press, 2003.

Danner, Mark. *Torture and Truth: America, Abu Ghraib and the War on Terror.* New York: New York Review of Books, 2004.

Greenberg, Karen J. and Joshua L. Dratel, eds. *The Torture Papers: The Road to Abu Ghraib.* New York: Cambridge University Press, 2005.

Levinson, Sanford, ed. *Torture: A Collection.* New York: Oxford University Press, 2004.

Nguyen, Tram. *We Are All Suspects Now: Untold Stories from Immigrant Communities After 9/11.* Boston: Beacon, 2005.

Strum, Philippa, ed. *Muslims in the United States: Identity, Influence, Innovation.* Washington, DC: Woodrow Wilson International Center for Scholars, 2006.

The Letter: An American Town and the "Somali Invasion." 2003. Film. Hamzeh, Ziad H., writer and director. 76 min. Color. English/Somali w/English subtitles. Arab Film Distribution, 10035 35th Ave NE, Seattle, WA 98125.

INDEX

About the Authors

JILL NORGREN is Professor Emeritus of Government at John Jay College of Criminal Justice and the Graduate Center, the City University of New York. Her research has been supported by the Rockefeller Foundation, NEH, the ACLS, and the Woodrow Wilson Center for International Scholars. She has also published (with Petra T. Shattuck) *Partial Justice: Federal Indian Law in a Liberal Constitutional System*; *The Cherokee Cases*; and a biography of pioneering American lawyer and presidential candidate Belva Lockwood. She is currently writing on the topics of Native American law and the legal treatment of women.

SERENA NANDA is Professor Emeritus of Anthropology at John Jay College of Criminal Justice. She is the author (with Rich Warms) of *Cultural Anthropology*, a widely used undergraduate text now in its 9th edition; *Neither Man nor Woman: The Hijras of India*; *Gender Diversity: Crosscultural Variations*; and *Forty Perfect New York Days: Walks and Rambles in and around the City*. Her current work is on the politics of cultural identity.

87159720R00170

Made in the USA
Middletown, DE
03 September 2018